SECOND EDITION

SPORTS ETHICS
FOR SPORTS MANAGEMENT PROFESSIONALS

Walter T. Champion, Jr., Esq.
George Foreman Professor of Law
Thurgood Marshall School of Law
Texas Southern University
Houston, Texas

and

Adjunct Professor of Sports Law
South Texas College of Law Houston
Houston, Texas

Richard T. Karcher, Esq.
Associate Professor
School of Health Promotion and Health Performance
Eastern Michigan University
Ypsilanti, Michigan

Lawrence S. Ruddell, PhD
Dean of Academics
Belhaven University at Houston
Houston, Texas

and

Founder and President
The Global Institute for Ethical Leadership

JONES & BARTLETT
LEARNING

World Headquarters
Jones & Bartlett Learning
25 Mall Road
Burlington, MA 01803
978-443-5000
info@jblearning.com
www.jblearning.com

Jones & Bartlett Learning books and products are available through most bookstores and online booksellers. To contact Jones & Bartlett Learning directly, call 800-832-0034, fax 978-443-8000, or visit our website, www.jblearning.com.

Substantial discounts on bulk quantities of Jones & Bartlett Learning publications are available to corporations, professional associations, and other qualified organizations. For details and specific discount information, contact the special sales department at Jones & Bartlett Learning via the above contact information or send an email to specialsales@jblearning.com.

Production Credits
VP, Product Management: Amanda Martin
Director of Product Management: Cathy L. Esperti
Product Manager: Sean Fabery
Product Assistant: Andrew LaBelle
Senior Project Specialist: Vanessa Richards
Digital Project Specialist: Rachel Reyes
Director of Marketing: Andrea DeFronzo
VP, Manufacturing and Inventory Control: Therese Connell
Composition: Exela Technologies

Project Management: Exela Technologies
Cover Design: Michael O'Donnell
Rights & Media Specialist: Maria Leon Maimone
Media Development Editor: Troy Liston
Cover Image (Title Page, Part Opener, Chapter Opener):
© Robert Daly/OJO images/Getty Images
Printing and Binding: Gasch Printing
Cover Printing: Gasch Printing

Library of Congress Cataloging-in-Publication Data
Names: Champion, Walter T., Jr., 1950- author. | Karcher, Richard T., author. | Ruddell, Lawrence S., author.
Title: Sports ethics for sports management professionals / Walter T. Champion Jr., Richard T. Karcher, Lawrence S. Ruddell.
Description: Second edition. | Burlington, MA : Jones & Bartlett Learning, 2019. | Revised edition of: Sports ethics for sports management professionals / Patrick K. Thornton, Walter T. Champion, Jr., Lawrence S. Ruddell. | Includes bibliographical references and index.
Identifiers: LCCN 2018052617 | ISBN 9781284171303 (paperback)
Subjects: LCSH: Sports administration. | Sports–Moral and ethical aspects. | BISAC: SPORTS & RECREATION / General.
Classification: LCC GV713 .T565 2019 | DDC 796.06/9–dc23
LC record available at https://lccn.loc.gov/2018052617

6048

Printed in the United States of America
26 25 24 23 22   10 9 8 7 6 5 4 3

To my friend Patrick Thornton, rest in peace.

–Walter T. Champion, Jr.

To all of the college athletes in commercialized sports who sow but do not reap.

– Richard T. Karcher

To my dad, Joe Ruddell, who was a star performer on the Virginia Tech basketball team of the 1940s, and brothers Pres (who played Minor League Ball with the Twins), Jim, and Bill, and my kids, Preston and Anna.

– Lawrence S. Ruddell

Brief Contents

Contents

Preface

As you can probably guess, the gist of a book titled *Sports Ethics for Sports Management Professionals* is ethics, or rather the lack thereof, in sports.

Penn State, which is no stranger to the ethics in sports debate, hired Robert Boland as its Athletics Integrity Officer. To begin with, Athletics Integrity, is an oxymoron, just like Jumbo Shrimp or Military Intelligence. The book's major instruction for sports management professionals (SMPs) is to make the right decision when confronted with difficult ethical questions. One wonders what is meant by the phrase "Athletics Integrity."

Should an athlete have more (or less) integrity than a regular student? Some might argue that most athletes are more inherently responsible than your run-of-the-mill students because they are involved with an extracurricular activity that demands a heightened sense of commitment and dedication. Should the onus of integrity be more profound with athletes?

As the *Second Edition* goes to press, there appears to be an ethical malaise currently surrounding big-time college athletics after the Baylor football scandal. However, the infractions at Baylor were of such a heinous invasive quality that it should not have merely instigated a sea-change in our opinions on athletic integrity. If anything, the Baylor scandal should invoke a discussion on feminism in our society as a whole, not just a titillating, myopic witch-hunt against college athletics.

In the past, there were certainly more dramatic ethical mishaps in college sports, such as the sad case of Jack Molinas, who fixed college (and professional) basketball games for a living. These days appear to be over, ironically, as a result of legalized sports betting and daily fantasy sports. This more civilized view on legalized sports gambling is a result of education, which could be the answer to the alleged problem of athletic integrity: "Teach your children well."

The term *ethics* covers a broad spectrum of disciplines in today's society. Business ethics, medical ethics, legal ethics, environmental ethics, and, yes, even sports ethics are prevalent in today's culture. Sports ethics confronts many issues that are common in our society within the context of the sports world. Race and discrimination, gender-equity issues, privacy, intellectual property, gambling, violence, and drug use and drug testing are all significant topics in the study of sports ethics.

SMPs will be confronted with many ethical decisions during their careers. It is essential that they be equipped to make the right decision when faced with a difficult situation. This book was written with an eye toward the SMP, who will certainly encounter many tough decisions during his or her career. It is one of the goals of this book to assist the SMP in making the right decision when the situation arises. Ethical situations can arise for the sports manager under a variety of circumstances: In the employment process, in the administration of an athletic program at both the amateur and professional levels, in youth sports, and in the everyday decisions that an SMP must make in fulfilling his or her duties and responsibilities.

▶ Organization of This Text

In Chapter 1, several ethical models are presented that the SMP may use as a platform to make ethical decisions. Chapter 1 also presents several practical cases ("tough calls") for the SMP relating to discrimination in the workplace, eligibility and participation issues, disability issues in sports, and ethical issues confronting the SMP in collegiate and professional sports. Each case allows the student to apply the ethical decision-making process to a sports-related ethical dispute.

In Chapter 2, the concepts of sportsmanship, gamesmanship, and cheating are examined. Is there a difference between them? If so, what are the differences, and how are they applied in the sporting world? Every sport has rules by which all participants (fans, players, coaches, referees, and parents) must abide. However, rules are often broken, particularly by the participants. Sometimes, this is even done intentionally. Should sports tolerate the intentional breaking of the rules of the game or sport? America's national pastime of baseball seems to tolerate the concept of gamesmanship more than other sports, and Chapter 2 further explores the differences between sportsmanship, gamesmanship, and cheating in this context. No one likes a cheater; that is a simple proposition. The concept of cheating is explored in the second chapter. How is cheating actually defined, and what should be done to prevent cheating in sports? Spying and espionage have always been present in sports. Trying to figure out the "secrets" of another athlete's success can be valuable information for a competitor. Those concepts are developed and discussed fully in Chapter 2. "Trash talking" and profanity have become prevalent in both professional and amateur sports. Is it ever acceptable to engage in either, and if so, under what circumstances? The limits of this kind of behavior are also discussed for all levels of sports.

Gambling has been present in sports ever since participants have thrown or passed a ball. It is a simple, but true, statement: Individuals like to play games of chance with the hope of winning money. But, is gambling good for a sport? Every professional sport league regulates gambling to a certain extent. Many experts agree that gambling diminishes the integrity of the sport. Chapter 3 explores the influence that gambling has had on players, teams, referees, and leagues at both the professional and amateur levels and what has been done to reduce the influence of gambling in sport.

All those involved in sports have an ethical calling. Coaches should perform their duties ethically and responsibly. Sports officials have a moral and ethical duty to be fair and unbiased in all of their rulings. These concepts are explored in Chapter 4. Coaches must supervise and instruct athletes properly to prevent injury, and they must refrain from violent and abusive behavior toward the athletes they coach. It is an understatement that sports officials have a tough job, but they must perform it without bias and with consideration for the safety of all participants and fans.

Chapter 5 discusses two of the most important participants at any sporting event—parents of youth sports participants and fans. Parents are becoming more involved in their children's sporting events, and along with that increased involvement come ethical duties. Parents should conduct themselves appropriately and be good examples for youth sports participants at all events. "Parental rage" has become a major issue, both legally and ethically, at the youth sports level. Chapter 5 discusses this concept in depth. Every sporting event needs enthusiastic fans. Without fans, no sport can survive. Fans love to cheer their team to victory, but it must be done in an ethical and certainly a nonviolent manner. Fans at sporting events owe an ethical duty to others at the sporting event to conduct themselves appropriately while enjoying the sporting event and refrain from "fan rage," violent behavior, "over the top" heckling, or stalking athletes. All of these concepts and ethical issues are explored in Chapter 5.

Violence in sports is a major ethical issue facing almost every major sport. Violence is tolerated in many sports and even encouraged in others. Issues of how much violence at all levels of sports should be tolerated are explored in Chapter 6. Both civil and criminal sanctions can be levied against violent athletes to attempt to curb inappropriate behavior. The sport of professional hockey tolerates, and in some cases even encourages, fighting and has clearly stated so. Unfortunately, athletes sometimes also engage in "off-the-field" violence. Leagues, teams, and managers may have to deal with off-the-field violent and nonviolent issues as well, determining appropriate punishment for the offenders.

It seems that no topic has been explored and discussed more in the sporting world in the last few years than drug use and drug testing. Chapter 7 explores drug testing and use and its ethical implications in the context of both professional and amateur sports. Steroid use has become prevalent in sports and is a controversial issue. This topic presents major ethical dilemmas for athletes and for the SMP. Congress has become involved in professional sports leagues to try to "clean up" the sport. Ethical issues abound in this area for the sports manager, athlete, coach, and athletic association as well as for professional teams and leagues.

Race has a long history in sports. In Chapter 8, race and discrimination issues are discussed. Racial issues are present at all levels of sports and involve all participants, sports officials, coaches, and parents. In this chapter, cases and case studies explore issues dealing with race in the employment context as well as with eligibility issues.

Sports agents arrived on the sports scene in the late 1960s, primarily because of the increasing salaries for professional players. In Chapter 9, numerous ethical issues facing sports agents are examined. Agents are in a trust or fiduciary relationship with clients, and they must abide by certain ethical and legal rules when performing their duties. Agents have many responsibilities and obligations to their clients, including contract negotiations, endorsements, tax advice, and legal advice. All of these duties must be performed in an ethical and legal manner. The issue of attorneys also acting as agents is explored. Many entities regulate sports agents: The NCAA, states, player unions, and universities. Any regulation of agents must be fair and ethical, and any discipline levied against unethical agents must comport with the agent regulatory system.

Chapter 10 discusses gender discrimination and Title IX. For many years, women did not have the same opportunities as men to participate and be involved in sports. Many antiquated attitudes existed—and some still do—about the "fragile" woman who is unable to participate in sports and "can't keep up with the boys." Unfortunately, discrimination and abuse against women in sports have become very significant issues for all involved in sports. An SMP will be called upon to make ethical decisions dealing with both sexual harassment and sexual abuse of female athletes. Title IX has done a lot to make women's sports "equal" to men's sports, but there is still room to grow. An SMP working at the collegiate level will certainly be faced with ethical issues related to Title IX and must understand the reasons behind its implementation. Compliance issues dealing with Title IX are also explored.

In Chapter 11 sports ethics is discussed in the context of sports media. Sports fans can access sports games and news in a wide variety of forms. Reporters, writers, and producers all owe a duty to perform their jobs in an ethical manner including producing factually accurate and truthful stories and to verify the facts of any story. The production of the story must be done in a truthful and forthright manner, presenting all sides of an issue. Ethical and legal issues can arise in reporting stories of athletes. The media must immediately issue a retraction for any statement or story that is untrue and also issue an apology. That is the ethical thing to do. Media outlets should be aware of how the individuals in a story are portrayed and refrain from stereotyping any groups or individuals during their presentation of the news or a journalistic piece. Social media has now become a form of art, and ethical issues abound in this area. These are explored in depth as well.

In Chapter 12, sports ethics is discussed in the context of the NCAA's collegiate model of athletics. The model was formulated by Myles Brand, former NCAA president, as a way to recommit to the academic success of intercollegiate athletics, to respect the concept that the student-athlete is central to the enterprise, and to reconnect athletics programmatically and financially with the rest of the universities. The chapter explores exactly how Brand planned on using the model to reach these goals and how he tried to steer clear of intertwining with a professional model so that student athletes maintain their amateurism. Brand believed that this was a preeminent step in his goal of reform and advocacy, but many critics would say otherwise; this is also discussed in Chapter 12. The chapter looks at ethical concerns that are related to the big money sports. The NCAA is the center of discussion as to whether the major money college sports only care about making money and the athlete is forgotten. It is true that some college coaches earn up to $10,000,000 per year, but college-athletes earn nothing. Another truism is that 80% of all professional athletes are broke in 6 years. The question is whether universities are about education or sports.

This chapter discusses the NCAA's "Collegiate Model of Athletics" to ascertain its viability and ethical righteousness.

It is our hope that this book will assist you in furthering your understanding of ethics and, more specifically, sports ethics. We also hope that it provides you with some practical decision-making skills to assist you in your career in the sports industry.

Good luck in your study of sports ethics.

▶ New to the *Second Edition*

In crafting the *Second Edition*, we have generally followed the same format as the previous edition. With that said, global changes and chapter revisions include the following:

- Many of the "Case Studies" and "Cases" have been deleted and replaced with new ones containing more recent and updated material.

- The material in the "Notes and Discussion Questions" following each chapter have also been updated. However, the notes and questions are now dispersed throughout the chapter rather than being grouped together at the end of each chapter. Additionally, since Chapter 1 serves primarily as an introduction to the text and contains no "Cases" or "Case Studies," the "Notes and Discussion Questions" for Chapter 1 have been retained at the end of the chapter.

- Chapter 1 includes more material on the principles, concepts, and theories that provide the foundation for analyzing ethical dilemmas in sport. The material in Chapter 1 on the topic of cheating has been deleted or moved to other chapters where appropriate.

- The material on the topic of violence previously found in Chapter 2 has been moved to Chapter 6.
- The section on gambling in amateur sports in Chapter 3 now includes a discussion of the results of the NCAA's survey given to college athletes on the subject of gambling.
- The title of Chapter 4 has been changed to "Ethical Issues Involving Coaches," reflecting that the sections on sports officials' ethics and participant ethics have been removed. These subjects are covered in other chapters.
- Chapter 7 includes new material on the World Anti-Doping Agency (WADA) and the WADA Code, as well as some "Cases" and "Case Studies" involving rulings of the Court of Arbitration for Sport (CAS).
- The first edition's chapter on intellectual property in sports has been removed.
- Chapter 12, "The Commercialization of Amateur Sports," is new to this edition and addresses both the "collegiate model of athletics" and principles of "amateurism" and the student-athlete.

▶ Instructor Resources

The following resources are available for instructors to use in conjunction with the text:

- Test Bank
- Slides in PowerPoint format
- Instructor's Manual

Acknowledgments

A good book needs input from a variety of people, and this book is no exception. There are many people to thank for this project. This is the second edition and we proudly acknowledge the debt to our late friend Patrick Thornton. He is greatly missed.

Much of the information in this book has been collected through research as well as experiences we have had in the sports industry, classroom teaching, and even by watching sports. Of course, a great deal of thanks and credit goes to my co-authors in the second edition of *Sports Ethics*, Richard T. Karcher and Lawrence S. Ruddell. Richard is a former baseball player and Larry is a former Marine Chaplain. It is a pleasure to work with these ethical scholars. I was taught sportsmanship very early in life by my family and through youth sports. But, I also observed "sports ethics" while watching fans pelt Santa Claus with ice balls at an Eagles game. As far as someone who was ethical and exhibited sportsmanship at all times, my hat has to go off to Walter Payton. More specifically, thanks goes to my research assistant Valarie Cortez, who played collegiate soccer, and generally super lawyer Nick Nichols who played point guard at Rice University and won big for Rudy Tomjanovich in *The Punch* by establishing an ethical standard of behavior for professional basketball and, in fact, for all sports.

—*Walter T. Champion, Jr.*

I'd like to acknowledge all of my former students who have had to put up with me over the years. I hope you've learned as much from me as I've learned from you.

—*Richard T. Karcher*

I'd like to thank my colleagues Walter T. Champion and Richard T. Karcher for including me in this important project; Chip Mason, Dean of the College of Business at Belhaven University for his support and encouragement to write; and my coaches throughout the years (Sink, Purcell, Holland, and many others) who taught me sports ethics and sportsmanship as a way of life.

—*Lawrence S. Ruddell*

Case Study Rubric

We have prepared many case studies for your use in the study of sports ethics. We believe that the case studies in the book will assist you greatly in your study and teaching of sports ethics. The following guidelines will assist you with the case studies in the book. Most of the studies are based on actual events in the sporting world. We have referenced each one so you can do further research and study if you so desire. You should find them very helpful in developing your own ethical decision-making skills. For the instructor, they are arranged so they can be assigned to students to write papers, develop questions, or used as extra credit assignments that will further develop knowledge of sports ethics.

When examining the case studies, the following questions should be asked:

1. What is the ethical dilemma or dilemmas posed in this case study?
2. What should be the goal of the sports management professional (SMP) when first addressing the problem?
3. What is the best ethical model to use to approach the ethical situation posed?
4. As an SMP, what other information would you need to have to make an ethical decision?
5. What other individuals would you need to consult to achieve a fair and ethical decision?
6. Does this ethical problem require a form of alternative dispute resolution such as a mediator? If so, how should you proceed, and what should be the goal of the mediator?
7. If this ethical problem cannot be resolved between the parties, what specific compromises can be offered in an attempt to resolve the problem?
8. Does the situation present legal issues that require the assistance of an attorney to arrive at a fair and ethical decision?
9. What cultural, social, or race issues need to be addressed by the parties involved in the scenario?
10. What are the possible consequences of making an unethical decision in this situation?

Reviewers

Donald Cragen, DSM
Professor and Chair
School of Business
Business and Management Program
Thomas College
Waterville, Maine

Eric Forsyth, PhD
Professor
Department of Human Performance,
   Sport, and Health
Bemidji State University
Bemidji, Minnesota

John R. Malmo, PhD
Assistant Professor
School of Professional Studies
Department of Business
Rogers State University
Claremore, Oklahoma

William Nowlan, EdD
Assistant Professor
Sport Management Program
School of Business
Lasell College
Auburndale, Massachusetts

Joe Santa, MPE
Adjunct Professor
Sport Management Program
Department of Business
Huntington University
Huntington, Indiana

Linda J. Schoenstedt, EdD
Associate Professor
Department of Sports Studies
College of Professional Sciences
Xavier University
Cincinnati, Ohio

Eddie G. Walker II
Assistant Professor
Sport and Recreation Management Program
Department of Business
University of Minnesota Crookston
Crookston, Minnesota

CHAPTER 1

Ethical Concepts in Sports

▶ Sports in Society

Americans are sports-crazed, but they are not alone in their love of sports. The world is connected by a sports culture with millions of individuals in Spain, India, Australia, New Zealand, Canada, Colombia, China, and many other countries watching and participating in sports each year. Participating in sports can bring new challenges to an individual and teach valuable life lessons along the way. Americans participate in a variety of sports, including; golf, basketball, cycling, tennis, baseball, soccer, and ice hockey. Parents are enrolling their children in youth sports at an ever-increasing rate so they might learn time-honored concepts such as hard work, dedication, team building, competition, and sportsmanship with the hope that they transfer those skills to their personal life. All are good societal values and help build character in youths.

Youth sports have never been more popular. In the United States, millions of kids participate in a variety of sports beginning as toddlers. Before their children can even bounce a ball, swing a club, or run in a straight line, overzealous parents have them in the sports arena learning how to kick a ball, take a charge, or throw a spiral. Kids participate in sports for a variety of reasons, some healthy and some not. Many participate because their friends are playing, others because their parents insist, and some even participate just for fun! When sports stop being fun, kids tend to drop out. The benefits of youth sports include increased confidence, fitness (less time for video games), social awareness, moral development, and problem-solving skills. Choosing sides, nominating a team captain, and shaking hands with an opponent after a match are all good character traits for a young athlete to develop, although organized sports have taken some of these basic tasks away from the youth participant. Many youth sports programs involve "select" or All-Star teams, in which certain players are picked to play additional games.

Sports at the high school level are increasing in popularity and watching collegiate sports is extremely popular in the United States. With universities offering scholarships in a variety of sports, including basketball, bowling, lacrosse, football, ice hockey, rowing, and swimming, parents hope that their child will be a superstar.

People flock to stadiums around the world to watch sports. American fans love to watch football, both amateur and professional, collegiate and professional basketball, ice hockey, and of course, America's national pastime, baseball. The business of sport has become an extremely lucrative business and it is increasingly clear that sport is a growing industry. Head football coaches at Football Bowl Subdivision (FBS) institutions earn more than the President of the university and, for that matter, the President of the United States. In professional sports, athletes can earn millions of dollars playing their favorite sport. Professional sports franchises are valued at more than $1 billion and college football games can draw more than 110,000 fans.

Some fans may take sports a little too seriously, including many parents involved in youth sports. Ardent fans spend hours each day ruminating over statistics for their individual fantasy leagues while others paint their bodies the color of their favorite team and "tailgate" for hours before NFL games. The contemporary sports world is fraught with "over-the-top parents" and fans alike.

Consider the following comments that appeared in the *New York Times* in 1895 concerning Americans' infatuation with sports:

> Is there not a certain defect of gaiety in contemporary sport? We Americans seem nowadays to take ours excessively hard. We take some of our soberer matters very easily. We giggle over heresy trials and have endless patience for the shortcomings of politicians, but we hold our breath over the reports of football games and yacht races and lose our sleep over intricacies in the management of those events. We worried nearly as much last September over the international yacht races as our fathers did a generation ago over Mason and Slidell and the affair of the Trent.[1]

Ethical, business, and legal issues abound in both professional and amateur sports. It is important for the sports management professional (SMP) to keep these three "buckets" in mind when thinking critically about issues and decisions since each entails different considerations that often conflict with one another. In other words, a business decision motivated solely by financial gain or success might not be an ethical one; moreover, just because an act or decision is legal or in compliance with a rule does not necessarily make it ethical—indeed, a law or rule in and of itself may be unethical.

▶ Why Study Sports Ethics?

Is there a specific discipline of sports ethics as there is for business, legal, or medical ethics? Many think so. A good deal of scholarship has been produced on the subject of sports ethics.[2] Several noted scholars have been appointed sports ethics fellows and some universities have created centers for the study of sports ethics. Is there a practical reason for studying sports ethics? Race and ethnicity are at the forefront of social issues in sports. Other issues, such as gambling, drug testing, athletic eligibility, gender equity, and violence in sports all present serious issues for an intellectual debate on sports ethics. U.S. collegiate sports are fraught with ethical issues ranging from the commercial exploitation and low graduation rates of athletes to on- and off-field misconduct of athletes, coaches, and administrators.

There is a clear advantage for the SMP who studies sports ethics along with a study of management and law. Sports executives need to have a solid grasp of the ethical decision-making process to perform their duties honestly, professionally, and ethically. Whether that individual is an athletic director, coach, general manager, business owner, agent, or sports executive, all must deal with significant ethical and legal concepts prevalent in sports.

Sports morality and ethics were much debated topics, even in the early years of the 20th century.[3] All-pro defensive end Bill Glass wrote a book in the late 1960s titled "Don't Blame the Game," with chapters including "Win at Any Cost," "Booze Makes It Better,

"Trainers Are Junkies," and "Racism Is Everywhere." An excerpt from the book states: "You know the type, 'Broadway' Joe, Dave Meggyesy, Bernie Parrish, Jim Bouton – a handful of professional athletes whose escapades on and off the field have cast a shadow across the entire sport world." Glass did not do himself any favors by naming specific players although he says the "swingers" are really not representative of the majority of professional sport personalities.[4] One wonders what Glass thinks of today's sports world.

This book contains numerous cases and case studies involving ethical issues in sports. For a quick overview of some of the issues involved, consider the following scenarios and the types of ethical decision-making processes that may be required of the SMP:

1. NBA player Gilbert Arenas said he faked an injury in a preseason game to allow a teammate to get more playing time.[5]
2. NFL Houston Texans team owner Bob McNair ordered his team's staff to search the players' locker room to make sure they were not using any banned substances.[6]
3. The University of Mississippi's new mascot, the "Rebel Black Bear," replaced its former mascot, "Colonel Reb."[7]
4. In November 2008, Grapevine Faith, a small Christian school in Dallas, played a football game against Gatesville, a state school at a maximum-security correctional facility for male teenage felons. The Gatesville players were required to travel in handcuffs. Grapevine's coach, Kris Hogan, split his school's fans and cheerleaders into two groups with one group cheering for Gatesville. One Gatesville player said, "Lord, I don't know how this happened, so I don't know how to say thank you, but I never would've known there was so many people in the world that cared about us."[8]
5. In 2010, the Ladies Professional Golf Association (LPGA) voted to amend its constitution to allow transgendered players to participate.[9]
6. New York Yankees shortstop Derek Jeter faked that he was hit with a ball to get on base.[10]
7. New York Governor David Paterson was called before an administrative law judge to determine whether he violated ethics laws when he was able to secure tickets to the first game of the 2009 World Series at Yankee Stadium.[11]
8. The National Football League (NFL) banned the "Captain Morgan" (producer of rum) end zone celebration after Eagles tight end Brent Celek performed it on a Sunday night telecast after catching a touchdown pass. The Captain Morgan Rum Company had intended to offer charity contributions each time a player was caught on camera striking the "Captain Morgan" pose.[12]
9. A high school wrestler was charged with sexual assault after performing a novel move called the "butt drag" on a teammate during a practice.[13]
10. In 1982, with the game between the NFL Patriots and Dolphins tied at 0–0, the Patriots coach ordered snowplow operator Mark Henderson to clear a spot for the New England kicker. The 33-yard field goal was good and the Patriots won 3–0. Dolphins coach Don Shula called the NFL commissioner and said "it was the most unfair act that had ever happened in a football game."[14] Henderson, a convicted felon, was on a work release program at the time of the game. He received a game ball from the Patriots.
11. In 2010, five football players at Ohio State University purportedly violated National Collegiate Athletic Association (NCAA) rules by selling championship rings, game gear, and personal awards for cash and/or tattoos. They were not suspended

by the NCAA for the Sugar Bowl, but instead were suspended for the first five games of the 2011 season.[15]

12. After a game between the Dallas Cowboys and the Philadelphia Eagles, Cowboys running back Tashard Choice asked Eagles quarterback Michael Vick to sign a glove for a family member who was a big fan of Vick's. Choice said, "I don't want anybody to think I was disrespectful. . . . My teammates, coaches, and Jerry [Jones] know where my heart is. I care about football. I meant no disrespect."[16]

13. Six-year-old Kennedy Tesch was tossed off the flag football cheerleading squad when her parents objected to the cheer "Our backs ache, our skirts are too tight, we shake our booties from left to right." Her parents thought the cheer was inappropriate for 6-year-old girls. After a team meeting, other parents voted to kick Kennedy off the squad because of her parents' objections.[17]

▸ Ethical Reasoning and Ethical Models

Any individual faced with an ethical or moral decision must make that decision based on certain guiding principles and a number of tough questions must be addressed:[18] How are ethical decisions to be made; which guiding principles should be employed in the decision-making process; should individuals merely do what they believe is right; should individuals employ the "Golden Rule"—"Do unto others as you would have them do unto you"—in all decisions and in their conduct when dealing with others; are there any guiding religious principles that should affect the choices made by the decision maker; should an ethical decision maker be concerned solely with what is legal and discard all other relevant

principles, or should other factors come into play; and can an action be considered legal but be immoral?

This introductory chapter discusses how ethical standards serve as the basis for sports ethics. This topic is a fundamental introduction for encouraging an environment that highlights the essence of sports: fair play, character development, and excellence. Sport, just as any other endeavor, places much emphasis on rules and regulations.

Ethics is considered to be a branch of philosophy since it is concerned with what is morally right and wrong. The challenge lies in finding the standard by which one determines what is right and wrong. The philosophy of ethics is intimately connected with metaphysics, specifically with ontology, or the study of being. These disciplines try to answer questions such as where do we come from; why are we here; what is our purpose; how do we determine a standard of right and wrong; and what universal ideas do we embrace that help us make sense out of particular situations that we face in life? As we make choices in day-to-day situations that we face, why do we make certain choices and not others?[19]

Two separate techniques that can be utilized to assess whether something is right or wrong are "universality" and "reversibility."[20] Universalizing the case means to apply it to all cases within the context and see if it leads to a permissible result. For example, when analyzing the ethical dilemma posed by the NCAA's amateurism rules, the question is: Would it be permissible if all universities entered an agreement to cap the value of graduate assistants working in all college athletic departments and that any institution violating that agreement would be sanctioned? Would it be permissible if all companies doing business in any other industry (i.e. the auto industry) entered an agreement to cap the value of human capital? One might answer: All of the clubs in the NFL have entered such an agreement;

however, it is permissible in that context only because the clubs have negotiated the cap with the individuals who are capped and they have expressly accepted and agreed to it. This is not the case in the NCAA. Reversing the case means to apply it to *you* and ask if the same decision or action would be acceptable or permissible to you. So the question would be: How would I feel if I was restricted from capitalizing on a unique talent and skill that has huge monetary value and is in high demand in a multi-billion dollar industry?

Ethical Theories and Principles

Ethical theories are divided into three general subject areas: metaethics, normative ethics, and applied ethics.[21] Metaethics examines the origins of theoretical concepts and notions and what they mean. Are ethics merely a social invention? Are they more than expressions of our individual emotions? The answers to these types of questions focus on issues of universal truth, God's will, and the role reason plays in ethical decision making defining ethical terms themselves.

Normative ethics takes on a more practical task. In normative ethics the inquiry is intended to determine what moral values or standards regulate right and wrong conduct and behavior.[22] This search for the ideal litmus test for proper conduct focuses on the duties and rules individuals should follow or the consequences that behavior or conduct have on other individuals. An example of normative ethics is the aforementioned Golden Rule. What systems or ideas are put forth to guide an individual's conduct and assist him or her in determining right from wrong? Subfields of normative ethics include deontological (duty) theories, consequential (utilitarian) theories, evolutionary ethics, and virtue theories.[23] Consequential ethical normative theory focuses on social benefit and achieving the greatest amount of good (usually at the expense of others), oftentimes applying a cost-benefit analysis to support or justify a decision, policy, or action.

Applied ethics examines specific, unresolved, controversial issues such as environmental concerns, social inequality, capital punishment, abortion, and racial discrimination.

Distinguishing between metaethics, normative ethics, and applied ethics can be a difficult task. In metaethics, it is argued that God or a form of Supreme Being provides the foundation of all ethical decision making. In normative ethics, it is argued that the foundation for ethical thought and decision making originates from agreements between individuals, from duty or virtue, or from consideration of the consequences of various actions on individuals or groups. In applied ethics, controversial issues such as capital punishment, stem cell research, gun ownership, and personal control over end-of-life are addressed.

Normative principles that can be applied uniformly, are not too narrowly focused, and take into account varying points of view include the following:

- Benevolence: assisting those in need.
- Honesty: not deceiving or lying to others.
- Autonomy: acknowledging an individual's bodily freedom.
- Justice: honoring an individual's right to due process and to live in a fair and just society.
- Paternalism: assisting others to achieve what is in their best interests when they are unable to do so.
- Harm: do no harm and prevent harm to others.
- Social benefit: acknowledging that certain actions are beneficial to society as a whole.
- Rights: acknowledging an individual's right to autonomy, privacy, free expression, and personal safety.
- Lawfulness: understanding that the rule of law benefits individuals and society as a whole.

These traditional normative principles (or moral values) are derived from several ethical approaches and can be applied to almost every ethical dilemma.

Non-Moral Values and Rationalization

All of those involved in sports—managers, executives, players, agents, sports officials, fans, and owners—face tough ethical decisions. Sports ethics is concerned with what the right thing is to do in sports for all those involved.[24] But how do we determine what is right and wrong? Making an ethical decision begins with a recognition of our motives. A motive is something that causes a person to act in a certain way or do a certain thing—it is what drives our decisions and actions. A motive typically takes the form of a non-moral (amoral) value. Non-moral values are objective-based measures of life or social worth that have no relation to morality, *i.e.* they are neither moral nor immoral. The list of non-moral values is endless and include: money, success, good grades, winning, power, fame, convenience, and self-gratification. They are not good or bad nor right or wrong, they just are. We all desire money, success, good grades, winning, etc., but the key is *how* we obtain them. It is the tension between these non-moral and moral values (honesty, justice, harm, rights, etc.) that creates ethical dilemmas.[25]

Ethical decision making requires striking the proper balance between non-moral and moral values. When we put too much weight and emphasis on non-moral values, we have a tendency to act solely out of self-interest; *i.e.*, what's in it for me? One scholar explains:

"In developing a reasoned view, we must grow beyond, 'What's in it for me?' Rather, our goal should be to consider the ramifications of each decision in relation to other people who may be affected by our action. This becomes even trickier in the sport management world because profit will veil and darken our perspective."[26]

An overemphasis on non-moral values leads one to *rationalize* their failure or refusal to act in accordance with moral values (normative principles). People often rationalize their avoidance of moral values by speculating, generalizing, making assumptions, blaming others, finger-pointing, or making excuses. They rationalize by saying things like: "everyone else is doing it," "business is business," "I can't change it on my own," "I personally think it's wrong but it doesn't matter what I think," "market forces require it," "we have always done it that way," or "when you make your bed, you must lie in it."

One aspect of sports ethics addresses how individuals and teams conduct themselves when competing or preparing to compete in sporting events.[27] In this case, the major concern is competing hard, yet doing so in the right way. In youth sports, the goal is character development and ethical concerns center on hard work, honor, teamwork, diligence, courage, and self-discipline. In competitive sports, including professional sports, the goal is to win (a non-moral value) through effort and excellence rather than by cheating. This is more a personal ethical matter but there can be strong influences from others including: coaches, teammates, friends, family, and fans.

The business aspect of sports applies to youth league organizations as well as to professional sports. How do organizations manage their sports programs and sporting events? Is the sports organization as a whole following ethical guidelines and making ethical decisions? This is where sports ethics intersects with business ethics. Corporations face increasing competition in a rapidly changing global economy and with that change comes more pressure to develop unethical ways to compete. Many times this pressure leads to the notion that "business is business" and an "anything goes" attitude;[28] unfortunately, this same mind-set can sometimes be found in the sports world. Individuals and teams often face increased competition and, like corporations, the challenges and pressures can come from several entities, including: government, sports governing organizations, agents, fans, parents, coaches, other athletes, and other clubs. To change this mind-set, organizations must understand the long-term benefits of ethics to individual, team, and organizational success. It is easy to believe that it is necessary to cut corners ethically to succeed in sports. Everyone connected with sports must realize that this reflects a short-term view of success that often ignores the potential for long-term consequences. Unethical viewpoints and conduct must be replaced by the realization that sound ethical principles are good for sports and for the individuals and clubs participating in sports.

Collaborative Ethics

The key to sports is competitive cohesion wherein the nexus between athletes and fans should be collaborative as opposed to adversarial. There are many examples of both the collaborative model and the adversarial model. In the collaborative model, athletes play with sportsmanship and enthusiasm while showing respect for fans, management, opposing players, and referees. For example, an outfielder practicing before the game will throw the last ball to a young fan. In the collaborative model, professional athletes visit hospitals and chat with sick children at every opportunity and fans respect the athlete's privacy and do not use profane, rude, or disrespectful language. The ethical fan appreciates the time and energy athletes spend pursuing goodwill. Conversely, the adversarial model is typified by the spoiled athlete and the obnoxious fan. The athlete will not readily sign autographs and takes on an adversarial persona. The obnoxious fan will taunt the athlete, drink to excess, "pester" the athlete, and does not respect his or her privacy.

The standard between athletes and fans should be one of collaborative ethics. All parties involved in sports should work together to maintain the integrity of the sport and the greater glory, pride, and self-esteem of the team and the team's city, or country. The inherent value of a sports contest is its capacity to produce a quality experience for the participants and the fans that is deemed good in and of itself.

▸ The Role of the SMP in Ethical Decision Making in the Workplace

The SMP faces many difficult situations in the workplace, especially in the employment context—many times, he or she is required to work with the human resources department to resolve difficult personnel issues and resolve disputes that inevitably occur. No company wants to end up in a dispute or lawsuit with an employee. An SMP must be able to bring to the workplace a multitude of skills for negotiating with employees. One of the most needed skills is that of dispute resolution or conflict management. A skilled professional must be able to resolve disputes ethically, fairly, and as quickly as possible.[29] The old adage "you can't please everyone" may be true, but a good-faith effort must be put forth to satisfy all the parties involved in any dispute. An SMP must be able to understand different cultures and points of view when attempting to resolve any workplace disputes. Effort must be made to understand each party's viewpoint and not favor one person over another when seeking fair resolution of any employment dispute. To maintain an ethical decision-making process, the SMP must develop and implement an understanding of another person's point of view, even though it may be different from their own.

"Team loyalty" is a valuable asset to a company. One of the most important responsibilities of an SMP is to contribute to the success of his or her employer. Towards this end, the SMP must be able to build morale, loyalty, and enthusiasm among employees. It is essential to employee morale that they feel that the company is on their side and understands their viewpoint. Granting every employee's wish is not realistic, and keeping every employee "happy" is not always achievable; however, individuals who enjoy their work will certainly be more productive. Unfair treatment in the employment context can lead to low employee morale, poor job performance, "back-biting" among employees, and even lawsuits. Although some lawsuits cannot be avoided, a lawsuit against the company is not a positive step. In an effort to stop a lawsuit before it happens, SMPs must be able to interact with a diverse population of individuals in the workplace and make ethical decisions in the context of that culture.

The discipline of business ethics applies to sports in the same way it applies to corporate America. All club personnel, from the leaders on down, face ethical decisions on a daily basis in their jobs. Corporate decision-makers, including those in the sports industry, are faced with ethical issues relating to employees, fans, clients, and customers. Sport organizations (professional teams, leagues, university athletic departments, etc.), as with any business or company, have a "mission statement" which details why the organization exists and what it wants to achieve. It often includes a statement of the organization's philosophy and values and provides a sense of direction for everyone in the organization.[30]

Most SMPs think of themselves as ethical people and it has been argued that being ethical in business is no different from being ethical in one's private life. Treating people with respect and dignity, being concerned for the welfare of others, and treating people like you want to be treated are all simple propositions that can and have been translated into the corporate culture by many successful companies. On a broader scale, high-level managers have responsibility for the creation and maintenance of an ethical corporate culture that protects against unethical and illegal conduct by employees and customers as well. Each person in a corporation, from the president of the club to the ticket-taker at the entrance to the ball-park, occupies a specific role and is charged with specific duties that must be undertaken in a fair, reasonable, and ethical manner. Some positions may encounter more difficult problems, but ethical decisions must be made regardless of an individual's status, wage, or position within a company.

▶ Summary

Business activity takes place within an extensive framework of laws, and some hold the view that the law determines whether an activity or conduct is ethical—in other words, if an activity is legal, then it is by definition ethical. However, obtaining approval from a company's legal department does not always translate to the solution of a business problem in an ethical and fair manner. In a more practical sense, SMPs need to consider both the ethical and the legal aspects of a situation when making a decision. Not every immoral act may be considered illegal. For example, taking credit for someone else's work (unless it constitutes plagiarism) is not necessarily illegal, but most people would agree that it is unethical. Conversely, just because a certain action is legal or complies with a rule does not make it ethical. For example, league or association rules that do not provide a fundamentally fair process for resolving a disciplinary matter or eligibility dispute would be deemed unethical; therefore, it is important for the SMP to be aware of the three "buckets" (ethical, business, and legal) when thinking critically about issues and decisions and to use the guiding principles and standards in their decision-making process in order to determine what is right and wrong under each circumstance.

▶ Notes and Discussion Questions

Sports in Society

1. How are business ethics and sports ethics inter-related? Are there overlapping principles applicable to both?
2. What are some examples of ethical decisions that SMPs have to make in the sports industry?[31]
3. What are some examples of ethical decisions corporations are required to make in the sports industry?[32]
4. Which principles from business ethics could be adopted by sports ethics?[33]
5. What can be done to further promote the concept of sports ethics?[34]
6. How are sports ethics principles applied differently to SMPs, coaches, and participants?
7. Are there any sports ethics principles that can be considered "universal"?
8. How should sports ethics be addressed at the international level? Do sports ethics differ in other cultures?[35]
9. What human rights issues are reflected in sports ethics?[36]

Ethical Decision Making and the SMP

10. What are the major ethical dilemmas facing the SMP today?[37]
11. What is the best training (military or work experience) and education (degree in business administration, sports management, liberal arts or law or a combination of several of these qualifications) for an SMP to enable him or her to deal with the important issues they will face in the workplace?
12. What are the essential elements of a corporate ethics program?[38] In the sports industry, how would this program differ from that in other industries such as financial, manufacturing, sales, or service?
13. Should every corporation establish an ethics hotline? Would this be a good idea for a professional sports franchise?
14. What are the essential skills needed by an SMP to develop an ethical decision-making model?

▶ References

1. "We Take our Sports too Seriously: While Soberer Matters are Treated with Unbecoming Levity," *New York Times*, November 5, 1895.
2. Robert L. Simon, *Fair Play: The Ethics of Sport* (Boulder, CO: Westview Press, 2003); Claudio Tamburrini, *Values in Sport: Elitism, Nationalism, Gender Equality and the Scientific Manufacturing of Winners (Ethics and Sport)* (New York: Taylor & Francis, 2000); William J. Morgan, *Ethics in Sport* (Champaign, IL: Human Kinetics, 2007); Tommy Boone, *Basic Issues in Sports Ethics: The Many Ways of Cheating* (Lewiston, NY: Edwin Mellen Press, 2009).
3. Sol Metzger, "Sport Ethics Grow Cleaner at 4 Colleges," *Chicago Daily Tribune*, January 2, 1916, B4; Bernie Lincicome, "From Nero Down, Sports Cheaters Are Rife," *Denver Rocky Mountain News*, September 19, 2007.
4. "Bill Glass Answers the Sport World Swingers in "Don't Blame the Game,"" *Chicago Tribune*, January 21, 1973, F6.
5. "Gilbert Arenas Says He Faked Injury," ESPN.com, October 12, 2010.
6. *Associated Press*, "Texans Searched Locker Room," ESPN.com, October 29, 2010.
7. Sandra Knispel, "University of Mississippi Introduces New Mascot," www.npr.org, October 15, 2010.
8. Joe Lemire, "The Decade in Sportsmanship," *Sports Illustrated*, December 22, 2009.
9. Ryan Ballengee, "LPGA Votes to Amend Constitution to Allow Transgender Players," *NBC Sports*, November 20, 2010.

10. "The Jeter School of Acting," *Sports Illustrated*, September 16, 2009.
11. "Paterson Won't Attend Ethics Hearing on Yankees Tickets," *Wall Street Journal*, August 16, 2010. David M. Halbfinger, "Paterson Fined $62,125 over World Series Tickets," *New York Times*, December 20, 2010.
12. Charles Robinson, "NFL Shipwrecks Captain Morgan Campaign," *Yahoo! Sports*, November 12, 2009.
13. Jesse McKinley, "Wrestler Sees Legal Move; Prosecutor Sees Assault," *New York Times*, December 18, 2010.
14. Mike Reiss, "'Snowplow Game' Still Stings Shula," ESPN.com, January 28, 2010.
15. "Bowl CEO Wanted Buckeyes Eligible," FoxSports.com, December 29, 2010; Pat Forde, "NCAA Ruling Defies Common Sense," ESPN.com, December 23, 2010.
16. Tim MacMahon, "Michael Vick Signs Cowboys RB's Glove," ESPN.com, December 12, 2010.
17. Joshua Rhett Miller, "Girl, 6, Removed from Cheerleading Team After Parents Object to 'Booty' Cheer," *Fox News*, September 15, 2010.
18. Ronald C. Arnett and Clifford Christians, *Dialogic Confession: Bonheoffer's Rhetoric of Responsibility* (Carbondale, IL: Southern Illinois University Press, 2005); Dietrich Bonheoffer, *Letters & Papers from Prison* (New York: Touchstone, 1997).
19. "Five Steps of Principled Reasoning, an Ethical Decision-Making Model" (Los Angeles, CA: Josephson Institute, 1999).
20. Angela Lumpkin, Sharon Kay Stoll, and Jennifer M. Beller, *Practical Ethics in Sport Management 12* (Jefferson, NC: McFarland & Company, Inc., 2012).
21. Steven M. Cahn and Peter Markie, *Ethics: History, Theory, and Contemporary Issues*, 4th ed. (New York: Oxford University Press, 2008).
22. Tara Smith, *Ayn Rand's Normative Ethics: The Virtuous Egoist* (New York: Cambridge University Press, 2006).
23. Michael Ruse, "Evolutionary Theory and Christian Ethics: Are They in Harmony?" *Journal of Religion & Science* 29, no. 1 (1994): 5–24.
24. Mike McNamee, "Sports, Ethics and Philosophy; Context, History, Prospects," *Sports, Ethics and Philosophy* 1, no. 1 (2007).
25. Angela Lumpkin, Sharon Kay Stoll, and Jennifer M. Beller, *Practical Ethics in Sport Management* (Jefferson, NC: McFarland & Company, Inc., 2012).
26. *Id.* at 14-15.
27. J. Brent Crouch, "Gender, Sports, and the Ethics of Teammates: Toward an Outline of a Philosophy of Sport in the American Grain," *Journal of Speculative Philosophy*, New Series 23, no. 2 (2009):118–127.
28. Laura Hartman, *Perspectives in Business Ethics*, 3d ed. (New York: McGraw-Hill, 2004).
29. Lawrence Van Gelder, "On the Job: Conflict Resolution Made Simple," *New York Times*, March 25, 2001. Andrew Greiner, "Student Suspended for Facebook Teacher Slam," *NVC Chicago*, February 22, 2010.
30. Daniel Covell and Sharianne Walker, *Managing Intercollegiate Athletics*, 2d ed. (Scottsdale, AZ: Holcomb Hathaway, Publishers, Inc., 2016).
31. Joy Theresa DeSensi and Danny Rosenberg, *Ethics and Morality in Sport Management* (Morgantown, WV: Fitness Information Technology, 2003).
32. D. Stanley Eitzen, "Ethical Problems in American Sport," *Journal of Sport and Social Issues* 12, no. 1 (1988):17–20.
33. Mary A. Hums, Carol A. Barr, and Laurie Gullion, "The Ethical Issues Confronting Managers in the Sports Industry," *Journal of Business Ethics* 20, no. 1 (1999):51–66.
34. Robert Simon, *Fair Play: The Ethics of Sport* (Boulder, CO: Westview Press, 2003).
35. Cui Jiang, "China's Traditional Sports Ethics: Thought and the Value of Rebuilding Morals of Modern Sports," CNKI.com.cn, February 29, 2006; Francois-Xavier Mbopi-Keou, *Health and Sports in Africa: A Challenge for Development* (Esher, Surrey, UK: John Libbey Eurotext, 2008).
36. Bruce Kidd and Peter Donnelly, "Human Rights in Sports," *International Review for the Sociology of Sport* 12, no. 2 (2000):131–148.
37. Hums, Barr, and Gullion, "The Ethical Issues Confronting Managers in the Sports Industry."
38. Jeanne M. Logsdon and Donna J. Wood, "Global Business Citizenship and Voluntary Codes of Ethical Conduct," *Journal of Business Ethics* 59, nos. 1-2 (2005):55–67.

CHAPTER 2

Sportsmanship, Gamesmanship, and Cheating

▶ How People Win

Everyone likes to win! Adults and children alike enjoy the exuberance of winning, but it is also clear that some people like to win more than others. The subject of this chapter is *how* people win. Should we concern ourselves with how people get into the winner's circle, or by what means they use to prevail? After all, no one remembers who finished second in the Super Bowl.

Cheating, rule breaking coupled with the intent to avoid detection, violates the normative principle of honesty. Why do people cheat in general and what nonmoral values drive people to cheat? Cheating occurs outside of the sports world, such as by students in colleges and universities—they may see others doing it and want to "level the playing field"—while others do it out of ignorance or simply the desire to avoid doing work. One example that is not always well understood by college students is plagiarism. Students have also found creative ways to cheat in the technological age by using text messaging to get answers or "Googling" during exams.

Cheating in one's private life ultimately leads to negative outcomes for the cheater while affecting other people and business interests. Cheating in one's personal life can translate to lost income—this can certainly occur if you are a world-class athlete. Professional Golf Association (PGA) golfer Tiger Woods' marital infidelities were splashed across world headlines when his conduct was exposed. Since he is one of the most famous people in the world, this was considered newsworthy, and it cost him dearly. His celebrity endorsements decreased by an estimated $22 million in 2010. Most celebrity and athlete endorsement contracts contain moral clauses; after the Woods scandal, insurers were inundated with inquiries from corporations anxious to protect their name and brands. Dan Trueman, head of the enterprise risk department at R.J. Kiln and Company, the managing agent for Lloyd of London Insurance Company, said, "Tiger Woods has made people think about their reputations. These days, people don't worry about the office burning down, but instead about their intellectual property being damaged."

The stock price of seven publicly held companies that had dealt with Woods lost approximately $12 billion in market value in the months after he announced he was taking a break from golf.[1] There is no doubt that, in some cases, personal unethical behavior affects others and also has a direct effect on business.

Why do people cheat in sports and what is their motivation? Some of the reasons for the unethical behavior of athletes, owners, and coaches are:

- An overemphasis on winning, which fosters a "winning at all costs" attitude.
- Participants in the sports industry seek prestige or financial wealth.
- Athletes are pressured to perform at a higher level by coaches, universities, parents, and alumni.
- A lack of emphasis on sportsmanship and teamwork at amateur levels.
- The lack of role models in sports, although many believe athletes should not serve as role models.
- The "commercialization" of sports participants at the collegiate level.
- A misplaced emphasis on the significance of sports in society in general.

Most everyone in sports would consider cheating to be ethically or morally wrong. Gamesmanship, however, occupies a gray area between good sportsmanship and outright cheating. Gamesmanship utilizes legal tactics that are morally dubious and are designed to unsettle opponents—these tactics usually are not technically against the rules. With millions of dollars at stake at the professional and collegiate levels, gamesmanship can sometimes take precedence over sportsmanship.

Former National Football League (NFL) player Bob Whitfield said, "Everybody cheats. After that initial handshake, anything goes. The code of honor and respect probably ends when they toss the coin."[2] After all, sports are about competition, with athletes competing on the field, court, or ice to determine a winner. Winning is the most important goal of an athlete at

all levels of competition, especially as a professional. What club owner is going to tolerate a player who does not do everything within his or her power to win? Certainly, sports can be played on a non-competitive basis just for fun; however, even a pickup basketball game among friends can be fiercely competitive.

Competition in most sports is a zero-sum game—there has to be a winner and a loser. Furthermore, competitive sports have a set of rules players must abide by during the game. If a player violates the rules to win, many will say that the player did not "legally win" because he or she failed to play by the rules. Most fans do not like cheaters, but what about those players who straddle the line between fair play and cheating? One example of gamesmanship is trash talking. Perhaps the most infamous trash talking statement was made by boxer Mike Tyson: "When I'm ready I'm going to rip out his heart and feed it to him. . . . My style is impetuous, my defense is impregnable and I'm just ferocious. I want your heart. I want to eat your children. Praise be to Allah." The overwhelming majority of high schools, along with the National Collegiate Athletic Association (NCAA), prohibit trash talking and "excessive celebration." Nevertheless, athletes continue to berate, trash talk, showboat, and needle their opponents, hoping to gain an edge—but the remarks are sometimes inciting, profane, offensive, or demeaning.

Other examples of gamesmanship include taking an inordinate amount of time between points in a tennis match and calling an unnecessary time-out to "freeze" an opponent before a crucial foul shot in basketball or a field goal in football. The strategic foul is also a form of gamesmanship which may be committed to prevent an opponent from scoring an easy layup. Unlike outright cheating, these types of fouls are *openly* committed in the expectation that a penalty will be imposed. What about a manager who intentionally gets himself ejected from a game to motivate his team?[3] Gamesmanship tactics are, at a minimum, a violation of the spirit of the game, but when does it cross over the line from strategy to cheating? Are there certain times in sports when it is acceptable to intentionally break the rules to try to win? Should players try to gain an advantage any way they can, even if it means bending the rules just a little? Gamesmanship is not cheating per se since it typically lacks the element of secrecy or cover-up, but it definitely falls short of sportsmanship. A fine distinction can be made between sportsmanship and some forms of gamesmanship. Stephen Potter, in his seminal work on golf gamesmanship, states that gamesmanship had its origin in the sport of tennis.[4] There is no doubt that gamesmanship is an art and comes in all forms[5]—gamesmanship occurs in a variety of other industries as well, including the legal profession.[6]

There have been many definitions of sportsmanship, but scholar James Keating has set forth one of the more notable definitions:

> Sportsmanship is not merely an aggregate of moral qualities comprising a code of specialized behavior; it is also an attitude, a posture, a manner of interpreting what would otherwise be only a legal code. Yet the moral qualities believed to comprise the code have almost monopolized consideration and have proliferated to the point of depriving sportsmanship of any distinctiveness. Truthfulness, courage, Spartan endurance, self-control, self-respect, scorn of luxury, consideration for another's opinions and rights, courtesy, fairness, magnanimity, a high sense of honor, cooperation, generosity. The list seems interminable. Whereas the conduct and attitude which are properly designated as sportsmanlike may reflect many of the above-mentioned qualities, they are not all equally basic or fundamental. A man may be law-abiding, a team player, well-conditioned, courageous, humane, and the possessor of sangfroid without qualifying as a sportsman. On the other hand, he may certainly be categorized as a sportsman without possessing Spartan endurance or a scorn of luxury. Our concern is not with those virtues that might be found in the sportsman. Nor is it with those virtues that often accompany the sportsman. Our concern is rather with those moral habits or qualities which are essential, which characterize the participant as a sportsman. Examination reveals that there are some that are pivotal and absolutely essential; others peripheral.[7]

Which "moral habits [and] qualities" is Keating referring to that characterize someone as a true sportsman? Does this definition fit the current sports industry in the United States?

Alternatively, gamesmanship has been defined as follows:

> The winning-at-all costs mentality; it is the way that sports may be, not how it should be. It includes: looking for exceptions to the rules; fake fouls; illegal head starts; taunting to gain an advantage; intentionally injuring another player; intimidation; and espionage.[8]

There is often a fine line between gamesmanship and sportsmanship, but gamesmanship is clearly present in sports, and always has been.

Most would agree that cheating involves breaking the actual rules of the game, with the hope of not getting caught; whereas gamesmanship focuses on the idea of winning at all costs. It embodies the concept that "it is only cheating if you get caught." It has been argued by one noted sports writer that American sports are consumed with gamesmanship and that players rarely value sportsmanship.[9] The attitude is "show me a good loser and I'll show you a loser." Everyone is looking for an edge up in competition, and athletes sometimes do not care how they get it. Many support the concept of gamesmanship and believe it to be a legitimate way to compete in sports.

Conceptually, we can think about sportsmanship, gamesmanship, and cheating on a sliding scale with sportsmanship and cheating on the opposite ends. Gamesmanship sits somewhere in the middle and tips the scale towards one side or the other depending upon the nature of the conduct.

Sportsmanship ◄ - - - - - - Gamesmanship - - - - - - ► Cheating

🔎 CASE STUDY 2-1 Enforcing the Letter of the Law

As South Pasadena High School's best pole vaulter, Robin Laird stood at the top of the runway preparing for her first vault of the day, a 7 feet 6 inch attempt. Robin was probably not thinking about the friendship bracelet on her left wrist, but someone else was—the coach of the opposing team. She completed her vault, giving her team a 66–61 victory and an apparent league title; however, opposing coach Mike Knowles began pointing at his wrist and gesturing toward Laird. A section of the National Federation of State High School Association (NFHS) rules states: "Jewelry shall not be worn by contestants," and further adds that competitors, if wearing jewelry, would be disqualified from competition. When Laird found out what happened, she burst into tears, blaming herself for her team's loss at the event and the league championship. Coach Knowles responded, "It's unfortunate for the young lady. But you've got to teach the kids rules are rules." Some questioned the coach's motives for such a strict enforcement of the rules.[10]

1. Does the adage "It is not whether you win or lose but how you play the game" still hold true?
2. Does sportsmanship still exist at all levels of sport, or has it become a winning at all costs attitude?
3. What is the purpose of the "no jewelry" rule? Is the penalty for violating the rule unjust?
4. Was the coach's strict enforcement of the rules a violation of the spirit of competition?

🔎 CASE STUDY 2-2 Ultimate Act of Sportsmanship

Western Oregon's Sara Tucholsky hit a three-run home run in the second inning of a game against Central Washington. As she rounded first base in her home run trot, she collapsed in the base path when her right knee gave way. Her coach was told by the umpire that a pinch runner could take her place but she would only be credited with a single and two RBIs; the home run would be erased. It was against the rules to allow her teammates to help her around the bases. It was Sara's only home run in four years. Central Washington's first baseman, Mallory Holtman, her conference's all-time home run leader, had a solution. There existed no rule prohibiting her teammates from carrying Sara around the bases and that is what they did—Western Oregon won the game 4–2.[11]

1. Were the actions of Holtman and her teammates sportsmanlike?
2. Should a participant ever assist an opponent to win in a competitive sport?
3. Did the actions of Holtman and her teammates destroy the integrity of the sport?

No one may have been better at gamesmanship than National Basketball Association (NBA) champion Bill Laimbeer of the Detroit Pistons. He was once referred to as the NBA's "consummate actor and psychiatrist." For whatever reason, Laimbeer just had a way of "getting under people's skin".

Brad Daugherty of the Cleveland Cavaliers said of Laimbeer, "If he is trying to get on people's nerves, he is doing a good job."[12] Laimbeer elbowed, fought, pleaded, annoyed, and cajoled his way to two NBA championships while he had others thinking about how "annoying" he was. One *Sports Illustrated* writer put it succinctly: "As the baddest of the Detroit Pistons' Bad Boys in the late 80s, Laimbeer was as famous for being a crybaby jerk as he was for his contributions to the Pistons' back-to-back championships."[13] He played the "villain" well and no one was a better actor than Laimbeer, who could "flop" with the best in the league. At 6 feet 11inches and 260 pounds, Laimbeer provoked a long list of NBA Hall of Fame players. Laimbeer's wife once said, "People are always coming up to me and saying how nice I am and how could I be married to such a jackass. . . . You just have to get to know him. Don't take any of his bull-____, you just can't let him bug you." But many people did, and Laimbeer got two NBA rings while opponents were consumed with Laimbeer's annoying behavior.

When the St. Louis Blues were ready to take on the Detroit Red Wings in the 1996 Stanley Cup playoffs, they had a surprise waiting for them at Detroit's Joe Louis Arena. The Red Wings had been thoughtful hosts and had just painted the Blues' locker room. Just painted meaning one hour before the Blues arrived! How thoughtful, you might say; however, one player remarked: "While the nice, white appearance would have gotten Martha Stewart's seal of approval, the fumes from the paint could have choked a cow." The next year the Red Wings did the same thing again. Blues defenseman Marc Bergevin told reporters, "It looks nice, though."[14]

Tennis player Andy Murray was accused of using gamesmanship tactics to "rattle" his opponent when his opponent claimed Murray had faked an injury. Murray responded:

> That's very disappointing to hear. I never once used any of the rules that certain players have used to try to gain an upper hand in a match or to slow my opponent down. Definitely, when I played him at Queen's, this was not the case. I didn't know there was a problem but I couldn't grip the racket the following day. There are so many things

in matches where guys take toilet breaks, injury time-outs, delay you sometimes when you are trying to serve, and take a little bit longer between the points than they are allowed. It happens all the time. It's just part of the sport.[15]

Murray said he never had to resort to gamesmanship saying, "It's a form of cheating. It's bending the rules to gain advantage. It's a bit like diving in football. It does go on and certain players do it and certain players don't. I'm one of the guys who doesn't do it."[16]

Minnesota Twins first baseman Kent Hrbek was a big man, physically. In a controversial play in the 1991 World Series, Hrbek pulled Atlanta Braves player Ron Gant (172 lbs) off first base and Hrbek (253 lbs) tagged him out. The Braves called it cheating. Hrbek said, smiling, "I didn't get away with anything. . . . I just kept my glove on his leg, and his leg came off the base."[17]

Gamesmanship exists even in the gentlemanly game of golf. In the 1947 United States Open, PGA players Sam Snead and Lew Worsham were battling for the title. Just as Snead was about to putt on the 18th green, Worsham stopped him and called for a measurement. The officials brought out a tape measure and it was discovered that Snead was, in fact, farther from the hole (30.5 in. to 29.5 in. for Worsham) so Snead had the honor of putting first. After a delay of five minutes, Snead missed his putt and Worsham subsequently made his putt and won the tournament. Worsham broke no rules in asking for the measurement. Was Worsham a poor sport under the circumstances?[18] In another gamesmanship moment from golf, in the 1971 U.S. Open, on the first tee, PGA golfer Lee Trevino pulled a three foot rubber snake from his golf bag, held it up, wiggled it for the amazed gallery, and then tossed it at Jack Nicklaus's feet. Trevino won the playoff hole and the U.S. Open.

🔍 CASE STUDY 2-3   *The Spitter and Me*

Gaylord Perry was a good baseball pitcher. He was an expert at "doctoring" a baseball—or was he? Did he just make batters think he was throwing a "spitball"? Over his career Perry was noted for applying a variety of foreign substances to the ball, including Vaseline, baby oil, hair tonic, spit, and a few other substances that were unknown even to Perry. Perry is in the baseball Hall of Fame and has been called baseball's most notorious cheater. He won two Cy Young awards and went to five All-Star games. Perry once stated, "When my wife was having babies, the doctor would send over all kinds of stuff and I'd try that too. Once I even used fishing line oil." The title of his biography is "Me and the Spitter".[19]

1. Did Gaylord Perry's conduct constitute cheating?
2. If it is cheating, why is cheating tolerated in baseball in certain contexts?
3. If Perry did cheat (as he admitted), should he be treated any differently than a player who took performance-enhancing drugs?[20]
4. When a cardboard fingernail file came flying out of Minnesota Twins pitcher Joe Niekro's back pocket during a 1987 game, many accused him of cheating. Niekro said he needed the emery board to file his fingernails. He was suspended by Major League Baseball (MLB) for ten games. Should filing the laces on the baseball be viewed any differently than applying a foreign substance?

🔍 CASE STUDY 2-4   *"Creative Cheating"*

Mark Schlereth was an offensive lineman for the National Football League (NFL) Denver Broncos. To gain an advantage in a playoff game, he and his fellow linemen coated their arms and the backs of their jerseys with Vaseline. All the linemen were "slimy," and no one could grab onto them. The Broncos won the game 14–12. Schlereth stated, "Did I grease up my jersey and use sticky substances on my gloves? You're damn right. . . . What you call cheating is a fine line. It's an interesting line. What we did, in the locker room, is called being creative. Certain cheating is snickered at, or applauded."[21]

1. Where should the line be drawn between strategy and blatant cheating?
2. Does the answer to this question depend on whether there is a violation of a written rule? Does the NFL need a rule that states, "No player shall apply any artificial substance to game apparel"?

🔍 CASE STUDY 2-5   *When is Enough, Enough?*

Beginning in September 2006, Connecticut high school football teams were subject to a "50 Point Rule." Football coaches who were found to be running up the score when their team was ahead by 50 points or more were subject to sanctions. The first week of the season, Bridge Central beat Bassick 56–0. At halftime the score was 49–0. The third touchdown was scored by a third string player. The loss was Bassick's fourth in a row. The Bassick coach noted that Dave Cadelina, coach of the Bridgeport team, had acted in a sportsmanlike manner while coaching the game. A three-member panel examined the actions of the coach and exonerated him, finding he did not engage in any unsportsmanlike acts.[22]

1. Do you favor a rule similar to the 50 Point Rule? What is the purpose of the rule?
2. Would you distinguish between professional and amateur sports?
3. Should different rules apply to different sports such as soccer, baseball, football, and hockey?
4. As a coach, should you ever instruct a player not to score or play to the fullest extent of their ability?

🔎 CASE STUDY 2-6   Poor Taste or Academic Brilliance?

The Rice University Marching Owl Band (the MOB) has always been a little esoteric, even for the elite. Their "act" is usually received well, even though only a selected few may truly understand their intended purpose. Todd Graham was the head football coach for the second smallest school in Division I-A football, the Rice Owls. He left that job after one year to go to the NCAA's smallest Division I-A football program, Tulsa. The following year, Tulsa defeated Rice in the last game of the season at Rice Stadium in Houston. During the halftime show, the MOB's performance became the subject of an investigation by Conference USA. The overriding theme of the performance was a search by the MOB through the nine circles of hell based on Dante's *Divine Comedy*. The band suggested that "Graham's shredded contract was found in the fourth circle of hell with the greedy and the avaricious—also claiming that former Texas A&M coach Dennis Franchione was in that circle." They also claimed "the coach could be found beyond hell's greatest depths behind a door marked 'Welcome to Tulsa.'"[23] The skit ended with the public address announcer calling Graham a "douchebag." The MOB later apologized, saying the skit was meant to be funny.[24]

1. Should the university or the band be sanctioned for their behavior, or, should their behavior be viewed as an artistic expression in the form of parody?
2. How many spectators do you think understood what the performance was actually about anyway?

🔎 CASE STUDY 2-7   "Icing" the Kicker

"Icing" the kicker has become a term of art in American football. Coaches attempt to call a time-out seconds before a kicker lines up to kick an important field goal. If a high school placekicker lines up to kick the winning field goal and, just as he begins his kick, the opposing coach calls a time-out, is that considered a strategic move or poor sportsmanship? Should time-outs be used in such a fashion? If time-outs are at the discretion of the coach, does that, by definition, make it ethical? Does it matter if this occurs in a professional or amateur game?[25] One study shows that placekickers in the NFL made 77.3% of field goals kicked in the final two minutes or in overtime when no time-out was called and made 79.7% when a time-out was called by the opposing coach, notwithstanding the distance of the kick.[26]

▶ Rules and Regulations

The main principle of sportsmanship is to conduct yourself in such a manner as to increase rather than decrease the pleasures found in a sporting activity—both for yourself and your opponent. Sportsmanship involves the value of fair play, which implies adherence to the letter and spirit of equality as indicated in the rules, regulations, and customs that control play of the sport in question. Many rules and customs regulate sportsmanship; for example, the NCAA attempts to foster sportsmanship in intercollegiate sports. The association has a myriad of rules dealing with eligibility and personal conduct policies for fans, parents, coaches, and participants. In addition, every sport has customs which are usually not written rules. For example, although not officially in the rulebook, a baseball player who hits a home run should run at a fairly quick pace around the bases and not at a slow trot. A player who takes his time may be seen as "showing up" the pitcher and could be subject to retaliation by the opposing club.

Rules and regulations are promulgated by state athletic associations, professional and amateur sports leagues and associations, and under state laws. Consider the ethical dilemmas presented for all participants and the sports officials in the following cases.

🔍 CASE STUDY 2-8 Trippin' Coach

There is no doubt that New York Jets strength coach, Sal Alosi, is a competitor both on and off the field. Alosi showed his own strength in a game on Monday Night Football when he tripped Miami Dolphins player Nolan Carroll as Carroll ran by the Jets bench during the game. He was suspended for the remainder of the season and fined $25,000 by the NFL. Alosi said "I accept responsibility for my actions and respect the team's decision . . . You are asking me to give you a logical explanation for an illogical act."[27]

1. Did the league take enough disciplinary action against the coach for his unethical conduct?
2. Was the fine too little, considering the coach could have severely injured the Dolphin player?
3. Does your assessment of the disciplinary action in this case depend upon whether there is a league rule that prohibits sideline tripping?

Consider Case 2-1, in which a boxer allegedly used a foreign substance in his hand-wraps in violation of professional boxing rules.

⚖ CASE 2-1 Margarito v. State Athletic Commission

2010 WL 4010605

1. The Parties

Margarito is a professional boxer who has fought more than 30 times across the United States, including more than half a dozen championship fights. Margarito was licensed by the Commission as a professional boxer in California from the mid-1990's until 2009 when his license was revoked.

The Commission is the agency with sole jurisdiction over professional boxing in California and is responsible for adopting and enforcing the professional boxing rules in this state. The Commission has the authority to issue, suspend, and revoke boxing licenses . . .

2. The Illegal Hand Wraps

Margarito was scheduled to fight Shane Mosley (Mosley) in a welterweight championship boxing contest in Los Angeles on January 24, 2009. Margarito's trainer, Javier Capetillo (Capetillo), was responsible for preparing the hand wraps, bandages, and tape used to protect Margarito's hands during the contest. Capetillo was a professional trainer who had worked with many professional boxers during his 38-year career as a trainer. During his 11 years as Margarito's trainer, Capetillo was the only person who wrapped Margarito's hands before a boxing contest.

Before the contest with Mosley, Capetillo was wrapping Margarito's hands while four Commission inspectors and Mosley's trainer observed the process. After Capetillo finished wrapping Margarito's right hand, Mosley's trainer asked the inspectors to physically inspect a pre-made gauze "knuckle pad" insert that Capetillo was about to wrap over Margarito's left hand. The inspectors found that the inner layers of the pad were discolored and that the pad felt harder than it should have. In a report prepared after the inspection, Commission Inspector Che Guevara (Guevara) described the gauze pad removed from Margarito's left hand as "dirty-looking" and smeared with a white substance that looked like plaster and was hard to the touch. Concluding that the pad violated the rules, the inspectors confiscated the pad and instructed Capetillo to prepare a new one.

Mosley's trainer then asked the inspectors to examine the gauze insert in Margarito's already wrapped right hand. Margarito insisted there was nothing in the right hand wrapping, and held his hand out saying, "Touch it. Feel it. Go ahead. There is nothing in it." The inspectors ordered the wrapping removed and found a similar improperly hardened pad, which they confiscated. After Capetillo prepared two new knuckle pads, the inspectors approved Margarito's hand wraps and allowed Margarito to proceed with the boxing match.

In a letter dated January 27, 2009, the Commission notified Margarito that his boxing license was temporarily suspended pending a final determination of the case. The Commission explained the reason for the suspension as follows:

> This action is taken because of your recent participation in what appears to be a violation of rule 323. Rule 323 limits the use of gauze and tape on an athlete's hands and requires that both contestants be represented while the gauze and tape are applied. The rule also prescribes the manner in which the gauze and tape is applied to an athlete's hands. Here, it appears that a foreign substance was used in the hand-wraps in violation of Rule 323. Additionally, Commission rule 390 allows the commission to revoke, fine, suspend or otherwise discipline any licensee who 'conducts himself or herself at any time or place in a manner which is determined by the Commission to reflect discredit to boxing.'

The Commission set a formal hearing on the matter for February 10, 2009.

3. Administrative Hearing

At the February 10, 2009 hearing, Commission Inspectors Guevara, Dean Lohuis (Lohuis), and Mike Bray (Bray) all testified that they felt the knuckle pads Capetillo initially placed in Margarito's hand wraps before the Mosley fight and that the pads felt harder than allowed by the applicable rules and were confiscated. After feeling one of the confiscated pads at the hearing, Margarito admitted that he felt something hard. Capetillo admitted that the confiscated pads violated the applicable rules, and acknowledged that had they been used, they could have seriously injured Margarito's opponent.

The commissioners at the hearing inspected one of the pads that had been confiscated from Margarito's hand wraps and compared it to the soft gauze that is used to wrap a boxer's hand before a contest. The other confiscated pad was sent to the Department of Justice's forensic laboratory for evaluation, where it was photographed under a microscope at six times magnification. The photographs were presented as evidence at the hearing.

At the conclusion of the hearing, all seven commissioners voted unanimously to revoke Margarito's license.

4. The Commission's Decision

In a written decision issued on March 31, 2009, the Commission found that the knuckle pads removed from Margarito's hand wraps before the Mosley fight on January 24, 2009, had been adulterated with a white plaster-like substance. The Commission concluded that the use of adulterated knuckle pads by a boxer seriously endangers the boxer's opponent and gives the boxer an unfair advantage that causes discredit to boxing. The Commission further concluded that "[b]ecause [Margarito] violated Commission Rule 323, there is sufficient cause for revocation of [Margarito's] boxing license . . .

The Commission rejected Margarito's argument that he could not be held responsible for violating rule 323 because he did not know that Capetillo had inserted the illegal pads into his hand wraps and noted that "[t]he Commission's laws and rules, enacted to protect public health and safety, do not require either knowledge or intent for a violation to occur." The Commission stated: "Because of the serious physical consequences which could have resulted to the other boxer from the use of boxing gloves loaded with illegal knuckle pads, the appropriate penalty is revocation."

. . . the Commission has adopted professional boxing rules. (Cal.Code Regs., tit. 4, § 201.) Rule 323 specifies the materials that may be used to wrap a boxer's hands during a contest and prescribes the manner in which those materials may be applied. It states:

> "Bandages shall not exceed the following restrictions: One winding of surgeon's adhesive tape, not over one and one-half inches wide, placed directly on the hand to protect that part of the hand near the wrist. Said tape may cross the back of the hand twice but shall not extend within one inch of the knuckles when hand is clenched to make a fist. Contestants shall use soft surgical bandage not over two inches wide, held in place by not more than ten yards of surgeon's adhesive tape for each hand. Not more than twenty yards of bandage may be used to complete the wrappings for each hand. Bandages shall be applied in the dressing room in the presence of a commission representative and both contestants. Either contestant may waive his privilege of witnessing the bandaging of his opponent's hands."

1. Were the actions of the State Athletic Commission appropriate? Was revocation of Margarito's boxing license an appropriate penalty in this case?
2. Do you think there was an actual violation of the rules by the *boxer* under these circumstances?

Margarito v. State Athletic Commission, U.S. Supreme Court.

⌕ CASE STUDY 2-9   Injury Lists

NFL teams are required to submit to the league office a list of injured players for the next week's game. Under NFL rules, a player is listed as "probable" if he has a better than 50% chance of playing in the next week's game. Players who are listed as "questionable" by the club are 50–50, and "doubtful" means the player has a 75% or greater chance of not playing in the next game. "Out" means exactly that: the player will not play. Teams and coaches have been fined for failing to follow the NFL guidelines in reporting injuries. Former Dallas Cowboys coach Jimmy Johnson stated, "If you want to be real technical about it you could list the majority of your team because in a sport as violent as pro football, nearly all players have something that's not 100%." Former Pittsburgh Steelers coach Bill Cower stated, "Sometimes when a guy had an ankle (injury), I might list it as a knee, just because I didn't want people knowing where to take shots at my players." Jimmy Johnson further stated, "Scanning injury reports rarely had an effect on our preparation, unless it's a key player like a quarterback, and even then, it's iffy."

1. What is the purpose of the NFL's injury reporting rules?
2. Did coach Cower's actions really protect his players, or do you consider them a form of cheating?

🔍 CASE STUDY 2-10 Draft Lottery Systems and Playing to Lose

The NFL Arizona Cardinals have had a horrible season. The Cardinals are 2–13 (post Kurt Warner era) going into the final game against the Seattle Seahawks, who are 9–6 and looking for a wild card spot. The Houston Texans are also 2–13 and are playing the 13–2 Bears, which need to win their final game to gain home field advantage in the playoffs. The Cardinals hold the tie breaker with the Houston Texans, so if they both lose, the Cardinals will get the first draft pick. The number one draft pick is certainly going to be Joe Savage, a "can't miss" NFL quarterback who by all accounts will be a sure Hall of Famer. Early in the fourth quarter, the Cardinals are beating the Seahawks 20–7 when the coach, at the request of the owner, inserts a rookie quarterback into the game who had never played in the NFL. The Cardinals lose 28–20 and get the first draft pick.

1. Should a team ever try to lose a game purposefully? Does it tarnish the integrity of the game if they attempt to do so?
2. How do you view the actions of the Cardinals coaching staff or the owner?
3. Should all leagues adopt a lottery draft system to discourage teams from "tanking"? In a lottery draft system, the top picks are decided by a lottery and are chosen from the teams that do not make the playoffs.

The NFL experienced a legal quagmire involving the Patriots' deflating footballs during the 2015 playoffs, which became widely known as "Deflategate." The controversy resulted in Patriots quarterback Tom Brady being suspended for four games the following season and the team being fined $1 million and losing two draft picks. The matter ultimately ended up in federal court, where Judge Richard M. Berman vacated Brady's suspension, which allowed him to play the entire 2015 season; however, following the conclusion of the season, the Second Circuit Court of Appeals reversed the lower court and reinstated Brady's four-game suspension, which became effective for the 2016 regular season. The 2016 season concluded with the Patriots winning the Super Bowl and Tom Brady being named MVP of the game.

⚖ CASE 2-2 NFL v. NFLPA and Tom Brady

820 F.3d 527 (2nd Cir. 2016)

On January 18, 2015, the New England Patriots and the Indianapolis Colts played in the American Football Conference Championship Game at the Patriots' home stadium in Foxborough, Massachusetts to determine which team would advance to Super Bowl XLIX. During the second quarter, Colts linebacker D'Qwell Jackson intercepted a pass thrown by Brady and took the ball to the sideline, suspecting it might be inflated below the allowed minimum pressure of 12.5 pounds per square inch. After confirming that the ball was underinflated, Colts personnel informed League officials, who decided to test all of the game balls at halftime. Eleven other Patriots balls and four Colts balls were tested using two air gauges, one of which had been used before the game to ensure that the balls were inflated within the permissible range of 12.5 to 13.5 psi. While each of the four Colts balls tested within the permissible range on at least one of the gauges, all eleven of the Patriots balls measured below 12.5 psi on both.

On January 23, the National Football League announced that it had retained Theodore V. Wells, Jr., Esq., and the law firm of Paul, Weiss, Rifkind, Wharton & Garrison to conduct an independent investigation into whether there had been improper ball tampering before or during the game. That investigation culminated in a 139–page report released on May 6, which concluded that it was "more probable than not" that two Patriots equipment officials—Jim McNally and John Jastremski—had "participated in a deliberate effort to release air from Patriots game balls after the balls were examined by the referee." Specifically, the Report found that McNally had removed the game balls from the Officials' Locker Room shortly before the game, in violation of standard protocol, and taken them to a single-toilet bathroom, where he locked the door and used a needle to deflate the Patriots footballs before bringing them to the playing field.

In addition to videotape evidence and witness interviews, the investigation team examined text messages exchanged between McNally and Jastremski in the months leading up to the AFC Championship Game. In the messages, the two discussed Brady's stated preference for less-inflated footballs. McNally also referred to himself as "the deflator" and quipped that he was "not going to ESPN . . . yet," and Jastremski agreed to provide McNally with a "needle" in exchange for "cash," "newkicks," and memorabilia autographed by Brady. The Report also relied on a scientific study conducted by Exponent, an engineering and scientific consulting firm, which found that the underinflation could not "be explained completely by basic scientific principles, such as the Ideal Gas Law," particularly since the average pressure of the Patriots balls was significantly lower than that of the Colts balls. Exponent further concluded that a reasonably experienced individual could deflate thirteen footballs using a needle in well under the amount of time that McNally was in the bathroom.

The investigation also examined Brady's potential role in the deflation scheme. Although the evidence of his involvement was "less direct" than that of McNally's or Jastremski's, the Wells Report concluded that it was "more probable than not" that Brady had been "at least generally aware" of McNally and Jastremski's actions, and that it was "unlikely that an equipment assistant and a locker room attendant would deflate game balls without Brady's" "knowledge," "approval," "awareness," and "consent." Among other things, the Report cited a text message exchange between McNally and Jastremski in which McNally complained about Brady and threatened to overinflate the game balls, and Jastremski replied that he had "[t]alked to [Tom] last night" and "[Tom] actually brought you up and said you must have a lot of stress trying to get them done." The investigators also observed that Brady was a "constant reference point" in McNally and Jastremski's discussions about the scheme, had publicly stated his preference for less-inflated footballs in the past, and had been "personally involved in [a] 2006 rule change that allowed visiting teams to prepare game balls in accordance with the preferences of their quarterbacks."

Significantly, the Report also found that, after more than six months of not communicating by phone or message, Brady and Jastremski spoke on the phone for approximately 25 minutes on January 19, the day the investigation was announced. This unusual pattern of communication continued over the next two days. Brady had also taken the "unprecedented step" on January 19 of inviting Jastremski to the quarterback room, and had sent Jastremski several text messages that day that were apparently designed to calm him. The Report added that the investigation had been impaired by Brady's refusal "to make available any documents or electronic information (including text messages and emails)," notwithstanding an offer by the investigators to allow Brady's counsel to screen the production.

National Football League, Defendant–Appellant, v. Tom Brady, Counter–Claimant–Appellee, U.S. Supreme Court.

In its ruling upholding Brady's four-game suspension, the Court of Appeals stressed that the collective bargaining agreement failed to contractually stipulate the procedural safeguards that Brady and the NFL Players Association believed ought to exist.

▶ Ethical Choices in America's National Pastime

It is probable that no other sport blurs the thin line between gamesmanship and sportsmanship more than baseball.[28] Stealing signs, pitchers scuffing balls, batters corking bats, phantom tags, ejected managers disguising themselves in the dugout to go undetected by umpires, brushback pitches, and head games have always been part of the national pastime. Whether before, during, or after the game, baseball has seen its share of gamesmanship and blatant cheating.[29]

Baseball is a game of rules—in some regards they are very strict. It is played on a diamond between two distinct white lines and is dominated by statistics and numbers. Notwithstanding this structure, baseball also has its share of *unwritten* rules that players are encouraged to follow. Baseball's list of unwritten rules has included the following:[30]

1. Don't swing at the first pitch after back-to-back home runs.
2. Don't "work the count" when your team is winning or losing by a wide margin.
3. When a batter is hit by a pitch, the batter should never rub the mark that is made by the baseball.
4. A batter should never stand on the dirt cutout at home plate while a pitcher is warming up.
5. A player should never walk in front of a catcher or umpire when getting into the batter's box.
6. A player should never help the opposition make a play.
7. A relief pitcher should "take it easy" when pitching to another relief pitcher.
8. A player should follow the umpire's Code when addressing an umpire on the field.
9. Pitchers should always stay in the dugout until the end of the inning in which they get "pulled."
10. Pitchers should never show up their fielders.

An ESPN poll of baseball's unwritten rules asked readers the following questions: In your opinion are these tactics a violation of baseball's unwritten rules? Do they constitute unsportsmanlike conduct?

1. A batter calls time-out when the pitcher is in the middle of his wind-up.
2. A batter stands at home plate and admires a home run.
3. A batter flips the bat or takes an excruciatingly slow home run trot.
4. A batter runs across the mound while the pitcher is standing on it.
5. A batter bunts to break up a no-hitter.
6. A batter peeks back at a catcher's setup or gets signs relayed to him from a teammate on second base.
7. A batter intentionally leans over the plate to be hit by a pitch.
8. A batter takes a big cut at a 3–0 pitch when his team is way ahead.[31]

Are players required to abide by these unwritten codes? Does the amount of money professional athletes earn entice them to break the unwritten codes of a sport? Do you consider breaking an unwritten code unsportsmanlike? (After all, it is unwritten!) Is it cheating or just gamesmanship to do so? Should a player announce to other players that he will no longer be abiding by the sport's unwritten code? Should amateur players (including youth sports participants) have an unwritten code of rules as well?

CASE STUDY 2-11   Alex Rodriguez "Ha!"

In a game between the Yankees and the Blue Jays in May 2007, Alex Rodriguez, as a base runner for the Yankees yelled "ha!" in an effort to distract Toronto third baseman Howie Clark from catching a fly ball. It worked, and the ball dropped in for a run-scoring single. Baseball has no rules against what Rodriguez did. The Toronto manager commented, "I haven't been in the game that long. Maybe I'm naïve. But, to me, it's bush league. One thing, to everybody in this business, you always look at the Yankees and they do things right. They play hard, class operation, that's what the Yanks are known for. That's not Yankee baseball." Rodriguez's actions were viewed by many in baseball as a "bush league" tactic. Rodriguez responded, "We're desperate. We haven't won a game in a little bit now. We won the game."[32]

1. Are Rodriguez's actions considered to be more unsportsmanlike since he was baseball's highest paid player at the time?[33]
2. Are Rodriguez's actions merely gamesmanship or can you make the argument that it was cheating? Why not just blame Howie Clark for missing an easy fly ball?
3. As the most visible and highest paid player on arguably the world's most famous sports club, doesn't he have to give his club every chance to win? Yankees management did not criticize the actions of Rodriguez.

The list of gamesmanship episodes in baseball is long, but a few examples worth noting are presented in the following case studies.

CASE STUDY 2-12   The "Phantom Tag"

A "phantom tag" has been defined by *The Dickson Baseball Dictionary* as "a missed tag or a tag from a glove without the ball in it, either one of which is mistakenly credited as a legal tag." Dustin Pedroia is an All-Star second baseman for the Boston Red Sox. Certainly, he knows he needs to tag a base runner with the baseball for that runner to be called out by the umpire. Pedroia supposedly tagged Orioles centerfielder Felix Pie as Pie slid into second base. The only problem was, the baseball was in Pedroia's left hand and he only tagged Pie with his empty glove. With a quick sleight of hand, Pedroia placed the ball in his glove and showed it to the umpire, who immediately declared Pie out. Did Pedroia cheat? He obviously knew what he was doing and even made an attempt to cover up his illegal actions. Could his actions be viewed as a veteran ballplayer doing whatever he needed to do to help his team win a game in a heated pennant race? Pedroia was not being paid to be a "good sport" by his club but was being paid to win. Should Pedroia have come clean, admitted his trick to the umpire, and allowed the umpire to correct his mistake? If Pedroia admitted his intentional breaking of the rules to the umpire, what would Red Sox management have said to Pedroia? Possibly, "Excellent job, Dustin, you have kept the integrity of the national pastime intact"? Most likely not. On the contrary, Pedroia was probably congratulated by his teammates in the clubhouse for his deceptive actions on the diamond.[34]

The Major League Baseball Uniform Player's Contract mentions fair play, sportsmanship, and good citizenship:

In consideration of the facts above recited and of the promises of each to the other, the parties agree as follows:

Loyalty

3.(a) The Player agrees to perform his services hereunder diligently and faithfully, to keep himself in first-class physical condition and to obey the Club's training rules, and pledges himself to the American public and to the Club to conform to high standards of personal conduct, *fair play* and good *sportsmanship*. (emphasis added)

TERMINATION ...
By Club

7.(b) The Club may terminate this contract upon written notice to the Player (but only after requesting and obtaining waivers of this contract from all other Major League Clubs) if the Player shall at any time: (1) fail, refuse, or neglect to conform his personal conduct to the standards of *good citizenship* and good sportsmanship . . . (emphasis added)

A Major League Baseball player is contractually obligated to engage in fair play and sportsmanship and be a good citizen. How does that affect your viewpoint of gamesmanship and sportsmanship if the player is contractually bound to perform such duties?

🔎 CASE STUDY 2-13 Baseball's Showman

There is no doubt Bill Veeck was the showman of baseball and proved it over many years in the game with his creative ideas. He used gimmicks and many other strategies to get fans to the ballpark. He also wanted to win.[35] On August 19, 1951, Veeck's last place St. Louis Browns were playing the Detroit Tigers in the second game of a double header in St. Louis. Veeck was looking for something to spice up his club's last place position. He found it in Eddie Gaedel. Unbeknownst to others, Veeck had signed Gaedel to a major league contract. Veeck instructed Browns' manager, Zack Taylor, to send Gaedel to the plate in the first inning as a pinch hitter. Using a pinch hitter in the first inning may seem odd in baseball circles; however, what was so unique about Gaedel was that he was only 3 feet 7 inches tall. Prior to his baseball career, Gaedel had been working in "show business."[36] Tigers pitcher Bob Cain threw four straight balls to Gaedel, who set his bat down and dutifully walked to first base.[37]

There are no height or weight requirements for players in baseball. With that in mind, consider the following:

1. Do you consider Veeck's actions demeaning to Gaedel or to the integrity of the game of baseball, or both?
2. If Gaedel had a good chance of getting on base when he batted, would it be acceptable for a club to use him in strategic situations during the game?
3. Should Veeck's actions be considered gamesmanship or cheating or simply boorish, discriminatory, demeaning, strategic, poor sportsmanship, or unprofessional? Perhaps this was merely a marketing ploy by a desperate owner to attract fans to a last place club.

When Veeck owned the Cleveland Indians in the 1940s, he had a movable fence installed in the outfield that could be shifted as much as 15 feet. How much Veeck moved it depended on how the Indians matched up against an opponent. Veeck could find no rule against it, although the American League eventually adopted one in 1947 in response to Veeck's actions, decreeing that outfield fences be kept in a "fixed" position during the season. Is this cheating? Must there be a violation of an express rule in order to constitute cheating?

🔎 CASE STUDY 2-14 Actor – Derek Jeter

MLB official rules allow a batter to take first base if he is struck by a pitched ball. It would seem to be simple to determine if a player has been hit by a ball thrown by the pitcher, but that has not always been the case. New York Yankees shortstop Derek Jeter was undoubtedly *not* hit by a pitched ball, but pretended as if he were. He was so convincing, the umpire awarded him first base.[38] Former major league catcher Tim McCarver said, "What upset some people, perhaps, is that he was so demonstrative when it hit the bat, but to think that quickly is remarkable . . . You can't say, 'No, the ball didn't hit me.' You're trying to get on base; you're trying to win the game." "It's gamesmanship," said Bob Costas, another veteran baseball commentator, approvingly of Jeter's actions. "This is completely different from steroids or stealing signs with a pair of binoculars."[39] Is Costas right? Why is it completely different from stealing signs with binoculars?

▶ The Ethics of Spying and Espionage in Sports

Spying and gaining access to an opponent's strategies is a long-standing issue in sports. The question is, when does it go too far? Should one team try to spy on another team's practice to gain valuable information for the next game? It seems to be acceptable in baseball to steal signs legally, which, of course, is an oxymoron; however, even in baseball, there is a line that can be crossed. MLB player Miguel Tejada was accused of "tipping" pitches to friends on opposing teams and also allowing balls his friends hit to get past him at shortstop during games with lopsided scores. No hard evidence was ever produced and Tejada vehemently denied the charges. Some Oakland Athletics (A's) players had major concerns and called a team meeting over the issue. Pitcher Livan Hernandez said, "If I knew someone

was doing that, I would fight them there, right on the field."

Significant in the eyes of some of the players was an incident in the second game of a series against Toronto. Tejada did not get to an easy ground ball hit by Tony Batista (a friend of Tejada's from the Dominican Republic), off reliever Mark Guthrie with the A's leading 8–2. When the inning was over, A's players fumed on the bench. If the charges were proven, what should happen to Tejada? If the score was not close, is it still an issue? Could Tejada's actions have been deemed unethical or cheating? Like other major league players, Tejada has a loyalty clause in his contract. Could the A's terminate Tejada's contract for his disloyalty based on his actions if it was proven that he was assisting opposing players?[40]

The scenario presented in Case Study 2-13 deals with the NFL's loyalty clause, which states in part: "Club employs player as a skilled football player. Player accepts such employment. He agrees to give his best efforts and loyalty to the club . . ." (NFL Player Contract, paragraph 2.)

🔎 CASE STUDY 2-15 Traitor or Loyal Teammate?

The Jacksonville Jaguars (Jags) had an upcoming game against the Pittsburgh Steelers, their division rival. In anticipation of the game, the Jags signed linebacker Marquis Cooper from the Steelers practice squad, which they are allowed to do under league rules. They signed him on November 27 and released him

December 6, after the game. During the brief time he was on the Jags, Cooper said Jacksonville coaches "asked him many questions about the Steelers, with particular interest in some of their players." Everything Jacksonville did was according to NFL rules. Did they do anything that could be deemed unethical? If a team follows the rules, does that mean they were acting ethically?[41] The player has no more legal obligations to his former club—he is now playing under a contract that requires him to give his best effort and loyalty to the new club. If he has information that can help his new club, should he be willing to share that information? For example, the Redskins signed quarterback Andre Woodson away from the New York Giants. Woodson said, "Right now, anything to help the Redskins out, I'm willing to do."[42] Would a quarterback be familiar with all the plays run by the offense, including audibles? Do you place this in the "legalized spying" category? How would you view this situation if Woodson had only stayed on the Redskins roster for the game against the Giants and then had his playing contract terminated?

Businesses develop trade secrets and make every effort to protect those secrets from their competitors. Trade secrets are non-public information, a valuable piece of intellectual property to any business. If a competitor attempts to misappropriate a trade secret, they can be sued. A trade secret is defined by the Uniform Trade Secrets Act (UTSA) as follows:

> Information, including a formula, pattern, compilation, program device, method, technique, or process, that: (i) derives independent economic value, actual or potential, from not being generally known to, and not being readily ascertainable by proper means by other persons who can obtain economic value from its disclosure or use, and (ii) is the subject of efforts that are reasonable under the circumstances to maintain its secrecy. U.T.S.A. §1(4).

Is sports competition the same as business competition? Is there any information in sports that can be protected under the trade secret law? What about a team's play signs or signals being relayed during a game? Hall of Famer Christy Mathewson wrote in 1912, "All is fair in love, war, and baseball except stealing signals dishonestly."[43] Former major league pitcher Bert Blyleven could be classified as an artist. He commented on sign stealing, "Stealing signs or noticing when a pitcher is unintentionally tipping his pitches is not cheating, that's just baseball. You try to get an advantage over your opponent any way you can."[44]

There is nothing in baseball's rulebook about sign stealing, but stealing signs with the use of technological equipment is a no-no. In 2001, MLB Vice President Sandy Alderson issued the following memo:

> No club shall use electronic equipment, including walkie-talkies and cellular telephones, to communicate to, or with, any on-field personnel, including those in the dugout, bullpen, field and–during the game–the clubhouse. Such equipment may not be used for the purpose of stealing signs or conveying information designed to give a club an advantage.

In 2017, the Yankees filed a complaint with the MLB commissioner's office that included a video they took of the Red Sox dugout during a three-game series in Boston showing a member of the Red Sox training staff looking at his Apple Watch in the dugout. As it turned out, the Red Sox were stealing hand signals from the Yankees' catcher, and the Yankees were not the only victims of this illicit scheme. The Red Sox admitted to the commissioner that their trainers were receiving signals from video replay personnel and then relaying messages to players in the dugout, who, in turn, would signal teammates on the field about the type of pitch that was about to be thrown.[45] The Red Sox were fined an undisclosed amount that would be given to hurricane relief efforts in Florida. If sign stealing has always been a part of the game and considered merely gamesmanship, why does the use of technological equipment to steal signs constitute cheating?

Should a team's playbook be considered a trade secret?[46] In November 2010, a Connecticut high school football coach was suspended for using an opposing quarterback's missing arm-band to assist his defense. The opposing player had misplaced the armband during the first half of the game. The principal of the high school suspended the coach after the coach admitted using the list of coded plays.[47]

Although certain actions may be unethical and even acknowledged as unethical by the parties involved, that does not necessarily mean the law provides a remedy for that behavior. Consider the now infamous NFL "spygate" episode involving the New England Patriots and coach Bill Belichick. Carl Mayer, a New York Jets season ticket holder, argued that the ticket he purchased stated that any game would "be played in accordance with NFL rules and regulations" and furthermore that as a ticket holder he "fully anticipated and contracted for a ticket to observe an honest match that would be played accordingly to NFL rules." He asked the court to award him (and other Jets fans who were in the same situation) $61,600,000, which was the amount paid by New York Jets ticket holders to watch eight "fraudulent games between the New England Patriots and the New York Jets" between 2000 and 2007. In a word, the court said "no" to Mr. Mayer and other Jets fans.

⚖ CASE 2-3 *Mayer v. Belichick*

605 F.3d 223 (3rd Cir. 2010)

This highly unusual case was filed by a disappointed football fan and season ticket-holder in response to the so-called "Spygate" scandal. This scandal arose when it was discovered that the Patriots were surreptitiously videotaping the signals of their opponents.

[Carl Mayer alleges that] Bill Belichick, during a game with the New York Jets on September 9, 2007, instructed an agent of the New England Patriots to surreptitiously videotape the New York Jets coaches and players on the field with the purpose of illegally recording, capturing and stealing the New York Jets signals and visual coaching instructions. The Patriots were in fact subsequently found by the National Football League (NFL) to have improperly engaged in such conduct. This violated the contractual expectations and rights of New York Jets ticket-holders who fully anticipated and contracted for a ticket to observe an honest match played in compliance with all laws, regulations and NFL rules.

Mayer, a New York Jets season ticket holder, contends that in purchasing tickets to watch the New York Jets that, as a matter of contract, the tickets imply that each game will be played in accordance with NFL rules and regulations as well as all applicable federal and state laws. Mayer [and others] contend that the Patriots tortuously [sic] interfered with their contractual relations with the New York Jets in purchasing the tickets. They further claim that the Patriots violated the New Jersey Consumer Fraud Act and the New Jersey Deceptive Business Practices Act. They also claim that the Patriots violated federal and state racketeering laws by using the NFL as an enterprise to carry out their illegal scheme. Because the Patriots have been found in other games to have illegally used video equipment, Mayer sought damages for New York Jets ticket-holders for all games played in Giants stadium between the New York Jets and the New England Patriots since Bill Belichick became head coach in 2000.

[Court's Decision]

At their most fundamental level, the various claims alleged here arose out of the repeated and surreptitious violations of a specific NFL rule. This rule provides that "'no video recording devices of any kind are permitted to be in use in the coaches' booth, on the field, or in the locker room during the game'" and that "all video for coaching purposes must be shot from locations 'enclosed on all sides with a roof overhead.'" In a September 6, 2007, memorandum, Ray Anderson, the NFL's executive vice president of football operations, stated that "'[v]ideotaping of any type, including but not limited to taping of an opponent's offensive or defensive signals, is prohibited on the sidelines, in the coaches' booth, in the locker room, or at any other locations accessible to club staff members during the game.'"

On September 9, 2007, the Jets and the Patriots played the season opener in Giants Stadium, East Rutherford, New Jersey. Mayer possessed tickets and parking passes to this game, and the Patriots ultimately won, 38–14. ESPN.com then reported that the NFL was investigating accusations that an employee of the Patriots was actually videotaping the signals given by Jets coaches at this game. Specifically, NFL security reportedly confiscated a video camera and videotape from an employee during the course of the game, and this employee was accused of aiming his camera at the Jets' defensive coaches while they were sending signals out to the team's players on the field.

This was not the first time a public accusation of cheating or dishonesty had been made against the Patriots. A man wearing a Patriots credential was found carrying a video camera on the sidelines at the home field of the Green Bay Packers in November 2006. Admittedly, "[t]eams are allowed to have a limited number of their own videographers on the sideline during the game, but they must have a credential that authorizes them to shoot video, and wear a yellow vest." However, this particular individual evidently lacked the proper credential and attire and was accordingly escorted out of the stadium by Packers security.

With respect to the 2007 incident, the Patriots denied that there was any violation of the NFL's rules. A Patriots cornerback named Ellis Hobbs told the press that he was unwilling to believe that his team had cheated and that he was standing by the team and its coaches. However, he also admitted that, "[i]f it's true, obviously, we're in the wrong." Belichick apologized to everyone affected following the confiscation of the videotape. But, at a weekly press conference on September 12, 2007, he refused to take questions from reporters about the NFL investigation and stormed out of the room.

On September 13, 2007, "the NFL found the [Patriots] guilty of violating all applicable NFL rules by engaging in a surreptitious videotaping program." It imposed the following sanctions: (1) the Patriots were fined $250,000.00; (2) Belichick was personally fined $500,000.00; and (3) the Patriots would be stripped of any first-round draft pick for the next year if the team reached the playoffs in the 2007–2008 season and, if not so successful, the team would otherwise lose its second- and third-round picks. Roger Goodell, the commissioner of the NFL, characterized the whole episode as "a calculated and deliberate attempt to avoid longstanding rules designed to encourage fair play and promote honest competition on the playing field."

He further justified the penalties imposed on the team on the grounds that "Coach Belichick not only serves as the head coach but also has substantial control over all aspects of New England's football operations" and therefore "his actions and decisions are properly attributed to the club."

The owner of the Patriots, Robert Kraft, refused to comment on the NFL's sanctions, and the New York Jets issued a statement supporting the commissioner and his findings. On September 13, 2007, Belichick stated the following: "Once again, I apologize to the Kraft family and every person directly or indirectly associated with the New England Patriots for the embarrassment, distraction and penalty my mistake caused. I also apologize to Patriots fans and would like to thank them for their support during the past few days and throughout my career." However, he then "bizarrely…attempted to deny responsibility, stating: 'We have never used sideline video to obtain a competitive advantage while the game was in progress…[.] With tonight's resolution, I will not be offering any further comments on this matter. We are moving on with our preparations for Sunday's game.'" But, at least according to Mayer, Jets ticket-holders have refused to "move on."

The Patriots and Belichick deployed their surreptitious videotaping program during all eight games played against the Jets in Giants Stadium from 2000 through 2007. Beginning in 2000 when Belichick became head coach, they commenced an ongoing scheme to acquire the signals of their adversaries and then match such signals to the plays on the field, in alleged violation of the "NFL rules that are part of the ticketholders' contractual and/or quasi contractual rights." On the other hand, Jets fans collectively spent more than $61 million on tickets to watch these purportedly honest and competitive games between the two teams.

In 2000, Matt Walsh, an employee in the team's videography department, was hired by the team to videotape the signals of opponents. Relying specifically on statements made by Walsh to the New York Times and United States Senator Arlen Specter, Mayer made a series of allegations with respect to this Patriots employee. Walsh claimed that he received his videotaping instructions directly from Ernie Adams, Belichick's own special assistant. The purpose of the videotaping program was to capture signals for use in games against the same opponent later in the season, and the program was later expanded to include teams that the Patriots could encounter in the playoffs. The first instance of taping occurred in a 2000 preseason game against the Tampa Bay Buccaneers. When the two teams played again in the regular season opener, the Patriots appeared to use the acquired signals. Walsh specifically asserted "that this was the first time he had seen quarterback Drew Bledsoe operate a 'no huddle' [offense] 'when not in a two-minute or hurry situation'" and that, when he asked an unnamed quarterback if the taped signals were helpful, the player replied that, "'probably 75 percent of the time, Tampa Bay ran the defense we thought they were going to run.'" Although Walsh left the videotaping program after the 2002 Super Bowl, "he [as a Patriots season ticketholder] witnessed Patriots employee Steve Scarnecchia continue the same taping practices in multiple games in the 2003, 2004, and 2005 seasons." Walsh was further instructed by the Patriots organization to conceal his actions and misrepresent his activities if challenged on the field by: (1) intentionally breaking the red operating light on the video camera, (2) telling any person questioning "the use of a third video camera on the field" that he was filming tight shots or highlights, and (3) "if asked why he was not filming action on the field, he was to say he was filming the down marker." Finally, at the 2002 American Football Conference championship game against the Pittsburgh Steelers, Walsh was instructed not to wear a team logo while filming.

Walsh's attorney, Michael Levy, likewise released a statement describing the team's method "of securing and tying coaching signals to plays." As reported in the New York Post, the lawyer provided the following description of a videotape made during an October 7, 2001, game against the Miami Dolphins:

> "[It] contains shots of Miami's offensive coaches signaling Miami's offensive players, followed by a shot from the end-zone camera of Miami's offensive play, followed by a shot of Miami's offensive coaches signaling Miami's offensive players for the next play, then edited to be followed by a shot of the subsequent Miami offensive play," Levy told ESPN.com. "And that pattern repeats throughout the entire tape, with occasional cuts to the scoreboard."

Citing again to the New York Post, Mayer further alleged that the NFL wrongfully destroyed the illicit videotapes themselves:

> Other tapes produced to the NFL (and later destroyed by order of Commissioner Roger Goodell) include defensive signals from Miami coaches in a game on Sept. 24, 2000, signals from Bills coaches from a Nov. 11, 2001, game, signals from Browns coaches from a game on Dec. 9, 2001, two tapes of signals from Steelers coaches from the 2001 AFC Championship game on Jan. 27, 2002, and signals from Chargers coaches from a game Sept. 29, 2002.

Walsh provided at least eight videotapes to the NFL, while the Patriots likewise furnished at least six tapes to the league. The commissioner claimed that he ordered the destruction of the videotapes to prevent their use by the Patriots, even though the NFL allegedly had a legal duty to preserve these items pursuant, inter alia, to the Sarbanes-Oxley Act and the NFL's own antitrust exemption.

Here, Mayer undeniably saw football games played by two NFL teams. This therefore is not a case where, for example, the game or games were cancelled, strike replacement players were used, or the professional football teams themselves did something nonsensical or absurd, such as deciding to play basketball.

Nevertheless, there are any number of often complicated rules and standards applicable to a variety of sports, including professional football. It appears uncontested that players often commit intentional rule infractions in order to obtain an advantage over the course of the game. For instance, a football player may purposefully commit pass interference or a "delay of game." Such infractions, if not called by the referees, may even change the outcome of the game itself. There are also rules governing the off-field conduct of the football team, such as salary "caps" and the prohibition against "tampering" with the employer-employee relationships between another team and its players and coaches. A team is apparently free to take advantage of the knowledge that a newly hired player or coach takes with him after leaving his former team, and it may even have personnel on the sidelines who try to pick up the opposing team's signals with the assistance of lip-reading, binoculars, note-taking, and other devices. In addition, even Mayer acknowledge[s] that "[t]eams are allowed to have a limited number of their own videographers on the sideline during the game."

In fact, the NFL's own commissioner did ultimately take action here. He found that the Patriots and Belichick were guilty of violating the applicable NFL rules, imposed sanctions in the form of fines and the loss of draft picks, and rather harshly characterized the whole episode as a calculated attempt to avoid well-established rules designed to encourage fair play and honest competition. At the very least, a ruling in favor of Mayer could lead to other disappointed fans filing lawsuits because of "a blown call" that apparently caused their team to lose or any number of allegedly improper acts committed by teams, coaches, players, referees and umpires, and others.

Professional football, like other professional sports, is a multi-billion dollar business. In turn, ticket-holders and other fans may have legitimate issues with the manner in which they are treated. ("It is common knowledge that professional sports franchisees have a sordid history of arrogant disdain for the consumers of the product.") Fans could speak out against the Patriots, their coach, and the NFL itself. In fact, they could even go so far as to refuse to purchase tickets or NFL-related merchandise. However, the one thing they cannot do is bring a legal action in a court of law.

In light of the *Mayer v. Belichick* case, consider the following questions:

1. Do you think the fans who attended the Jets–Patriots games from 2000 through 2007 were defrauded as a result of the unethical and illegal actions of the Patriots team and administration?
2. Do you think the commissioner of the NFL did enough to penalize New England and Coach Belichick for their improper actions?
3. Do you consider the actions of the Patriots team and their coaching staff unethical or was it merely gamesmanship at its highest level? Do you think their actions could constitute criminal conduct?[48]
4. The Patriots did break league rules by spying, but is that always translated to be an unethical act?
5. Can Jets' fans still claim that they saw a dishonest match if the Jets won the game?
6. Do you consider Mayer and other Jets' fans 'victims' as they argued to the court?
7. Do you believe the alternative remedies suggested by the court, such as never going to another NFL game, are realistic?

Mayer v. Belichick, U.S. Supreme Court.

Is spying on another club always wrong? In November 2010, the Denver Broncos and their former coach, Josh McDaniels, were both fined $50,000 in what many deemed "spygate 2". McDaniels was an assistant coach for the Patriots when the first spygate incident occurred in 2007. The Broncos team video operations director had filmed a San Francisco's 49ers practice one month before, in violation of league rules. After being presented with the film, McDaniels refused to view it, but the league still fined him for failing to properly report it. McDaniels was fired by the Broncos within a month after the incident.[49]

▶ Summary

Is too much emphasis placed on winning in sports? With so much money at stake and big contracts available in professional sports, players have more of a "win at all costs attitude" and most owners want nothing less. Unfortunately, this same mentality has filtered down into college, high school, and youth sports. As this chapter illustrates, sportsmanship, gamesmanship, and cheating issues arise in many aspects of sport management, from coaching to developing rules and policies, to imposing appropriate discipline and sanctions. Sportsmanship, gamesmanship, and cheating issues arise at all levels of sport and it is important for the sport management professional (SMP) working at any level to have a firm grasp of these concepts.

▶ References

1. Reed Albergotti, "How Tiger's Top Man Is Managing the Crisis," *Wall Street Journal*, December 7, 2009; "Tiger's Endorsements Down Estimated $22 Million," *Washington Street Journal*, July 21, 2010; "Sports Players Facing Moral Clauses in Contracts," *Lawyers Weekly*, May 28, 2009; Ken Belson and Richard Sandomir, "Insuring Endorsements Against Athlete's Scandals," *New York Times*, February 1, 2010.

2. George Vecsey, "Sports in the Times; When Gamesmanship Blurs to Cheating," *New York Times*, September 23, 2006.

3. Michael Bleach, "La Russa Denies Gamesmanship Charge," *Cardinals.com News*, June 30, 2010.

4. Stephen Potter, *The Theory and Practice of Gamesmanship: Or the Art of Winning Games Without Actually Cheating* (Kingston, RI: Moyer Bell, 1998).

5. John Paul Newport, "The Art of Gamesmanship," *Wall Street Journal*, January 10, 2009.

6. Juha Nasi and Pasi Sajasalo, "Consolidation by Game-Playing: A Gamesmanship Inquiry into Forestry Industry," *The Evolution of Competitive Strategies in Global Forestry Industry*, World Forest 4, no. 3 (2006): 225–256; Daphne Patai, "Gamesmanship and Androcentrism in Orwell's 1984," *PMLA* 97, no. 5 (October 1982): 856–870; Frederick R. Struckmeyer, "God and Gamesmanship," *Religious Studies* 7, no. 3 (September 1971): 233–243; Betty Lehan Harragan, *Games Mother Never Taught You: Corporate Gamesmanship for Women* (New York: Warner Books, 1978).

7. James W. Keating, "Sportsmanship as a Moral Category," *Ethics* 75, no. 1 (October 1964): 29.

8. Eugene F. Provenzo, John P. Renaud, and Asterie Baker Provenzo, *Encyclopedia of the Social and Cultural Foundations of Education*, vol. 2 (New York: Sage Publications, 2008): 325.

9. "Gamesmanship vs. Sportsmanship," *Sports Illustrated*, September 1, 1999.

10. Modified from Dave Wielenga, "Where's the Sportsmanship? Girl Disqualified for Wearing Bracelet," *Sports Illustrated*, May 11, 2010.

11. Modified from Graham Hays, "Central Washington Offers the Ultimate Act of Sportsmanship," *ESPN.com*, April 28, 2008.

12. Clifton Brown, "Gamesmanship or Dirty Play?" *New York Times*, February 7, 1989.

13. Jeff Pearlman, "Detroit Pistons Center Bill Laimbeer," *Sports Illustrated Vault*, November 10, 1997.

14. Chuck O'Donnell, "Playing Those Mind Games—Gamesmanship in National Hockey League Playoffs," *Hockey Digest*, Summer 2001.

15. Steve Bierley, "Andy Murray Accused of Using Gamesmanship to Upset Opponent," *Guardian.co.uk*, June 24, 2009.

16. Ibid.

17. Bill Plaschke, "Hrbek Wins Game of Gamesmanship," *Los Angeles Times*, October 21, 1991.

18. Al Barkow, "Golf's Gamesmanship is as Subtle as a Controlled Slice," *New York Times*, June 13, 1993.

19. Modified from Derek Zumstag, "Perry Greased Batters with His Stuff," *ESPN.com*, May 16, 2002; Jack Curry, "In Perry's Book, a Brown Smudge Is Not a Black Mark," *New York Times*, October 24, 2006.

20. Derek Zumsteg, *The Cheater's Guide to Baseball* (Boston, MA: Houghton Mifflin, April 2007); Dave Krieger, "Integrity? In Baseball, it no Longer Exists," *Denver Rocky Mountain News*, February 17, 2007.

21. Lance Pugmire, "Cheating in Sports: The Fine Art of Getting Away with it," *Los Angeles Times*, August 20, 2006.

22. Modified from Hal Levy, "Connecticut: 50-Point Rule Gets Tested," *MaxPreps High School Sports*, September 28, 2006; John Dankosky, "High School Team Tests 50-Point Run-Up Rule," *NPR*, December 14, 2007.

23. Associated Press, "Rice Band's 'Todd Graham's Inferno' Not a Hit at Tulsa," *ESPN.com*, November 27, 2007.

24. Modified from Sarah Rutledge, "MOB Makes National Headlines in Wake of Tulsa Outrage," *The Rice Thresher*, November 30, 2007.

25. Judy Battista, "New Way to Ice the Kicker: It's Legal, but is it Sporting?" *New York Times*, October 21, 2007.

26. Modified from Michael David Smith, "When Icing the Kicker Can Backfire," *Wall Street Journal*, September 22, 2010.

27. Modified from Greg Bishop, "Contrite Jets Suspended Coach after Sideline Trip to Dolphin," *The New York Times*, December 13, 2010. Also see Kevin Seifert, Dirty Laundry: Trippin' Over Tripping, *ESPN*, October 29, 2009.

28. James Wolfe and Mary Ann Presman, *Curse? There Ain't No Stinking Chicago Cubs Curse and Other Stories about Sports and Gamesmanship* (Charleston, SC: BookSurge Publishing, 2009).

29. Jerry Crasnick, "Cheating Done Rather Subtly in Baseball Nowadays," *ESPN.com*, August 9, 2007.

30. "The 'Code': Ten Unwritten Baseball Rules You Might Not Know," *Yahoo.com*, May 5, 2010.

31. "Vote: Baseball's Unwritten Rules," *ESPN.com*, May 9, 2010. Also see Jason Turbow and Michael Duca, *The Baseball Codes: Beanballs, Sign Stealing, and Bench-Clearing Brawls: The Unwritten Rules of America's Pastime* (New York: Pantheon Books, 2010); Ross Bernstein, *The Code: Baseball's Unwritten Rules and its Ignore-at-Your-Own-Risk Code of Conduct* (Chicago, IL: Triumph Books, 2008).

32. Modified from Tyler Kepner, "Rodriguez Says 'Ha,' but Jays Aren't Laughing," *New York Times*, May 31, 2007. Also see Craig Calcaterra, "A-Rod, Dallas Braden and Baseball Etiquette," *NBC Sports*, April 23, 2010.

33. "A-Rod's Antics: Bush League or Major Play?" *Associated Press*, May 31, 2007.

34. Modified from Ryan Hogan, "Dustin Pedroia's Prestidigitation: Cheating or Gamesmanship?" *Bombasticsports.com*, July 1, 2009; David W. Rainey, Janet D. Larsen, Alan Stephenson, and Torry Olson, "Normative Rules among Umpires: The 'Phantom Tag' at Second Base," *Journal of Sport Behavior* 16 (1993).

35. "Bill Veeck was no Baseball Midget," *Los Angeles Times*, January 4, 1986.

36. Richard Goldstein, "Jim Delsing, 80, Pinch-Runner for Midget in Baseball Stunt Dies," *New York Times*, May 9, 2006; Mike Brewster, "Bill Veeck: A Baseball Mastermind," *Bloomberg Business Week*, October 27, 2004.

37. Modified from Jim Tootle, "Bill Veeck and James Thurber: The Literary Origins of the Midget Pinch Hitter," *NINE: A Journal of Baseball History and Culture* 10, no. 2 (Spring 2002). Also see Arthur Daley, "Where's the Strike Zone," *New York Times*, August 19, 1951; Dave Hoekstra, "Valparaiso Outfielder Gaedel Comes from Proud—Albeit Short—Baseball Lineage," *Chicago Sun Tribune*, August 6, 2010.

38. Kenneth Plutnicki, "Derek Jeter's Emmy-Worthy Performance," *The New York Times*, September 16, 2010.

39. Ben Shpigel, "Reviews are in on Jeter's Role as a Hit Batsman," *The New York Times*, September 16, 2010.

40. David Waldstein, "Friendship or Betrayal from Inside the Lines," *New York Times*, August 30, 2009.

41. Modified from Ed Bouchette, "The Games Some NFL People Play When You Get Right Down to it, Bill Belichick not the Only One Working the Shadows Looking for an Edge on Game Day," *Pittsburgh Post-Gazette*, December 16, 2007.

42. Associated Press, "Giants Think Woodson Spilling Secrets," *ESPN.com*, September 7, 2009.

43. Christy Mathewson, *Pitching in a Pinch: or, Baseball from the Inside* (Lincoln, NE: University of Nebraska Press, 1994).

44. Bert Blyleven, "Blyleven: The Do's and Dont's of Stealing Signs," *NBC Sports*, October 4, 2009.

45. Michael S. Schmidt, "Boston Red Sox Used Apple Watches to Steal Signs Against Yankees," *New York Times*, Sept. 5, 2017.

46. J. Rice Ferreille Jr., "Combating the Lure of Impropriety in Professional Sports Industries: The Desirability of Treating a Playbook as a Legally Enforceable Trade Secret," *Journal of Intellectual Property Law* (2003–2004); Jason Reid and Jason La Canfora, "Photo of Playbook Concerns Coach," *Washington Post*, September 16, 2008.

47. Associated Press, "Aaron Hernandez' Brother Suspended from H.S. Coaching Gig for Play-Stealing," *Boston Herald*, November 10, 2010.

48. Samuel J. Horovitz, "If You Ain't Cheating You Ain't Trying: Spygate and the Legal Implications of Trying too Hard," *Texas Intellectual Property Law Journal* (2008–2009).

49. Associated Press, Broncos, McDaniels Fined $50K Each, *ESPN.com*, November 28, 2010.

CHAPTER 3

Gambling in Sports and Society

▶ Introduction

Gambling, whether sports leagues want to admit it or not, has been a part of sports for over a century.[1] A plethora of episodes exists in sports regarding gambling, but no sport seems to despise gambling and its repercussions more than baseball.

> Baseball club owners are "sensible business men," Colonel Jacob Ruppert, joint owner of the New York American League Club, once said. "You can bank on the fact that they will conduct their clubs as business men. They must do this to protect their investments. Now, if they permitted gambling to get a hold they would destroy the game and with it their property, their business, would go to ruin. For that reason we have always tried to eliminate any form of gambling. We don't let known gamblers enter the ball park. Instructions are given the gatemen to look out for them."[2]

Gamblers were present at the earliest stages of the American sporting world and baseball has certainly had its share of gambling scandals, with the most notable being the Black Sox Scandal of 1919. ESPN's list of the 25

"hoaxes, cheats, and frauds," names the "Black Sox Scandal" as number one. This scandal involved Chicago White Sox players allegedly gambling away the World Series and is one of the most infamous events in sports history. Ballplayers from the White Sox club allegedly took money from gamblers to "throw" the games. The White Sox lost the 1919 World Series to the Cincinnati Reds, 5 games to 3.[3] Another notorious gambling scandal centered around Pete Rose, baseball's all-time hit leader, when he was the manager of the Cincinnati Reds and was eventually banned from baseball.[4] Besides Rose, baseball players Leo Durocher, "Shoeless Joe" Jackson, Ty Cobb, Tris Speaker, and Hal Chase were all involved in gambling scandals.

Gambling in sports is replete with unethical motives and practices. It is anathema to the continued integrity of sports but has a long history and association with sports. Players gambling on the outcome of their own games strikes at the very core of the "integrity of the game." It was the Black Sox Scandal that caused club owners to hire their first league commissioner, Kenesaw Mountain Landis, and he was granted the authority to do whatever he deemed to be in the "best interests of the sport." The trial of the Black Sox players commenced in June 1921 and, with no proof that any crime had been committed, the jury returned "not guilty" verdicts after deliberating for less than three hours.[5] One day after the verdict, Commissioner Landis banned all eight White Sox players for purportedly betting against their team and issued the following statement:

> Regardless of the verdict of juries, no player that throws a ball game; no player that undertakes or promises to throw a ball game; no player that sits in a conference with a bunch of crooked players and gamblers where the ways and means of throwing ball games are planned and discussed and does not promptly tell his club about it, will ever play professional baseball. . . . Just keep in mind that, regardless of the verdict of juries, baseball is competent to protect itself against crooks, both inside and outside the game.[6]

Gambling on the outcome of games by players is a form of cheating, an act through which the conditions for winning in a sports contest have been unfairly changed in favor of one participant over another. As a result, the principle of the equality of chance based on an even match of skill and strategy is destroyed. Gambling poses major ethical dilemmas for leagues, fans, players, coaches, and society in general. Gambling by players on their own *successful* athletic performance is not unusual. Certain sports, such as golf, tennis, horse racing, automobile racing, and rodeo, essentially reward the winners with prize money. The participants in these sports oftentimes pay entry fees either in total or as augmented by tournament sponsors.

Illegal gambling in sports has reached nearly pandemic proportions. The few headlines of suspensions and indictments are the exception rather than the rule, and this is combined with a laissez-faire attitude that is the legal betting fortress of the Las Vegas sports booking empire. The media reports point-spreads, player and team information, injury reports, and a myriad of other statistics and advertising, making gambling more accessible. Like it or not, sports and gambling are inherently linked to each other through a relationship between injury reports, bookmakers' and those who like to wager.

Gambling is a big business in the American sports world and in international sports as well. Gambling creates ethical issues at both the professional and amateur ranks of sports. For example, every March, millions of employees across the United States enter "office pools" and wager sums of money hoping to pick the "Final Four" college basketball teams and the eventual winner. Should these "office pools" be considered gambling? Just ask former University of Washington head football coach, Rick Neuheisel, who lost his head coaching job because it was decided he gambled in violation of NCAA rules. Neuheisel won $25,000 in an "office pool" based on the NCAA basketball tournament. Neuheisel, an attorney as well as a coach, later prevailed in court against the university.[7]

The most popular professional and college sports betting events in the United States are football- and basketball-related and include the Super Bowl, NFL playoff games, college football bowl games, and March Madness.[8] The NFL draws more gamblers than any other sport. The Super Bowl creates a frenzy of betting every year with betters wagering millions in Nevada's sports books. Of the total amount of money wagered on the Super Bowl, only about 1.5% is wagered legally (by a person over 21 years of age who was physically present in the state of Nevada). A 2018 Supreme Court decision discussed later in this chapter allows states to regulate sports betting as they see fit. Of course, everyone likes to win and every gambler seems to have a strategy for success, but, of course, a good strategy does not always translate to winning.

Sports gambling is an ethical issue on the international level as well.[9] Globally, the World Cup is one of the largest gambling sporting events.[10] In Pakistan in 2010, some of that country's leading cricket players were alleged to have committed one of the biggest frauds in the game's history. The International Cricket Council (ICC) and its Anti-Corruption Security Unit investigated sports betting allegations wherein three Pakistani cricket team members were accused of fixing matches and underperforming in a match between England and Pakistan. ICC Chief Executive Hansie Cronje said, "The integrity of the game is of paramount importance."[11]

Many argue there is too much gambling in sports and in society in general. Is there a valid reason gambling was essentially banned in the United States for many years? Should there be a limit on the amount of money individuals can wager? Are people responsible for their own actions, and if they want to gamble, then so be it? The gambling industry keeps growing, and it seems there is no way to stop it. Notwithstanding its growth in popularity, some scholars argue that gambling is associated with both moral and social costs.

▶ Gambling in Professional Sports

Professional sports leagues have implemented rules and regulations prohibiting gambling and gamblers. All professional sports leagues prohibit players from gambling and from associating with gamblers. Leagues want to ensure the integrity of the sport and provide an event that is based on the skill of the participants rather than on a certain outcome. Every sporting event contains an element of luck, but no fan wants to see a "rigged" or "fixed" match. Fans want to see an athlete vying to be a champion without the presence of a gambling element. The coin toss that starts every NFL game is exactly that, a "flip of the coin," but after that, the skills of the participants should produce the eventual winner, with some luck of course.

Professional sports leagues have taken tough stances against those who engage in or associate with gambling. When an individual or entity is charged with wrongdoing or misconduct, it involves the "justice" normative principle, in particular, procedural justice— the perceived fairness of the process and procedures used to determine disciplinary action. Leagues will typically suspend, fine, or even ban those who engage in gambling or associate with gamblers. Such was the case of former NBA player Jack Molinas. In *Molinas v. National Basketball Association (NBA)*, professional basketball player Jack Molinas was suspended for life because he gambled on the outcome of sporting matches. What ethical dilemma did this present for the NBA and Molinas?

⚖ CASE 3-1 *Molinas v. National Basketball Association*

190 F. Supp. 241 (S.D.N.Y. 1961)

Jack Molinas is a well-known basketball player. In 1953, upon his graduation from Columbia University, he was 'drafted' by the Fort Wayne Pistons, then a member of the National Basketball Association (now the Detroit Pistons). Subsequently, in the fall of 1953, he signed a contract to play with the Pistons. In January of 1954, however, he admitted, in writing, that he placed several bets on his own team, the Pistons, to win. The procedure he followed was that he contacted a person in New York by telephone, who informed him of the 'point spread' on the particular game in question. Molinas would then decide whether or not to place a bet on the game. He admitted that he received some four hundred dollars as a result of these wagers, including reimbursement of his telephone calls to New York. After he admitted this wagering, Mr. Podoloff, the president of the league, acting pursuant to a clause in Molinas' contract and a league rule prohibiting gambling, indefinitely suspended him from the league. This suspension has continued until the present date. Since the suspension, Molinas [made] several applications, both oral and written, for reinstatement. All of these [were] refused, and Mr. Podoloff testified that he [would] never allow him to re-enter the league. He has characterized [Molinas] as a 'cancer on the league' which must be excised.

In the meantime, Molinas attended and graduated from the Brooklyn Law School, and was then admitted to the New York State Bar. He had also been playing basketball for Williamsport and Hazelton of the Eastern Basketball League.

In 1954, shortly after the suspension, Molinas brought an action in the New York State Supreme Court, alleging that he had been denied notice and hearing prior to the suspension, and that there was no authority for the indefinite suspension imposed by Mr. Podoloff. The court, after a trial, found against Molinas, holding that since he had engaged in reprehensible and morally dishonest conduct, he was not entitled to seek the aid of an equity court. The court also found that even if a hearing was required by league rules, it would have been a futile formality in this case, since Molinas had admitted violations of his contract and the league rules.

In the action before the court, Molinas allege[d] that the National Basketball Association had entered into a conspiracy with its member teams and others in restraint of trade, and thus violated the antitrust laws. It is further alleged that the suspension of Molinas by the league, and its subsequent refusal to reinstate him, is the result of a conspiracy in violation of these laws. Finally, he charge[d] that the league has, through this conspiracy, imposed certain collateral restraints upon him, affecting his opportunities to play in 'exhibition games' against league personnel.

Molinas sought treble damages in the sum of three million dollars and reinstatement to the league.

With respect to Molinas' suspension from the league in January of 1954, and the subsequent refusal by the league to reinstate him, he failed to establish an unreasonable restraint of trade within the meaning of the anti-trust laws. A rule, and a corresponding contract clause, providing for the suspension of those who place wagers on games in which they are participating, seems not only reasonable, but necessary for the survival of the league. Every league or association must have some reasonable governing rules, and these rules must necessarily include disciplinary provisions. Surely, every disciplinary rule which a league may invoke, although by its nature it may involve some sort of a restraint, does not run afoul of the anti-trust laws. And, a disciplinary rule invoked against gambling seems about as reasonable a rule as could be imagined. Furthermore, the application of the rule to Molinas' conduct is also eminently reasonable. He was wagering on games in which he was to play, and some of these bets were made on the basis of a 'point spread' system. Molinas insists that since he bet only on his own team to win, his conduct, while admittedly improper, was not immoral. But I do not find this distinction to be a meaningful one in the context of the present case. The vice inherent in his conduct is that each time he either placed a bet or refused to place a bet, this operated inevitably to inform bookmakers of an insider's opinion as to the adequacy or inadequacy of the point-spread or his team's ability to win. Thus, for example, when he chose to place a bet, this would indicate to the bookmakers that a member of the Fort Wayne team believed that his team would exceed its expected performance. Similarly, when he chose not to bet, bookmakers thus would be informed of his opinion that the Pistons would not perform according to expectations. It is certainly reasonable for the league and Mr. Podoloff to conclude that this conduct could not be tolerated and must, therefore, be eliminated. The reasonableness of the league's action is apparent in view of the fact that, at that time, the confidence of the public in basketball had been shattered, due to a series of gambling incidents. Thus, it was absolutely necessary for the sport to exhume gambling from its midst for all times in order to survive.

The same factors justifying the suspension also serve to justify the subsequent refusal to reinstate. The league could reasonably conclude that in order to effectuate its important and legitimate policies against gambling, and to restore and maintain the confidence of the public vital to its existence, it was necessary to enforce its rules strictly, and to apply the most stringent sanctions. One can certainly understand the reluctance to permit an admitted gambler to return to the league, and again to participate in championship games, especially in light of the aura and stigma of gambling which has clouded the sports world in the past few years. Viewed in this context, it can be seen that the league was justified in determining that it was absolutely necessary to avoid even the slightest connection with gambling, gamblers, and those who had done business with gamblers, in the future. In addition, conduct reasonable in its inception certainly does not become unreasonable through the mere passage of time, especially when the same factors making the conduct reasonable in the first instance, are still present. At any rate, Molinas must show much more than he has here in order to compel a conclusion that the [league's] conduct was in fact unreasonable. The proof established at most that several league owners, coaches or players may have felt that it was unwise, possibly because of the likelihood of adverse publicity, to participate in a game, in which [Molinas], an admitted gambler, was also involved. This falls far short of the conspiracy required to establish a violation of the anti-trust laws. [Molinas was not reinstated.]

Molinas v. National Basketball Association, 190 F. Supp. 241 (S.D.N.Y. 1961). U.S. Supreme Court.

Jack Molinas was sentenced to 10–15 years in prison and served 5 years. He became the inspiration for the film, *The Longest Yard*, starring Burt Reynolds.[12] Molinas died in 1975 at the age of 43, when he was killed by a gunshot to the head. Molinas was an interesting fellow—he was a lawyer, outstanding college and professional player, and, by all accounts, a "crooked" player. Unfortunately, his life ended in tragedy and his murder remains unsolved.

1. Did the NBA's banishment of Molinas preserve the integrity of the game? Was the league's decision to ban Molinas a correct course of action for the league?
2. From an ethical standpoint, does it make a difference if a player only bets on his team *to win*?
3. Should a player be reinstated into a league if they receive counseling for their gambling addiction?

🔍 CASE STUDY 3-1   League Regulation of Gambling by Players

The "Integrity of Game" clause in Paragraph 15 of the NFL Standard Player Contract provides:

INTEGRITY OF GAME. Player recognizes the detriment to the League and professional football that would result from impairment of public confidence in the honest and orderly conduct of NFL games or the integrity and good character of NFL players. Player therefore acknowledges his awareness that if he accepts a bribe or agrees to throw or fix an NFL game; fails to promptly report a bribe offer or an attempt to throw or fix an NFL game; bets on an NFL game; knowingly associates with gamblers or gambling activity; uses or provides players with stimulants or other drugs for the purpose of attempting to enhance on-field performance; or is guilty of any other form of conduct reasonably judged by the League Commissioner to be detrimental to the League or professional football, the Commissioner will have the right, but only after giving Player the opportunity for a hearing at which he may be represented by counsel of his choice, to fine Player in a reasonable amount; to suspend Player for a period certain or indefinitely; and/or terminate this contract.

Pursuant to Section 5(d) of the NBA Uniform Player Contract, players agree to be bound by Article 35 of the NBA Constitution, which states the following with regard to gambling:

Any Player who, directly or indirectly, wagers money or anything of value on the outcome of any game played by a Team in the league operated by the [NBA] shall, on being charged with such wagering, be given an opportunity to answer such charges after due notice, and the decision of the Commissioner shall be final, binding and conclusive and unappealable. The penalty for such offense shall be within the absolute and sole discretion of the Commissioner and may include a fine, suspension, expulsion and/or perpetual disqualification from further association with the Association or any of its Members.

1. The NFL's "Integrity of Game" clause, similar to the NBA Constitution, prohibits players from gambling on the outcome of a game played by *any team in the league*. Should professional players be allowed to bet on sports they do not play as well as the college sport that they play professionally?
2. What discipline should be assessed against professional players who have been found betting on a team in the league (other than their own team)? Is it fact specific?
3. What is the NBA Constitution referring to when it says "directly or indirectly"?

Although participants, coaches, and managers determine the game on the field, the decision of the sports official has a much more immediate impact. If sports officials are paid by professional gamblers to affect the outcome and point-spread of the game, then the integrity, honesty, and ethics of the game will forever be in doubt. That was the case with long-time NBA referee Tim Donaghy. The effect of the Tim Donaghy scandal on the integrity of professional basketball was devastating. It is considered by many to be one of the most serious gambling scandals in the history of professional sports. NBA referee Tim Donaghy provided gamblers with picks during the 2006–2007 season. He was sentenced to a 15-month prison term for his involvement in the betting scandal. He pled guilty to felony charges of wire fraud and transmission of wagering tips through interstate commerce. He admitted to betting on NBA games, but investigators never found that he bet on games he had refereed.[13] Does that make a difference? Should a sports official go to federal prison for his or her involvement in a gambling scandal?[14]

⚖ CASE 3-2   USA v. James Battista

575 F.3d 226 (2nd Cir. 2009)

[Tim] Donaghy began his career as an NBA referee in September 1994 and continued in that position for thirteen seasons. He first began placing bets on NBA games, including games he officiated, during the 2003 to 2004 season through his friend Jack Concannon. The conspiracy at issue here, however, began in December 2006 and continued until April 2007. Donaghy provided "picks" on NBA games, again including games he officiated, to co-conspirators Battista and Martino. Battista agreed to pay Donaghy a fee for each game in which Donaghy correctly picked the winner. Donaghy provided the picks to Martino, Martino relayed the information to Battista, and Battista placed the bets. According to the government, Donaghy and Martino devised a code for communicating picks over the telephone using the names of Martino's two brothers. If Donaghy mentioned Martino's older brother, the pick would be the home team; if Donaghy referred to Martino's younger brother, the pick would be the visiting team.

In making his picks, Donaghy relied on, among other things, nonpublic information to which he had unique access by virtue of his position as an NBA referee. This information included his knowledge of the officiating crews for upcoming NBA games, the interactions between certain referees, players, and team personnel, and the physical condition of players. During the course of the conspiracy, Martino met with Donaghy in several cities for the primary purpose of paying Donaghy for his correct predictions.

After the government discovered the gambling scheme, Donaghy agreed to cooperate with its investigation. Thereafter, in August 2007, Donaghy pleaded guilty to conspiracy to commit wire fraud and conspiracy to transmit wagering information. In February 2008, Battista and Martino were both charged with conspiracy to commit wire fraud and conspiracy to transmit wagering information. As pertinent here, the indictment alleged that Martino and Battista committed the following overt acts in furtherance of the conspiracy to transmit wagering information:

A.　On or about December 13, 2006, MARTINO spoke with the NBA referee [Donaghy] by telephone regarding the NBA referee's pick for an NBA game.
B.　On or about December 14, 2006, BATTISTA and MARTINO met with the NBA referee in Pennsylvania and gave a cash payment to the NBA referee.
C.　On or about December 26, 2006, MARTINO spoke with the NBA referee by telephone regarding the NBA referee's pick for an NBA game.
D.　On or about March 11, 2007, MARTINO met with the NBA referee in Toronto, Canada, and MARTINO gave a cash payment to the NBA referee.

A few months later, Martino pleaded guilty to the wire fraud conspiracy charge and Battista pleaded guilty to the wagering conspiracy charge. Battista described his criminal conduct during his plea allocution:

[F]rom December of 2006 to March 2007, I was engaged in the business of sports betting, and I agreed with Tom Martino and Tim Dona[ghy] to use the telephone across state lines to obtain information to assist me in wagering on sporting events, on NBA basketball games. I received information from Tom Martino, who received his information from the NBA referee Tim Donaghy. This agreement was formed during a meeting between the three of us, in a hotel in December of 2006. During the course of this agreement from time to time I directed Mr. Martino to do certain things such as having meetings with Mr. Donaghy.

Battista further admitted that he had met with Donaghy in Pennsylvania for payment.

The NBA, and the United States on its behalf, sought restitution against all three. The NBA requested restitution for (1) Donaghy's compensation for the portions of the 2003–04, 2004–05, 2005–06, and 2006–07 seasons when he officiated games in which he had a financial interest; (2) that portion of the salaries of NBA employees attributed to reviewing the tapes of the games Donaghy refereed; and (3) attorneys' fees incurred by the NBA in connection with assisting the government in its investigation and prosecution.

After a comprehensive and particularized discussion of each restitution claim asserted by the NBA, the district court ordered the defendants to pay restitution in the total amount of $217,266.94.

Specifically, the government contends that the conduct underlying the wagering conviction was Battista's dealings with Donaghy and Martino as part of a scheme to defraud the NBA of Donaghy's honest services by using NBA insider information to place wagers on NBA games. The district court generally agreed, observing that "the success of Battista's wagering was dependent on Donaghy's fraudulent conduct." In support of its position, the government points to statements made by Battista during his plea allocution and the factual allegations set forth in the indictment, asserting that they demonstrate that Battista's transmittal of wagering information was intertwined with the fraudulent gambling scheme.

The [law] defines [a] "victim" as:

a person directly and proximately harmed as a result of the commission of an offense for which restitution may be ordered, including, in the case of an offense that involves as an element a scheme, conspiracy, or pattern of criminal activity, any person directly harmed by the defendant's criminal conduct in the course of the scheme, conspiracy, or pattern.

On the facts presented in this case, we conclude that the NBA was "directly and proximately harmed" by Battista committing the crime of conspiracy to transmit wagering information and Battista's use of nonpublic information solely belonging to the NBA (conveyed to him by the co-conspirators) to place illegal wagers on its games. Moreover, we must look at Battista's "offense" of conspiracy, in which his criminal conduct encompasses not just his own acts but also those of his co-conspirators. By this standard, Battista's crime plainly harmed the NBA.

1. Do you consider the NBA a victim of Donaghy's gambling scheme?
2. Is restitution a proper remedy under the circumstances?
3. Was the NBA damaged by Donaghy's actions? If so, how?
4. What are the necessary steps the NBA needed to take to prevent this from happening again?

USA v. James Battista, U.S. Supreme Court.

🔍 CASE STUDY 3-2   Lee Durocher, Baseball Manager

Brooklyn Dodgers manager Leo Durocher was suspended for the entire 1947 season by Baseball Commissioner Happy Chandler for consorting with gamblers. Commissioner Chandler's decision to suspend Leo Durocher from baseball for the 1947 season read as follows:

On 15 March 1947, L. S. MacPhall, president of the American League Baseball Club of New York, Inc., placed in the hands of the Commissioner a request for a hearing to determine whether: [A] certain statements appearing in the public press, alleged to have been made or issued by Branch Rickey, President, and Leo Durocher, Manager of the Brooklyn Baseball club, and [B] articles appearing in the Brooklyn Daily Eagle, under the by-line of Leo Durocher, were authentic, and whether Mr. Rickey and the Brooklyn club might be held responsible, and whether their publication might be considered conduct detrimental to baseball.

The incident in Havana, which brought considerable unfavorable comment to baseball generally, was one of the series of publicity-producing affairs in which Manager Durocher had been involved in the last few months.

Managers of baseball teams are responsible for the conduct of players off the field. Good managers are able to insure the good conduct of the players on the field and frequently, by their example, can influence players to be of good conduct off the field.

Durocher has not measured up to the standards expected or required of [a] manager of our baseball teams. As a result of the accumulations of unpleasant incidences in which he has been involved, which the commissioner construes as detrimental to baseball, Manager Durocher is hereby suspended from participating in professional baseball for the 1947 season... Club owner, manager, players and all others connected with baseball have been heretofore warned that association with known and notorious gamblers will [not] be tolerated and that swift disciplinary action will be taken against any person violating the order.

All parties to this controversy are silenced from the time this order is issued.

Respectfully submitted, A. B. Chandler, Commissioner.

The Durocher affair was important because, unlike the Black Sox scandal, a respected coach—the leader of his team—was implicated and associated with gambling.[15] As bad as it is to have athletes who shave points, is it more damaging to the integrity of the game to have coaches and managers betting on games? Pete Rose, "Charlie Hustle," wowed baseball fans for many years with his exploits on the field. He was also a noted gambler and was suspended by the commissioner for his gambling activities as a coach.

⚖ CASE 3-3 *Rose v. Giamatti*

721 F. Supp. 906 (S.D. Ohio 1989)

For the last several weeks, the charges against Pete Rose have focused enormous public attention on gambling and the possible corruption of the game. Now that Pete Rose has aired these charges by bringing suit, it has become critical for the Commissioner's Office to act promptly to maintain public confidence in the integrity of the game. If every action by the Commissioner to investigate and determine matters affecting the integrity of the game were to be subject to court intervention and delay, the Commissioner's ability to safeguard the integrity of the game would be destroyed. The action of the court below threatens the very reputation of Major League Baseball, and deprives the Commissioner of the power to protect the integrity of the game.

[Rose], field manager of the Cincinnati Reds baseball club, has been under investigation for allegations of gambling on baseball. The Commissioner of Baseball is empowered to investigate and act on such allegations under the Major League Agreement and [Rose's] contract with the Cincinnati Reds.

In this instance the Commissioner enlisted special counsel, John Dowd, to investigate the allegations against [Rose]. Mr. Dowd conducted an extensive investigation and submitted a comprehensive report to the Commissioner consisting of 225 pages and eight volumes of exhibits.

On May 11, 1989, the Commissioner provided a copy of the Report to [Rose] and scheduled a hearing on the matter for May 25, 1989. [Rose] requested from the Commissioner an extension of thirty days in which to prepare for the hearing. This request was granted and the hearing was rescheduled for June 26, 1989.

Rather than prepare for the hearing before the Commissioner, [Rose] filed suit on June 19, 1989, seeking a temporary restraining order, preliminary injunction, and permanent injunction, as well as other relief. After two days of testimony, the trial court granted the temporary restraining order on June 25, 1989, concluding that there is substantial evidence the Commissioner has prejudged [Rose's] case and cannot serve as a fair and impartial decision maker. The trial judge enjoined the Commissioner and the Cincinnati Reds baseball club from taking any disciplinary action whatsoever against [Rose] during the 14-day life of the order. Where a voluntary association has yet to conduct a disciplinary hearing or to render a decision, judicial intervention to enjoin the association's proceeding or to disqualify the decision maker is unprecedented.

The court below has erred on a fundamental matter of law by restraining the Commissioner of Baseball from even holding a hearing with respect to the serious allegations that Pete Rose was gambling on Major League Baseball games.

The sole basis for the court's action was Judge Nadel's finding that Commissioner Giamatti had prejudged the matter of Pete Rose's guilt.

This finding, too, is incorrect. The single item of evidence relied upon by Judge Nadel was a letter, dated April 18, 1989, drafted by the Commissioner's Special Counsel John M. Dowd, signed by Commissioner Giamatti and sent to the Honorable Carl Rubin, who was about to sentence one of Pete Rose's accusers, Ron Peters. The letter recites that "[b]ased upon other information in our possession, I am satisfied Mr. Peters has been candid, forthright and truthful with my special counsel." As discussed in [Giamatti's] Brief, the claim of prejudgment based on this letter is not sustainable as a matter of law or fact.

The unrefuted evidence was that the letter was drafted by Mr. Dowd, reflected only his preliminary assessment of the quality of the testimonial and documentary evidence provided to him by Mr. Peters, represented no independent assessment of evidence by the Commissioner, and did not in any manner constitute a ruling on the ultimate issue which would be before the Commissioner.

Moreover, the type of "prejudgment" about which [Rose] complains forms an insufficient basis as a matter of law for disqualifying decision makers. If the rule were otherwise, judges who made preliminary findings of credibility in preliminary injunction matters, or in connection with warrants in criminal cases would be forever disqualified from subsequent proceedings over the same or related matters. This is plainly not the case.

In supervising the investigation of Pete Rose, the Commissioner was acting pursuant to specific powers given him under the Major League Agreement to investigate conduct not in the best interests of Baseball. The Commissioner will inevitably make certain judgments in the course of his investigations, but there is no reason that his investigatory function should preclude the exercise of his adjudicatory function. The combination of such functions is routine in government agencies, and is certainly not inconsistent with natural justice and fundamental fairness.

Judges repeatedly issue arrest warrants on the basis that there is probable cause to believe that a crime has been committed and that the person named in the warrant has committed it. Judges also preside at preliminary hearings where they must decide whether the evidence is sufficient to hold a defendant for trial. Neither of these pretrial involvements has been thought to raise any constitutional barrier against the judge's presiding over the criminal trial and, if the trial is without a jury, against making the necessary determination of guilt or innocence.

Judge Nadel's suggestion that the hearing of this matter would be futile, given the supposed prejudgment of the Commissioner, is contradicted by the facts before him, and is also inconsistent with the appropriate legal standard. This rule against judicial interference in the decision-making process of a private association cannot be avoided by "[a] mere averment that a remedy is futile or illusory."

The subject of Pete Rose's gambling activities and the extent of gambling on Major League Baseball has been the focus of widespread speculation and intense public concern, putting a cloud over Major League Baseball and its administration. The trial court's issuance of the temporary restraining order has now raised substantial doubt as to baseball's ability to police itself and the Commissioner's power to enforce its rules. The integrity of the game has been damaged by the lower court's ruling and it will continue to suffer as long as the temporary restraining order remains in effect.

It is vital that the Commissioner be allowed to hear the evidence on the allegations against [Rose] and reach a determination as quickly as possible. Indeed, the sport of baseball will be severely damaged if the Commissioner is barred from completing his investigation and taking the actions he sees as appropriate-steps consistent with his mandate to uphold the integrity of the game. The image of a sport no longer capable of policing itself in a matter as serious as a manager betting on his own team's games could only erode public confidence in and respect for the national pastime. The ability of the Commissioner to protect the integrity of baseball, the purpose for which his office was created, is at stake.

Rose v. Giamatti, 721 F. Supp. 906 (S.D. Ohio 1989). U.S. Supreme Court.

The Baseball Commissioner, A. Bartlett Giamatti, and Pete Rose settled their dispute by entering into an agreement pursuant to which Rose accepted the penalty imposed on him by the Commissioner ("permanently ineligible") and agreed not to challenge that penalty in court or otherwise. Importantly for Rose, it contained the following provision: "Nothing in this agreement shall be deemed either an admission or a denial by Peter Edward Rose of the allegation that he bet on any Major League Baseball game."[16]

1. Should Pete Rose be banned from baseball for life because of his gambling activities?
2. Should he be refused admission to Baseball's Hall of Fame because of his admitted gambling on baseball games? If he is banned, is it unethical not to ban other players who engage in misconduct, other than gambling, such as illegal steroid use?
3. Rose said he always bet on his team to win; does that make a difference?
4. Should a coach, manager, or sports official be treated differently than a player for violations of a league gambling policy?

The Black Sox scandal of 1919 is the most famous gambling episode in sports. With pressure building, White Sox players Eddie Cicotte was the first player to step forward and admit his wrong-doing in the series. Cicotte first went to the office of the club's attorney, Alfred Austrian. In the presence of White Sox owner Charles Comisky, White Sox manager Kid Gleason, and attorney Austrian, a destroyed Cicotte admitted he took money to fix the series. Cicotte was then taken to the criminal courts building where Assistant State's Attorney Hartley Replogle questioned Cicotte in front of Judge McDonald and the grand jury. Cicotte confessed his part in throwing the 1919 World Series saying, "I was a fool," as he exited the jury room.[17] The *New York Times* reported Cicotte's testimony as follows:

I've lived a thousand years in the last year. . . In the first game at Cincinnati I was knocked out of the box. I wasn't putting a thing on the ball. You could have read the trademark on it when I lobbed the ball up to the plate. . . In the fourth game, played at Chicago, which I also lost, I deliberately intercepted a throw from the outfield to the plate which might have cut off a run. I muffed the ball on purpose. At another time in the same game I purposely made a wild throw. All the runs scored against me were due to my own deliberate errors. I did not try to win.

The day before I went to Cincinnati I put it up to them squarely for the last time, that there would be nothing doing unless I had the money.

That night I found the money under my pillow. There was $10,000. I counted it. I don't know who put it there, but it was there. It was my price. I had sold out 'Conny.' I had sold out the other boys, sold them for $10,000 to pay off a mortgage on a farm, and for the wife and kids.

If I had reasoned what that meant to me, the taking of that dirty crooked money—the hours of mental torture, the days and nights of living with an unclean mind, the weeks and months of going along with six of the seven crooked players and holding a guilty secret, and going along with the boys who had stayed straight and clean and honest—boys who had nothing to trouble them—say, it was a hell.

I got the $10,000 cash in advance, that's all.

Joe Jackson was next, confessing to his part in the scandal, testifying he was promised $20,000 but only got $5,000. Jackson's story was a confirmation of Cicotte's. He said he was given $5,000 by White Sox pitcher Lefty Williams while the club was in Chicago, and when he threatened to talk about it to the grand jury, White Sox players Chic Gandil, Lefty Williams, and Swede Risberg told him, "You poor simp, go ahead and squawk. Where do you get off if you do? We'll all say you're a liar, and every honest baseball player in the world will say you're a liar. You're out of luck. Some of the boys were promised a lot more than you, and got a lot less." Jackson's story was summarized in the *Chicago Daily Tribune*:

Jackson's Story
Joe Jackson last night described his confession to the grand jury as follows:

"I heard I'd been indicted. I decided that these men couldn't put anything over on me. I called up Judge McDonald and told him I was an honest man, and that he ought to watch this thing. He said to me, 'I know you are not.' He hung up the receiver on me.

I thought it over. I figured somebody had squawked. I got the idea that the place for me was the ground floor. I said 'I'll tell him what I know.'

He said, 'Come on over and tell it to me.' I went over."[18]

At one point the *New York Times* reported that Jackson testified to the grand jury he either struck out or hit easy balls when hits would mean runs. Jackson never testified in front of the grand jury in such a manner. The Black Sox scandal of 1919 is infamous and immortalized in the films *Eight Men Out* and *Field of Dreams*. Even though the ballplayers were acquitted, they were still permanently suspended from baseball. Was that fair? Joe Jackson and Eddie Cicotte confessed that they were part of the scheme to "throw" the World Series. Their confessions were later "lost," and their written confessions could not be used against them at the trial.

▶ Gambling in Amateur Sports

Gambling is also very popular in the amateur sports world. Of course, bookies create point-spreads and establish the odds in college sports as well as in professional sports. Over the last 75 years, many point-shaving schemes involving college athletes have been uncovered by the NCAA in both basketball and football. Some have even resulted in criminal prosecutions. In 1945, two Brooklyn College basketball players were arrested in the home of two bookmakers. They had accepted $1,000 in return for intentionally losing a game against Akron University.[19] One of the most infamous gambling episodes in college sports was the "rigging" of Boston College basketball games in 1978 and 1979. Gangster Henry Hill (of *Goodfellas* fame) convinced Boston College players to "shave" points during the season while he ran a

gambling ring.[20] The 1951 college basketball betting scandal involved seven schools and 32 players, with 7 being indicted on bribery and conspiracy charges.[21]

"Article 10.3 Sports Wagering Activities" of the NCAA bylaws prohibits college athletes and staff members of an institution's athletics department or conference office from participating in sports wagering activities or providing information to individuals involved in or associated with any type of sports wagering activity concerning intercollegiate, amateur, or professional athletics competition. The prohibition applies to "any institutional practice or any competition (intercollegiate, amateur, or professional) in a sport in which the [NCAA] conducts championship competition, in bowl subdivision football, and in emerging sports for women."

1. Compare the scope of the NCAA's prohibition against sports wagering to the professional league rule. Is the NCAA's prohibition too broad? Should it be limited to *intercollegiate* competition and to the sport in which the athlete or coach participates?
2. Which normative principles support Article 10.3? Does Article 10.3 compromise any normative principles?

What type of gambling activity meets the definition of "sports wagering"? Article 10.3 does not define sports wagering but imposes a different sanction on athletes depending upon the activity. An athlete who engages in activities designed to influence the outcome of a contest or in an effort to affect win-loss margins ("point-shaving") or who participates in any sports wagering activity involving the athlete's institution shall be *permanently* ineligible; whereas an athlete who participates in any sports wagering activity through the Internet, bookmaker, or a parlay card shall be ineligible for a minimum period of one year. Should participation in March Madness pools and fantasy leagues be deemed a "sports wagering activity"?

🔍 CASE STUDY 3-3   Rick Neuheisel, Coach and Attorney-at-Law

Rick Neuheisel was the football coach at the University of Washington. He had a 33–16 record in four seasons with the Huskies and had five years remaining on a six-year contract that was to pay him $1.4 million a year. He reportedly won $25,000 in a 2002 office pool when he correctly picked Maryland to win the men's NCAA basketball tournament. Neuheisel eventually entered into a $4.5 million settlement with the NCAA and the university.

Neuheisel argued that NCAA investigators acted improperly because they had not advised him they would ask about his gambling in an auction-style pool on NCAA basketball games. NCAA president Myles Brand said he believed the NCAA acted properly. The NCAA infractions committee had found that Neuheisel violated NCAA rules against gambling but did not sanction him. The university had argued that Neuheisel's contract allowed him to be fired for acts of dishonesty. School officials said he was fired for gambling on NCAA basketball and for lying when first questioned by NCAA investigators.[22]

The NCAA has always been concerned about gambling activity involving college athletes, including point-shaving, and for good reason[23]—every four years, the NCAA surveys approximately 20,000 athletes across all three NCAA divisions in order to study the trends in their gambling behavior and attitudes. In the 2012 survey, 4.6% of Division I men's basketball players reported having been contacted by outside gamblers.[24] In the 2016 survey, 55% of male athletes reported gambling for money within the past year and 24% of male athletes reported violating NCAA bylaws within the previous year by wagering on sports for money (9% reported wagering on sports once per month or more).[25] Also in the 2016 survey, 11% of Division I football players and 5% of men's basketball players reported betting on a college game in their sport (but not involving their team). It seems that a root cause for the large number of college athletes wagering on sports is that they don't see anything wrong with it. The 2016 survey revealed that 54% of men and 31% of women think sports wagering is a harmless pastime, and these figures are substantially higher (76% and 61%) among those athletes who wager on sports. Additionally, half of men and one-quarter of women who bet on sports think they can consistently make a lot of money on the activity.

In 1998, gambling and agent representative for the NCAA, Bill Saum, testified before the U.S. Congress regarding gambling issues and the NCAA.

Testimony of NCAA Representative Bill Saum

Gambling and Agent Representative
National Collegiate Athletic Association
Before the National Gambling Impact Study Commission
November 10, 1998
Las Vegas, Nevada

Impact on the Integrity of the Sports Contest

As a sports organization, the NCAA is well aware of the direct threat sports gambling poses to the integrity of each intercollegiate contest. In the late 1940's, the academic community and the public were shocked to learn that the City College of New York basketball team was involved in a point-shaving scandal. Sadly, today the scandals appear to be occurring more frequently. Within the last ten months, the public learned of point-shaving scandals in the campuses of Arizona State University and Northwestern University. The magnitude of these and similar incidents should not be underestimated. According to federal law enforcement officials, more money was wagered in the Arizona State case than on any point-shaving scam in the history of intercollegiate athletics; however, when it comes to sports gambling on college campuses, this is just the tip of the iceberg.

In 1995, four Maryland football players and one men's basketball player were found to have bet on collegiate sporting events. Two years ago, 13 football players at Boston College were involved in sports gambling activities, four admitted to betting against their own team.

Just last year, a basketball player at Cal-State Fullerton was approached by a student after a practice and offered $1000 per game to shave points. Earlier this year, law enforcement dismantled a large sports gambling ring that was operating, in part, out of a Columbia University fraternity house.

Obviously, the influence of sports gambling is far reaching and sports organizations continually live in fear that gambling will infiltrate and undermine the contest itself.

Impact on Student-Athletes

As the NCAA staff person responsible for conducting sports gambling investigations at our member institutions, I am acutely aware of the impact that sports gambling can have on the lives of college student-athletes. I have seen students, their families, and institutions publically humiliated. I have watched students be expelled from college, lose scholarships worth thousands of dollars, and jeopardize any hope of a career in professional athletics. In most cases, the scenario is strikingly familiar. Student-athletes who have begun gambling on sports incur losses beyond their means to repay and, as a result, become vulnerable to point-shaving schemes. Sometimes they participate in such schemes voluntarily in a desperate attempt to erase their outstanding debt, other times they are compelled by the threat of personal injury. In the latter cases, organized crime is often involved. In many cases, student bookmaking operations can be traced back to organized crime.

The profile of the typical college student who gambles is someone who believes he can control his own destiny, someone who is willing to take risks, and someone who believes he possesses the skill to be successful in the endeavor. If looked upon in a positive light, these qualities are reflected in many college athletes—this may, in part, explain why some student-athletes are drawn to sports gambling. Environmental factors may also be playing an influential role. One of the Boston College football players involved in the school's betting scandal stated, "The attitude was: 'It's just part of the college experience.' To tell the truth, it never crossed my mind it was illegal, it was so commonplace." Other statements from student-athletes involved in sports gambling scandals reveal that their gambling habits were developed well before college. One of the athletes involved in the Northwestern University point-shaving case admitted that gambling has been a part of his life ever since he was a youngster. He stated that he remembered "guys younger and older saying, 'let's bet $5 to see who is better in one-on-one.' I saw gambling every day in the inner city. People were playing cards and shooting dice. It was normal."

Our NCAA investigations have revealed that there is a very high incidence of gambling among college students. Student bookies are present at every institution. There is certainly no dispute that the impact of sports gambling is being felt on college campuses across the country.

1. In addition to preserving the integrity of intercollegiate athletics, one of the goals of the NCAA in preventing gambling is to ensure the well-being of student-athletes. Do you agree with this goal?
2. Which is more unethical: college players or professional players gambling on the outcome of their own games? Is it more damaging in college sports because of the participants involved, their relative youth, and the amateur nature of the match? What about the fact that college athletes are unpaid and professional athletes are highly paid employees who owe a fiduciary duty to their employer?
3. Do college athletes have more of an incentive, or reason, to gamble than professional athletes? Would paying college athletes curb illegal gambling behavior?

z

▶ Legalizing Sports Betting

In 2018, the Supreme Court (Case 3-4) struck down as unconstitutional the Professional and Amateur Sports Protection Act (PASPA) of 1992, a federal statute that essentially made Nevada the only state where someone could legally bet on the results of a single game. In 2017, more than $4.8 billion was bet at Nevada sportsbooks.

⚖ CASE 3-4 Murphy, Governor of New Jersey et al. v. NCAA et al.

138 S. Ct. 1461 (2018)

The State of New Jersey wants to legalize sports gambling at casinos and horseracing tracks, but a federal law, the Professional and Amateur Sports Protection Act, generally makes it unlawful for a State to "authorize" sports gambling schemes.[28] U. S. C. §3702(1). We must decide whether this provision is compatible with the system of "dual sovereignty" embodied in the Constitution.

. . . .Sports gambling, however, has long had strong opposition. Opponents argue that it is particularly addictive and especially attractive to young people with a strong interest in sports, and in the past gamblers corrupted and seriously damaged the reputation of professional and amateur sports. Apprehensive about the potential effects of sports gambling, professional sports leagues and the National Collegiate Athletic Association (NCAA) long opposed legalization.

By the 1990s, there were signs that the trend that had brought about the legalization of many other forms of gambling might extend to sports gambling, and this sparked federal efforts to stem the tide. Opponents of sports gambling turned to the legislation now before us, the Professional and Amateur Sports Protection Act (PASPA). 28 U. S. C. §3701 *et seq.* PASPA's proponents argued that it would protect young people, and one of the bill's sponsors, Senator Bill Bradley of New Jersey, a former college and professional basketball star, stressed that the law was needed to safeguard the integrity of sports. The Department of Justice opposed the bill, but it was passed and signed into law.

PASPA's most important provision, part of which is directly at issue in these cases, makes it "unlawful" for a State or any of its subdivisions, "to sponsor, operate, advertise, promote, license, or authorize by law or compact . . . a lottery, sweepstakes, or other betting, gambling, or wagering scheme based . . . on" competitive sporting events. §3702(1). In parallel, §3702(2) makes it "unlawful" for "a person to sponsor, operate, advertise, or promote" those same gambling schemes—but only if this is done "pursuant to the law or compact of a governmental entity." PASPA does not make sports gambling a federal crime (and thus was not anticipated to impose a significant law enforcement burden on the Federal Government). Instead, PASPA allows the Attorney General, as well as professional and amateur sports organizations, to bring civil actions to enjoin violations. §3703.

At the time of PASPA's adoption, a few jurisdictions allowed some form of sports gambling. In Nevada, sports gambling was legal in casinos, and three States hosted sports lotteries or allowed sports pools. PASPA contains "grandfather" provisions allowing these activities to continue. §3704(a)(1)–(2).

. . . .The legislative powers granted to Congress are sizable, but they are not unlimited. The Constitution confers on Congress not plenary legislative power but only certain enumerated powers. Therefore, all other legislative power is reserved for the States, as the Tenth Amendment confirms. And conspicuously absent from the list of powers given to Congress is the power to issue direct orders to the governments of the States. The anti-commandeering doctrine simply represents the recognition of this limit on congressional authority.

. . . .The PASPA provision at issue here—prohibiting state authorization of sports gambling—violates the anti-commandeering rule. That provision unequivocally dictates what a state legislature may and may not do. And this is true under either our interpretation or that advocated by respondents and the United States. In either event, state legislatures are put under the direct control of Congress. It is as if federal officers were installed in state legislative chambers and were armed with the authority to stop legislators from voting on any offending proposals. A more direct affront to state sovereignty is not easy to imagine.

. . . . The legalization of sports gambling is a controversial subject. Supporters argue that legalization will produce revenue for the States and critically weaken illegal sports betting operations, which are often run by organized crime. Opponents contend that legalizing sports gambling will hook the young on gambling, encourage people of modest means to squander their savings and earnings, and corrupt professional and college sports.

The legalization of sports gambling requires an important policy choice, but the choice is not ours to make. Congress can regulate sports gambling directly, but if it elects not to do so, each State is free to act on its own. Our job is to interpret the law Congress has enacted and decide whether it is consistent with the Constitution. PASPA is not. PASPA "regulate[s] state governments' regulation" of their citizens, *New York*, 505 U. S., at 166. The Constitution gives Congress no such power.

The judgment of the Third Circuit is reversed.

It is so ordered.

As a result of the Supreme Court's ruling, any state can now get in on the action and legalize sports betting within their state. Is the Supreme Court's ruling inconsistent with any ethical (normative) principles? Keith Whyte, Executive Director of the National Council on Problem Gambling, addresses some of the ethical dilemmas:

> If the leagues are going to directly profit from sports betting, they also need to protect people with gambling problems. . . . I do think in the past, gambling addiction has not been something the leagues have gotten engaged with. That's for people who operate and profit from gambling. Now they're in that boat. If they're interested in benefiting from legalized sports betting, they need to step up their game to minimize gambling-related harm.[26]

Should sports betting be allowed in every state? Is it proper for states to view sports gambling as a "savior" to bail them out when they are having financial difficulties?

✎ CASE STUDY 3-4   *Should States Get in on the Action?*

Review the following article that addresses the pros and cons of legalized gambling on sports:

Arguments against Illegalizing Gambling

Those who argue that sports gambling should remain legal argue, among other reasons, that economic benefits can be derived from the conduct, that sports gambling reflects consumer approval of the legality of the activity, and that sports betting has yet to bring on the "demise" of any sport.

A. Sports Gambling Brings an Economic Benefit

On-site sports betting has brought unprecedented economic success to Las Vegas and the popularity of internet sports betting has increased that success. Those who support keeping sports betting legal argue that if the U.S. were to completely ban sports betting, the sports books would move out of the country or would move "underground," forcing astronomical costs in monitoring that potentially new illegal activity. Also, with sports betting being illegal, cities like Las Vegas would not be able to receive the tax benefits that come with the gambling profits. Further, the *Indian Gaming Regulatory Act* limits the use of those profits to fund tribal government operations or programs, provide for the general welfare of Indian tribes, and to promote tribal economic development—all goals that would be much more difficult to achieve without the money from sports books.

This argument parallels those made for years by persons attempting to legalize certain types of drugs and prostitution. For example, prostitution and drug use and distribution occur frequently, regardless of their illegality. Additionally, cities do not receive tax benefits from these activities and spend millions of dollars enforcing the laws enacted to keep them illegal.

Most states and the federal government have kept drugs and prostitution illegal because they are worried legalization would lead to the exploitation of children and women, as well as the increased health problems associated with these activities. Like drugs and prostitution, sports gambling is addictive and leads to exploitation as well. Further, the economic benefit that the country might realize by completely legalizing sports gambling is far outweighed by the potential risks and harm associated with the activity.

B. Sports Gambling Reflects Consumer Approval

Proponents of legalized sports gambling cite the success of sports books and the growth of Las Vegas as consumer approval of the activity. Each year, the number of sports books and off-shore internet sports gambling web sites increases exponentially with revenues rising rapidly. Like the economic benefits argument above, the consumer approval argument is also flawed. Many illegal activities, like drug distribution, make huge profits each year. The profits reflect "consumer approval," yet just because the consumer participates in the activity, it does not mean that the millions of people not involved with sports gambling should be required to pay for the bankruptcies and thefts that occur to feed gambling addictions.

C. Sports Gambling Has Not Led to the Demise of Sports

Although there have been a few well-publicized sports betting scandals, those in favor of keeping sports betting legal contend that a few isolated incidents have not brought about the end of competitive sports. They argue that people go to sporting events to be entertained and that the "purity of sport" is the last thing on most fans' minds. They further contend that point-shaving scandals happen so rarely that even sports purists should not worry about sporting events being tainted by athletes not giving their best efforts.

It is true that, over the years, relatively few reported scandals have arisen compared with the thousands of games played every year; however, it is unclear how many athletes have not been caught for their involvement in point-shaving schemes. For example, how many times have athletes unexpectedly fumbled balls without getting touched, or missed wide-open lay-ups during undecided games? With the ability for people to gamble on sporting events comes the possibility that any athlete could be involved in assisting organized crime or sports bookies. If all sports betting were illegal, it would remove all incentive for athletes to intentionally throw games. The NCAA has made it completely illegal for any athletes to bet on any intercollegiate sports, but the monetary incentive for the athletes remains present.[27]

1. Would it tarnish the integrity of a sport if fans could legally bet on a match at the stadium where the games are played?
2. If customers approve of legalized gambling, does that make it ethical? Are you just giving the customers what they want?
3. Does organized crime necessarily follow if legalized gambling is allowed in sports?
4. If a state decides to legalize sports betting, what should be the scope of lawful activity? Consider the following:
   a. Should online sports gambling be regulated differently than other forms of gambling?[28]
   b. Do you agree with writer Justin Wolfers, who says, "Legalizing wagering on which team wins or loses a particular game, while banning all bets on immaterial outcomes like point spreads, would destroy the market for illegal bookmakers and make sporting events less corruptible by gamblers"?[29]
   c. Should fans be allowed to place bets at the stadium before and during a game/match?
   d. Illegal gambling in collegiate sports is a billion-dollar business.[30] Should college and professional sports be regulated differently? If so, how and why?

▶ Summary

Players gambling on the outcome of their games, or accepting payment from a bookie to affect a game's outcome, strikes at the very core of the "integrity of the game" and violates the normative principles of honesty and lawfulness. It is a form of cheating—an act through which the chance of winning based on skill and strategy in a sports contest has been destroyed and unfairly altered in favor of one participant over another. Both professional and college sports have a history of dealing with gambling activity involving players, including point-shaving, and are concerned for good reason. Legalizing sports betting raises an ethical dilemma, as states need to determine whether there is a social benefit to legalization that outweighs the harm that legalization can bring to gambling addicts and their families. Those interested in benefiting from legalized sports betting have an ethical responsibility to minimize gambling-related harm, as some of the profits from legalized gambling will come from the pockets of people with gambling problems.

▶ References

1. Paul Blumenau Lyons, *The Greatest Gambling Stories Ever Told: Thirty-One Unforgettable Tales of Risk and Reward* (Guilford, CT: Lyons Press, 2004); Charley Rosen, *Scandals of '51: How the Gamblers Almost Killed College Basketball* (New York: Holt, Rinehart and Winston, 1978).
2. Modified from William L. Crenery, "Why Gambling and Baseball Are Enemies," *New York Times*, October 3, 1920.
3. Christopher H. Evans and William R. Herzog II, *The Faith of 50 Million* (Louisville, KY: Westminster John Knox Press, 2002).
4. Aaron Kuriloff, "25 Great Hoaxes, Cheats and Frauds in Sports," *ESPN.com*, April 17, 2005.
5. Lamb, W. F. (2013). *Black Sox in the Courtroom: The Grand Jury, Criminal Trial and Civil Litigation.* eBook
6. Schiff, L. H., and Jarvis, R. M. (2016). *Baseball and the Law: Cases and Materials 103* (Durham, NC: Carolina Academic Press).
7. Associated Press, "Neuheisel Said He Feels Vindicated by Settlement," *ESPN.com*, March 8, 2005.
8. Michael McCarthy, "Gambling Madness can Snag Court Fans," *USA Today*, March 28, 2007, citing to Danny Sheridan, Top 10 Betting Favorites, *USA Today*.

9. Robin Insley, Lucia Mok, and Tim Swartz, "Issues Related to Sports Gambling," *Australia & New Zealand Journal of Statistics* 46, no. 2 (June 2004): 219–232; Timothy J. Brailsford, Philip K. Gray, Stephen A. Easton, and Stephen F. Gray, "The Efficiency of Australian Football Betting Markets," *Australian Journal of Management* 20, no. 2 (December 1995): 167–197; Warren D. Hill and John E. Clark, "Sports, Gambling, and Government: America's First Social Compact?" *American Anthropologist* 103, no. 2 (June 2001).

10. William Spain, "The World Cup: Biggest Gambling Event in History?" *MarketWatch*, June 1, 2010; Kate O'Keefe, "Macau Gambling Revenue Jumps," *Wall Street Journal*, August 3, 2010.

11. Tom Wright and Jonathan Clegg, "Cricket Allegations Deliver Blow to Pakistan," *Wall Street Journal*, August 31, 2010.

12. Joe Goldstein, "Explosion II: The Molinas Period," *ESPN Classic*, November 19, 2003.

13. Michael S. Schmidt, "League Finds Donaghy Was Sole Referee Culprit," *New York Times*, October 3, 2008.

14. Jon Saraceno, "Gambling Case Fallout Remains as Donaghy Reports to Prison," *USA Today*, September 23, 2008. For further study, see Lawrence B. Pedowitz, "Report to the Board of Governors of the National Basketball Association," October 1, 2008; Howard Beck, "Lawyer Will Examine NBA Gambling Rules," *New York Times*, August 22, 2007.

15. A. B. (Happy) Chandler, John Underwood, "Dunned Down by the Heavies: Durocher's Suspension Triggered Chandler's Downfall. The Owners Didn't Mind Losing Leo-But They Didn't Want a Strong Commissioner," *Sports Illustrated*, May 3, 1971.

16. "Rose's Road Back," *CBC Sports*, January 7, 2003

17. "Admit Guilt," *Chicago Daily Tribune*, September 29, 1920, p. 1.

18. "Jackson's Story," *Chicago Daily Tribune*, September 29, 1920, p. 2.

19. Joe Goldstein, "Rumblings: The Brooklyn Five," *ESPN.com*, November 19, 2003.

20. Henry Hill, "How I Put the Fix In," *Sports Illustrated*, February 16, 1981

21. Joe Goldstein, "Explosion: 1951 Scandals Threaten College Hoops," *ESPN.com*, November 19, 2003.

22. Associated Press, "Neuheisel Said He Feels Vindicated by Settlement," *ESPN.com*, March 7, 2005; Ray Glier, "A Coach Is Ousted, This One for Betting," *New York Times*, June 13, 2003.

23. Michael McCarthy, "Point-Shaving Remains a Concern in College Athletics," *USA Today*, May 9, 2007.

24. NCAA, "NCAA Student-Athlete Gambling Behaviors and Attitudes: 2004-2012: Executive Summary" (May 2013).

25. NCAA, "Trends in NCAA Student-Athlete Gambling Behaviors and Attitudes: Executive Summary" (November 2017).

26. Jeremy Fuchs, "What to Expect in a World Where States Can Legalize Sports Betting," *Sports Illustrated*, May 14, 2018.

27. Brent J. Goodfellow, "Betting on the Future of Sports: Why Gambling Should Be Left off the Field of Play," *Willamette Sports Law Journal* (Fall 2005) (footnotes omitted).

28. Anthony N. Cabot and Robert D. Faiss, "Sports Gambling in the Cyberspace Era," *Chapman Law Review* (2002); Lori K. Miller and Cathryn L. Claussen, "Online Sports Gambling: Regulation or Prohibition?" *Journal of Legal Aspects of Sport* (2001).

29. Justin Wolfers, "Blow the Whistle on Betting Scandals," *New York Times*, July 27, 2007.

30. Aaron J. Slavin, "The 'Las Vegas Loophole' and the Current Push in Congress Towards a Blanket Prohibition on Collegiate Sports Gambling," *University of Miami Business Law Review* 715(2002).

CHAPTER 4

Ethical Issues Involving Coaches

▶ Introduction

Coaches must behave in an ethical manner towards the athletes under their charge and in their relationships with superiors, employers, sports officials, media personnel, and security. Ethical behavior includes refraining from committing unnecessary violent acts, properly instructing and supervising players, and abiding by all applicable rules and regulations of the relevant governing body (e.g., the National Collegiate Athletic Association or state high school athletic associations) and the university.

Like participants, coaches must make correct ethical choices. There are unique ethical problems in the administration and organization of sports that coaches must face. The goal of this chapter is to grasp the meaning of ethical conduct and what constitutes misconduct for coaches. The main task of ethics is to evaluate the standards of right or wrong that people assign to behavior, motives, and intentions.[1]

Confusion often exists between the terms *ethics* versus *morals*. Ethics is the set of theories or principles that determine right from wrong[2] whereas morals involve the practice of ethical theories or principles. Coaches must often double as teachers and employ all of the characteristics and virtues of a good teacher. The ethical coach insists on discipline, hard work, and proper behavior from student-athletes similar to a teacher, since any misstep in the educational process might result in serious injury or even death.[3]

▶ Student-Athlete Issues and Team "Chemistry"

Team unity is vital to any team's success at all levels of sports. If a team works together, they are more likely to be successful on the field of play. A team must have the right "chemistry" between the players to win. With that in mind, when is it acceptable for a high school player to voice his or her opposition to the way a team is being run? When does this constitute an unacceptable act of insubordination (*i.e.* defiance or disobedience)? The following case involves the expulsion of several high school student-athletes from the team after they started a petition attempting to get their coach fired.

⚖️ *CASE 4-1   Lowery v. Euverard*

497 F.3d 584 (6th Cir. 2007)

Derrick Lowery, Jacob Giles, Joseph Dooley, and Dillan Spurlock were students at Jefferson County High School in Tennessee during the 2005 to 2006 school year. All four were members of the Jefferson County varsity football team. Euverard became the head varsity football coach at Jefferson County in 2004. During the 2005 season, many of the Jefferson County football players became dissatisfied with Euverard's coaching methods. They allege that Euverard struck a player in the helmet, threw away college recruiting letters to disfavored players, humiliated and degraded players, used inappropriate language, and required a year-round conditioning program in violation of high school rules.

In early October of 2005, after discussions with Dooley and Lowery, Giles typed the following statement: "I hate Coach Euvard [sic] and I don't want to play for him." Giles and Dooley asked other players to sign the petition, which would be held until after the football season. Giles and Dooley intended to then give the petition to Schneitman, the principal of Jefferson County, in order to have Euverard replaced as head coach. Eighteen players eventually signed the petition, including Spurlock.

Euverard learned of the petition on October 7, 2005. Darren Whitehead, another player on the team, told Assistant Coach Ricky Upton about the petition, who then told Euverard. Euverard called an all-coaches meeting on October 9. Schneitman was also present at the meeting. At the meeting, the coaches discussed how to deal with the petition. The coaches decided to question the players individually to learn more about the petition.

When the players arrived for practice on October 10 they were told to sit in front of their lockers and remain quiet. Players were then taken one by one into an office in the weight room where they were interviewed by Euverard. Assistant Coach Brimer was also present in the office, taking notes. All the players were asked the same questions: (1) Have you heard about the petition? (2) Did you sign it? (3) Who asked you to sign it? and (4) Do you want to play football with Coach Euverard as coach?

When Wesley Lee, a player who had signed the petition, was called for his interview, Lowery called out, "Are you alright?" Assistant Coach Pippenger then asked Lowery to come over. At first, Lowery refused and then walked over to Pippenger. Lowery told Pippenger "don't put your hands on me," or words to that effect, and refused to go outside with Pippenger. Giles and Dooley then got up and stood by Lowery. Pippenger took the three of them into the weight room and told Euverard about the situation. Euverard attempted to interview the three boys individually, but they said they would only meet with Euverard as a group. Euverard told them that if they were going to be that way, they could pick up their things and leave. Giles, Dooley, and Lowery gathered their belongings and left. As they were leaving, Dooley said to the other players, "I know how much you hate him, and you guys need to leave with us right now."

Spurlock was not at school on October 10. Euverard interviewed Spurlock on October 11, and Spurlock told Euverard that he signed the petition. Euverard asked Spurlock if he still felt that way, and Spurlock answered that he loved football. Euverard then asked Spurlock if he wanted to play football with Euverard as head coach. Spurlock said no, but that he wanted to play for Jefferson County. Euverard told Spurlock to get his stuff, and that he was no longer on the team. Players who signed the petition but apologized to Euverard and told him they wanted to play for him were allowed to remain on the team.

In the 1986 movie Hoosiers, Gene Hackman plays Norman Dale, the new basketball coach at a small Indiana high school. On the first day of practice Dale makes an introductory speech to the players. All of the players attentively listen to Dale except two, who are talking to each other. Dale notices the two players talking, and the following dialogue ensues:

Dale: Basketball is a voluntary activity. It's not a requirement. If any of you feel you don't want to be on the team, feel free to leave right now. Did you hear what I just said?

Player: Me?

Dale: Yes, you.

Player: Sure, I'm just kinda curious to know when we start.

Dale: We start when I say so.

Player: OK, would you kinda let me know, 'cause I'm kinda getting tired of standing.

Dale: Alright. Out. Out of here. Right now.

One of the purposes of education is to train students to fulfill their role in a free society. Thus it is appropriate for students to learn to express and evaluate competing viewpoints. The goal of an athletic team is much narrower. Of course, students may participate in extracurricular sports for any number of reasons: to develop discipline, to experience camaraderie and bonding with other students, for the sheer "love of the game," etc. Athletic programs may also produce long-term benefits by distilling positive character traits in the players. However, the immediate goal of an athletic team is to win the game, and the coach determines how best to obtain that goal. As this Court has recognized:

> Unlike the classroom teacher whose primary role is to guide students through the discussion and debate of various viewpoints in a particular discipline, [the role of a coach] is to train his student athletes how to win on the court. The plays and strategies are seldom up for debate. Execution of the coach's will is paramount.

The success of an athletic team in large part depends on its coach. The coach determines the strategies and plays, and "sets the tone" for the team. The coach, particularly at the high school level, is also responsible for providing "an educational environment conducive to learning team unity and sportsmanship and free from disruptions and distractions that could hurt or stray the cohesiveness of the team." The ability of the coach to lead is inextricably linked to his ability to maintain order and discipline. Thus attacking the authority of the coach necessarily undermines his ability to lead the team. In this case, Spurlock admitted that signing the petition was equivalent to saying he had no respect for Euverard ... coaches are entitled to respect from their players. The circulation of a petition stating "I hate Coach Euvard [sic] and I don't want to play for him" was a direct challenge to Euverard's authority, and undermined his ability to lead the team. It could have no other effect.

In addition to challenging Euverard's authority, the petition threatened team unity. In most instances, school officials would be more likely to fire a coach who had a horrible season than one who had a successful season. Thus players advocating the removal of a coach would have a powerful incentive to give less than one hundred percent. The Court is not accusing the [players] of this behavior; they all claim to have played their hardest despite their feelings for Euverard. However, after every missed block, dropped pass, or blown tackle, it would only be natural for other players, knowing the situation, to question the [players] motivation. This would inevitably increase the tension on the team.

The circulation of the petition necessarily divided players into two camps, those who supported Euverard and those who didn't. Although team chemistry is impossible to quantitatively measure, it is instrumental in determining a team's success. Joakim Noah, a player on the University of Florida basketball team that won consecutive NCAA championships in 2006 and 2007, stated that "the difference between winning and losing is so, so small . . . It's teams that really play together that win. Team chemistry is such a sensitive thing, but we really, really have it." See Paola Boivin, "Gators Bare Their Championship Teeth," *Arizona Republic*, Mar. 19, 2007, 11.

Mutual respect for the coach is an important ingredient of team chemistry. The Detroit Tigers were the talk of the baseball world during the 2006 season, due to their remarkable turnaround and run to the World Series. An opposing player attributed the Tigers' success to "a manager they all trust and respect and that they are behind, and a team chemistry that seems pretty unified." See John Lowe, "Add in Some Hot Bats, and the Tigers Have Found Their Swagger," *Detroit Free Press*, Oct. 16, 2006, 5. See also Mark

Gaughan, "Expectations Low in an Uncertain Era," *Buffalo News*, Sep. 7, 2006, C11 ("I truly believe there is team chemistry. I believe the players truly believe and respect Coach Jauron."); David Boyce, "Central Missouri State Working for Series Title," *Kansas City Star*, May 10, 2002, D8 ("We have a deep respect for our coaches. We know they know what they are doing. We have a good team chemistry.").

Conversely, conflict between a player and the coach can shake "the very foundation of team chemistry." See Greg Boeck, "Revolution on Court: Players' Defiance Upsets NBA Leadership Picture," *USA Today*, Dec. 21, 2000, C1. One sportswriter has noted that:

> The feud between [the player and coach] ultimately tore at the fabric of team chemistry and may have contributed to [the team's] postseason failure. At best, the constant discord created an uncomfortable atmosphere on the team. At worst, it forced players to choose between a coach and a teammate, creating a fissure of distrust and disunity.

See Glenn Nelson, "Ready to Blow? Enigmatic George Karl Can't Understand Why He's Misunderstood," *Seattle Times*, Nov. 1, 1995, H3.

Conflict between a player and coach has also been described as a "cancer." See Selena Roberts, "From Sleepless to Selfless," *The New York Times*, Dec. 10, 1996, B13.

The Court does not have an idealized, pristine view of athletic teams. Athletic teams are a family of sorts, and, like any family, it is inevitable that there will be some squabbles. Games are emotional affairs, and players and coaches may exchange angry words in the heat of the moment. From time to time, players may also vent their frustrations over play calls, lack of playing time, etc. The petition in this case, however, cannot be characterized as an isolated expression of dissatisfaction. The petition, stating "I hate Coach Euvard [sic] and I don't want to play for him," was part of a concerted effort to have Euverard fired. Such a petition would necessarily force players to choose between Euverard and the players that opposed him.

Lowery v. Euverard, U.S. Supreme Court.

Of course, student-athletes do not completely waive their First Amendment rights when they join a team. A coach could not dismiss a player simply because the player had religious or political views that were unpopular with his teammates or in a "whistleblower" situation where a player had reported legitimate improprieties.

After reviewing the facts of Case 4-1, how would you answer the following questions?

1. Should student-athletes be dismissed from the team for writing and signing the petition? Do the student-athletes have any free speech rights to be considered?
2. If you were the principal or athletic director, how would you handle the allegations against the coach? How would you determine whether the allegations are true?
3. Would you initiate an investigation and, if so, how would it be conducted?
4. How much leeway should a coach be given to discipline players?
5. Should the coach be disciplined or fired if any of the allegations are proved to be true?
6. The district court ruled the players could challenge the coach under the circumstances, which was reversed by the Sixth Circuit Court of Appeals. What normative principle(s) supports the court of appeals' decision?

How could litigation have been avoided in this situation? The Sports Management Professional (SMP) is required to hear all sides of an issue and make a decision that is fair to all parties involved. Resolving disputes in any industry is a difficult task. Therefore, every SMP must have the requisite skills to solve problems and must be able to resolve them within the bounds of ethical behavior and achieving fairness for all involved. How is the next case different from the Euverard case?

⚖ CASE 4-2 Wildman v. Marshalltown School District

249 F.3d 768 (8th Cir. 2001)

In January 1998, Rebecca Wildman was a sophomore student at Marshalltown High School in Marshalltown, Iowa and a member of the school's basketball team.

Wildman hoped to play on the varsity team and she testified that Coach Rowles, the high school girls' varsity basketball coach, promised in conversations with her before the season that he would promote her to the varsity team. When the promotion never materialized, Wildman testified that she "became frustrated and decided to write a letter to [her] teammates" and that her "purpose was to find out what they thought of the situation and Coach Rowles." She composed a letter on her home computer and distributed it to her teammates in the school's locker room on Saturday, January 24, 1998. The letter stated:

> To all of my teammates:
>
> Everyone has done a great job this year and now is the time that we need to make ourselves stronger and pull together. It was a tough loss last night but we will get it back. We have had some bumps in the road to success but every team does and the time is here for us to smoothen it out. Everyone on this team is important whether they think so or not. After watching last nights [sic] Varsity game and seeing their sophomores play up I think and I think [sic] that some of you are think [sic] the same thing. I think that we have to fight for our position. Am I the only one who thinks that some of us should be playing Varsity or even JV? We as a team have to do something about this. I want to say something to Coach Rowles. I will not say anything to him without the whole teams [sic] support. He needs us next year and the year after and what if we aren't there for him? It is time to give him back some of the bullshit that he has given us. We are a really great team and by the time we are seniors and we ALL have worked hard we are going to have an AWESOME season. We deserve better then [sic] what we have gotten. We now need to stand up for what we believe in!
>
> She included below her statement a poem about geese in flight titled "We Makes Me Stronger."

Wildman v. Marshalltown School District, U.S. Supreme Court.

After reviewing Case 4-2, answer the following questions:

1. How would you handle the situation in which a student is disrespectful to a coach on his or her social media page? Is that poor sportsmanship or improper conduct that merits discipline? What about a coach who slams players and parents? Royal Oak Michigan varsity soccer coach, Jason Windsor, resigned after he used his Facebook page to threaten players and disparage players' parents. Some of his comments included: "3 words my varsity soccer parents will get used to this week. BENCH, JV, CUT. You will all be taught a lesson you sh—stirring pri—!!!!!!!" and "(certain) Parents are the worst part of kid's sports" and finally "great set of results on the field today! Shame certain soccer moms make soccer so negative."[4]

2. Should every school have a code of conduct which states student-athletes must respect and abide by all reasonable decisions of the coach? Rebecca Wildman lost her case in federal district court. She appealed her case to the federal court of appeals, which once again ruled against her in favor of the school. The court stated in part: "Marshalltown had in place a handbook for student conduct in 1997–1998, as well as a Marshalltown Bobcat Basketball Handbook, drafted by Coach Rowles and distributed to Wildman and her teammates at the start of the season. Both handbooks indicated that disrespect

and insubordination will result in disciplinary action at the coach's discretion." It also stated, "Wildman's letter, containing the word 'bullshit' in relation to other language in it and motivated by her disappointment at not playing on the varsity team constitutes insubordinate speech toward her coaches."

3. How much credibility do you give to Rebecca Wildman and her cause, considering the numerous typographical and grammatical errors in her letter?

4. Would there be a difference if Rebecca Wildman had emailed her letter to her teammates instead of distributing the letter to her teammates on school property?

5. Should the use of the word "bullshit" in her letter automatically disqualify her from the team?

A growing trend (or some might argue, a disturbing trend) in intercollegiate athletics is head coaches banning social media usage by their players during the season. For example, it has become standard practice for Clemson University head football coach Dabo Swinney to impose upon his players a season-long social media ban on the first day of fall camp, which begins in the first week of August.[5] Perhaps the business reason, or non-moral value, supporting such a ban would be to remove distractions and keep players focused on football during the season. What normative principle(s) supports social media bans? What normative principle(s) oppose social media bans?

A college coach must "be an instructor, fundraiser, recruiter, academic coordinator, public figure, budget director, television and radio personality, alumni 'glad-hander,' and whatever else the university's athletic director or president may direct the coach to do in the best interests of the university's athletic program."[6] Professional coaches and collegiate football and basketball coaches at nationally-known institutions receive large salaries and extensive benefits. But coaches do not belong to unions and, while they often have "buy-out" clauses that pay them a specified sum of money if fired, they rarely have contract protection (*i.e.* "guaranteed contracts"), similar to that of professional athletes.[7]

The mission and goals of youth sport organizations are to teach sport-specific skills and game strategies and to instill values of physical fitness, teamwork, fair play, dedication, discipline, and good work ethics. Youth sport coaches have an ethical duty and responsibility to make the mission and goals a reality, and SMPs working for youth sport organizations must ensure that coaches act accordingly. As explained by Lumpkin, Stoll, and Beller (2012), ethical issues in youth sport in general can be categorized into five areas: "(1) age/size/height-appropriate equipment, fields, courts, and arenas; (2) developmental motor skills and physical fitness; (3) appropriate training of coaches and officials; (4) injury recognition and care; and (5) parental interest and control versus program goals."[8] Coaches at the youth level essentially have two primary ethical duties: a duty of safety and one of supervision and instruction.

▶ Ethical Duty of Safety

A coach has a duty to provide for the safety of those under his or her charge and this is even more so in youth sports. At the professional level, players have access to doctors, agents, team and league personnel, and unions that monitor safety issues. It is essential at the youth sports level that coaches provide for the safety of the players under their tutelage and they have an ethical duty to do so.

The following safety tips for coaches should be employed:

1. Inspect the field or ice prior to the game and practice sessions.

2. Inspect playing equipment.

3. Have first aid available at all times, including someone who is certified in cardiopulmonary resuscitation (CPR).

4. Beware of players who are struggling physically.

5. Assign coaches to watch any players who are struggling physically or mentally.

6. Observe the weather at all times for extreme heat, lightning, and other adverse conditions.
7. Ensure all participants are accounted for when traveling.
8. Ensure all equipment is fitted properly.
9. Ensure all participants know how to use the equipment properly and safely.
10. Address all safety issues immediately and notify all safety personnel when appropriate.
11. In youth sports, beware of individuals who are uninvited to practice or loitering around the playing field.
12. Keep informed of any serious medical conditions of athletes.
13. Ensure all participants are placed in positions on the field that are appropriate for their size and skill level.

Coaches have an absolute duty to care for the players under their charge.[9] In August 2008, 15-year-old Max Gilpin collapsed at football practice and died the next day. His coach, Jason Stinson, was charged with "wanton endangerment and reckless homicide" for Max's heat-related death. In 2009, coach Stinson was found not guilty in the first case of its kind in which a coach had been charged with criminal conduct for failure to remove a player from the field for safety reasons.[10] In 2010, Declan Sullivan, a 20-year-old student manager for the University of Notre Dame football team was killed during a Notre Dame football practice after an "extraordinary burst of wind" toppled a video tower in which Sullivan was working. In an amazing statement, Notre Dame President, the Rev. John Jenkins, sent an e-mail to students, faculty, staff, and alumni saying the university was responsible for the student's death. He stated, "Declan Sullivan was entrusted to our care, and we failed to keep him safe . . . We at Notre Dame and ultimately I, as President are responsible. Words cannot express our sorrow to the Sullivan family and to all involved."[11] Regulators began investigating whether the University of Notre Dame violated safety rules. Should the Notre Dame football coach ultimately be held responsible for this situation?

Coaches often face difficult ethical dilemmas involving player health and safety issues. Put yourself in the following situation: You are a college head football coach who is well respected and trusted by the players on your team. It is the middle of the season and one of your top players predicted to be selected in the early rounds of the NFL draft comes to your office one day to speak with you privately. He breaks into tears and says, "My doctor just informed me that I am HIV-positive and I don't know what to do. But please, please keep this strictly confidential." What would you do as head coach in this situation? What normative principles can you apply to assist you in making an ethical decision?

The next case shows the extent to which some coaches will go in order to win. A cycling coach lied to his athletes about drugs he gave to them, saying they were legal when they were not. Violating the normative principles of honesty and harm, the coach failed to act in the best interests of the athletes he was responsible for coaching.

⚖ CASE 4-3 *Strock v. USA Cycling, Inc.*

2006 WL 1223151 (D. Colo. 2006)

Greg Strock and Erich Kaiter were both members of the United States' junior cycling team in early 1990. The United States' cycling program is operated by USA Cycling, Inc. That organization hired Rene Wenzel to be head coach of the junior national team (Junior National Team). Wenzel served in this capacity for all relevant times in this lawsuit.

In April 1990, the Junior National Team traveled to Europe to train and compete. Strock rendezvoused with the team shortly thereafter upon his return from racing in Spain. While in Spain, a local physician prescribed antibiotics to Strock to treat an illness. When he convened with the Junior National Team, however, Wenzel allegedly gave Strock a substance to be taken in lieu of the antibiotics. Strock maintains that he inquired of Wenzel about the substance, and Wenzel indicated it was a mixture of extract of cortisone and vitamins. Strock further asserts Wenzel represented the mixture as safe and legal, and that Wenzel informed Strock he should not question the good judgment of the coaching staff.

Strock's health appeared to improve, and that July he competed in the world championship in Cleveland, England. There, both Strock and Kaiter allege they were injected up to three times per day with unknown liquids by USAC staff under Wenzel's supervision. In all, Kaiter maintains he received forty-two to forty-eight injections during the world championship period. When Strock and Kaiter inquired as to the substance in the injections, Wenzel purportedly told them it was the safe and legal extract of cortisone/vitamin mixture. Kaiter also claims he followed instructions from Wenzel to take several non-steroidal anti-inflammatory drugs (NSAIDs) such as Motrin each day.

Following the world championship, in August 1990 Wenzel allegedly gave Strock and Kaiter each a box of twenty ampules of liquid to help them prepare for the upcoming Washington Trust race in Spokane, Washington. Strock maintains he was injected with the liquid in a hotel room there by USAC coaching staff. According to Strock, Wenzel implied the liquid was the same extract of cortisone/vitamin mixture Strock had consumed in April and during the world championship.

Around this time, Kaiter began to notice blood in his stool. He was diagnosed with Crohn's disease several months later in July 1991. Strock claims he was overwhelmed by illness in March 1991. After initially suspecting he had HIV or lymphatic cancer, doctors that summer diagnosed him with human parvovirus. Although Strock subsequently raced with the Amateur Banesto Team, both Strock and Kaiter attribute the end of their elite cycling careers to parvovirus and Crohn's disease, respectively. In 1993 Wenzel informed Strock about a rumor Wenzel had doped Junior National Team riders.

Following a bout with depression, Strock matriculated at Indiana University's medical school. While taking a pharmacology class there in November 1998, Strock claims he learned there was no such thing as "extract of cortisone" that Wenzel had allegedly given him in 1990. Strock insists this was the first time he had reason to believe he had been administered steroids by USAC coaching staff. Strock discussed the alleged doping in a nationally televised interview in September 2000. Kaiter contends this was the first time he learned that he, too, may unwittingly have been administered steroids.

Strock v. USA Cycling, Inc., U.S. Supreme Court.

In *Strock v. USA Cycling, Inc.*, applying the normative principles, what unethical actions were taken by the coach? What disciplinary measures should be taken against him for his improper actions?

▶ Ethical Duty to Supervise and Instruct

Coaches have the responsibility to properly supervise and instruct their charges with special consideration to dangers inherent to the activity as well as the age, skill, and maturity of the participants. A properly-coached, -trained, and -equipped athlete consents to the blows and bodily contact that are an integral part of the sport. In contrast, inadequate instruction and improper training could cause serious injury and, in extreme cases, death. Coaches should not ignore any technical aspects of instruction, fail to emphasize proper training methods, or fail to implement any necessary safety measures to prepare athletes physically and mentally for their sport. For example, in *Stehn v. Bernarr MacFadden Foundations, Inc.*, 434 F. 2d 811 (C.A. Tenn. 1970), a wrestling coach instructed other wrestlers to use the "Agura" maneuver but failed to explain a method of escape or a defense to the hold. Coaches should also inspect all equipment before the sporting contest begins and ensure the equipment is state-of-the-art and presents no safety issues to the participants.[12]

The failure of a duty to supervise and instruct can cause serious injury or be fatal to a youth sports participant. One aspect of a coach's duty to supervise is to properly remove injured athletes from further participation. This concept is explored fully in the following case.

⚖ CASE 4-4 Welch v. Dunsmuir Joint Union High School District

326 P.2d 633 (Cal. App. 1958)

Prior to the opening of school on August 29, Welch was given a physical examination by a Doctor Reynolds and found to be physically fit. The coaches were on the field directing or supervising the play and there were no "game officials" there. The teams alternated in carrying the ball, and after each sequence of plays the coaches stopped the activity and instructed the players. Welch took the ball on a "quarterback sneak" and was tackled shortly after he went through the line. As he was falling forward another player was coming in to make the tackle and fell on top of him. After this play Welch was lying on his back on the field and unable to get to this feet. [Welch] was moved by eight boys, four on each side; with no one directing the moving . . . [Welch] is [now] a permanent quadriplegic caused by damage to the spinal cord at the level of the fifth cervical vertebra. . . . The removal of Welch from the field without the use of a stretcher was an improper medical practice in view of the symptoms.

1. How should coaches respond to an injured player?
2. What procedures and policies should be put in place regarding injured athletes?

Welch v. Dunsmuir Joint Union High School District, U.S. Supreme Court.

Do you believe the high school football coaches in the next case satisfied their ethical duties of safety and to supervise and instruct

when they provided their players with protective equipment and instruction?

⚖ CASE 4-5 Vendrell v. School District No. 26C, Malheur County

376 P.2d 406 (Cal. 1962)

August 24, 1953, a week before classes assembled in the high school, Louis Vendrell registered for football practice and play. He shortly enrolled in the school as a freshman. October 9, about six weeks after he had turned out for football and while playing as a member of the Nyssa High School team against the Vale High School team, he was injured. At the time of his injury [Vendrell claimed] (1) he was "an inexperienced football player"; (2) . . . weighed 140 pounds; (3) . . . was "not physically coordinated"; (4) his injury befell him when he was "tackled hard by two Vale boys"; (5) . . . had not received "proper or sufficient instructions"; and (6) . . . had not been furnished with "the necessary and proper protective equipment" for his person.

[A] coach or physical education instructor is required to exercise reasonable care for the protection of the students under his supervision. Before entering Nyssa High School Vendrell had completed the course of study offered by Nyssa Junior High School. The latter maintains a football team, two coaches and scheduled games. While a student in that school Vendrell had constantly been a member of its football team. He played the position of left half-back, the same position that he was playing at the time of his injury. Nyssa High School has about 300 students, two football coaches and a manager for the team. It played scheduled games with other high schools. Vendrell was 15 years of age when he entered the high school—one year older than most pupils. He sustained his injury during the close of the fourth quarter of a game in which Nyssa's opponent was the Vale High School team. He was injured when he was tackled by two Vale players while he was carrying the ball.

As a witness Vendrell described as follows what happened: "And I saw the Vale players in front of me and I knew I couldn't go any further so I put my head down and just ran into em and that is when I heard my neck snap." At that moment he suffered the injury for which he seeks redress in damages. It consists of a fracture of the fifth cervical vertebra of the neck.

Thomas D. Winbigler, football coach of the Bend High School, saw the Nyssa-Vale game and the play in which Vendrell sustained his injury. Referring to that play and Vendrell's handling of it, he testified: "It was a well-executed play. I will say that. Any play that will go for that much yardage is a well-executed play."

Before Vendrell had turned out on August 24, 1953, for football practice he had played for two years as a member of the football team of Nyssa Junior High School. Evidently, the training given to the football squad in the junior high school is substantial, for Vendrell mentioned that the squad was taught how to tackle, block, stiff-arm, carry the ball and keep the ball from the opponent. While a member of the junior high school football team Vendrell played in games against Adrian, Vale, Payette, and Parma.

Before any student was accepted as a member of the Nyssa High School football squad it was necessary for him to be pronounced physically fit by a physician and for his parents to give their written consent. Vendrell met both requirements. He had worked in the preceding summer upon farms and deemed himself in good condition. More than one of the witnesses spoke of him as a promising football player, and none referred to him in any other way. He concedes that he was generally the first member of the squad present for football practice and the last to leave the training field.

Football practice was conducted every afternoon, Monday through Thursday, for about two hours. No practice was maintained on Fridays because that was the day upon which the team played its games. The training for football play which [Vendrell], as a member of the Nyssa High School football squad, underwent was, of course, dependent somewhat upon the competency of the school's coach. All other coaches who mentioned the subject described Nyssa's head coach, Howard Lovelace, as competent and well regarded. Thomas D. Winbigler, aforementioned, was the football coach of Weiser High School in 1953 but at the time of the trial was the football coach of Bend High School. He testified: "I have a high regard for Howard in his ability to coach and his teams were well coached."

The training of the squad consisted of a program of calisthenics, classes on physical conditioning and training rules. The calisthenics were intended to strengthen the body. One of them was called bull-neck exercise. It was engaged in for several minutes each day and was designed to strengthen the neck. Vendrell described it as hard. The training program was also intended, Vendrell said, to enable the players to learn the plays and the fundamentals of football such as tackling, running, blocking and the proper position of the head and body while in play. We observe that the players engaged in scrimmage, line play, dummy tackling, and backfield movements. Vendrell conceded that the coaches stressed the necessity for each player to learn "the fundamentals of football" and told them that otherwise they could not enjoy the game or play it successfully. The coaches stated that calisthenics, training and hard work were essential for self-protection.

The players were instructed in the manner of gaining protection from blows and taking them on their protective equipment. Mr. Winbigler testified that the school's program of drills, practice and exercises was proper and adequate. He also expressed the belief that the Nyssa High School team was well coached.

Vendrell practiced, so he testified, "most of the time" with what he termed the "varsity" team. He attended every practice session. Since in junior high school he played the position of left half-back, the same as in the senior high school, he conceded that when he was injured he was playing that position for the third year. His testimony upon that subject was:

Question: "So this was your third year in that particular position?"

Answer: "Yes."

Before Vendrell played in the game against Vale he had played (1) in the preceding two year period in several games as a member of the football team of Nyssa Junior High School, (2) as a member of the Nyssa High School's "A" team for a few plays against the John Day High School team, and (3) as a member of Nyssa High School's "B" team in games against Ontario, Parma, and Vale. Vendrell claims that the Vale team was powerful and that it contained many players of outstanding skill. Before Vendrell entered the game in the fourth quarter the score was 48 to 0 in Vale's favor. The Vale team believed that with that score it could not lose the game, and, accordingly replaced virtually all of its best players with substitutes. One of its players, Kay Smith, who was a sophomore and left half-back, testified that at the time of Vendrell's injury, "we had most of our freshmen and sophomore players in the ballgame." He added, "They were pretty close evenly matched," that is, the two teams that were then in the field. Smith was one of the players who tackled him.

Vendrell weighed 140 pounds. Smith, Vale's half-back who tackled him, weighed 130 to 135 pounds. Don Savage was a junior in Nyssa High School and, like Vendrell, was a left half-back upon its team. He played in the Vale-Nyssa game. When he was taken out of the game Vendrell replaced him. He weighed, so he swore, "125 to 130 pounds" at that time. Dirk Rhinehart, another backfield player upon the Nyssa team, weighed 120 pounds. Mr. Winbigler testified:

Question: "And I believe you said that on a man-to-man basis, the Vale and Nyssa teams were pretty much equal—about the same?"

Answer: "That's right."

The following was given by Don Savage who was a member of the Nyssa football team at the time of Vendrell's injury.

Question: "Will you describe his physical co-ordination and how he handled himself, generally?"

Answer: "Well, he was a pretty fast boy. He was—ah—not too awkward, but he certainly wasn't as well co-ordinated as some of the other members of the team—the older ones."

Question: "What do you mean in 'co-ordinating'? Will you describe it?"

Answer: "Well, I mean the way that he would run with the ball and things of that nature."

Vendrell made the outstanding gain of the game for Nyssa and Mr. Winbigler swore that the run in which he made the gain was a well executed play. Vendrell saw the tacklers charging upon him and realized that he could not escape them. One of the tacklers (Smith) was to the side and rear of him. The other tackler (Carl Gustafson) came from the front. He came into contact with Vendrell before Smith did.

A day after August 24 when Vendrell enlisted for football practice, the protective equipment was distributed to the players. The manager supervised its allotment and the coaches were present. The equipment consisted of helmets, shoulder pads, rib pads, and hip pads together with the uniforms. The quantity was larger in amount than the number of players. The gear was placed upon tables and the lettermen were given first choice. Next came the seniors and finally the freshmen. Vendrell testified that after he had chosen the equipment he wanted, "I just took it to my locker and put it on." He added, "Whatever didn't fit, I'd bring it back and try—until I'd get the right deals and the right equipment." Although the coaches in some other schools helped their players fit their equipment, Nyssa's coaches did not. The Nyssa coaches were present, however, when the players made their selections and tried on their equipment. Vendrell did not testify that he needed help in order to determine whether the gear which he chose fitted him. The helmet which he selected in August was discarded several weeks later when he split it in a game by running head-on into an opposing player. He then returned to the equipment room and selected another helmet. Concerning it he said, "It was just a little bit loose." He admitted that he did not try on all of the available helmets before he took the one that "was just a little bit loose," but described as "old" the helmets which he did not try on. He also testified that one of his shoulder pads was loose because the string which was intended to draw it into a snug position was broken and therefore too short. Other strings were readily available. The two complaints just mentioned are the only ones that [Vendrell] voiced concerning his equipment. He made no claim that his equipment was defective nor did he find any fault with his uniform. All of the equipment was regularly inspected; defective parts were discarded and replaced with new. Vendrell conceded that he did not mention to the manager, the coaches, or any other school representative the fault that he found with his gear. He also conceded that he had the privilege of returning any of his equipment and of selecting a substitute. He testified that when he played in a game, such as the Nyssa-Vale game, he wore a jersey and that since it fitted tight it held the shoulder pad well in place . . . the complaint did not aver any shortcoming in the protective equipment. If it was in any way unsuitable to [Ventrell's] needs he was intimately familiar with that fact and voluntarily decided to proceed.

The playing of football is a body-contact sport. The game demands that the players come into physical contact with each other constantly, frequently with great force. The linemen charge the opposing line vigorously, shoulder to shoulder. The tackler faces the risk of leaping at the swiftly moving legs of the ball-carrier and the latter must be prepared to strike the ground violently. Body contacts, bruises, and clashes are inherent in the game. There is no other way to play it. No prospective player need be told that a participant in the game of football may sustain injury. It draws to the game the manly; they accept its risks, blows, clashes and injuries without whimper.

No one expects a football coach to extract from the game the body clashes that cause bruises, jolts and hard falls. To remove them would end the sport. The coach's function is to minimize the possibility that the body contacts may result in something more than slight injury. The extensive calisthenics, running and other forms of muscular exercise to which the coaches subjected the squad [to] were intended to place the players in sound physical condition so that they could withstand the shocks, blows and other rough treatment with which they would meet in actual play. As a further safeguard for the players' protection the [school district] provided all of the players with protective equipment. Each player was taught and shown how to handle himself while in play so that a blow would fall upon his protective equipment and not directly upon his body. We have also noticed the fact that every player was instructed in the manner of (1) running while carrying the ball, (2) tackling an opposing player, and (3) handling himself properly when about to be tackled. For example, Vendrell testified:

Question: "Now, if you would stiff-arm properly, or run properly, with your tail down and your legs underneath you, with your head up and your back straight, wouldn't the coach point this out to you? Wouldn't he work with you and discuss these matters with the various backs?"

Answer: "Yes, he did."

Question: "At any time, in your coaching by Mr. Lovejoy or Mr. McGinley, were you ever told that you should either strike a dummy or an opposing player with your head?"

Answer: "No, but, see I had done it in practice. In actual scrimmage. I had done that very same thing in practice-in scrimmage and nobody had ever told me any different."

The purpose of the extensive instructions and arduous practice was to enable the player not only to make for his team the maximum yardage but also to reduce to the minimum the possibility that an injury would befall him. All of the football coaches who testified upon the subject swore that the instructions and practice which were given to the school's football squad were adequate and were similar to that which they gave to their own players. No criticism was offered of the instructions and practice. Had Vendrell followed the instructions that were given to him about holding his head up, his injury would not have occurred, assuming, of course, that the failure to hold up his head was the cause of his injury.

But Vendrell says that the school's coaches had not told him that if he used his head as a battering ram an injury might befall him. One of the first lessons that an infant learns when he begins to toddle about on his feet is not to permit his head to collide with anything. Not only do his parents, playmates and teachers unite in teaching him that lesson, but every door, chair and other protruding object that is in the child's presence becomes a harsh but effective teacher that injury occurs if he bumps his head upon something. Less than two weeks before his lamentable injury befell him, Vendrell was taught the lesson again that he had learned in his infancy. This time it was taught to him when he ran head-on into a player in the Parma game and split his head gear. When he discarded his ruined helmet and borrowed one from a teammate he saw from the split helmet in his own hands what could have happened to his head. No coach could have spoken to him more effectively.

The school's coaches were Vendrell's teachers. He had the right—in fact, the duty—to ask the coaches questions concerning any matter which was not clear. In turn, the coaches had the right to assume that he possessed the intelligence and stock of information of a normal young man. Thus, they had the right to assume that he knew of the possibility of injury that comes to an individual who uses his head as a battering ram. Vendrell swore that he lowered his head when he saw that he was about to be tackled.

Vendrell assumed the risk attendant upon being tackled. The risk of injury that was inherent in being tackled was obvious. He was thoroughly familiar with it. He had been tackled scores of times and had been the tackler many many times. The tackle in question was made fairly and according to the rules.

The school's coaches gave to the football squad adequate, standard instruction and practice. The school's coaches did not negligently omit any detail; certainly the school's coaches did not omit to perform any expected duty. Vendrell assumed all of the obvious risks of which tackling was one.

1. Do you agree with the court that the equipment was adequately and properly distributed to the players? Did the coaches satisfy their ethical duty of safety in that regard?
2. In what ways does the court say that Louis Vendrell was at fault for his injuries? Do you agree with the court?
3. What duty of instruction does a football coach owe to his players? Does the duty of instruction owed differ with regard to the age of the participants?
4. As an SMP (athletic director), how would you determine if a coach has met the standard required for the duty of supervision and instruction?
5. In *City of Miami v. Cisneros*, 662 So.2d 1272 (Fla. 1995), a 78-lb 11-year-old broke his leg tackling another player who weighed 128 lbs. Did the coach violate an ethical duty by allowing two players with such disparate weight to compete against each other?

Vendrell v. School District No. 26C, Malheur County, U.S. Supreme Court.

▶ Coach Abuse

Abuse by coaches can take the form of mental or physical abuse, emotional abuse, unreasonable confinement, and excessive punishment. Sexual abuse and harassment by coaches, which is covered more extensively in Chapter 10, must yield a zero-tolerance policy and be reported to the appropriate officials and law enforcement as soon as reported or discovered. The following case demonstrates that a coach can abuse a student-athlete even when just playing or "messing around".

⚖ *CASE 4-6 Spacek v. Charles*

928 SW 2d 88 (Tex.App.-Houston [14 Dist.] 1996)

Spacek and Ramsey, athletic coaches at New Waverly High School (the coaches), called Joshua Maxey, a fourteen-year-old junior high school student, into Spacek's office during school hours to talk to Maxey about improving his grades so that when he entered high school he could participate in sports. Spacek allegedly threatened to hang Maxey if he did not improve his grades. Maxey also claims that Spacek reached for a white extension cord, told him to look at the ceiling, and attempted to grab him. Ramsey allegedly retrieved what Maxey believed to be a hand-gun, placed Maxey in a headlock, put the weapon against Maxey's head, and threatened to kill him if his grades did not improve.

The coaches maintain that, as teachers, they were acting within the scope of their employment and exercising their discretion and judgment in encouraging Maxey to improve his grades.

[Coach Spacek said,] "I never threatened to hang him and Ramsey, who was present during most of this encounter, which lasted a few minutes, never threatened to shoot him. . . . I did not discipline Maxey. I used no force upon him. He suffered no bodily injury in my presence." Likewise, Ramsey stated, "I never threatened Maxey and I did not hear Spacek threaten him. . . . I observed no discipline of any kind of Maxey during this incident. He was not physically harmed in any way."

Superintendent Davis said Spacek admitted reaching for the extension cord, but claimed that he was "just playing" with Maxey and trying to establish a rapport with him. An excerpt from Spacek's testimony reflects that Spacek portrayed he and Maxey as "laughing it up" while in his office. In testifying before the school board, Spacek said he playfully responded to Maxey's dare that he couldn't catch him by picking up the extension cord and saying, "[Y]es, I will catch you and I will tie you up and we will whip you."

"In determining whether force or confinement is reasonable for the control, training, or education of a child, the following facts are to be considered:

(a) whether the actor is a parent; (b) the age, sex, and physical and mental condition of the child; (c) the nature of his offense and his motive; (d) the influence of his example upon other children of the same family or group; (e) whether the force or confinement is reasonably necessary and appropriate to compel obedience to a proper command; (f) whether it is disproportionate to the offence, unnecessarily degrading, or is likely to cause serious or permanent harm."

Consistent with the public policy of Texas to give teachers the necessary support to enable them to efficiently discharge their responsibilities, teachers may use reasonable force not only to punish wrongful behavior, but also to enforce compliance with instructional commands. However, "a teacher may not use physical violence against a child merely because the child is unable or fails to perform, either academically or athletically, at a desired level of ability, even though the teacher considers such violence to be 'instruction and encouragement.'"

Although the facts of this case do not involve paddling or spanking or other physical force typically associated with corporal punishment, allegations that a teacher restrained a child in a headlock and placed a weapon against his head, and that another teacher attempted to grab the student to hang him with an extension cord, undoubtedly raise a question of excessive force.

1. Do you believe the coaches in *Spacek* used excessive force which constituted physical and mental abuse?
2. As an SMP, what acts would you have taken to ensure this conduct never occurs again?
3. Should the coaches have been fired for their conduct?

Spacek v. Charles, U.S. Supreme Court.

What rules should be in place regarding the physical contact of a student by a coach? Should a coach be required to always seek permission before he or she touches a player? In the next two cases, the coaches inflicted serious injury on their players without intending to do any harm. In Case 4-7, a middle school wrestling coach engaged in friendly horseplay with one of his players.

⚖ CASE 4-7 Reaume v. Jefferson Middle School

2006 WL 2355497 (Mich. App. 2006)

On January 7, 2003, Matthew Reaume, a middle school student, went to the Jefferson Middle School gym for wrestling practice. As Reaume waited in the gym for the rest of the team and the coaches to arrive, he talked to his friends with his back to the entrance. Nadeau, an assistant wrestling coach, entered the gym, came up behind Reaume and, allegedly without alerting or informing Reaume, wrapped his arms around Reaume's chest and took Reaume to the ground. Once on the ground, Nadeau performed a wrestling roll. As the roll ended, Reaume posted his arm on the floor to right himself. However, Nadeau performed a second roll. During the second roll, Reaume's elbow was fractured and required surgery to repair it. During Reaume's recuperation, he developed osteomyelitis. Although Reaume was a middle school student, he was an experienced wrestler. He had wrestled since he was six-years-old in both school and non-school athletic programs using freestyle, folk-style, and modified folk-style wrestling techniques. Nadeau had been Reaume's coach since Reaume was in the third grade. Nadeau was a qualified coach . . .

Reaume v. Jefferson Middle School, U.S. Supreme Court.

⚖ CASE 4-8 Koffman v. Garnett

574 S.E.2d 258 (2003)

In the fall of 2000, Andrew W. Koffman, a 13-year-old middle school student at a public school in Botetourt County, began participating on the school's football team. It was Andy's first season playing organized football, and he was positioned as a third-string defensive player. James Garnett was employed by the Botetourt County School Board as an assistant coach for the football team and was responsible for the supervision, training, and instruction of the team's defensive players.

The team lost its first game of the season. Garnett was upset by the defensive players' inadequate tackling in that game and became further displeased by what he perceived as inadequate tackling during the first practice following the loss. Garnett ordered Andy to hold a football and "stand upright and motionless" so that Garnett could explain the proper tackling technique to the defensive players. Then Garnett, without further warning, thrust his arms around Andy's body, lifted him "off his feet by two feet or more," and "slamm[ed]" him to the ground. Andy weighed 144 pounds, while Garnett weighed approximately 260 pounds. The force of the tackle broke the humerus bone in Andy's left arm. During prior practices, no coach had used physical force to instruct players on rules or techniques of playing football…

The disparity in size between Garnett and Andy was obvious to Garnett. Because of his authority as a coach, Garnett must have anticipated that Andy would comply with his instructions to stand in a non-defensive, upright, and motionless position. Under these circumstances, Garnett proceeded to aggressively tackle the much smaller, inexperienced student football player, by lifting him more than two feet from the ground and slamming him into the turf. According to the Koffmans' allegations, no coach had tackled any player previously so there was no reason for Andy to expect to be tackled by Garnett, nor was Andy warned of the impending tackle or of the force Garnett would use.

Receiving an injury while participating in a tackling demonstration may be part of the sport. Andy's injury, however, goes beyond the circumstances of simply being tackled in the course of participating in organized football. Here Garnett's knowledge of his greater size and experience, his instruction implying that Andy was not to take any action to defend himself from the force of a tackle, the force he used during the tackle, and Garnett's previous practice of not personally using force to demonstrate or teach football technique signify that his actions were imprudent and taken in utter disregard for the safety of the player involved.

How should Coach Garnett be disciplined for his actions?

Koffman v. Garnett, U.S. Supreme Court.

⚖ CASE 4-9 Moore v. Willis Independent School Dist.

233 F.3d 871 (5th Cir. 2000)

In February 1997, fourteen-year-old Aaron Moore was an eighth-grade student at Lynn Lucas Middle School in the Willis (Texas) Independent School District. Aaron was a student athlete who had just finished the season playing on the school's basketball team and was looking forward to trying out for the track team. He and approximately eighty other boys were enrolled in an elective gym class of which Allen Beene was one of the teachers. On the day in question, Beene observed Aaron talking to a classmate during roll call, a violation of a class rule. As punishment, Beene told Aaron to do 100 "ups and downs," also known as squat-thrusts. Aaron had not been subjected to similar punishment before, but he understood that if he stopped during this punishment, he either would be made to start over or would be sent to the principal's office. A classmate counted the 100 repetitions.

Aaron then participated in approximately twenty to twenty-five minutes of weight lifting required of the gym class that day. He did not complain to Beene of pain or fatigue, fearing that would make matters worse.

In the following days, however, Aaron was diagnosed with rhabdomyolysis and renal failure; he also developed esophagitis/gastritis. Aaron was hospitalized and missed three weeks of school. He continues to experience fatigue, and has been unable to participate in school sports or physical education class.

Nancy Moore, Aaron's mother, states that Beene told her the "ups and downs" were a means of punishment necessary to control middle school students. Mrs. Moore also states that Beene told her that he had intentionally inflicted pain on her son, explaining: "With high school kids you can have them do two ups and downs and they remember the next time. With junior high kids, you have to inflict pain or they don't remember." Mrs. Moore further states that the school district's athletic director, Ron Eikenberg, told her that "the coaches at the junior high were out of control and they did their own thing." By now, every school teacher and coach must know that inflicting pain on a student through unreasonably excessive exercise poses a risk of significant injury.

1. Were the actions of the coach in *Moore v. Willis Independent School Dist.* physically and/or mentally abusive?
2. Is it ever appropriate to discipline a student with excessive physical exercise?

Moore v. Willis Independent School District, U.S. Supreme Court.

🔎 CASE STUDY 4-1 Kelly v. North Highlands Recreation and Park District

2006 WL 1652667 (E.D.Cal.)

Adam G. Kelly was thirteen years old at the time of the events in question. . . . Ralphelia B. Grandinetti is Adam's foster mother and legal guardian. Adam is a "special needs" foster child who has the mentality of a child of six to eight years of age and who also has epilepsy and some physical abnormalities. Adam was a member of [the] North Highlands Recreation & Park District's ("District") swim team, the "Highlander Dolphins Swim Team."

On June 14, 2004, Adam was participating in his scheduled swimming practice . . . Christine Bagley ("Bagley"), a swim coach for the team, placed or forced Adam to sit on a hot metal folding chair in direct sun in approximately 100 degree weather as some sort of discipline. Adam was forced to remain on the hot metal chair for approximately 35–45 minutes while Bagley yelled at Adam only inches from his face. When Adam complained that the hot metal chair was hurting him and got up from the chair, Bagley yelled at Adam that he had to remain in the chair and physically forced Adam back into the chair . . . as a result of these events, Adam became seriously ill and was treated at the Mercy San Juan Hospital Emergency Room that evening and into the next morning.

How should this coach be disciplined?

▶ The Coach as a Role Model

Coaches function as role models to players and student-athletes at both the professional and amateur levels. At the collegiate and high school levels especially, coaches have a major influence over the lives and well-being of student-athletes. Indeed, many college athletes have coaching career aspirations and coaches must understand that they function as a role model for their players in this regard. Unfortunately, too many college coaches allow the non-moral values of fame, winning, and compensation to take priority over the well-being of their players. As explained by Lumpkin, Stoll, and Beller (2012), these coaches control their players by resorting to intimidation tactics in the form of negative feedback:

> Intimidation has long been used as a means to control the behavior of others. Coaches often use intimidation practices to motivate athletes

to behave in certain ways—that is, to be more aggressive during competition or to attend to and meet the responsibilities of being an athlete. The moral agent, in this case the coach, believes that intimidation will motivate the athlete to act in a certain fashion, through fear of what otherwise might occur. Typical intimidation methods can range from mild tactics, such as glaring at the athlete or raising the pitch and tone of the voice to stronger physical and emotional tactics, such as cursing, throwing objects, kicking, berating, grabbing the jersey or face mask, pushing the athlete, or spitting in their faces. In the psychology literature, these forms of motivation are typically called negative feedback. . . . Often, however, these forms of negative feedback set a motivational climate that is outcome/ego oriented—one whereby the focus is on the individual in relation to the win, the goal, rather than a performance/task/mastery environment—whereby the focus is on individual performance goals and mastery of skills, strategies, and so forth. Positive motivation (positive feedback) tends to set a climate focused towards the performance/task/mastery environment. Thus, according

to researchers, performance is best improved if the motivation climate is set using positive feedback.[13]

Is it ethical for a coach to use intimidation in order to make his or her athletes act in a certain fashion, knowing that they are complying out of "fear of what otherwise might occur." What might otherwise occur if they don't comply? Does the NCAA's "collegiate model of athletics" and all of its unilaterally imposed rules give these extremely high paid coaches too much power and control?

In *Nydegger v. Don Bosco Preparatory High School*, 495 A.2d 485 (1985), a high school soccer coach urged his athletes to compete in an "aggressive and intense manner," which allegedly led to an injury when one of the players on the opposing team was injured. If the coach urged the players to play aggressively while inferring that they should ignore the risk of injury or that they should intentionally cause injury, is the coach's behavior unethical?

Review the following model code of ethics for coaches. What are your impressions of the code of ethics? Is there anything missing? What would you add or delete from the code?

▶ Model Code of Ethics for Coaches

The function of a coach is to educate students through participation in competition. An athletic program should be designed to enhance academic achievement and should never interfere with opportunities for academic success. Each student-athlete should be treated with respect and dignity, and his or her welfare should be the utmost concern of the coach at all times.

The coach shall be aware that they have a tremendous influence (good or bad) on the education of the student-athlete and should never place the value of winning above the value of instilling the highest ideals of character in the student-athlete.

The coach shall uphold the honor and dignity of the profession. The coach shall strive to set an example of the highest ethical and moral conduct for all.

The coach shall take an active role in the prevention of drug, alcohol, and tobacco abuse by student-athletes.

The coach shall avoid the use of alcohol and tobacco products when in contact with players.

The coach shall promote the entire academic program of the school and direct his or her program in harmony with the total school academic program.

The coach shall master the contest rules and shall teach them to his or her team members. The coach shall not seek an advantage by circumvention of the spirit or letter of the rules.

The coach shall exert his or her influence to enhance sportsmanship by spectators.

The coach shall respect and support contest officials. The coach shall not indulge in conduct which would incite players or spectators against the officials. Public criticism of officials or players is unethical.

Before and after contests, coaches for the competing teams should meet and exchange cordial greetings to set the correct tone for the event.

A coach shall not scout opponents by any means other than those adopted by the league and/or state high school athletic association.

As an SMP, do you believe all coaches should be required to sign the following "Coaches' Ethics Code Agreement"?

I, the undersigned coach, have read and agree to abide by the Coaches' Ethics Code.

I understand that violations of the Coaches' Ethics Code may result in full or partial forfeiture of my coaching privileges.

I further understand that lack of awareness or a misunderstanding of an ethical standard on my part is not a defense to a charge of unethical conduct.

🔍 *CASE STUDY 4-2   Regulating a Coach's "Off-Field" Conduct*

There is no doubt former Louisville head basketball coach Rick Pitino can coach basketball. He had been a successful college basketball coach for many years; however, some of his off-court conduct became an issue at a criminal trial of a woman who was convicted of attempting to extort money from Pitino after he admitted having an affair with her in 2003. He had given the woman $3,000 to help her get medical care—the woman later had an abortion. Pitino apologized for his indiscretions. Pitino's coaching contract with the University of Louisville contained a morals clause that gave Louisville the right to fire Pitino for acts of "moral depravity."[14]

1. Should the university have terminated coach Pitino's contract for his actions?
2. Should a coach's "off the field" conduct ever be subject to regulation by the university?

In *O'Brien v. Ohio State University*, 2007 Ohio 4833, 2007 Ohio App. LEXIS 4316, former Buckeyes basketball coach Jim O'Brien gave $6,000 to the mother of a recruit who had just lost her husband in a war-torn region of the former Yugoslavia. The coach's conduct in making the loan to the family of the recruiting prospect, and then failing to report it to the university's athletic director, violated NCAA's rules and Ohio State University terminated their employment relationship with O'Brien. Evaluate O'Brien's conduct using the normative principles from Chapter 1. Do you need any additional information? Would the additional facts that it was O'Brien's own money and that the prospect, Alex Radojevic, never played for Ohio State change your opinion regarding the ethical choices that O'Brien made?

Under NCAA by-laws, head coaches are "presumed to be responsible" for the unethical conduct of assistant coaches and administrators and are required to monitor their activities. In 2017, Rick Pitino was in the spotlight once again when the NCAA Division I Committee on Infractions found that he did not monitor the activities of his former operations director.

🔍 *CASE STUDY 4-3   Encouraging Aggressive Play or Ordering Intentional "Hits"?*

In 2005, Temple suspended its men's basketball coach, John Chaney, for the remainder of the regular season, 3 days after he ordered a player to commit "hard fouls" that resulted in a broken arm for St. Joseph's forward, John Bryant. Coach Chaney said he regretted ordering a little-used player to commit rough fouls against St. Joseph's without having taught the difference between hard fouls and flagrant fouls.[15]

1. From an ethical standpoint, is there a difference between "hard fouls" and "flagrant fouls"?
2. Is it the severity of Bryant's injury that makes Coach Chaney's actions unethical?
3. Should Coach Chaney have been terminated?
4. Is it acceptable for a baseball coach to direct a pitcher to intentionally hit a batter?

Coach Chaney did not actually order any of his players to *injure* an opponent. The New Orleans Saints Bounty Scandal was probably the most highly publicized, scrutinized, and complex commissioner disciplinary authority dispute in all of the professional sports leagues. In 2010, the NFL investigated whether the New Orleans Saints coaches were financially incentivizing their defensive players to injure opposing players. NFL Commissioner Roger Goodell concluded that the bounty system existed and, in 2012, stripped the Saints of two second-round draft picks, imposed a $500,000 fine on the club, and suspended the general manager as well as multiple players and coaches for various lengths of time. All four suspended players appealed and requested that Goodell recuse himself from deciding the appeal. Goodell agreed to recuse himself and designated former NFL Commissioner Paul Tagliabue to hear the appeals in his place and Tagliabue vacated the suspensions of all four players. While Tagliabue, for the most part, did not dispute Goodell's factual findings surrounding the scandal, he felt the Saints organization was to blame and the players' suspensions were inappropriate:

> Unlike [the] Saints' broad organizational misconduct, player appeals involve sharply-focused issues of alleged individual player

misconduct in several different aspects. My affirmation of Commissioner Goodell's findings could certainly justify the issuance of fines. However, this entire case has been contaminated by the coaches and others in the Saints' organization.[16]

Do you agree with Tagliabue that the players' suspensions were inappropriate? Is it more unethical for the Saints coaches to offer financial incentives for injuring opposing players than for the Saints players to accept the money after they injure them?

▶ Summary

Coaches must behave in an ethical manner toward their players and recruits, players and coaches on opposing teams, parents, fans, sports officials, media personnel, and athletic department staff and administrators. At the amateur level, ethical decision making requires coaches to consider their important function as a teacher and role model. This chapter addressed some of the unique ethical problems in the administration and organization of sports that coaches must face at all levels of sport, including ethical issues pertaining to safety and health, regulating athletes' speech, supervision and instruction, coach abuse, and regulating "off-field" conduct.

▶ References

1. Sheryle Bergmann Drewe, "Coaches, Ethics, and Autonomy," *Sport, Education, and Society* 5, no. 2 (October 2000): 147–162.

2. Moisekapenda Bower, "Fleeing Coaches Leave Many Feeling Empty," *Houston Chronicle*, December 5, 2007, C1.

3. Robert Simon, *Fair Play: The Ethics of Sport* (Boulder, CO: Westview Press, 2004).

4. Marilisa Kinney Sachteleben, "Royal Oak High School Soccer Coach Resigns After Facebook Confrontations,"Associated Content from Yahoo, October 15, 2010.

5. Scott Keepfer, "Shutting it Down: Clemson Players Ready for Season without Social Media," *USA Today*, August 14, 2015.

6. Martin Greenberg, *Sports Law Practice* (Charlottesville, VA: Lexis Law Publishing, 1993).

7. Walter Champion, *Fundamentals of Sports Law* (Rochester: Thomson West, 2004).

8. Angela Lumpkin, Sharon Kay Stoll, and Jennifer M. Beller, Practical Ethics in Sport Management (Jefferson, NC: McFarland & Company, Inc., 2012).

9. "Athlete Death Blamed on Excessive Coaching," *United Press International*, August 27, 2008; "Parent,

Player Blame Coach for High School Football Injuries," *KTVB.com*, August 20, 2010.

10. Lindsay English, "Former PRP Football Coach Found Not Guilty on All Charges," *Wave 3*, September 17, 2009; "After Player's Death, High School Football Coach Charged with Homicide," *Wall Street Journal*, January 23, 2009.

11. Associated Press, "Notre Dame President: School Responsible in Student Death," *Sports Illustrated*, November 5, 2010.

12. Allan Korpela, "Tort Liability of Public Schools and Institutions of Higher Learning for Injuries Resulting from Lack or Insufficiency of Supervision," *American Law Reports* (1971); Andrew McCasky and

Kenneth Biedzynski, "A Guide to the Legal Liability of Coaches for a Sports Participant's Injuries," *Seton Hall Journal Sport Law* (1996).

13. Angela Lumpkin, Sharon Kay Stoll, and Jennifer M. Beller, Practical Ethics in Sport Management (Jefferson, NC: McFarland & Company, Inc., 2011).

14. Modified from Eamonn Brennan, "Uh Oh, Rick Pitino's Contract Contains a Morality Clause," *Yahoo! Sports*, August 12, 2010.

15. Jere Longman, "Temple Increases Suspension for Chaney," *New York Times*, February 26, 2005.

16. NFL.com. "Paul Tagliabue Vacates Saints Player Bounty Suspensions." December 11, 2012.

CHAPTER 5

Ethical Considerations Involving Parents and Fans

▸ Introduction

Parents and fans are essential to any successful sports program or franchise; however, ethical concerns abound, with abusive parents injuring coaches and children and out-of-control fans engaging in unethical conduct. Parents are a significant part of any youth sports organization. Many serve as volunteers and are necessary for the administration and eventual success of the league. Ethical parents are supportive of coaches, participants, and other parents. They teach young athletes respect for coaches, other participants, and sports officials. Parents set the tone for their young athlete by setting an example of a true sportsman. Fans are essential to professional sports; after all, they buy tickets! Ethical fans are not abusive—they are, in essence, good sports.

Negative comments or acts of displeasure from parents or fans toward the coach, visiting team, or officials undermine the sporting efforts of all involved. Ethical standards attempt to mold good behavior on the part of parents and fans. These standards usually come into play as punishment for unacceptable behavior, with the hope that these penalties will act as a deterrent to future acts of bad behavior or poor sportsmanship by both parents and fans.

▸ Parental Ethics

Parental involvement in youth sport creates huge problems for coaches of teams and administrators of leagues and associations. The joy of being a parent of a young athlete comes from watching your child compete in athletic events and, of course, winning; however, too many parents place far too much emphasis on winning. No one likes to lose, but for a young athlete it is inevitable—the athlete must learn to lose and be a good sport in the process. That is a tough task for a 9-year-old, but sometimes an even tougher task for the parents of that child who have already begun thinking about a college athletic scholarship.

Amateur sports leagues and associations sometimes have a difficult job ensuring that parents set good examples for their children, play within the rules, act ethically, and conduct themselves properly at sporting events. Many parents are enthralled with the idea of their child hitting the winning home run, scoring the winning touchdown, or making the winning goal. When that doesn't happen, some parents lose focus or perspective and think their child is not being treated fairly or is being denied an opportunity.

Standard of Appropriate Behavior for Parents

Ethical parents view the participation of their child in sports as a part of the educational process. Participation in interscholastic or youth sports is a learning experience for students—kids will make mistakes and parents must understand that. Ethical parents praise their childrens' attempts to improve as dedicated students, athletes, and citizens. Parents must operate as role models for their children in all areas of life, and that includes sports participation. Parents should encourage good sportsmanship by demonstrating positive support for all players, coaches, and officials at every game or practice. Parents' conduct is considered unethical if they "misbehave." Parents would do well to follow these suggestions:

1. Stress good sportsmanship. Talk to youth participants about what it means to be a good sport. Stress that "winning isn't everything," especially at the early stages of youth involvement in sport.
2. Watch for "teachable" moments. If a scenario arises where youth sports participants can learn a lesson, step in and instruct.
3. Teach how to lose gracefully. Shaking hands with the opposing team and teaching youth participants how to accept defeat is a giant step toward good sportsmanship.
4. "Check yourself." If emotions are getting out of control, step away from the field and perform a self-evaluation of your own conduct.

In recent years, hostile and abusive parents at youth sporting events are a far too common occurrence. For whatever reason, Little League baseball and youth sports in general, seem to bring out the worst in some parents. Whether it is the dad who sends "nasty" emails to his son's t-ball coach, or the mom who complains about how everything is organized but does nothing to support the team, irate and negative parents come in all forms. The majority of parents are well-behaved, but a few disruptive parents can sour youth sports for the good people. Everyone cannot be Chrissy Lisle, Little League Mom of the Year (although we wish they could be). Stephen D. Keener, President and Chief Executive Officer of Little League Baseball and Softball, said of Ms. Lisle:

> "This year's Mom of the Year truly represents the majority of Little League Moms. Growing up with baseball as part of her life, Chrissy Lisle has a special appreciation for the game and what Little League is about. As a parent, she has embraced the role of Little League volunteer by simply enjoying the experience. Serving as a team mom, while supporting her children and husband during this special time in all their lives, has shown her to be an impactful role model. Little League International is pleased to honor her with this special award."[1]

In contrast to Ms. Lisle is Matthew Collins, an out-of-control parent who assaulted a coach after a Little League baseball game.[2] Criminal acts have even occurred at youth sports, sometimes involving weapons. With tight family schedules and kids playing 40-plus games in a short season, taking music lessons, playing video games, and sometimes even doing homework, parents, kids, and coaches are under extreme pressure.[3]

Former MLB Most Valuable Player, Dale Murphy, knows a thing or two about playing baseball and being a good sport. His "I Won't Cheat Foundation" is "on a mission to encourage young players to avoid shortcuts":

> It takes courage, and we encourage kids to speak up. . . . Kids especially need as many

people as possible to say: You don't want to do that. You want to do it the right way to be successful. Kids see the short-term gain, that's kind of the challenge with all of us at any age—you see the short-term gain; you don't see the long-term consequences.[4]

What parents say to their children can have a major effect on their sports experience. Six-year-olds do not need to be told they are showing "lack of effort," are "dogging it," or are not giving it "110 percent." After all, sports are supposed to be fun (at least to a certain point). Little League parents would be wise to consider how the sport of baseball is played and the pace of the game. Nine players waiting in a field to hopefully get a chance to "muff" a "soft" ball is not exactly an activity the average 5-year-old considers as enticing. Parents should keep in mind the nature of the sport when "encouraging" their child to be successful. What about penalizing disruptive parents and keeping them a certain distance from the field? About a hundred yards

to be exact! That is what happened to a parent in one Maryland soccer league. The league president said:

> The league's disciplinary board has had better luck barring individual parents from attending games in the past three years rather than fining them, because the parents would pay the money and continue the bad behavior. We have taken a strong stance. It's important. This isn't the World Cup . . . and for the parents to be shrieking on the sidelines and belittling people goes against everything we're trying to do . . . it's not acceptable behavior.[5]

Parental Choices

There are many ethical issues involving parents in youth sports, and many of them arise in the context of religion and gender. Examine the following two case studies dealing with girl participants in a boys' league and prayer before a youth sports game.

CASE STUDY 5-1 Co-Ed Participation

At what levels should girls no longer be allowed to participate in a boys' league, if ever? What ethical issues arise when parents insist that their high school daughter is capable of playing football? Little League allows girls to play youth baseball.[6]

Check out one response to 12-year-old Jaime, a girl who was "dominating" a boys' basketball league:

> They were great . . . until she blocked the first shot. Then they were like, "Hey, we don't want this big kid coming out and making us look bad," said Michael Abraham, Jaime's coach. After parents complained, The Hoop, a private league that organizes the games, told Jaime she could no longer play with the boys, citing a rule that bars mixed-gender teams.[7]

Consider the following questions regarding Jaime's participation on the boys' basketball team.

1. What actions, if any, should be taken?
2. What reasons can you provide that Jaime should not be able to play basketball with the boys? What reasons can you give in support of her participation?
3. What would you do about the parents who do not want her making their sons look bad on the court?
4. Is there an age limit at which girls should no longer participate in a boys' league?

🔍 CASE STUDY 5-2   "There's No Religion in Baseball"

Expression of religion in youth sports can present multiple problems that need to be resolved fairly and ethically with parents. Consider the issue faced by the Little League in Medford, Oregon. A parent pulled his son from Coach Chris Palmer's baseball team because the parent said Palmer "forced" religion on the kids by leading them in prayer and quoting Bible verses. "All I wanted was for my daughter to sign up and play baseball this spring. Not to have religion or prayer shoved down her throat. There's a time and place for prayer—and baseball isn't it," said Mike, a former assistant coach for Palmer. Coach Palmer said, "I just pray that the Lord will watch over us. . . . I've never had anyone raise a stink about it."[8]

Consider the following questions as they relate to the place of prayer in youth sports.

1. Are there any concerns with a short solemn prayer for the safety of children notwithstanding which higher power you choose to worship?[9]
2. Would a prayer at a youth sporting event be acceptable if it uses neutral language, specifying no particular religion, during the prayer?[10]
3. Should prayer be allowed under any circumstances? What if a child is severely injured? Is prayer appropriate under those circumstances?[11]
4. What consideration should people of different faiths be given in this scenario?[12]
5. What role should religion play in youth sports, if any? Consider the debate over whether cheerleaders could use Bible verses on the banner a football team runs through when they enter the playing field. The principal of the school stated:

   As a Christian I would not have liked it if they had used verses from the Quran, and if I had known about it, I probably would not have approved of them doing so . . . that's the basis of the court's ruling . . . if you allow Christian verses then you have to allow Buddhist, or Jewish, and everything else. And to be perfectly honest with you, that would have been a problem here.[13]

Parental Rage

People, and especially parents, can become angry—sometimes at the smallest things. The issue becomes urgent when parents or fans fail to control their anger and it boils over to rage, with negative consequences. "Rage" has become a term of art. Sports rage has been defined as "within the context of an organized athletic activity, any physical attack upon another person such as striking, wounding, or otherwise touching in an offensive manner, and/or any malicious, verbal abuse, or sustained harassment which threatens subsequent violence or bodily harm."[14] Parental rage can cause major ethical dilemmas for youth sports organizations and even present serious legal concerns.[15]

Parental rage has taken youth sports to a new level. Anyone who has ever coached a youth sports team knows it can be tainted by one "raging" parent. It would be naïve to think youth sports coaches and officials, which consist primarily of volunteers (the key word being "volunteer"), will not be subject to criticism—they will; however, violent acts are different than verbal criticism.[16] Parental abuse or rage can include any of the following:

- Profanity
- Improper touching of a participant, referee, coach, or other parent
- Abusive language (including profanity) that demeans, ridicules, or belittles a participant's physical make-up, sex, national origin, gender, religion, skin color, skill level, sexual orientation, or parental heritage
- Entering the playing field uninvited
- Making derogatory comments to coaches, parents, officials, league officials, or other participants
- Failing to follow the rules and regulations of the league[17]

As an SMP, what should be done to control a "raging" parent? What steps would you recommend?[18] In the following case, an out-of-control parent threatened violence against a young player. When is that ever appropriate? The simple answer: never.

⚖ CASE 5-1 *Hale v. Antoniou*

2004 WL 1925551

Jordan Hale was thirteen at the time of the incident. When Jordan was in the seventh grade, he signed up to play in the Casco Bay hockey league. On December 10, 2001, Jordan's team played another team on which Michael Antoniou was a player. Jordan knew Michael and they were friends. Jordan also knew Michael's father, Demetri Antoniou.

Towards the end of the hockey game, Jordan and Michael collided. Jordan had lowered his shoulder and checked Michael. Michael went down onto the ice. Michael took a while to get up, and Jordan could tell Michael had been jarred by the hit. Michael returned to his team bench, and the game ended about ten seconds later. No penalty was called against Jordan.

From Demetri's perspective, it appeared as if Jordan drove his hockey stick onto Michael's "right jaw and right neck." Demetri testified that he thought his son might have suffered a concussion. In fact, Michael was injured as a result of the hit.

After the game, the teams went to their respective locker rooms. Jordan was in the locker room for about five minutes and had already started getting out of his hockey equipment when he saw Demetri at the doorway of his team's locker room. . . .

Scalia [Jordan's coach] testified that Demetri asked him where Jordan was, came into the locker room with a "hockey stick under—a bag on his shoulder, a hockey stick under his arm."

In his affidavit, Jordan testified that after the incident, when he tried to stand up, his knees buckled and he had to sit back down.

The court denied Demetri's motion for summary judgment, because Jordan's claims for civil assault and intentional infliction of emotional distress are allowed to go forward, their punitive damages claim were not barred by the absence of an underlying tort.

Jordan showed that there is a dispute regarding whether Demetri's alleged actions were motivated by ill will toward Jordan or so outrageous that malice towards Jordan as a result of that conduct can be implied. The court cites Scalia's testimony that Demetri asked him where Jordan was, came into the locker room with a "hockey stick under a bag on his shoulder, a hockey stick under his arm," and said, "Jordan Hale is an asshole."

Express malice exists when the defendant's tortuous conduct is motivated by ill will toward the plaintiff and that implied malice exists when deliberate conduct by the defendant, although motivated by something other than ill will toward any particular party, is so outrageous that malice toward a person injured as a result of that conduct can be implied.

Consider the following questions regarding Case 5-1.

1. Even though this parent did not physically strike Jordan, it is clear that he was "enraged." What disciplinary measures should be assessed against the parent and who should assess them?
2. Should a police report have been made in this case?
3. Should the parent be made to apologize to all involved?
4. Should the parent be forced to take anger management classes before he can come back to the league?

Hale v. Antoniou, U.S. Supreme Court.

The "hockey dad" case study that follows involves the tragic death of a parent.

🔍 *CASE STUDY 5-3   Thomas Junta, Hockey Dad*

The most notable occurrence of parental rage resulted in the death of a young hockey player's father at a Massachusetts hockey rink. The encounter between Thomas Junta, known as the "Hockey Dad," and Michael Costin occurred on July 5, 2000. Costin was supervising a hockey practice for 10-year-old boys, including his three sons and Junta's son. Junta was in the stands observing his son in a non-contact scrimmage.

During the scrimmage, Junta became upset when he saw players acting rough and engaging in what he thought was unnecessary "body-checking." Junta then left the stands and went onto the ice, yelling at Costin for allowing the rough play between the boys. Costin was in his protective hockey gear and attacked Junta by choking him with Junta's necklace and then kicking Junta's shins and feet with the 3-inch blades of his ice skates. After the physical altercation, a rink employee separated Junta and Costin and requested that Junta leave the rink. Junta left the rink with his son and later returned to pick up his son's two friends.

When Junta returned to the rink, he once again ran into Costin. A second argument ensued and both men "squared off" and began punching each other. Junta threw Costin to the floor and repeatedly beat Costin in the head and the neck. Upon their arrival at the rink, paramedics found Costin without a pulse. At the hospital, he fell into a coma and was placed on a ventilator. A day after the incident, Michael Costin was declared brain dead, was removed from the ventilator, and died. Junta surrendered to the police and was arrested for manslaughter.

In January 2002, Junta's trial began with jury selection, which consisted of asking potential jurors if they had children, if their children played on sports teams, and if they ever had witnessed an incident of parental rage at a youth sports game. Junta was found guilty of involuntary manslaughter and sentenced to 6 to 10 years in prison.[19] The jury refused to find him guilty of the more serious charge of manslaughter, which would have sentenced Junta to 20 years in prison.[20]

Why do you suppose the jury refused to find Junta guilty of the more serious charge of manslaughter?

Parents should be supportive of their student-athlete. Any violence or abusive language is anathema to the desired goal of the ethical parent. When the stakes appear to be higher for the parents than for the children, parents have an obligation to examine their own behavior and to refrain from unethical conduct.

⚖ *CASE 5-2   Bill Brantley v. Bowling Green School*

2003 WL22533643 (E.D. Louisiana)

Bill Brantley was injured while working as a referee at a high school boys' basketball game at Bowling Green School. Frank Glenn came onto the court and began assaulting Brantley's referee partner, Charlie Ackerman. Apparently, this occurred when Glenn's minor son was ejected from the game because of a technical foul. Glenn allegedly was joined in his assault of Ackerman by Donald McGehee. When Brantley tried to stop the assault, McGehee allegedly punched, clawed, and battered him. In the melee that ensued, McGehee was soon joined by two other McGehees, who allegedly punched, kicked, and beat Brantley until he was unconscious. Brantley alleges that his injuries were caused by the intentional acts of Glenn, Bowling Green School, and the three McGehees. Here, Glenn's alleged acts occurred at a high school sports event where Brantley and his fellow referee were charged with officiating and keeping order.

Consider the following questions with regard to Case 5-2.

1. Should there be a harsher penalty for the parent who assaults a sports official?
2. Should criminal charges be brought in this case?
3. Does the school's athletic department bear any responsibility for what happened in this case?

Bill Brantley v. Bowling Green School, U.S. Supreme Court.

Preventing Parental Rage

What can be done to ensure parents are kept under control? If they are not held in check, it could lead to dire consequences and possible legal action.

◎ CASE STUDY 5-4   *Parents' Ethics Course*

A youth athletic league in Florida is adding a requirement for kids who want to be sports participants. Their parents must learn how to behave on the sidelines as well.

The Jupiter-Tequesta Athletic Association is requiring parents to take an hour-long mandatory ethics course. Jeff Leslie, the volunteer President of the association and father of four, stated: "We just want to try to de-escalate the intensity that's being shown by the parents at these games." The program, Parents Alliance for Youth Sports (PAYS) of the National Alliance for Youth Sports, costs $5 and attendance will be required for at least one parent or guardian from each family. It states the roles and responsibilities of a parent of a youth athlete in a 19-minute video and a handbook. The first season had many parents enrolled in the class.

It is always good to ask an expert. Joey Scherperborg, an 8-year-old who plays in the White Oak League, puts it succinctly when discussing parental misconduct: "It makes it not as fun. . . . I wish parents wouldn't do that."[21]

▶ Fan Ethics

Fans can be adamant about supporting a team. They like to go to the stadium or park and have a good time; however, sometimes a "good time" can get out of hand. Just as any other participant in a sporting contest, fans must regulate their conduct to conform to societal expectations. Although fans should have a good time at the ballpark, there is a line that cannot be crossed. Getting 100,000 fans or more together in a large stadium with alcohol present and enthusiasm running high can create a lot of excitement. Teams and stadium owners have both a legal and an ethical duty to their fans to ensure that spectators conduct themselves in a proper manner so as not to offend others. Some conduct inappropriate in a restaurant may be perfectly acceptable at an outdoor sporting event. The key is knowing when a spectator has crossed the line into inappropriate or unethical conduct.

What should happen if a fan crosses the line? Should stadium officials Taser them?[22] How about an out-of-control, intoxicated heckler at a golf match? Is a Taser appropriate under these circumstances?[23] Should kids ever be "tasered"?

Fans can become overly boisterous and rowdy, even violent. Fans have a responsibility to act in accordance with the rules and to control their behavior at sporting events. Unnecessarily violent behavior is anathema to the proper conduct of ethical fans. Fans, like participants, must make ethical decisions. They can choose the ethical course or allow themselves to lose their sense of perspective by abusive heckling or even violent interactions with participants, coaches, referees, or other sports officials.

Appropriate Standards for Fan Behavior

Enthusiastic hockey fans banging on the glass during a game is generally considered part of the game. Good natured "ragging" of a player by a fan is generally accepted, but cursing, profane, or abusive language is not. Stadium owners want fans to come back to the ballpark. They have an investment in ensuring fans behave themselves. The fan has a responsibility for behaving ethically during a sporting contest. Spectators at sporting events are encouraged to (in a reasonable manner) yell, scream, and cheer in an effort to provide support to their team and express their opinion to sports officials. (Again, only if done reasonably.) This behavior is done to encourage and motivate the players.

The spectator and fan should be enthusiastic but fair, and adhere to the tenets of good sportsmanship. Committing a violent, drunken, or criminal act will not be tolerated and is considered inappropriate fan conduct. This behavior can be punished by expulsion from the stadium as well as the fan suffering legal consequences

of his or her actions. Owners want fans excited about their team, but only if fans do so ethically and follow the rules of conduct set down by the owner and society in general.

Professional leagues and teams have recently begun to publish codes of conduct for fans. The following is a model:

Fan Code of Conduct

The club expects all who enter the stadium and surrounding parking lots to adhere to the fan code of conduct. Failure to follow this Code will result in possible ejection from the stadium, revocation of ticket privileges, and arrest. Although Season Ticket Holders may give their tickets to others, the account holder is responsible for the actions of those using their tickets.

The following actions are prohibited at the stadium and in surrounding parking lots:

- Fighting, taunting, or engaging in any action that may harm, threaten, or bring discomfort to anyone in the stadium
- Sitting in a seat other than one's ticketed seat location or refusing to produce one's game ticket upon request by stadium personnel
- Possession or use of any illegal drugs or irresponsible use of alcohol
- Loitering in concourses, aisles, tunnels, or stairs
- Smoking in the stadium
- Use of foul, abusive, or obscene language or gestures
- Damage, destruction, vandalism, or theft of any property of other fans or the club
- Failure to follow the directions of law enforcement, security, ushers, ticket takers, or any other stadium personnel
- Unauthorized use of any seating designed for persons with a disability
- Engaging in any action that causes a disruption, creates an unsafe environment, interferes with the game, or hinders the enjoyment of the game for other fans
- Mistreatment of visiting team fans, including verbal abuse, harassment,

profanity, confrontations, intimidation, or threatening behavior

- Refusal to remove or turn inside-out clothing deemed offensive or obscene upon request by stadium personnel[24]

Consider the following with regard to the model code of fan conduct:

1. Is the code of conduct complete? If not, what would you add?
2. Under what circumstances should club officials remove a fan?
3. How do you define "irresponsible use of alcohol"?

In 2008, the NFL adopted a fan code of conduct which prohibits the following:

- Behavior that is unruly, disruptive, or illegal in nature
- Intoxication or other signs of alcohol impairment that result in irresponsible behavior
- Foul or abusive language or obscene gestures
- Interference with the progress of the game (including throwing objects onto the field)
- Failing to follow instructions of stadium personnel
- Verbal or physical harassment of opposing team fans[25]

Fan Heckling

"Heckling" is very common in baseball as well as other sports. As long as it does not get out of hand, it is considered acceptable behavior. Is it a "fair comment" when fans heckle a player when the player is not playing well? Should athletes be subject to heckling in a public place? LeBron James was heckled at a wedding reception and also at an amusement park.[26] Evidently, there is an art form to heckling.[27] The question is, when does a heckler go too far? One expert has stated it well:

Heckling players is not an act of sportsmanship and should be avoided. While many players will ignore most verbal heckling, it is a little more difficult to avoid items that are being thrown. Noise is acceptable at certain spectator events and taboo at others. Dealing with noise is a challenge for many athletes. Although at times it may be distracting, noise is considered a big advantage by a home team's athletes and coaches. At spectator events such as football, baseball, and basketball, it is considered appropriate to yell and cheer for your team. It is not considered appropriate to yell comments about a player's family, race, or any other disparaging remark. In the game of golf, however, noise is disrespectful. One golfer, following a noisy tournament, commented: "I'm certainly not going to go out and disrupt a business person in their business life and they shouldn't disrupt our game."

Another inappropriate behavior by spectators is running out on fields and floors after their teams win. While this was previously done only when a team was ranked and played a ranked team, it now happens for no apparent reason. Fans should consider taking this bit of advice: "Try winning like you've done it before."[28]

How a player reacts to a heckler may dictate whether the heckler will continue his or her verbal barrage. Charles Albert "Chief" Bender was a great Native American baseball player during the first two decades of the 20th century and is in Baseball's Hall of Fame. At the time he was playing, African American players were prohibited from playing. Bender was subject to racial prejudice when he played the game. He was known for handling racial taunts gracefully and with a little wit. When fans heckled him or greeted him with "war whoops" when he came onto the field, he responded with his own style, yelling back, "Foreigners, Foreigners."[29]

Are certain subjects off-limits for fans and hecklers? How much should a fan be able to say about an athlete's personal life? There was much debate about this issue when Tiger Woods returned to the golf course in 2010.

Some fans made comments about Woods's off-course activities.[30] There are ethical guidelines for hecklers.[31] Legal constraints impose obligations on fans that mandate appropriate behavior and fans can also be ejected for poor sportsmanship and conduct.

🔎 CASE STUDY 5-5 Ultra Spectator Michael Katz

Michael Katz, a spectator who heckled coach Isiah Thomas of the New York Knicks, received a warning card from a security guard to stop what he was doing or he would be ejected from Madison Square Garden. Katz, an accountant, said he was not cursing or swearing but merely yelling critical remarks at Thomas. Katz said his comments were within the boundaries of "fair comment." Representatives of the Knicks and the NBA said the warning was "routine" and part of a league-wide effort to control fan behavior that was instituted after a brawl in 2004 involving the Detroit Pistons, the Indiana Pacers, and some spectators. Verbal criticism of Thomas had been common in 2004, with some Knicks fans sometimes chanting "Fire Isiah!"

The card given to Katz featured blue letters on a white background and read: "You are being issued a warning that the comments, gestures, and/or behaviors that you have directed at players, coaches, game officials, and/or other spectators constitute excessive verbal abuse and are in violation of the NBA Fan Code of Conduct. This is the first and only warning that you will receive. If, after receiving this warning, you verbally abuse any player, coach, game official or spectator, you will be immediately ejected from the arena without refund."[32] After receiving the warning, Katz said he moved to a different seat and was not ejected from the Garden.

Consider the following questions related to Katz's behavior.

1. Is giving a fan a warning card if they engage in improper conduct a good idea?
2. Should there be different levels of warning to fans before they are ejected?
3. For what conduct should a fan be ejected?
4. Would a fan commenting on the sexual harassment lawsuit against Isiah Thomas while he was the general manager of the New York Knicks be considered "fair comment"? It is, after all, a public record.
5. Should warning systems for abusive fans be applied to youth sports similar to that of the NBA? In youth sports, what should the warnings contain?

Should a fan be ejected for "negative cheering"? The Wisconsin Interscholastic Athletic Association (WIAA), a high school athletic association, decided that chanting by student sections directed at opponents during sporting events was getting out of hand. In December 2015, the WIAA sent the high school athletic directors the following email:

"Seasons Greetings,

I hope everyone has a Merry Christmas and a Happy New Year, as well as the opportunity to take a short breather.

Heading into the New Year, with the holiday tournaments and conference schedules ramping up, and the winter sports Tournament Series soon to follow, we want to identify a point of emphasis for sportsmanship this season.

As we reviewed the fall tournaments and the sportsmanship evaluations and observations, we want to address concerns with a noticeable increase in the amount of chants by student sections directed at opponents and/or opponents' supporters that are clearly intended to taunt or disrespect.

Not wanting to restrict creativity or enjoy-ment, an enthusiastic and boisterous display of support for a school's team is welcomed and encouraged at interscholastic events when directed in a positive manner. However, any action directed at opposing teams or their spectators with the intent to taunt, disrespect, distract or entice an unsporting behavior in response in not acceptable sportsmanship. Student groups, school administrators and event managers should take immediate steps to correct this unsporting behavior.

Some specific examples of unsporting behavior by student groups including[sic] chants directed at opposing participants and/or fans. Among the chants that have been heard at recent high school sporting events are: "You can't do that," "Fundamentals," "Air ball," "There's a net there," "Sieve," "We can't hear you," The "scoreboard" cheer, and "Season's over" during tournament series play.

Thanks for your assistance![33]

In response, a girls' basketball player at Hilbert High School in Wisconsin posted on her twitter account, "Eat Shit WIAA." The school district imposed a five-game suspen-sion for the tweet. Did the WIAA make an ethical decision by banning chants in student sections that are "clearly intended to taunt or disrespect"? According to scholars, reg-ulating fan speech raises First Amendment issues for public institutions such as public high schools and state universities.[34] Did the school district make an ethical decision by suspending the high school athlete five games for expressing her opinion about the WIAA's new policy?

The national pastime can sometimes bring out the worst in baseball fans.[35] Baseball fans can be very loyal to their team and hos-tile to visitors. Consider the following case in which a heckler provoked a player.

⚖ CASE 5-3 *Manning v. Grimsley and the Baltimore Baseball Club*

643 F.2d 20 (1st Cir. 1981)

On September 16, 1975, David Manning, Jr., was a spectator at Fenway Park in Boston for a baseball game between the Baltimore Orioles and the Boston Red Sox. Ross Grimsley was a pitcher for Baltimore. During the first three innings, Grimsley was warming up by throwing a ball from a pitcher's mound to a plate in the bullpen located near the right field bleachers. The spectators in the bleachers continuously heckled Grimsley. On several occasions immediately following the heckling, Grimsley looked directly at the hecklers, not just into the stands. At the end of the third inning, Grimsley, after his catcher had left his catching position and was walking over to the bench, faced the bleachers and wound up or stretched as though to pitch in the direction of the plate. Instead, the ball traveled from Grimsley's hand at more than 80 miles per hour at an angle of 90 degrees to the path from the pitcher's mound to the plate and directly toward the hecklers in the bleachers. The ball passed through the wire mesh fence in front of the bleachers and struck Manning.

Manning v. Grimsley and the Baltimore Baseball Club, U.S. Supreme Court.

It is not illegal for hecklers to heckle temper-amental relievers; however, it was certainly illegal for Grimsley to intentionally throw a "pitch" into the grandstands where the hecklers were situ-ated. What ethical duty does this case present for teams, leagues, and stadium operators?

In the following case, some minor league baseball players decided to take matters into their own hands with a heckler, who ended up suing the major league club that employed the minor league players.

⚖ CASE 5-4 *Simmons v. Baltimore Orioles, Inc.*

712 F. Supp 79 (W.D. Va. 1989)

Simmons, along with a friend, attended the Fourth of July, 1988 game between the Martinsville Phillies and the Bluefield Orioles, a Baltimore farm team, at Bluefield, Virginia. Bluefield was not having a good year, and whether for this or some other reason Simmons moved down to the third baseline along about the eighth inning, and started to heckle the Oriole players sitting in the bullpen. Champ [Orioles player] stated in his deposition that Simmons was accusing the ballplayers of stealing the local women, and that he (Simmons) would show the Orioles what West Virginia manhood was like by blowing the players' heads off. Whatever was precisely said, the pitching coach [of the Orioles] then asked Simmons to leave. After the game (Bluefield lost, 9–8, stranding three runners in the bottom of the ninth), Champ encountered Simmons in the parking lot. Simmons . . . offers no details of what ensued other than that he was punched and kicked by Champ and then hit in the jaw by a baseball bat wielded by Hicks [Orioles player], causing his jaw to be broken in two places. Champ's version was that Simmons saw him carrying a bat, made a gesture as if he were shooting Champ with his finger, and said "Oh, so you need a bat, huh?" Champ said "No, I don't," and threw his bat down. Simmons gestured toward his car and said, "Let's go over to my car, and I'll blow your head off." Another player tried to intervene, and Champ said, "Just get out of here." Simmons then advanced threateningly upon him, and Champ hit Simmons in the face. Simmons was unfazed, and Champ kicked him in the chest, causing Simmons to stagger back. According to Champ he then smiled and said "I'm drunk. I didn't feel that." Champ turned to walk away, and at that point . . . Hicks hit Simmons. Simmons says Hicks hit him with a bat, but Hicks says that he used only his fist. Hicks had not been near any of the heckling and says he intervened because he was afraid Simmons was about to pull a gun on Champ.

1. Could the stadium operators have done something to prevent this from happening?
2. Do the Baltimore Orioles have a responsibility to discipline Champ and Hicks? What would be a fair disciplinary action?
3. What can the Orioles do to make sure something like this doesn't happen again?
4. If a fan merely has a license to be on the premises, under what circumstances could the license be revoked?

Simmons v. Baltimore Orioles, Inc., U.S. Supreme Court.

What actions should be taken against players who enter the stands and assault hecklers? In a highly publicized incident, in November 2004, a spectator threw a beverage that struck Indiana Pacers player Ron Artest during a game against the Detroit Pistons. Artest and two of his teammates, Stephen Jackson and Anthony Johnson, ran up into the stands and fought with several spectators. Another Pacers player, Jermaine O'Neal, attempted to enter the stands and was restrained by an arena official, but O'Neal pushed the official away and then struck a spectator who had descended from the stands onto the court. The NBA Commissioner suspended Artest for the remainder of the season, Jackson for thirty games, O'Neal for twenty-five games, and Johnson for five games. The players association appealed to an arbitrator who upheld the suspensions of Artest, Jackson, and Johnson but found that O'Neal's suspension of twenty-five games was not supported by just cause and reduced it to fifteen games.[36]

Fan Rage

Fan rage is much like parental rage—it should never be tolerated and stadium personnel should take immediate action to remove abusive fans from the premises. In the fourth quarter of a 1995 NFL game between the Giants and the Chargers, fans began throwing snowballs from their seats and one struck Chargers equipment manager Sid Brooks in the face, rendering him unconscious for 30 seconds. A melee ensued with fourteen fans being arrested, 175 ejections, and 15 injuries. It was reported, "Early in the fourth quarter, an ice ball sent in the direction of the San Diego bench hit Brooks in the left eye. 'He went down like a ton of bricks,' said Paul Black, the Chargers' doctor, rendering him unconscious. As the teams were called off the field and the crowd was warned a cancellation was imminent, ugly got uglier: more snowballs were hurled at the circle of trainers and players surrounding Brooks, out for thirty frightening seconds, down for two frightening minutes."[37]

A Bowie hunting knife with a 5-inch blade was thrown at California Angels rookie Wally Joyner after his team's 2–0 defeat of the Yankees. "Joyner was grazed on the left arm by the butt end of the weapon, escaping injury. Said Joyner, "I picked it up and gave it to [Angels' manager] Gene Mauch."[38]

A local disc jockey set up an anti-disco promotion to be held between games of a White Sox/Tigers doubleheader. Fans bringing a disco record were charged only 98 cents for admission. The thousands of records were then jammed into a large wooden box in center field and blown to pieces. A riot ensued on the field as about 7000 fans brawled and set off bonfires with the debris, forcing the postponement of the second game. Former major league player Rusty Staub said, "They

would slice around you and stick in the ground. It wasn't just one, it was many. Oh, God almighty, I've never seen anything so dangerous in my life. I begged the guys to put on their batting helmets."[39]

Even coaches are not immune to fan violence. An attack against Kansas City Royals first base coach Tom Gamboa was unprecedented. The "fan," William Ligue, Jr. and his 15-year-old son ran onto the field and attacked Gamboa from behind. Ligue had telephoned his sister before Thursday night's attack and told her to watch the White Sox game. Ligue was charged with aggravated battery—he told the police that he charged the field because he was angry that the White Sox were losing; however, the evidence strongly supports the fact that the attack was premeditated—shortly before he ran onto the field, he handed his keys, cell phone, and jewelry to another of his sons; he was wearing a pocketknife on his waistband when he ran on the field. His 15-year-old son was charged with two juvenile counts of aggravated battery; one for attacking Gamboa and the other for hitting a White Sox security guard who was an off-duty police officer. Gamboa was pummeled and received several cuts and a large bruise on his forehead.[40]

Fan Stalking

Stalking is a serious societal crime and should be treated as such. Although many women, including entertainers and sports stars, have been the victims of stalking, few actually report it.[41] Male athletes have been stalked as well. A man was found to be stalking Olympic gold medalist Shawn Johnson.[42]

Fans stalking sports stars has become a major problem in sports.[43] The *New York Times* reported:

> Whether they are obsessed fans fixating on celebrities or former romantic partners, stalkers . . . typically invoke spurned love—real

or imagined—to defend their actions. But stalkers seldom have to justify their behavior in the legal system because only one in three cases is ever reported to the authorities.[44]

In Case 5-5, Bob Uecker, "Mr. Baseball," had been stalked and procured a restraining order against his stalker.[45] She subsequently sued him for defamation.

⚖ CASE 5-5   Ladd v. Uecker and Milwaukee Brewers Baseball Club

780 N.W.2d 216 (2010)

Uecker is the radio broadcaster for the Brewers. In June 2006, Uecker petitioned the Milwaukee County Circuit Court for an injunction against Ladd, alleging a six- or seven-year pattern of harassment. Around the same time, Ladd, a self-described "devoted fan," was charged with felony stalking. The injunction petition hearing was held on July 3 and September 7, 2006. The court commissioner found probable cause and issued an injunction charge.

On September 8, 2008, Ladd filed a sprawling pro se complaint alleging that between June 1 and September 7, 2006, Uecker defamed her in the affidavit supporting the injunction petition; he and/or the Brewers published the allegedly defamatory affidavit to a website called thesmokinggun.com; the Brewers posted on their website a defamatory article regarding her removal from a spring training game in Maryvale, Arizona; and a claim for "false light invasion of privacy" for, among other things, making and republishing false, defamatory statements and photographing her in the stands at various baseball stadiums.

Ladd's September 8, 2008, complaint alleges that Uecker defamed her: (1) in the affidavit in support of his petition for the harassment injunction; (2) by publishing the affidavit to thesmokinggun.com; (3) during the two-day injunction hearing; and (4) in a media interview after the first day of the hearing. Distilled to its essence, Ladd's claim is that the false depiction of her as a stalker has damaged her personal and professional reputations. Except for the continued injunction hearing on September 7, 2006, however, all of these incidents occurred more than two years before Ladd filed her complaint.

Ladd also argues that, although Uecker and/or the Brewers allegedly posted his affidavit to thesmokinggun.com on June 2, 2006, the purportedly defamatory statements still can be accessed on the Internet today. She contends that the information therefore is republished each time someone visits that website or others to which the material has found its way, thus renewing her cause of action.

Ladd asserts, however, that Uecker's statements lost their absolute privilege through "excessive publication" on the Internet, because the "stalker label" "defame[ed][her] as a criminal" and because Uecker defamed her to law enforcement officials.

Ladd's complaints that the Brewers defamed her likewise fail. The Brewers advised Ladd in December 2006 that, in light of the harassment injunction, they would deny her entrance to the spring training facility in March 2007 should she purchase a ticket. Upon finding her in the stands, they were entitled to have her removed. As Ladd's ticket indicates, a ticket of admission to a place of amusement is simply a license to view a performance that the owner or proprietor may revoke at will.

Ladd included a photocopy of her ticket as an exhibit, evidently to show she had a right to be at the game. The ticket reads: "The license granted by this ticket to enter the Club baseball game is revocable."

Ladd then directs us to an allegedly defamatory March 20, 2007, article in the Brewers' online news archive about the Maryvale incident. Assuming, as Ladd contends, that the Brewers posted the story there, and accepting simply for argument's sake that the article is defamatory, this claim also fails. Before filing suit, Ladd did not give written notice to the Brewers providing them "a reasonable opportunity to correct the libelous matter."

Ladd alleges that the Brewers took photographs of her in the stands at baseball parks and disseminated her "mug shot" and information about the injunction and the spring training incident. None of these involved private places, using her likeness for advertising or trade, or depictions of nudity. Further, they are matters of public record.

Ladd had been hounding Uecker for six or seven years, sending him unusual gifts, seeking his autograph, and appearing at ball parks and hotels where he was staying.

Consider the following questions in light of the Uecker case.

1. What can be done to prevent crazy fans from stalking players?
2. What actions should stadium officials take to prevent such conduct? How could the stadium owners keep stalkers from entering the ball park?
3. Where is the ethical line drawn between an enthusiastic fan and a stalker?
4. The fan was banned from Brewers' home and road games. How can this be enforced?[46]

Ladd v. Uecker and Milwaukee Brewers Baseball Club, U.S. Supreme Court.

Other Inappropriate Fan Conduct

Going onto a playing field without permission constitutes criminal trespass and the fan can be arrested; however, that does not stop many fans from doing just that. Running on a sports field without permission is a crime and also creates multiple safety issues for fans, security personnel, and participants. In Case 5-6, Erica Eneman and Amy Nadler were crushed by persons attempting to come onto the playing field at Camp Randall Stadium at the University of Wisconsin after the 1993 Wisconsin/Michigan football game. They assert their injuries would not have occurred if certain gates had not been closed by security personnel at the conclusion of the game.

⚖ CASE 5-6   *Erica Eneman and Amy Nadler v. Pat Richter*

577 N.W.2d 386 (1998)

Camp Randall Stadium is the site used for football games and other outdoor events at the University of Wisconsin at Madison. The football field is encircled by a chain-link fence with a walkway between the fence and the bottom row of bleachers. Ingress and egress of the bleachers varies, depending on the section of the stadium. Sections O and P were at issue in this lawsuit. The lower rows of sections O and P exit to the walkway and then through the home team tunnel. It was also possible for those rows to exit to the field itself, even though security personnel directed spectators not to do so. Prior to the 1993 football season, access to the field was limited by handheld ropes, which provided no real barrier to a spectator determined to enter the field. In anticipation of the 1993 football season, the University installed metal gates that could be positioned to close off the walkway at the bottom of the bleachers in order to permit the team to exit the field into the tunnel without interference from the spectators. When the walkway was closed off by the gates, sections O and P spectators' means of egress was restricted, until the team had made its way through the tunnel and the gates were opened again.

On October 30, 1993, after the University of Wisconsin's football team defeated the University of Michigan's team at Camp Randall, many of the students in sections O and P attempted to come onto the playing field. However, a few minutes before the game's end, the gates had been closed and latched by security personnel. This provided a significant barrier to the spectators' egress onto the field, and it also created a dead end for tunnel egress from sections O and P, at a time when spectators were moving down the bleachers to exit the stadium or to push onto the field. The plaintiffs were crushed against a metal railing and the gates when security personnel were unable to quickly unlatch the gates to open them.

Ward and Richter had no personal responsibility to manage the crowd at the Camp Randall games. On the other hand, Riseling's, Green's and Williams's activities at Camp Randall were arguably within the scope of the Standard Operating Procedures for Camp Randall relating to crowd control. Additionally, prior to the Michigan game, and subsequent to the installation of the gates, Riseling knew that it was possible that the students might try to rush onto the field at the game's end. In response to this potential for congestion in the student sections, she formulated and issued a directive entitled, "Post Game Crowd Tactics," whose goal was "to prevent injury to people—officers, band members and fans." The plan outlined a general strategy to follow which, in her judgment, would have prevented injury. Although her plan was implemented by security personnel, it was not successful.

Riseling, as Chief of Police and Security did not ignore the potential danger. She, with the assistance of others, formulated a plan, the "POST GAME CROWD TACTICS," the goal of which was "to prevent injury to people—officers, band and fans."

The plan established no specific tasks that were to be performed at a certain time; rather, it made general statements and set general guidelines such as,

> We expect that if Wisconsin wins today, especially if it is a close game, there will be an attempt by fans to come onto the field.
>
> . . . .
>
> If there is a crowd surge, officers at that point will make the initial decision to move aside and begin pulling back to the goalpost assignment. Lt. Johnson will be observing from the press box and will make decisions on giving the command for all officers to pull back.
>
> . . . .
>
> There may be times during and after the game when people crowd the fence and put pressure against it. Actively encourage them to move back. If it seems there is danger of the fence breaking (it has in the past) move back to a safe position.

Here, the formation of the post-game crowd control plan represented Riseling's judgment about how best to reduce the potential for injury to persons at the game. Additionally, the implementation of the plan required Riseling, Green and Williams to respond to their assessment of what the crowd's actions required. By its very nature, the way the plan was effected had to change from moment to moment because the plan was responsive to the crowd. Reacting to the crowd also constituted the exercise of discretion. Furthermore, neither the documents nor the testimony contained in any of the portions of the depositions submitted in opposition to respondents' motion for summary judgment established a factual dispute about whether any specific acts were required of any of the respondents.

Here, documents provided establish no inconsistency between the actions of those respondents whose job duties took them personally into crowd control management activities, and the University's policy of safe management of the crowd at football games. Rather, they acted in accord with the General Operating Procedures for Camp Randall Stadium. Neither the formulation of the plan nor the implementation of it required highly technical, professional skills, such as a physician's.

Consider the following questions as they apply to the Camp Randall incident:

1. What ethical duties do stadium owners owe to fans? Were the fans at Camp Randall engaging in poor sportsmanship, criminal activity, or unethical conduct?
2. Did the university violate any ethical duty they had to the fans?
3. How could stadium owners prevent these tragic events in the future?

Erica Eneman and Amy Nadler v. Pat Richter, U.S. Supreme Court.

▶ Summary

While parents and fans are necessary components of any sports program or franchise, they sometimes become too emotionally involved and that can create problems for the SMP. The SMP is responsible for implementing policies and rules to deter inappropriate parental and fan behavior. As this chapter demonstrated, striking the appropriate balance of regulation and sanctions for violations often raises ethical considerations for the SMP, as well as practical problems with enforcement.

▶ References

1. "Chrissy Lisle Recognized as 2009 Little League Mom of the Year," *LittleLeague.org*, July 31, 2009.
2. Jason Lea, "Court Date Delayed Again for Man Accused of Attacking Little League Coach," *The News-Herald*, June 15, 2010. Skip Bayless, "Little League Is Out of Control," *ESPN.com*, August 31, 2006.
3. Bernie Augustine, "Big Demands on Little League Parents," *SILive.com*, August 26, 2009. Les Edgerton, *Surviving Little League: For Players, Parents, and Coaches* (New York: Taylor Trade Publishing, 2004).
4. Associated Press, "Former MVP Takes a Stand Against Cheating," *New York Times*, August 14, 2010.
5. Annie Gowen, "100-Yard Penalty on Players' Parents: Fans of Md. Soccer Team Banned After a Few Berate the Referee," *Washington Post*, April 21, 2009.
6. Dave Merchant, "Local Woman Changes Face of Little League Baseball," *Heritage Newspapers*, August 17, 2010; Bruce Weber, "Judge Sylvia Pressler, Who Opened Little League to Girls, Dies at 75," *New York Times*, February 17, 2010.
7. Kari Pricher, Lisa Fletcher, Nicole Young, and Stephanie Dahle, "Banned from Playing Basketball with the Boys," *ABC News*, May 24, 2008.
8. Associated Press, "Little League Calls Coach's Pre-Game Prayer Fair, Not Foul," *KCBY News*, May 3, 2010.
9. Dennis Collins, "Nearer My God to the Goal Line: 'Suppose I Pray to Win, and the Other Guy, He Prays to Win, What's God Gonna Do?'" *Washington Post*, November 19, 1978.
10. Charles S. Prebish, "'Heavenly Father, Divine Goalie': Sport and Religion," *The Antioch Review* 42, no. 3 (Summer 1984): 306–318.
11. Pat McManamon, "Major Gains for Boy Hit by Ball at Minor League Game," *Fanhouse.com*, July 26, 2010; Sara Pulliam Bailey, "Where God Talk Gets Sidelined: Sports Journalists Are Reluctant to Tackle Faith on the Field," *Wall Street Journal*, February 4, 2010.
12. "Kurt Warner: Jesus Brought Me Here," *Christian Post*, January 30, 2010; Hannah Karp, "Can Buddha Help Your Short Game?" *Wall Street Journal*, April 27, 2010.
13. L. Z. Granderson, "The Debate at Lakeview-Fort Oglethorpe," *ESPN.com*, October 6, 2009.
14. Gregg S. Heinzmann, "Parental Violence in Youth Sports: Facts, Myths, and Violence," *Youthsports.Rutgers.edu*.
15. Howard P. Benard, "Little League Fun, Big League Liability," *Marquette Sports Law Journal* (1997–1998).
16. Paulo David, "Young Athletes and Competitive Sports: Exploit and Exploitation," *International Journal of Children's Rights* 7 (1999): 53–81.
17. G. S. Heinzmann, "Parental Violence in Youth Sports: Facts, Myths, and Videotape," *National Recreation and Parks Association*; Joel Fish and Susan Magee, *101 Ways to Be a Terrific Sports Parent* (New York: Fireside, 2003).
18. Dianna K. Fiore, "Parental Rage and Violence in Youth Sports: How Can We Prevent Soccer Moms and Hockey Dads from Interfering in Youth Sports and Causing Games to End in Fistfights Rather Than Handshakes?" *Villanova Sports and Entertainment*

Law Journal (2003); Geoffrey G. Watson, "Games, Socialization and Parental Values: Social Class Differences in Parental Evaluation of Little League Baseball," *International Review for the Sociology of Sport* (1977).

19. "Hockey Dad Gets 6 to 10 Years for Fatal Beating," *CNN.com*, January 25, 2002.
20. Fox Butterfield, "Fatal Fight at Rink Nearly Severed Head, Doctor Testifies," *New York Times*, January 15, 2002, A9.
21. Richelle Thompson, "Youth Leagues Make Parents Play by the Rules," *Cincinnati Enquirer*, March 22, 2000.
22. Jason Gay, "Would Taser Boy Electrify Broadway?" *Wall Street Journal*, May 5, 2010.
23. Samuel Goldsmith, "Drunk Golf Fan Tasered for Heckling Tiger Woods at The Players Championship," *New York Daily News*, May 8, 2010.
24. © 2011 Little League Baseball, Incorporated. All Rights Reserved.
25. Michael McCarthy, "NFL Unveils New Code of Conduct for Its Fans," *USA Today*, August 6, 2008.
26. Chris Sheridan, "LeBron James Heckled at Carmelo's Wedding Reception," *ESPN.com*, July 12, 2010; Rick Chandler, "LeBron James Heckled at Amusement Park, Beaten by This Guy in 3-Point Shootout," *NBC Sports*, August 10, 2010.
27. Katlin Stinespring, "The Art of Sports Heckling," *The Charleston Gazette*, June 11, 2010.
28. Jeanette S. Martin and Lillian H. Chaney, "Sports Etiquette," *Proceedings of the 2007 Association for Business Communication Annual Convention.*
29. Frederick E. Hoxie, *Encyclopedia of North American Indians* (Boston, MA: Houghton Mifflin Harcourt, 1996), p. 66. Tom Swift, *Chief Bender's Burden: The Silent Struggle of a Baseball Star* (Lincoln, NE: Bison Books, 2010).
30. Larry Dorman, "Woods Is Getting Ready; So Are the Hecklers," *New York Times*, March 24, 2010.
31. Robin Ficker, "The Heckler's Code," *New York Times*, November 22, 2004.
32. Joe Lapointe, "NBA Gives Etiquette Warning to Fans," *International Herald Tribune*, December 14, 2007.
33. Modified from Des Bieler, "Wisconsin High Schoolers Banned from Chants Including 'Airball' and 'Scoreboard,'" *The Washington Post*, January 12, 2016; Ricardo Arguello, "Hilbert Athlete's Suspension Draws International Notice," *Post Crescent*, January 12, 2016.

34. Kelley Tiffany, "Cheering Speech at State University Athletic Events: How Do You Regulate Spectator Sportsmanship?" *Sports Law Journal* (2007). Jonathan Singer, "Keep It Clean: How Public Universities May Constitutionally Enforce Policies Limiting Student Speech at College Basketball Games," *University of Baltimore Law Review* (Winter 2010).
35. Ashby Jones, "The Happy Heckler Can't Be Heard Now in the Din at Tropicana Field," *Wall Street Journal*, October 25, 2008.
36. Richard T. Karcher, "The Commissioner's Power to Discipline Players for On- and Off-Field Misconduct," in Michael A. McCann (ed.), *The Oxford Handbook of American Sports Law* (New York, NY: Oxford University Press, 2017).
37. Ian O'Connor, "Giants Get Snowballed: Fans Show Disgusting Lack of Class," *New York Daily News*, December 24, 1995.
38. "Previous Examples of Fan Violence," *SI.com*, September 19, 2002.
39. Joe LaPointe, "The Night Disco Went Up in Smoke," *New York Times*, July 5, 2009.
40. Phil Rogers, "Two Fans Attack Coach during White Sox Game," *Chicago Tribune*, September 20, 2002.
41. Elizabeth Olson, "Though Many Are Stalked, Few Report It," *New York Times*, February 15, 2009.
42. Anthony McCartney, "Trial Begins for Accused Shawn Johnson Stalker," *USA Today*, June 8, 2010. Justin Scheck, "Stalkers Exploit Cellphone GPS," *Wall Street Journal*, August 3, 2010; Subhajit Basu and Richard Jones, "Regulating Cyberstalking," *Journal of Information, Law, and Technology* (February 2007).
43. Kimberly S. Schimmel, C. Lee Harrington, and Denise D. Bielby, "Keep Your Fans to Yourself: The Disjuncture Between Sport Studies' and Pop Culture Studies' Perspectives on Fandom," *Sport in Society* 10, no. 4 (July 2007): 580–600; J. Reid Meloy, Lorraine Sheridan, and Jens Hoffmann, *Stalking, Threatening, and Attacking Public Figures: A Psychological and Behavioral Analysis* (New York: Oxford University Press, 2008).
44. Barbara De Lollis, "ESPN's Erin Andrews to Fight for Stronger Federal Anti-Stalking Laws," *USA Today*, July 2010.
45. "Accused Bob Uecker Stalker Gets Restraining Order," *CBS Sports*, September 7, 2006.
46. Andrew Greiner, "Bob Uecker's Stalker Banned from Road Games," *NBC Chicago*, December 8, 2009.

CHAPTER 6

Violence in Sports

▶ Introduction

Violence is prevalent throughout sports. "Violence" is the use of physical force to effect harm or injury on another person in an unjust, unwarranted, or unlawful manner. Thus, when unintentional harm or injury occurs, it is not violence. Many sports are violent by nature, but instances of extreme violence in sports are becoming more of a common occurrence, both on and off the field. Whether it be an NFL linebacker making a late hit on a quarterback, an NHL enforcer protecting his star player, or a major league pitcher throwing a "beanball" at a batter, violence is a major part of the landscape of both professional and amateur sports. Bench clearing brawls in baseball, sticks to the head in hockey, and "helmet-to-helmet" contact in the NFL have become commonplace in the sports world. NHL commissioner Gary Bettman has even said fighting is a part of the game and the NHL tolerates fighting to a certain extent.

The news is filled with stories of athletes committing violent acts both on and off the field, with many commentators calling for stricter punishments for bad behavior by athletes. Leagues and clubs impose fines and suspensions in an attempt to stop violent and inappropriate behavior by athletes. The NFL has instituted a personal conduct policy as well

as a gun policy in an attempt to ensure better behavior from players both on and off the field.

Boxer Mike Tyson's act of biting off a part of Evander Holyfield's ear in a 1997 boxing match is probably the most infamous act of sport violence and may be one of the "lowest blows" ever dealt in the boxing world.[1] Tyson was disqualified from the match for his actions. He said he did it in response to Holyfield's constant head butts during the match that went unchecked. He said, "He butted me in the second round and he looked at me and butted me again. . . . No one deducted points. This is my career. What am I supposed to do? I've got children to raise."[2]

One of the more infamous violent incidents in NBA history, addressed in Chapter 5 on the topic of fan misconduct, occurred in November 2004 in a major brawl between the Detroit Pistons and the Indiana Pacers. Ron Artest of the Pacers fouled Ben Wallace of the Pistons. After the foul Wallace said something Artest did not like, so he pushed Wallace, who then grabbed Artest by the neck. When the fight had almost stopped, Artest, who was lying on the scorer's table with headphones on to "calm himself," was hit in the face by a paper cup thrown by a Detroit fan. Artest became enraged and stormed into the crowd, throwing punches and assaulting fans. The police were forced to use pepper spray to break up the melee.[3] The Oakland county prosecutor charged four Pacers' players with assault and battery. In 2005, Artest and other Pacer players pleaded no contest to criminal charges and were sentenced to one year of probation and a $250 fine. NBA league commissioner David Stern issued suspensions to nine players totaling 143 games as a result of the fight.

There have been numerous instances of violence at the amateur level as well. In 2006, one of the more excessive displays of violence occurred when a brawl broke out in a college football game between the University of Miami and Florida International University. Both benches were cleared with players swinging helmets at one another. The respective universities reviewed the film and 31 players were suspended from Florida International University, with 2 dismissed from the team permanently.[4]

🔍 CASE STUDY 6-1   1970 Major League Baseball All-Star Game

Pete Rose, "Charlie Hustle," was one of baseball's all-time greats and played the game at full speed no matter what he did. In the 1970 Major League Baseball All-Star Game, Rose ran over Ray Fosse of the Cleveland Indians at home to score the winning run for the National League. Fosse was injured in the play. Rose's actions were questioned by some as unnecessary considering it was an all-star game that had no impact on a club's record in the standings. Rose later commented about the incident, saying he did not know they changed the game to girls' softball between third base and home plate.[5]

Was Rose's aggressive and violent play inappropriate for an All-Star contest? Baseball awards home field advantage in the World Series to the league that wins the All-Star Game.

▶ Rules and Regulations

The purpose of rules and regulations in sports is to allow the participants to compete fairly with some assurance that it is safe to do so. The rules are in place to regulate competition, but all participants agree to a certain measure of contact during the competition, depending on the sport. The rules are in place to standardize play and protect participants, and sometimes to directly regulate participant violence; however, some rules are made to be broken. For instance, in hockey, fighting is prohibited by the rules and players are penalized when they engage in such conduct, but players still fight for various strategic reasons. There are even different categories of fighting in hockey, major and minor. The NHL accepts fighting as part of the game itself. In baseball, a player will try to break up a double play by intentionally sliding into another player, even though injuries can result from the play. In the NBA, a player may commit a "hard foul" to prevent a score, but all players understand it as a strategic play essential to the game.

Three types of rules have been developed for organized competitive sport to standardize play, regulate behavior, and attempt to prevent harm: (1) constitutive rules, (2) proscriptive rules, and (3) sportsmanship rules.[6]

Constitutive Rules

Constitutive rules give structure to sports and are designed to equalize competition and standardize the competitive environment and help to make games fair and provide equitable competitive opportunities.[7] Constitutive rules specify and regulate age, weight classes, skill level, gender, residence, academic performance and progress, recruiting practices, financial aid, roster size, eligibility, and length of games.

Proscriptive Rules

Proscriptive rules prohibit particular types of actions during the game. "Spearing" in football, "cleating" another player in baseball while sliding, "high sticking" in hockey, or using a "chop block" in the NFL are all prohibited, but all are still occasionally performed by participants trying to gain a competitive edge. These rules are in place for the safety of the participants and to prevent athletes from intentionally harming one another. Professional and amateur leagues and associations alike have instituted such rules.

Sportsmanship Rules

Sportsmanship rules are instituted to encourage participants to play within the rules in a sportsmanlike manner. These kinds of rules are put into place to promote ethical conduct and to prevent violent behavior. In golf, players must self-report if they touch or move a golf ball in play. They also keep their own score and must report themselves if they make a mistake in calculating their score. In baseball, players can be ejected from the game by the umpire for arguing a call too intensely. Some comments are tolerated by the umpire, but there is definitely a line that a player should not cross. The rule exists to allow a player to "blow off some steam" if he thinks he has been the subject of a bad call, as well as to control violence within the game. In college football, teams can be penalized for "excessive celebration" if they celebrate too much after scoring. This rule is in place to promote sportsmanship, to prevent trash talking, and to curb violent behavior.

Both professional and amateur athletic associations have instituted rules and regulations to establish fair play, encourage sportsmanship, prevent injuries, and establish proper decorum by participants on and off the field. Proscriptive rules and sportsmanship rules come into play during participant violence.

Civil and Criminal Sanctions

Civil Sanctions

Holding a violent athlete civilly liable is one way to deter violent behavior in sports. If violent offenders know they can be held responsible for any damages they might cause, they may think twice about engaging in violent behavior with an opponent on the court or ice. When Kermit Washington punched Rudy Tomjanovich in the face in an NBA game on December 9, 1977, Rudy T suffered fractures of the nose, jaw, and skull. He further sustained facial lacerations, a brain concussion and leakage of spinal fluid from his brain cavity. It may have been the most devastating punch ever thrown in a sporting event by a participant. Tomjanovich missed the remainder of the season due to the injury. Noted sports lawyer Nick Nichols[8] handled the case on behalf of Rudy T against the Lakers and won a multimillion-dollar lawsuit on behalf of his client, the first of its kind. The case was eventually settled for $1.8 million[9] and became the subject of a book, *The Punch*, by John Feinstein.

Criminal Sanctions

Criminal charges also can be used to punish an athlete's violent actions. The state has the authority to charge and hold athletes accountable for their criminal actions just as they do for any other individual.[10] Numerous cases exist in which the state has prosecuted criminal behavior that occurred in a sporting event.[11]

Standard of Conduct for Participants

The standard for participants in sports was at one time wed to Judge Cardozo's maxim that "the timorous may stay at home."[12] It was acknowledged that the restraints of civilization must accompany every athlete onto the playing field. In *Nabozny*, the court stated:

> When athletes are engaged in an athletic competition; all teams involved are trained and coached by knowledgeable personnel; a recognized set of rules governs the conduct of the competition; and a safety rule is contained therein which is primarily designed to protect players from serious injury, a player is then charged with a . . . duty to every other player on the field to refrain from conduct prescribed by a safety rule.[13]

Every participant should refrain from engaging in unsportsmanlike conduct. It is considered unsportsmanlike to act with a reckless lack of concern for the safety and well-being of other participants in an athletic contest. Numerous examples exist of participants who have veered from the path of being a true sportsman. Running the bases in

the sport of baseball can be fun, just ask any t-ball player. Running around in a circle to go "home" has a rather pastoral feeling. The great Ty Cobb always considered the bases his territory. His base-running skills were described as "wonderful."[14] Stealing a base in baseball is exactly that, "stealing," and most people do not like this! So how should baseball players run the bases?

Case 6-1, *Bourque v. Duplechin*, explores this question. Duplechin, an aggressive base runner, was under an ethical obligation to play softball in a sportsmanlike manner and not cause injuries to other participants. Duplechin breached this duty when he made a conscious decision to recklessly endanger Bourque by choosing not to slide and by taking a path 5 feet away from the base path. He put himself on a collision course with the second baseman, who was unable to protect himself. Duplechin's choice was clearly an unethical decision for a participant.

⚖ CASE 6-1 *Bourque v. Duplechin*

331 So.2d 40 (La. Ct. App. 1976)

On June 9, 1974, Bourque was playing second base on a softball team fielded by Boo Boo's Lounge. Duplechin, a member of the opposing team sponsored by Murray's Steak House and Lounge, had hit the ball and advanced to first base. A teammate of Duplechin's, Steve Pressler, hit a ground ball and Duplechin started to second. The shortstop caught the ground ball and threw it to Bourque who tagged second base and then stepped away from second base to throw the ball to first and execute a double play. After Bourque had thrown the ball to first base, Duplechin ran at full speed into Bourque. As Duplechin ran into Bourque, he brought his left arm up under Bourque's chin. The evidence supports the . . . factual conclusion that the collision occurred four or five feet away from the second base position in the direction of the pitcher's mound. Duplechin was thrown out of the game by the umpire because of the incident.

. . . Bourque, age 22 at the time of trial, testified that he is 5'7" tall. He was well out of the way when he was hit, standing four or five feet from second base and outside the base line. He knew there was a possiblity of a runner sliding into him but had never imagined what actually happened, which he regarded as unbelievable under the circumstances.

Gregory John Laborde, a student at Tulane Law School, testified that he witnessed the incident from the dugout along the first base line and saw Duplechin turn and run directly toward Bourque who was standing four or five feet from second base toward home plate. Duplechin did not attempt to slide or decrease his speed and his left arm came up under Bourque's chin as they collided. Duplechin had to veer from the base path in order to strike Bourque.

Donald Frank Lockwood, baseball coach at USL, testified as an expert witness that: softball is a noncontact sport; in a forced play to second such as this, the accepted way to break up a double play is by sliding.

Steve Pressler, who hit the ground ball that precipitated the incident, testified that the sides were retired as a result, because the collision was a flagrant violation of the rules of the game.

Duplechin admitted that he ran into Bourque while standing up in an attempt to block Bourque's view of first base and keep him from executing a double play. Duplechin also admitted that he was running at full speed when he collided with Bourque, a much smaller man. Duplechin attributed the accident to Bourque's failure to get out of the way.

Oral surgeon John R. Wallace saw Bourque following the accident and said the nature of the injury and the x-rays indicated that it was caused by a blow from underneath the jaw. Dr. Wallace characterized the injury as one that may have been common in football before the use of mouthpieces and faceguards.

There is no question that . . . Duplechin's conduct was the cause in fact of the harm to . . . Bourque. Duplechin was under a duty to play softball in the ordinary fashion without unsportsmanlike conduct or wanton injury to his fellow players. This duty was breached by Duplechin, whose behavior was, according to the evidence, substandard and negligent. Bourque assumed the risk of being hit by a bat or a ball. Bourque may also have assumed the risk of an injury resulting from standing in the base path and being spiked by someone sliding into second base, a common incident of softball and baseball. However, Bourque did not assume the risk of Duplechin going out of his way to run into him at full speed when Bourque was five feet away from the base. A participant in a game or sport assumes all of the risks incidental to that particular activity which are obvious and foreseeable. A participant does not assume the risk of injury from fellow players acting in an unexpected or unsportsmanlike way with a reckless lack of concern for others participating.

The trial court awarded . . . Bourque $12,000 for his pain and suffering and $1,496.00 for his special damages. There is no dispute about the amount awarded. Bourque's jaw was fractured; his chin required plastic surgery; seven teeth were broken and had to be crowned; and one tooth was replaced by a bridge.

. . . Bourque's injuries resulted from the negligence of . . . Duplechin; Bourque was not guilty of contributory negligence and did not assume the risk of this particular accident . . . CUTRER, Judge (dissenting):

As correctly stated in the majority opinion, Duplechin admitted that he ran into the [Bourque] in an attempt to prevent a double play. In essence the [Duplechin] testified that if the [Bourque] did not get out of the way he would run into him in order to prevent the double play. [Bourque] did not get out of the way and Duplechin did run into him. As a result [Bourque] received rather severe facial injuries, principally because of the difference in size between the two players; Duplechin was five feet, eleven inches tall and weighed two hundred ten pounds, while [Bourque] was five feet, seven inches tall and weighed one hundred forty pounds.

In the present case the danger of Duplechin colliding with [Bourque] and causing him injury was more than a foreseeable risk which a reasonable man would avoid. The collision and resulting injury were a substantial certainty, particularly in view of the fact that Duplechin was larger than [Bourque], was running in an upright position at full speed directly at [Bourque], and knew he would run over [Bourque] if the latter did not get out of his way.

Bourque v. Duplechin, U.S. Supreme Court.

It is a participant's ethical duty to act in a sportsmanlike manner and clearly, Duplechin was not acting in this way when he veered 5 feet out of the correct and ethical path to deliberately strike Bourque. Bourque assumed the risk of being hit by a bat or a ball and may also have assumed the risk of an injury resulting from standing in the base path and being "spiked" by someone sliding into second base; however, he did not assume the risk of Duplechin going out of his way to run into him at full speed when Bourque was 5 feet away from the base. A participant in a sport assumes all of the risks incidental to that sport that are obvious and foreseeable.

A participant does not assume the risk of injury from fellow players acting in unexpected or unsportsmanlike ways with a reckless lack of concern for other participants.

What action should be taken when a participant becomes unruly and engages in unsportsmanlike conduct? Should the player be banned from further participation? Should the participant be warned or fined?

Case 6-2 describes a situation where a soccer player is injured in a recreational soccer match. Is the fact that the player violated a rule of the game enough to conclude that he acted in an unethical and unsportsmanlike manner?

⚖ CASE 6-2   Lestina v. West Bend Mutual Insurance Company

501 N.W.2d 28 (1993)

Robert F. Lestina was injured in a collision with Leopold Jerger ... during a recreational soccer match organized by the Waukesha County Old Timers League, a recreational league for players over the age of 30.

[Lestina] (45 years of age) was playing an offensive position for his team and [Jerger] (57 years of age) was the goalkeeper for the opposing team on April 20, 1988, when the injury occurred. Shortly before [Lestina] was injured, he had scored the first goal of the game. After his goal [Lestina] regained possession of the ball and was about to attempt a second goal when [Jerger] apparently ran out of the goal area and collided with [him]. [Lestina] asserted that the [goalie] "slide tackled" him in order to prevent him from scoring. Although slide tackles are allowed under some soccer rules, this league's rules prohibit such maneuvers to minimize risk of injury. Jerger claimed that the collision occurred as he and [Lestina] simultaneously attempted to kick the soccer ball.

Lestina v. West Bend Mutual Insurance Company, U.S. Supreme Court.

The safety rule in Lestina that prohibits slide tackles is promulgated to ensure fair play. Although slide tackles are not prohibited in all soccer leagues, they were prohibited in this "Old Timers" league. The rule that mandates fair play here takes into consideration the age and skill of the participating athletes.[15]

Consider how the participants acted in the soccer match described in Case 6-3. Were their actions any different from those in the Lestina case noted above?

⚖ CASE 6-3   *Nabozny v. Barnhill*

334 N.E.2d 258 (Ill. 1975)

A soccer match began between two amateur teams at Duke Child's Field in Winnetka, Illinois. Nabozny was playing the position of goalkeeper for the Hansa team. Barnhill was playing the position of forward for the Winnetka team. Members of both teams were of high-school age. Approximately twenty minutes after play had begun, a Winnetka player kicked the ball over the midfield line. Two players, Jim Gallos (for Hansa) and Barnhill (for Winnetka) chased the free ball. Gallos reached the ball first. Since he was closely pursued by Barnhill, Gallos passed the ball to Nabozny, the Hansa goalkeeper. Gallos then turned away and prepared to receive a pass from Nabozny. Nabozny, in the meantime, went down on his left knee, received the pass, and pulled the ball to his chest. Barnhill did not turn away when Gallos did, but continued to run in the direction of Nabozny and kicked the left side of his head causing him severe injuries.

All of the occurrence witnesses agreed that Barnhill had time to avoid contact with Nabozny and that Nabozny remained at all times within the 'penalty area,' a rectangular area between the eighteenth yard line and the goal. Four witnesses testified that they saw Nabozny in a crouched position on his left knee inside the penalty zone. Nabozny testified that he actually had possession of the ball when he was struck by Barnhill.

[T]he game was played under 'F.I.F.A' rules… [E]xperts agreed that those rules prohibited all players from making contact with the goalkeeper when he is in possession of the ball in the penalty area. Possession is defined in the Chicago area as referring to the goalkeeper having his hands on the ball. Under 'F.I.F.A' rules, any contact with a goalkeeper in possession in the penalty area is an infraction of the rules, even if such contact is unintentional. The goalkeeper is the only member of a team who is allowed to touch a ball in play so long as he remains in the penalty area. The only legal contact permitted in soccer is shoulder to shoulder contact between players going for a ball within playing distance. The contact in question in this case should not have occurred. Additionally, goalkeeper head injuries are extremely rare in soccer. As a result of being struck, [Nabozny] suffered permanent damage to his skull and brain.

. . .

Individual sports are advanced and competition enhanced by a comprehensive set of rules. Some rules secure the better playing of the game as test of skill. Other rules are primarily designed to protect participants from serious injury. The safety rule in Nabozny is contained in a recognized set of rules governing the conduct of athletic competition.

This rule mandates the tenets of fair play and ethical behavior. Although, obviously, it is essential to good competition that the athletes try as hard as they can to achieve victory, the most vital aspect of competition is not in victory but in overcoming the challenge presented by a worthy opponent. The glue between opponents is the element of fair play. It is an ethical question, whether to choose to follow the stipulations of fair play between well-matched opponents following established rules and customs, or to allow the behemoth of "winning at all costs" to prevail.

Nabozny v. Barnhill, U.S. Supreme Court.

The player in *Nabozny v. Barnhill* also violated traditional notions of fair play due to his unnecessary roughness. Do you agree with the last statement made in the case? Is this proposition also applicable to youth sports?

Everyone likes to ski fast down the side of a mountain, but just like golf, some can do it and some cannot. Should you be aware of your skill level before you engage in a sport? Consider the following case in which an out-of-control skier killed another skier. Snow skiing has never really been thought of as a contact sport, except in some extenuating circumstances for the novice who has not yet learned the control necessary to be successful on the snow and ice. In the following case, a snow skier was criminally charged for his actions on the slopes.[16]

⚖ CASE 6-4 *State of Colorado v. Nathan Hall*

999 P.2d 207 (Col. 2000)

While skiing on Vail Mountain, Nathan Hall flew off of a knoll and collided with Allen Cobb, who was traversing the slope below Hall. Cobb sustained traumatic brain injuries and died as a result of the collision. On April 20, 1997, the last day of the ski season, Hall worked as a ski lift operator on Vail Mountain. When he finished his shift and after the lifts closed, Hall skied down toward the base of the mountain. The slopes were not crowded. On the lower part of a run called "Riva Ridge," just below where the trail intersects with another called "North Face Catwalk," Hall was skiing very fast, ski tips in the air, his weight back on his skis, with his arms out to his sides to maintain balance. He flew off of a knoll and saw people below him, but he was unable to stop or gain control because of the moguls. Hall then collided with Cobb, who had been traversing the slope below Hall. The collision caused major head and brain injuries to Cobb, killing him. Cobb was taken to Vail Valley Medical Center, where efforts to resuscitate him failed. Hall's blood alcohol level was .009, which is less than the limit for driving while ability impaired. A test of Hall's blood for illegal drugs was negative.

Hall was charged with manslaughter (a class 4 felony) and misdemeanor charges. At the close of the prosecution's case at the preliminary hearing, the state requested that, with respect to the manslaughter count, the court consider the lesser-included charge of criminally negligent homicide (a class 5 felony).

Judge Buck Allen, who serves as a judge for several mountain towns and lives in Vail, testified that he is an expert skier and familiar with Vail's slopes. He was making a final run for the day when he first noticed Hall on the slope. Allen was on part of the run called "Lower Riva," which is just below the "North Face Catwalk." From that part of the slope, Allen had a direct line of sight to the bottom of the run. Allen said that he could see other skiers traversing the slope below him at least from their waists up and that there were no blind spots on that part of the run.

Hall passed Allen skiing "at a fairly high rate of speed." Allen estimated that Hall was skiing about three times as fast as he was. Allen stated that Hall was "sitting back" on his skis, tips in the air, with his arms out to his sides in an effort to maintain his balance. Hall was skiing straight down the fall line; that is, he was skiing straight down the slope of the mountain without turning from side-to-side or traversing the slope. Hall "bounded off the bumps as he went," and "[t]he terrain was controlling [Hall]" rather than the other way around. In Allen's opinion, Hall was skiing too fast for the skill level he demonstrated, and Hall was out of control "if you define 'out of control' as [not] being able to stop or avoid someone." Although he watched Hall long enough to note Hall's unsafe skiing—approximately two or three seconds—Allen did not see the collision.

1. Do you consider Hall's actions criminal?
2. What is the appropriate punishment for Hall?
3. As an SMP, how do you prevent this kind of accident in the future?

State of Colorado v. Nathan Hall, U.S. Supreme Court.

Ice hockey distributes its own brand of justice. No other sport integrates fighting into the actual playing of the game the way ice hockey does. Because hockey is a sport where fighting is tolerated as part of the game, special considerations must be given to violence within the sport.[17]

🔍 CASE STUDY 6-2   Assault on Ice

The term "enforcer" does not appear in the NHL rulebook; however, every player, coach, and manager knows what the term means. Steve Moore, former Harvard captain and a player for the Vancouver Canucks, and Moore's parents sued NHL tough man Todd Bertuzzi, the Vancouver Canucks, and the partnership that owned the Canucks, for an on-ice incident that occurred between Moore and Bertuzzi on March 8, 2004.

The dispute between Moore and Bertuzzi actually began on February 16, 2004 when Moore checked the Canucks' Captain, Markus Naslund, in a regular season game between the two clubs. As a result of the check, Naslund received a concussion, facial lacerations, and suffered soreness to his wrist. No penalty was called on Moore and, after a review by the NHL, the hit was ruled a "clean" hit.

The next game scheduled between the two teams was March 3, 2004. Leading up to the game, Todd Bertuzzi made several statements to the effect that he or his teammates would retaliate against Moore. In fact, the threat became so publicized that NHL Commissioner Gary Bettman and Executive Vice President and Director of Hockey Operations, Colin Campbell, attended the March 3, 2004 match. However, no retaliation took place in that game. Bertuzzi was questioned after the game about why nothing occurred and he said that the game was too close, but added that other situations would present themselves.

The final regular season game between the two clubs was played just five days later. Moore's parents were watching the game from their home in Ontario. The NHL Director of Officiating contacted the game officials and warned them about possible retaliation against Moore. In the final period, the Canucks were in the middle of a line change when Bertuzzi confronted Moore. When Bertuzzi tried to get him to fight, Moore merely skated away. Bertuzzi continued to follow Moore the length of the ice and halfway back up the ice in the opposite direction. Bertuzzi finally struck Moore from behind, dropping him to the ice face first. Moore remained unconscious on the ice for some time and was taken to the hospital. He sustained massive injuries as a result of the assault, including a broken neck with fractures to the C3 and C4 vertebrae and a T1 avulsion fracture. Bertuzzi was suspended for the rest of the season. The Canucks were fined $250,000 by the league. The NHL eventually reinstated Bertuzzi after a 17-month suspension. The suspension cost Bertuzzi more than $500,000 in salary and $350,000 in endorsements. Bertuzzi was charged with assault by Canadian authorities and eventually pleaded guilty to "assault causing bodily harm" on December 22, 2004, in British Columbia.[18]

Hockey is clearly a rough sport. The league cannot and does not penalize or discipline players every time they cause injury to another player and neither do the courts. The Commissioner of the NHL has said: "I think fighting has always reached whatever level is appropriate in the game and has been a part of the game. And I don't have a problem with that."[19] Do you agree with his statements? Is this an ethical or a proper view of violence in hockey by the commissioner of a sports league? In the following civil lawsuit, a court said a "body check" is merely a part of the game of hockey.

⚖️ CASE 6-5   McKichan v. St. Louis Hockey Club

967 S.W.2d 209 (1998)

In 1988, Steve McKichan signed a contract with the Vancouver Canucks, a professional National Hockey League team. The team assigned him to its professional "minor league" International Hockey League (IHL) team, the Milwaukee Admirals. On December 15, 1990, the Milwaukee Admirals played the Peoria Rivermen in a regulation IHL game in Peoria, Illinois. The Peoria Rivermen is an IHL team affiliated with the St. Louis Hockey Club. IHL hockey is played on an ice rink measuring at least 200 feet by 85 feet with goals on opposing ends of the ice. The rink is surrounded by a wall made partially of clear Plexiglass, customarily referred to as the "boards." The rink is divided in two by a center line. On each side of the center line is a line called the "blue line." The blue lines are parallel to the center line and have to be at least 60 feet from the boards behind the goals. A game consists of three twenty-minute periods.

In the second period, an incident took place between McKichan and a Rivermen player. McKichan was penalized as a result of that incident. During the third period, McKichan and the Rivermen player were both playing and "on the ice." A videotape of the incident discloses that the Rivermen player was skating near center ice and McKichan was positioned in front of his goal. The hockey puck was shot in the general direction of McKichan's goal by a teammate of the Rivermen player. However, it traveled over the goal and the boards and out of play. As the puck was traveling, McKichan skated several yards to the side of the goal. A linesman blew his whistle stopping play. About this time, McKichan began turning his body toward the boards and moved closer to them. As he was moving away from the goal, the Rivermen player was skating from the near blue line toward McKichan. The Rivermen player continued skating toward McKichan after a second whistle. Holding his stick, the Rivermen player partially extended both arms and hit McKichan with his body and the stick, knocking him into the boards. He fell to the ice and was knocked unconscious. The Rivermen player received a "match penalty" from the referee and was suspended for a period of games by the IHL.

Rough play is commonplace in professional hockey. Anyone who has attended a professional hockey game or seen one on television recognizes the violent nature of the sport. In order to gain possession of the puck or to slow down the progress of opponents, players frequently hit each other with body checks. They trip opposing players, slash at them with their hockey sticks, and fight on a regular basis, often long after the referee blows the whistle. Players regularly commit contact beyond what is permitted by the rules, and, we are confident, intentionally. They wear pads, helmets, and other protective equipment because of the rough nature of the sport.

Professional hockey is played at a high skill level with well conditioned athletes, who are financially compensated for their participation. They are professional players with knowledge of its rules and customs, including the violence of the sport. In part, the game is played with great intensity because its players can reap substantial financial rewards. We also recognize that the professional leagues have internal mechanisms for penalizing players and teams for violating league rules and for compensating persons who are injured.

In summary, a severe body check is a part of professional hockey. This body check, even several seconds after the whistle and in violation of several rules of the game, was not outside the realm of reasonable anticipation. For better or for worse, it is "part of the game" of professional hockey.

McKichan v. St. Louis Hockey Club, U.S. Supreme Court.

Is it unethical or unsportsmanlike to intentionally injure a player? If you know you will only spend 2 minutes in the penalty box while putting the other team's star player out for the game or possibly the season, is it then deemed a good strategy?[20] Is intentional injury by a player for "strategic reasons" to be considered gamesmanship, unsportsmanlike conduct, criminal behavior, or just unethical? Is "retaliatory" violence ever ethical, even if it is allowed within the rules of the game? Consider such ethical dilemmas in light of the following case.

⚖ *CASE 6-6 Babych v. McRae*

567 A.2d 1269 (1989)

[O]n September 24, 1986, while employed as a professional hockey player for the Hartford Whalers, Dave Babych participated in a hockey game at the Hartford Civic Center against Ken McRae and the Quebec Nordiques hockey team of Quebec, Canada. On that date, he was struck across his right knee causing personal injury and financial losses. Babych contends that the injuries and losses were caused by McRae's negligence in one or more of the following ways: (1) that McRae swung his stick when he knew or should have known that such action could cause serious injury; (2) that such action was unnecessary; (3) that the action violated Rule 77 of the National Hockey League Rules; and (4) that the action was retaliatory.

1. Is hockey violence out of control? Is it good for the game of hockey?
2. Should hockey fighting be prohibited, or is it too much a part of the history of the game to remove it?
3. Why don't other sports have a "tradition" of fighting?
4. Do you consider hockey violence necessary to the continued success of the sport?
5. Does the NHL encourage players to fight? Is this an ethical stance for the league to take? Is allowing players to fight just giving the fans what they want to see? Is it really a marketing ploy on behalf of the NHL?

Babych v. McRae, U.S. Supreme Court.

Different cultures have varying views on sports violence. American courts have been less willing to criminally charge those who engage in violent behavior on the ice. Canadian prosecutors have charged some NHL hockey players with assault and battery involving violence on the ice. Dino Ciccarelli was the first NHL player to serve a limited jail term in 1988 for an on-ice assault of another player.[21] Marty McSorley was convicted of assaulting Vancouver Canucks' Donald Brasher, who suffered a grand mal seizure before regaining consciousness. McSorley was found guilty and placed on criminal probation for 18 months and, as mentioned above in Case Study 6-2, Todd Bertuzzi pleaded guilty to assault charges in 2004; however, most prosecutions have been unsuccessful, as the courts have generally recognized the defenses of self-defense and assumption of risk. For example, in dismissing an assault charge involving a spearing incident during an exhibition game in Ottawa between the Boston Bruins and the St. Louis Blues, the Canadian court in *Regina v. Green* noted:

Hockey is a game that is played at great speed, and we are here dealing with players from the National Hockey League, who are, I think by common consent, the best trained and probably the best hockey players anywhere. We have here men wearing the very best equipment, with one notable and totally incomprehensible omission, and that is the fact that most players do not wear helmets. But apart from that they are very well equipped, they are very well trained, and they are playing in the best surroundings and on the best possible ice surface. They also, in the very nature of the game, assume certain risks. . . .

[S]ince it is assumed and understood that there are numerous what would normally be called assaults in the course of a hockey game, but which are really not assaults because of the consent of the players in the type of game being played, where do you draw the line? It is very difficult in my opinion for a player who is playing hockey with all the force, vigor, and strength at his command, who is engaged in the rough and tumble of the game, very often in a rough situation in the corner of the rink, suddenly to stop and say, "I must not do that. I must not follow up on this because maybe it is an assault; maybe I am committing an assault." I do not think that any of the actions that would normally be considered assaults in ordinary walks of life can possibly be, within the context that I am considering, considered assaults at all.[22]

Ice hockey is certainly not the only sport in which assaults and batteries occur. In one of the more infamous cases in baseball violence, pitcher Juan Marichal struck catcher John Roseboro in the head with a baseball bat. Marichal was later sued by Roseboro and the case was settled for $6,000. Marichal was fined and suspended by the League.

Should "head-hunting" in baseball be outlawed considering the dangerous nature of a ball traveling at someone's head at approximately 100 miles an hour?[23] Intentionally throwing a ball at a batter in Major League Baseball is against the rules.[24]

Elite "fastballers" are able to throw a baseball in excess of 100 miles an hour, which could seriously injure or kill a batter.[25] Enter the "brushback" pitch, also referred to as the "beanball" in baseball circles. The brushback pitch has always been a part of the game of baseball. Some pitchers are well known for guarding the plate with an inside fastball. St. Louis Cardinals pitcher, Bob Gibson, was well known in baseball for intentionally throwing at hitters. After Gibson beaned a batter on opening day of the baseball season, Los Angeles Dodgers pitcher Don Drysdale commented: "Welcome to Bob Gibson's school of what you better do and what you better not do."[26] If anyone dared show him up on the field, Gibson took exception. Former player Dusty Baker once received some good advice from baseball's legitimate home run king, Hank Aaron. Aaron said: "Don't dig in against Bob Gibson, he'll knock you down. He'd knock down his own grandmother if she dared

to challenge him. Don't stare at him, don't smile at him, don't talk to him. He doesn't like it. If you happen to hit a home run, don't run too slow, don't run too fast. If you happen to want to celebrate, get in the tunnel first. And if he hits you, don't charge the mound, because he's a Gold Glove Boxer.' I'm like, 'Damn, what about my 17-game hitting streak?' That was the night it ended."[27]

Is the beanball gamesmanship or unnecessary violence on the part of the pitcher? If intentionally throwing a baseball at a player is in violation of the rules of baseball, should a player try to intentionally break the rules of the game, knowing he or she may only get a warning for the first brushback pitch they throw? Should a pitcher throw this type of pitch knowing that the batter may suffer a serious injury?

The brushback pitch has been around since the early days of baseball and has always been a strategic weapon in the pitchers' arsenal. If a batter "crowds" the plate, a pitcher may see that as an infringement of his territory and send a little "chin music" the batter's way. "Chin music" has been defined by the *Dickson Baseball Dictionary* as "a brushback or knockdown pitch that passes close to the batter's jaw. Thrown so high and inside that the batter supposedly can hear it 'buzz or sing.'" Scott Ostler (*Los Angeles Times*, March 31, 1978). When a pitcher throws inside on a batter causing breeze to whistle on his Adam's apple, baseball folks call it "chin music".

Dickson Baseball Dictionary's definition of the "brushback pitch" is as follows:

A pitch that comes so close to the batter's body that he is forced to step backward and thereby is unable to dig in at the plate. When a batter crowds the plate, taking away some of the pitcher's target area, a pitcher may throw a pitch close to the batter's body to encourage him to move back. The brushback pitch is not to be confused with a *beanball*, which is intentionally thrown at the batter's head.[28]

Should rules differ for a "brush-back" pitch at the amateur and professional levels?

In April 2009, Patrick Clegg, a high school player, tragically died after he was struck in the head by a pitched ball.[29] In *Avila v. Citrus Community College District*, a college baseball player was severely injured when he was struck in the head by a brushback pitch. In dismissing the case, the court ruled:

> For better or worse, being intentionally thrown at is a fundamental part and inherent risk of the sport of baseball. It is not the function of tort law to police such conduct. The conclusion that being intentionally hit by a pitch is an inherent risk of baseball extends only to situations such as that alleged here, where the hit batter is at the plate. Allegations that a pitcher intentionally hit a batter who was still in the on-deck circle, or elsewhere, would present an entirely different scenario.[30]

In football, the players essentially assault one another in every play, with consent, of course. NFL Hall of Famer Dick Butkus once joked, "I never set out to hurt anybody deliberately unless, it was, you know, important . . . like a league game or something."[31] Player injuries are assumed in professional football. There are certain rules in place that attempt to curb the violent behavior of NFL participants. For instance, the "chop block", or hitting below the knees within 15 yards of the line of scrimmage, is prohibited. The NFL does protect its quarterbacks very closely and prohibits certain kinds of contact with the quarterback. Is that a good rule, or should everyone on the field be "fair game"? For safety reasons, helmet-to-helmet contact is also prohibited. Players must abide by certain rules and guidelines or suffer the consequences, which can include fines, penalties, and possible expulsion from the League.

What are the limits on violent behavior between NFL players? In Case 6-7, one NFL player violently attacked another player.

⚖ CASE 6-7 *Hackbart v. Cincinnati Bengals*

601 F.2d 516 (10th Cir. 1979)

An injury occurred in the course of a game between the Denver Broncos and the Cincinnati Bengals, which was played in Denver in 1973. The Broncos' defensive back, Dale Hackbart, was injured by the Bengals' offensive back, Charles "Booby" Clark. . . . Clark had run a pass pattern to the right side of the Denver Broncos' end zone. The pass was intercepted by Billy Thompson, a Denver free safety, who returned it to mid-field. As a consequence of the interception, the roles of Hackbart and Clark suddenly changed. Hackbart, who had been defending, instantaneously became an offensive player. Clark, on the other hand, became a defensive player. Acting as an offensive player, Hackbart attempted to block Clark by throwing his body in front of him. He thereafter remained on the ground. He turned, and with one knee on the ground, watched the play following the interception.

Clark, "acting out of anger and frustration, but without a specific intent to injure . . . stepped forward and struck a blow with his right forearm to the back of the kneeling [Hackbart's] head and neck with sufficient force to cause both players to fall forward to the ground." Both players, without complaining to the officials or to one another, returned to their respective sidelines since the ball had changed hands and the offensive and defensive teams of each had been substituted. Clark testified at trial that his frustration was brought about by the fact that his team was losing the game. Due to the failure of the officials to view the incident, a foul was not called. However, the game film showed very clearly what had occurred. Hackbart did not, at the time, report the happening to his coaches or to anyone else during the game. However, because of the pain he experienced, he was unable to play golf the next day. He did not seek medical attention, but the continued pain caused him to report the incident to the Bronco trainer, who gave him treatment. Apparently, he played on the specialty teams for two successive Sundays, but after that, the Broncos released him on waivers. (He was in his thirteenth year as a player.) He sought medical help and it was then that it was discovered by the physician that he had a serious neck fracture injury.

Despite the fact that Clark admitted that the blow which had been struck was not accidental, that it was intentionally administered, the court ruled as a matter of law that the game of professional football is basically a business which is violent in nature, and that the available sanctions are imposition of penalties and expulsion from the game. Many fouls are overlooked, the game is played in an emotional and noisy environment, and [these kinds of] incidents are not unusual.

Applying the laws and rules which are a part of injury law to the game of professional football can be unreasonable, holding that one player has a duty of care for the safety of others. Hackbart had to recognize that he accepted the risk that he would be injured by such an act.

1. Was the player violence in *Hackbart* excessive, even for the NFL?
2. What limits should there be on violence in the NFL?
3. Was there any unethical conduct or violations of fair play by any of the parties in *Hackbart*?

Hackbart v. Cincinnati Bengals, U.S. Supreme Court.

Case 6-8 involves the suspension of Latrell Sprewell, who became enraged at a team practice and choked his coach, P. J. Carlesimo.

Sprewell said he didn't choke Carlesimo but did admit he attacked Carlesimo because he "couldn't take it anymore."[32]

⚖ CASE 6-8 *Sprewell v. Golden State Warriors*

266 F.3d 979 (9th Cir. 2001)

Latrell Sprewell joined the NBA in 1992 as a guard for the Golden State Warriors. During Sprewell's tenure with the Warriors, he played under four different head coaches, the last of whom was P. J. Carlesimo. Sprewell's star-crossed relationship with Carlesimo, while amicable upon its inception in June of 1997, quickly deteriorated over the ensuing six months to the point that both Sprewell and the Warriors openly entertained the possibility of trading Sprewell to another team.

Tensions between Sprewell and Carlesimo climaxed during a closed-door practice on December 1, 1997, during which Carlesimo told Sprewell to pass the ball to a teammate for a quick shot. Despite Sprewell's contention that he passed the ball "admirably, as one would expect of an All-Star," Carlesimo rebuked Sprewell for not putting more speed on his pass. When Carlesimo subsequently repeated his criticism, Sprewell slammed the ball down and directed several expletives at Carlesimo. Carlesimo responded with a similar showing of sophistication. Sprewell immediately either walked or lunged at Carlesimo and wrapped his hands around Carlesimo's neck. With his arms fully extended, Sprewell moved Carlesimo backwards, saying "I will kill you." Carlesimo offered no resistance. Sprewell grasped Carlesimo's neck for approximately seven to ten seconds—the time it took for other players and coaches to restrain Sprewell. Sprewell then left the practice floor, saying "trade me, get me out of here, I will kill you," to which Carlesimo countered, "I am here."

After showering and changing, Sprewell returned to the practice facility to again confront Carlesimo. Despite the efforts of two assistant coaches to restrain him, Sprewell was able to approach Carlesimo and throw an overhand punch that grazed Carlesimo's right cheek. Sprewell landed a subsequent blow to Carlesimo's shoulder, but it is uncertain whether it was intentional or the product of Sprewell's attempt to free himself from those restraining him. As Sprewell left the facility, he again told Carlesimo, "I will kill you."

That evening the Warriors suspended Sprewell for a minimum of ten games and expressly reserved its right to terminate Sprewell's contract. Two days later, the Warriors exercised that right and ended Sprewell's reign as a Warrior. The NBA subsequently issued its own one-year suspension of Sprewell after conducting an independent investigation of the matter.

On December 4, 1997, Sprewell invoked the arbitration provisions of his collective bargaining agreement ("CBA") by filing a grievance challenging both his suspension by the NBA and the Warriors' termination of his contract. The arbitrator held nine days of hearings, received testimony from twenty-one witnesses, accepted over fifty exhibits, and was presented with over 300 pages of pre and post-hearing briefs. The arbitrator found that the dual punishments issued by the NBA and the Warriors were permissible under the CBA, but found that: (1) the Warriors' termination of Sprewell's contract was not supported by just cause because after the Warriors' initial suspension of Sprewell, any residual interest of the Warriors was absorbed by the NBA's investigation of the matter; and (2) the NBA's suspension should be limited to the 1997–98 season.

Sprewell v. Golden State Warriors, U.S. Supreme Court.

Consider the following case involving an assault in a high school basketball game. What duties and responsibilities should the school have with regard to the violence that took place? What rules and procedures should be in place to prevent violent acts from occurring in amateur sports?

⚖ CASE 6-9 Baker v. Trinity-Pawling School

21 A.D.3d 272 (2005)

Rayon Baker, a student basketball player at Hotchkiss, was injured as the result of an assault by Carl Elliott, a student basketball player at Trinity. The assault followed a basketball game between the two schools at Hotchkiss on February 12, 2000. Baker was unaware of any rivalry between the schools and he had never been cited for any disciplinary problems while at Hotchkiss. During the course of the game, he was punched in the eye and elbowed in the mouth, although he was unaware which of the Trinity players hit him. He [stated] that Elliott threatened him at the postgame handshake and, as he was leaving the building, he was hit from behind and fell down, at which point Elliott jumped on top of him and began striking him. The Trinity coach also testified that there was no special rivalry between the schools, that Baker was hit with an inadvertent elbow by a player named Billy Allen, and that there had been a commotion in the handshake line. The coach stated that Baker and Elliott had words, and the assault by Elliott, according to some of his other players, was provoked by Baker, who had spit on Elliott. Elliott, the coach noted, also had no prior history of violent behavior. The Hotchkiss coach echoed Baker's claim that Baker had no history of behavior problems, and stated that Baker was not violent or aggressive, and that although the game was loud and intense, there was no excessive jeering or fouling. The coach maintained that there was a disruption in the handshake line between Elliott and Baker, but nothing physical occurred, although the coach later saw Baker upset and holding his face, while other players explained that Baker had been jumped.

Schools are under a duty to provide adequate supervision to ensure the safety of the students in their charge and are liable for foreseeable injuries which are proximately caused by the absence of adequate supervision …

… [t]here was no prior history of violent conduct or behavioral problems on the part of Baker or Elliott, or between the two teams, so as to have placed Trinity on notice of the conduct which caused Baker's injuries. In addition, there was no violent history between Baker and Elliott, and Elliott was concededly not part of either the elbowing or eye-punching incidents, which themselves were not shown to be outside the bounds of normal play. In sum, Trinity and Hotchkiss demonstrated they had no actual or constructive knowledge of dangerous conduct on the part of Baker's attacker, and, accordingly could not have reasonably foreseen the attack on Baker.

Baker v. Trinity-Pawling School, U.S. Supreme Court.

⌕ CASE STUDY 6-3   *Violence in Ice Skating*

Women's amateur ice skating would seem to be a sport free of violence, but that was not the case leading up to the 1994 Olympics. Tonya Harding and Nancy Kerrigan were both outstanding ice skaters and fierce competitors; however, Harding would take the competition just a bit too far. She conspired with her ex-husband Jeff Gillooly to attack her competitor, Nancy Kerrigan, at a practice session during the 1994 U.S. Figure Skating Championships. After she admitted to covering up the attack, the United States Olympic Committee (USOC) initiated proceedings against her to remove her from the 1994 U.S. Olympic team. She pled guilty to hindering the investigation of the attack and received three years' probation. The United States Figure Skating Association (USFSA) met to determine whether Harding had violated their code of ethics. The association code of ethics stated, in part: "Any person whose acts, statements, or conduct is considered detrimental to the welfare of figure skating is subject to the loss of the privilege of registration by the USFSA."[33] Harding later became a boxer.[34]

Is the sport of boxing too violent? Many boxers have died after bouts in the ring. The NCAA discontinued boxing championships after 1960. At the 1960 NCAA championships, Charlie Mohr from the University of Wisconsin Madison collapsed with a brain hemorrhage and passed away a week later. Should the NCAA allow boxing if they also allow wrestling, football, and ice hockey? Is football any less violent than boxing or hockey? Ultimate Championship Fighting (UCF) has become a very popular sport. At what age should kids be allowed to participate in mixed martial arts? Does it teach kids to be violent or just competitive?[35]

▶ Off-the-Field Violence

The creation of new media platforms and technologies—the Internet, twenty-four-hour cable television sports coverage, social media, and cell phone cameras—has put athletes in a fishbowl. The compensation of professional athletes has increased exponentially as well. The combination of these two developments during the last quarter century has had a profound impact on the societal view of athletes as "role models." The news is replete with stories of athletes allegedly engaging in improper conduct off the field. Whether in professional or collegiate athletics, off-the-field conduct of athletes is a concern for both professional leagues and universities. Drunk driving, drugs, domestic violence, assault, theft, and identity theft are all examples of off-the-field conduct. At the collegiate level, universities (not the NCAA or the conferences) are often forced to step in and take action against athletes who behave badly. Indeed, many are on a scholarship at the university and when they act poorly, it makes the news; however, sometimes a university seems to overlook problems a star player may have just to keep him or her on the field of play. And many believe that the penalties for professional athletes are not severe enough for their off-the-field misdeeds.

Professional sports teams must decide when to take action against their players and determine the appropriate sanction for off-the-field misconduct. New York Mets pitcher Francisco Rodriguez, a four-time all-star, was arrested and charged with third-degree assault and second-degree harassment after assaulting his girlfriend's father at CitiField. As a result of the assault on his girlfriend's father, Rodriguez tore a ligament in his hand. He had surgery and missed the remainder of the 2010 season. As a result, the Mets converted his guaranteed contract to a non-guaranteed contract as they are permitted to do under the terms of the contract and announced the club would not pay him until he was able to play again. The Players Association filed a grievance on Rodriguez's behalf that was eventually settled by the parties.[36]

No other issue seems to be in the news more than athletes beating up women. As noted by one scholar, "[d]omestic violence has been largely ignored by professional sports leagues. This inaction persists despite the fact that a survey revealed seventy-six percent of U.S. adults and eighty-two percent of teens think it is 'bad for society' to allow athletes to continue their sports careers when convicted of a violent crime."[37] Even coaches, front office people, and sportscasters are sometimes involved in domestic violence.

The NFL has had a formal personal conduct policy since 1997 that was enhanced in 2007, one year after Roger Goodell took over as League Commissioner. Goodell had demanded a stricter policy because, at that time, NFL players were perceived as being out of control. While the advent of 24-hour news distributed via a variety of media platforms certainly makes it seem that player arrests have been a growing problem in the NFL, there is virtually no evidence to suggest that this is the case. In 2014, the policy was again revised and strengthened. Goodell's emphatic view

that playing football in the NFL is a privilege led to numerous suspensions under his watch for personal conduct that both occurred away from the field and garnered substantial media attention and scrutiny. These suspensions included: Adam "Pacman" Jones (battery) and Michael Vick (dog fighting) in 2007; Donte Stallworth (DUI manslaughter) in 2009; Ben Roethlisberger (sexual assault) in 2010; Ray Rice (domestic violence) and Adrian Peterson (child abuse) in 2014; and Greg Hardy (domestic violence) in 2015.

Under the NFL's personal conduct policy, prohibited conduct (with or without a criminal conviction) includes, but is not limited to, the following:

- Actual or threatened physical violence against another person, including dating violence, domestic violence, child abuse, and other forms of family violence;
- Assault and/or battery, including sexual assault or other sex offenses;
- Violent or threatening behavior toward another employee or a third party in any workplace setting;
- Stalking, harassment, or similar forms of intimidation;
- Illegal possession of a gun or other weapon (such as explosives, toxic substances, and the like), or possession of a gun or other weapon in any workplace setting;
- Illegal possession, use, or distribution of alcohol or drugs;
- Possession, use, or distribution of steroids or other performance enhancing substances;
- Crimes involving cruelty to animals as defined by state or federal law;
- Crimes of dishonesty such as blackmail, extortion, fraud, money laundering, or racketeering;
- Theft-related crimes such as burglary, robbery, or larceny;
- Disorderly conduct;
- Crimes against law enforcement, such as obstruction, resisting arrest, or harming

a police officer or other law enforcement officer;

- Conduct that poses a genuine danger to the safety and well-being of another person; and
- Conduct that undermines or puts at risk the integrity of the NFL, NFL clubs, or NFL personnel.[38]

A first offense committed for assault, battery, domestic violence, dating violence, child abuse and other forms of family violence, or sexual assault involving physical force or committed against someone incapable of giving consent, is subject to a baseline suspension without pay of six games, with consideration given to any aggravating or mitigating factors.

In 2015, Major League Baseball and the Players Association reached agreement on a collectively-bargained domestic violence policy. Under the policy, the commissioner may place a player accused of domestic violence, sexual assault, or child abuse on paid administrative leave for up to seven days while the allegations are being investigated. The commissioner decides the appropriate discipline, with no minimum or maximum penalty set forth under the policy, and punishment is not dependent on whether the player was convicted of a crime or pled guilty. Unlike in the

NFL, where players have no right to appeal the Commissioner's decision to a neutral arbitrator or arbitration panel, MLB players can appeal before a 3-person arbitration panel comprised of a league representative, a players association representative, and an agreed-upon independent arbitrator.

Some scholars argue that professional athletes are treated more leniently when dealing with domestic violence issues.[39]

1. Are the NFL and other professional sports leagues doing enough to curb domestic violence and other violent criminal behavior by players?[40]
2. Do you believe it is just a few criminals in sports that are giving the majority of players a bad name?
3. What ethical duties, if any, do professional leagues owe to their fans to produce a criminal-free product? Unlike the NFL, the NCAA does not discipline players for off-the-field misconduct; the member institutions have decided that disciplinary action is within the sole discretion of the athlete's institution.
4. Does a double standard exist for professional players when it comes to off-the-field conduct, and specifically with regard to domestic violence?

🔍 CASE STUDY 6-4 *Gun Control in Sports and League Gun Policies*

Professional sports has seen its share of violence in recent years. NFL player Sean Taylor was murdered in a 2007 home invasion. Houston Texans player Dunta Robinson was robbed at gunpoint in his house. Denver Broncos player Darrent Williams was killed in a drive-by shooting in 2007. NFL player Plaxico Burress suffered a self-inflicted gunshot wound at a nightclub in 2008. In 2009, two NBA players drew guns on each other in the team's locker room over a gambling debt.[41] Many athletes claim they need firearms for their own protection. The NFL instituted a gun policy in 1994[42]—the current NFL gun policy states, in part:

Prohibitions. Whether possessed legally or illegally, guns and other weapons of any kind are dangerous. You and your family can easily be the losers if you carry or keep these items in your home. You must not possess these weapons while traveling on League-related business or whenever you are on the premises of the following:

- A facility owned, operated or being used by an NFL club (for example, training camp, dormitory, locker room, workout site, parking area, team bus, team plane, team hotel/motel);
- A stadium or any other venue being used for an NFL event (for example, a game, practice or promotion);
- A facility owned or operated by the NFL or any League company.

Put simply, the League, the Players Association, and law enforcement authorities urge you to recognize that you must not possess a gun or other weapon at any time you are performing any service for your team or the NFL.[43]

1. Do you find the NFL gun policy complete?
2. What actions should be taken against those who violate a league's gun policy?

In the following case study, an NFL player was charged with DWI manslaughter after he killed a pedestrian.

🔍 CASE STUDY 6-5   NFL Player Conduct

Donté Stallworth was a standout wide receiver in the NFL for the Cleveland Browns. On March 14, 2009, he struck and killed a 59-year-old man while driving his 2005 Bentley. Stallworth had been at a bar celebrating a $4.5 million roster signing bonus the night of the crash. His blood alcohol level of .126 was well above the .08 legal limit of the State of Florida. He pled guilty to DWI manslaughter, a second degree felony, and served 24 days in jail. He was placed on two years' probation and performed 1,000 hours of community service. Stallworth was suspended for the entire 2009 season by the NFL commissioner for his actions.[44]

1. Were the actions of the NFL commissioner proper and just?
2. Do you think Stallworth received preferential treatment by the justice system because he was a professional athlete? Compare Stallworth's sentence to that of Andrew Gallo, a 24-year-old construction worker who killed three people while driving drunk. One of the individuals he killed was Los Angeles Angels pitcher Nick Adenhart. Gallo was sentenced to "51 years to life" by a California judge. Gallo's blood alcohol level was three times the legal limit when he ran a red light at 65 miles per hour. At the time of the crash, Gallo was on parole for a felony DUI conviction.[45]

Corporations typically place a morals clause in contracts as corporate protection. When companies hire athletes as spokespersons for their products or services, they seek to increase exposure of their product as well as increase revenue. The company also assumes the risk that the sports celebrity may get into some trouble along the way. A morals clause typically allows a corporation to cancel an agreement in the event the athlete engages in conduct that brings the corporation into a "bad light" or tarnishes its image.[46] Accusations of sexual assault of a woman in a hotel room caused Kobe Bryant to lose endorsements with McDonalds, Spalding, Coca-Cola, and Nutella.[47]

Coaches' contracts usually contain a morals clause dealing with situations that occur both on and off the field, court, or ice. A typical morals clause in a coach's contract might stipulate that the coach be fired for the following reasons:

- Dishonesty with employer or university
- Acts of "moral depravity"
- Conviction of a felony or drug-related misdemeanor
- Intoxication
- Being under the influence of illegal substances when performing duties under their contract[48]

Should a college coach be terminated for violent acts against a player? How would you define a violent act? Would your definition of violence also include emotional violence against players? Should a distinction be made between professional and amateur coaches for the purposes of discipline?[49]

▶ Hazing

Hazing exists at all levels of sports. Some sports initiations are simple and just poke a little fun at rookies. When NFL player Tim Tebow joined the Denver Broncos, they gave him a new, rather unattractive haircut. That is not the kind of hazing discussed in this chapter. Multiple episodes of illegal behavior, abuse, and horrific acts ending in death and injuries have occurred on both college and high school campuses across the United States in the past few years, bringing this issue to prominence. Many of these episodes go unreported, but hazing incidents can result in a criminal indictment in many jurisdictions. Many times, the hazed individual sues the school district and the individuals who performed the hazing. Many student-athletes are suspended by the school for their participation in hazing.[50]

In the following case, members of a sports team were criminally charged with hazing.

⚖ CASE 6-10 *Haben v. Anderson*

597 N.E. 2d 655 (1992)

Nicholas E. Haben was an 18-year-old freshman at Western Illinois University in the fall of 1990. On October 18, 1990, Haben was a "rookie" in the Lacrosse Club, a recognized and sanctioned student activity at the University. Club membership was "a valued status." On October 18, 1990, between 3:00 p.m. and 10:30 p.m., the defendants participated in the "initiation" of new recruits of the Club known as "rookies," which included Haben.

It was alleged that during the initiation ceremony, the defendants caused or participated in causing various types and quantities of intoxicating beverages to be given and ingested by the rookie initiates of the Club. The rookies, including Haben, were required to engage in various strenuous physical activities, and submit to acts intended to ridicule and degrade them, including smearing their bodies, faces, and hair with various food and other materials. These activities allegedly violated the Hazing Act and University regulations. It was alleged that the hazing and drinking activities had been conducted by the Club members for a number of years and had become a "tradition of, and a de facto requirement for, membership in the Club," and that the pressure to consume dangerous quantities of alcohol created a hazardous condition threatening the initiate's physical welfare.

Haben became highly intoxicated and lost consciousness. He was carried to defendant Kolovitz's dorm room, where, in Kolovitz's presence, he was laid on the floor and then left alone. Kolovitz returned to the room on more than one occasion to check on Haben and heard him "gurgling." Haben was discovered dead about 9:00 a.m., on October 19, 1990. He died from acute ethanol intoxication, possessing a blood ethanol level in excess of .34.

Haben v. Anderson, U.S. Supreme Court.

Hazing seems to be viewed by team members as a legitimate "team building" exercise; however, there are important distinctions between the two. Hazing humiliates and degrades; team building promotes respect and dignity. Hazing tears down individuals; team building supports and empowers individuals. Hazing involves shame and secrecy; team building entails pride and integrity. Hazing is a power trip; team building is a shared positive experience.

A 1999 survey found that at least eighty percent of all college athletes were the subject of hazing.[51] What actions should an SMP take if confronted with a hazing situation? What can be done to prevent further hazing incidents at the high school or collegiate level?[52] As an SMP, what measures should be taken to limit hazing by athletes? What should be contained in a school district anti-hazing policy? How would you define hazing?

Consider the following Connecticut State law on hazing. Is it complete or are there additions or revisions that should be made?

Sec. 53-23a. HAZING

1. "Hazing" means any action which recklessly or intentionally endangers the health or safety of a person for the purpose of initiation, admission into or affiliation with, or as a condition for continued membership in a student organization. The term shall include, but not be limited to:
   a. Requiring indecent exposure of the body;
   b. Requiring any activity that would subject the person to extreme mental stress, such as sleep deprivation or extended isolation from social contact;
   c. Confinement of the person to unreasonably small, unventilated, unsanitary, or unlighted areas;
   d. Any assault upon the person; or
   e. Requiring the ingestion of any substance or any other physical activity which could adversely affect the health or safety of the individual. The term shall not include an action sponsored by an institution of higher education which requires any athletic practice, conditioning, competition, or curricular activity.

▶ Summary

Violence is, and always has been, prevalent in all levels of sport. This chapter highlighted some of the incidences of on- and off-the-field misconduct that have occurred in a variety of professional and amateur sports. Leagues and associations adopt proscriptive rules and sportsmanship rules as well as personal conduct policies to prevent violence. SMPs must decide when to take disciplinary action against players and determine an appropriate sanction for on- and off-the-field misconduct.

▶ References

1. Rick Weinberg, "30: Tyson Bites Holyfield's Ear in Rematch," *ESPN.com*, June 28, 1997.
2. Tom Friend, "Tyson Disqualified for Biting Holyfield's Ears," *New York Times*, June 29, 1997.
3. "Carlisle: 'I Was Fighting for My Life Out There,'" *ESPN.com*, November 19, 2004.
4. Charles Nocles, "31 Players Suspended for Miami-F.I.U. Brawl," *New York Times*, October 16, 2006.
5. Modified from Joel Sherman, "The Man Who Caught Rose's Shoulder—Fosse Isn't Bitter 18 Years After All-Star Game," *Los Angeles Times*, July 12, 1988.
6. Angela Lumpkin, Sharon Kay Stoll, and Jennifer M. Beller, Practical Ethics in Sport Management 75 (Jefferson, NC: McFarland & Company, Inc., 2012).
7. Angela Lumpkin, Sharon Kay Stoll, and Jennifer M. Beller, Practical Ethics in Sport Management 75-76 (Jefferson, NC: McFarland & Company, Inc., 2012).
8. www.abrahamwatkins.com (Mr. Nichols not only knew his way around the courtroom but the basketball court as well. He attended Rice University on a basketball scholarship).

9. "Lakers, Rockets Settle Suit," *New York Times*, August 29, 1979; "Basketball as Combat Sport," *New York Times*, December 16, 1977.

10. Michael McCarthy and Jodi Upton, "Athletes Lightly Punished After Their Day in Court," *USA Today*, May 4, 2006.

11. Jeff Yates, "The Problem of Sports Violence and the Criminal Prosecution Solution," *Cornell Journal of Law and Public Policy* (Fall 2002).

12. *Murphy v. Steeplechase Amusement Co.*, 250 N.Y. 479 (1929).

13. *Nabozny v. Barnhill*, 334 N.E.2d 258 (Ill. App. 1975), pp. 260–261.

14. "Ty Cobb's Sensational Base Running Helps Detroit Beat Cleveland in Thirteenth Inning," *New York Times*, September 11, 1911.

15. Hana R. Miura, "*Lestina v. West Bend Mutual Insurance Company*: Widening the Court as a Playing Field for Negligent Participants in Recreational Team Contact Sports," *Wisconsin Law Review*, 1994.

16. Associated Press, "Skier's Manslaughter Trial to Start," *ABC News*, November 13, 2009.

17. Tracey Oh, "From Hockey Gloves to Handcuffs: The Need for Criminal Sanction in Professional Ice Hockey," *Hasting Communications and Entertainment Law Journal* (Winter 2006). Arpon Basu, *NHL Enforcers: The Rough and Tough Guys of Hockey* (Montreal, Quebec, Canada: Overtime Books, 2006).

18. Modified from Patrick Thornton, "*Moore v. Bertuzzi*: Rewriting Hockey's Unwritten Rules," *Maine Law Review*, 61, no. 1 (2009).

19. "Bettman: Fighting Part of the Game," *USA Today*, March 26, 2007.

20. "H.S. Football Player Charged for Game Hit," *ABC News*, December 5, 2009; Charles Haray, "Aggressive Play or Criminal Assault? An In-Depth Look at Sports Violence and Criminal Liability," *Columbia Journal of Law & the Arts* (Winter 2002); Sean Bukowski, "Flag on the Play: 25 to Life for the Offense of Murder," *Vanderbilt Journal of Entertainment Law & Practice* (Winter, 2001); Jeff Yates and William Gillespie, "The Problem of Sports Violence and the Criminal Prosecution Solution," *Cornell Journal of Law and Public Policy* 12, no. 145 (2002).

21. Associated Press, "Ciccarelli Cited for Assault," *New York Times*, August 25, 1988.

22. Courtesy of Supreme Court of Canada.

23. Mike Sowell, *The Pitch That Killed* (Hoboken, NJ: John Wiley & Sons, 1994).

24. Major League Baseball Official Rules 2010, Rule 8.02(d), p. 142.

25. David Brown, Scout Clocks Reds' Pitching Prospect Chapman at 105 mph, Yahoo! Sports, August 28, 2010.

26. Chass Murray, "Drysdale Brushed Back Pitchers and Batters for Beanings," *New York Times*, July 12, 1987. Bob Gibson, Reggie Jackson, and Lonnie Wheeler, *Sixty Feet, Six Inches: A Hall of Fame Pitcher & A Hall of Fame Hitter Talk About How the Game Is Played* (Garden City, NY: Doubleday, 2009). "Reggie Jackson, Bob Gibson Slug It Out," *NPR*, October 12, 2009.

27. Bob Gibson—One of the Greatest MLB Pitchers Ever, *Black Sports: The Magazine*, September 2010, Volume 9.

28. Paul Dickson, The Dickson Baseball Dictionary Third Edition, W.W. Norton & Company, 2009, p. 140.

29. Associated Press, "High School Baseball Player Killed by Wild Pitch," *Fox News*, April 25, 2009. Mike Sowell, *The Pitch That Killed* (Hoboken, NJ: John Wiley & Sons, 1991).

30. Modified from Timothy Davis, "Avila v. Citrus Community College District; Shaping the Contours of Immunity and Primary Assumption of the Risk," *Marquette Sports Law Review*, 2006–2007.

31. Jonathan Rand, *300 Pounds of Attitude: The Wildest Stories and Craziest Characters the NFL Has Ever Seen* (Guilford, CT: Lyons Press, 2006).

32. Richard Sandomir, "Students Take Side in the Sprewell Debate," *New York Times*, December 11, 1997; Corky Siemaszko, "Sprewell Says He Didn't Choke Coach," *New York Daily News*, March 9, 1998. Jeff Benedict, *Out of Bounds: Inside the NBA's Culture of Rape, Violence, and Crime* (New York: Perennial Currents, 2004).

33. Richard Sandomir, "Harding Faces New Threat on Ethics," *New York Times*, February 4, 1994; Jere Longman, "Kerrigan Attacked After Practice, Assailant Flees," *New York Times*, January 7, 1994.

34. Stan Grossfel, "From the Rink, to the Rink," *The Boston Glove*, January 26, 2005.

35. "Outside the Lines . . . for Kids," *ESPN.com*, July 19, 2008; G.J. Buse, "No Holds Barred Sports Fighting: A 10 Year Review of Mixed Martial Arts Competition," *British Journal of Sports Medicine* (February 9, 2006).

36. "Union Files Grievance over Mets' Stance on K-Rod," *SI.com*, August 18, 2010; Adam Rubin, "Union Grievance on Francisco Rodriguez," *ESPN.com*, August 18, 2010.

37. Bethany P. Withers, "The Integrity of the Game: Professional Athletes and Domestic Violence," *Journal of Sports and Entertainment Law, Harvard Law School*, 1, no. 1 (Spring 2010).

38. National Football League, "Personal Conduct Policy," December, 2014.

39. Jeff Benedict, "A Double Standard When It Comes to Athletes and Domestic Violence," *SI.com*, August 18, 2010. Jeff Benedict, *Public Heroes, Private Felons: Athletes and Crimes Against Women* (Lebanon, NH: Northeastern University Press, 1997).

40. Anna L. Jefferson, "The NFL and Domestic Violence: The Commissioner's Power to Punish Domestic Abusers," *Seton Hall Journal of Sports*

Law (1997). Joel Michael Ugolini, "Even a Violent Game Has Its Limits: A Look at the NFL's Responsibility for the Behavior of Its Players," *University of Toledo Law Review* (Fall 2007); Jeff Benedict and Don Yaeger, *Pros and Cons: The Criminals Who Play in the NFL* (New York: Warner Books, 1998).

41. Peter Vecsey and David K. Li, "Wizards Gilbert Arenas and Javaris Crittenton Pull Pistols on Each Other," *New York Post*, January 2, 2010.

42. Mike Freeman, "For Athletes with Guns, There Are Few Controls," *New York Times*, August 11, 1997; David Barron, "Can There Be Gun Control in Pro Sports?" *Houston Chronicle*, December 7, 2008.

43. NFL Gun Policy, *ESPN.com*, May 2, 2008.

44. Modified from Stallworth Suspended for the Entire N.F.L. Season, *New York Times*, August 13, 2009.

45. Associated Press, "Nick Adenhart's Killer Sentenced," *ESPN*, December 22, 2010.

46. Daniel Auerbach, "Morals Clauses as Corporate Protection in Athlete Endorsement Contracts," *DePaul Journal of Sports Law & Contemporary Problems* (Summer, 2005).

47. Richard Sandomir, "Like Him or Not, Bryant the Brand Is Scoring, Too," *New York Times*, January 27, 2006.

48. Porcher L. Taylor III, Fernando M. Pinguelo, and Timothy D. Cedrone, "The Reverse-Morals Clause: The Unique Way to Save Talent's Reputation and Money in a New Era of Corporate Crimes and Scandals," *Cordozo Arts & Entertainment Law Journal* 28, no. 1 (2010): 65.

49. Cameron Jay Rains, "Sports Violence: A Matter of Societal Concern," *Notre Dame Law Review* 55 (1979–80): 796–813.

50. Maria Newman, "14 Girls Tied to Hazing Case Are Suspended from Team," *New York Times*, September 5, 2001. Michael S. Carroll, Daniel P. Connaughton, John O. Spengler, and James J. Zhang, "Case Law Analysis Regarding High School and Collegiate Liability for Hazing," *European Sports Management Quarterly* 9, no. 4 (December 2009): 389–410. Marc Edelman, "How to Prevent High School Hazing: A Legal, Social, and Ethical Primer," *North Dakota Law Review* 81 (2005).

51. "80% of College Athletes Victims of Hazing," *CNN.com*, August 30, 1999; Rehman Y. Abdulrehman, "The Cycle of Abuse in Sport Hazing: Is It Simply a Case of Boys Being Boys?" Dissertation, 2007; Sandra L. Kirby, "Running the Gauntlet: An Examination of Initiation/Hazing and Sexual Abuse in Sport," *Journal of Sexual Aggression* 8, no. 2 (July 2002); Joshua A. Sussberg, "Shattered Dreams: Hazing in College Athletics," *Cardozo Law Review* (2002–2003); Scott R. Rosner and R. Brian Crow, "Institutional Liability for Hazing in Interscholastic Sports," *Houston Law Review* (2002–2003); R. Brian Crow and Scott R. Rosner, "Institutional and Organizational Liability for Hazing in Intercollegiate and Professional Team Sports," *St. John's Law Review* (2002).

52. Melissa Dixon, "Hazing in High School: Ending the Hidden Tradition," *Journal of Law and Education* 30 (2001): 357, 359–360.

CHAPTER 7

The Ethics of Drug Use and Testing

▶ Introduction

The use of performance-enhancing drugs (PED) by athletes and drug testing—two distinct concepts that pose different ethical issues—have been two of the most debated ethical dilemmas in sports for years. Debate regarding the use of steroids has become prevalent among professional athletes, coaches, trainers, student-athletes, parents, and school administrators. The ethics of drug use and testing has been written about, debated, litigated, and discussed in all forms of media. Every week there seems to be a new revelation about an athlete who has attempted to improve his or her performance through the use of performance-enhancing drugs. Numerous sports leagues and associations, including the NCAA, Tour de France, MLB, NFL, Ultimate Fighting Championship, National Association for Stock Car Auto Racing (NASCAR), and the English Premier League, have instituted drug testing policies that test athletes for both performance-enhancing and recreational drugs. The two main purposes of drug testing are: (1) to prevent the use of artificial drugs by competitors,

and (2) to ensure that the competition is fair to all participants.

The use of performance-enhancing and recreational drugs in sports is not new. In 1971, it was reported, "Drug usage is quickly becoming as common among athletes as the wearing of white sweat socks."[1] Dave Meggyesy, a former NFL player, quit the league in 1969, claiming it was "dehumanizing" because NFL trainers were no better than the average junkie.[2] In 1973, U.S. Senator Birch Bayh noted a huge increase in the use of drugs by athletes, including those in amateur sports, and specifically addressed the use of steroids among athletes.[3] The subject of drug use by athletes was reported in the *New York Times* in 1971 as follows:

> The sport where the greatest variety as well as the greatest quantity of drugs are used is football—particularly professional football, although the use of drugs in football often extends all the way down to the Pop Warner Leagues. I recently had an irate and disgusted parent tell me how the star quarterback on his son's Pop Warner Team was given three injections of painkiller so he could play in the "championship" game. As startling as this

may seem, it is really not surprising, since, from the players on the field to the coaches on the sidelines, Pop Warner league participants dress and behave as miniature replicas of their heroes in the college and professional ranks.

Realistically, the Lombardi philosophy that "winning is the only thing" is likely to continue as the dominant one in American athletics. As long as there is an inordinate emphasis on winning, athletes will continue using drugs or any other aid they believe will contribute to the likelihood of victory.[4]

So while drug use is not a new problem, many believe drug use—specifically, the use of performance-enhancing drugs—has increased in both the professional and amateur ranks in recent years. The use of performance-enhancing drugs among athletes poses multiple ethical dilemmas and raises numerous questions, but before addressing the normative principles, the non-moral (or amoral) values associated with such use should be considered. The livelihood of the professional athlete depends on his or her achievement at the highest level. An athlete's career can be very short; therefore, many athletes are tempted to use performance-enhancing drugs to enhance their performance on the field as well as to gain or lose weight. Amateur and professional athletes clearly understand that the better they perform on the field of play, the greater potential they have to earn an athletic scholarship or make more money. In today's competitive sports market, players want to hit more home runs, score more touchdowns, or jump higher than their competitors since their performance will most likely be directly tied to their next playing contract or endorsement deal. The use of performance-enhancing drugs can also be motivated by improved physical appearance and greater self-confidence.

In recent years, it has almost become commonplace for sports stars to come forward and confess that they have used performance-enhancing drugs to improve their play. The list is long, but a few are noteworthy. Alex Rodriguez

of the New York Yankees was one of the highest paid players in MLB and one of the most recognized athletes in the world. Initially, Rodriguez claimed he never used steroids[5] but later admitted he did in fact use steroids for a three-year period beginning in 2001 while playing for the American League Texas Rangers. During an interview, he said, "Back then, [baseball] was a different culture. . . . It was very loose. I was young. I was stupid. I was naïve. And I wanted to prove to everyone that I was worth being one of the greatest players of all time. . . . I did take a banned substance. And for that, I am very sorry and deeply regretful."[6] Former track star Marion Jones admitted steroid use when she was preparing for the 2000 Summer Olympic Games in Australia.[7] New York Yankees slugger Jason Giambi injected himself with human growth hormone in 2003 and admitted using steroids for several seasons. Major league pitcher Roger Clemens is the subject of much debate when it comes to steroid use. Clemens denied any use of performance-enhancing drugs and subsequently filed a lawsuit for defamation against his former trainer, Brian McNamee, after McNamee claimed Clemens used steroids during his playing days. The Clemens lawsuit was eventually dismissed.[8]

Before discussing whether use of drugs to enhance athletic performance is ethical, it is important to establish what constitutes a "performance-enhancing drug" and how that determination is or should be made. The classification of substances as "performance-enhancing" is not always obvious. The term "performance-enhancing drugs" has been used to refer to a large group of drugs, including:

- Diuretics
- Sedatives
- Painkillers
- Stimulants
- Lean mass builders

Generally speaking, "performance-enhancing drug" refers to any aid, supplement, or substance prohibited by the rules (or spirit of the rules) used to gain a competitive advantage. Professional leagues and amateur sports associations have taken extreme measures to try to prevent the use of steroids by players and student-athletes;[9] however, enforcement of a drug testing policy at the high school or collegiate levels or even in the professional ranks is difficult. What constitutes a performance-enhancing drug, or "prohibited substance," can vary in each sport, particularly in the professional leagues. A substance banned as performance-enhancing in one sport may be allowed in another. This can lead to confusion over what is deemed a prohibited substance for any particular sport.

The issue of drugs in sports also calls into question the integrity of that particular sport. If existing rules prohibit the use of performance-enhancing drugs, is a player cheating if he or she takes them, or just breaking the rules like any other rule of the game?[10] Should athletes be able to use performance-enhancing drugs if they choose to with the full knowledge of the consequences of their use? The normative principle of autonomy would suggests they should. Steroids and their use may contribute to aggressive behavior on and off the playing field. There is some evidence that steroid users are more likely to engage in aggressive behavior, sometimes referred to as "roid rage."[11] Steroid usage can also lead to heart problems and sterility.[12] If steroids are not physically harming anyone but the athlete and the athlete is fully aware of the risks involved in taking performance-enhancing drugs, should sports governing bodies still institute policies to prevent their use? The normative principle of paternalism would say that sports organizations have a responsibility to keep athletes—at least youth athletes—from harming themselves by using performance-enhancing drugs. But should that responsibility trump an athlete's right to privacy and human dignity by demanding their bodily fluids and requiring that they be visually monitored when providing a urine sample, without probable cause or reasonable suspicion that the athlete even took

a banned substance? In addition to autonomy, the normative principle of right to privacy provides another argument against mandatory drug testing of athletes.

Is it unethical or could it be considered engaging in unfair play if some players are using illegal drugs and others are not? Many argue that steroids give the user a competitive edge over other athletes and, thus, a primary justification for drug testing is competitive equity. But what if performance-enhancing drugs were available to all athletes and regulated by a sport's governing body? Under those circumstances, would the taking of performance-enhancing drugs be considered cheating or unethical conduct?[13] If professional athletes were allowed to use performance-enhancing drugs during competition, do you believe that would influence younger athletes to use the same types of drugs? Would the pressure on athletes be increased towards the use of performance-enhancing drugs to obtain a college scholarship? Do you think the use of performance-enhancing drugs by professional athletes would be setting a bad example for younger athletes? How would that differ from an athlete who is in violation of a league's personal conduct policy? All of these questions raise issues under the normative principle of social benefit.

If the rules of a professional league prohibit the use of performance-enhancing drugs, should athletes compete against one another only in the context of those rules? Should an athlete's ability be measured solely by dedication, commitment, hard work, and training, without reference to the use of performance-enhancing drugs? If so, would it follow that an athlete's use of performance-enhancing drugs does not truly measure the competition between athletes, but instead measures the athlete's reaction to a certain substance rather than his or her true ability? What effects do the use of performance-enhancing drugs have on the process of athletic competition itself? What justification can be made for restricting the use of performance-enhancing drugs in athletic competition? These are all difficult ethical dilemmas to resolve.

When faced with ethical dilemmas and illegal behavior, the wrongdoers are, many times, one step ahead of the regulators. If professional sports leagues allowed doping, do you believe they might alienate fans? If leagues were to allow drug use by athletes, would they be held legally responsible for the long-term health conditions of those athletes? Sports in America drive amateur and professional athletes to succeed, sometimes at all costs. With an overemphasis on winning, athletes are sometimes tempted to do whatever is necessary to enhance their performance and this can include taking performance-enhancing drugs. Athletes can use masking agents to prevent the detection of drugs in their system, which is the ultimate act of cover up and deception (violating the normative principle of honesty).

Both professional and amateur athletes are faced with ethical dilemmas in the area of drug use and testing. Apply the normative principles discussed in Chapter 1 to help you answer the following questions:

1. If everyone else is taking them, does that provide greater incentive to an athlete to cheat in order to ensure his or her place on a club?
2. The governing body for that competition will have promulgated rules for drug use. Is it considered unethical for an athlete not to keep a promise to stay drug-free? If an athlete tells the coach, teammates, and governing body that he or she is "clean," when in fact the athlete is using drugs, is that an unethical act? Would you consider a broken promise to a teammate unethical or merely disloyal? What about personal responsibility to teammates, parents, and coaches?
3. Athletes do not always follow the rules of the sports in which they compete. Why should they be required to do so when it comes to taking performance-enhancing drugs?

4. Under which circumstances should an athlete who has used illegal drugs be banned from further competition?
5. Should professional athletes ever be allowed to use human growth hormone (HGH) during competitions?
6. Should more severe penalties exist for those athletes who attempt to hide their drug use through masking agents or other forms of deception?
7. Should an athlete be allowed to do whatever he or she chooses to do in order to improve athletic performance, as long as the athlete understands the health and legal risks involved?
8. Should an athlete always be responsible for what goes into his or her body, regardless of the circumstances? Imposing a strict liability standard (i.e. liability without any personal fault) for doping offenses raises difficult ethical questions, applying the normative principles of honesty, justice, social benefit, and harm. Try to balance these normative principles when reading the rationale for strict liability as explained in *USA Shooting and Q. v. Int'l Shooting Union (Quigley)*, an arbitration ruling involving a skeet shooter who tested positive for a banned substance in medication prescribed by a physician for bronchitis during a skeet shooting competition in Egypt:

It is true that a strict liability test is likely in some sense to be unfair in an individual case, such as that of Q., where the athlete may have taken medication as the result of mislabelling or faulty advice for which he or she is not responsible—particularly in the circumstances of sudden illness in a foreign country. But it is also in some sense "unfair" for an athlete to get food poisoning on the eve of an important competition. Yet in neither case will the rules of the competition be altered to undo the unfairness. Just as the competition will not be postponed to await the athlete's recovery, so the prohibition of banned substances will not be lifted in recognition of its accidental absorption. The vicissitudes of competition, like those of life generally, may create many types of unfairness, whether by accident or the negligence of unaccountable persons, which the law cannot repair.

Furthermore, it appears to be a laudable policy objective not to repair an accidental unfairness to an individual by creating an intentional unfairness to the whole body of other competitors. This is what would happen if banned performance-enhancing substances were tolerated when absorbed inadvertently. Moreover, it is likely that even intentional abuse would in many cases escape sanction for lack of proof of guilty intent. And it is certain that a requirement of intent would invite costly litigation that may well cripple federations—particularly those run on modest budgets—in their fight against doping.[14]

Many athletes know how to avoid a positive drug test, cycling on and off banned substances to avoid detection. Athletes can be pressured by society into making poor decisions; therefore, the sporting organization plays the role of decision-maker for the athlete to ensure that he or she makes the right decision. Does a professional sports union fulfill its role in this regard?

Education on the potential dangers of illegal and banned substances can prevent harm to athletes now and in the future. Consider the following questions from a policy-making standpoint:

- What steps should be taken to educate kids in youth sports about the problems of banned and illegal drugs?
- What are the potential psychological side effects for adolescents who use anabolic steroids?
- What comparisons can be made between an athlete's use of alcohol and use of illegal drugs? Should professional sports leagues and organizations make rules relating to both alcohol and illegal drugs for their players?
- Should players incur the same suspension for excessive use of alcohol as they do for illegal drug use, illegal gambling, or domestic violence?

- How should a professional sports league's personnel be treated with regard to drug and alcohol use? Is it unethical to suspend a player for using marijuana but not suspend coaches, administrators, or other office personnel for the crime of driving while intoxicated?[15]
- Do you believe if doping were legalized, it would lead to a more informed use of drugs in sports and an overall decline in health problems for the participants?
- What about having an "anything goes" professional league? Would fans object to the "unnatural" athletes or would they flock to stadiums to see them perform at a "higher level"?
- Do you believe the use of performance-enhancing drugs violates the traditional notions of sportsmanship and fair play?
- Some argue that the aim of fair play through drug testing is a noble goal, but that, to be effective, the science behind the tests needs to be more detailed and accurate. There are scientific problems dealing with drug testing at all levels. How does this affect the ethical dilemmas in drug testing?[16] Can drug testing regulations keep up with advancing technology to ensure the integrity of drug testing procedures?
- Who are the largest stakeholders when dealing with ethics in drug testing? In addition to ethical issues, what legal issues are present?

▶ Ethics of Drug Testing in Professional Sports

No sport has wrestled more with the issues of performance-enhancing drugs than America's National Pastime—baseball. Baseball's "steroid era", ranging from approximately 1988 to the early 2000s, featured inflated statistics, monstrous home runs, and some record-breaking moments. Mark McGuire and Sammy Sosa's home run duels brought millions of fans to the park. Barry Bonds's record-breaking season in 2001, in which he slugged 73 home runs, also packed stadiums. The hitters were in charge, driving the "era of pitchers" sky high. MLB National League Most Valuable Player (MVP) Ken Caminiti admitted he used performance-enhancing drugs in 1996, his MVP season.

Some players who played in the steroid era of baseball have suffered the effects of the bad behavior of others. Jeff Bagwell was a great ballplayer for the Houston Astros and certainly should be enshrined in the Baseball Hall of Fame at Cooperstown. It was reported:

> [Jeff] Bagwell, who has never been linked in any way to performance-enhancing drugs, received 41.7 percent, which bodes well for him in the future. But Bagwell was likely a victim of suspicion. The kid who left the Red Sox organization in 1990 in a deal with Houston for reliever Larry Andersen went from gap hitter to power hitter and racked up some very impressive numbers in his long career. Bagwell denied he ever used anything—and if he didn't, we're sorry, but blame his peers, some of whom got caught and some of whom didn't, they're the ones who created the suspicion.[17]

MLB had a notion that some players were using performance-enhancing drugs, but it was unable to take any action throughout the 1990s.[18] A labor dispute between players and management in 1994 cancelled the MLB World Series—after this, baseball needed all the goodwill it could generate. Fans began to come back to the game and all seemed right once again with baseball; however, a national scandal was looming right around the corner. The book, *Game of Shadows*, would change everything and eventually cause the Commissioner of Baseball to investigate further, employing the knowledge and skill of a former U.S. Senator. The publication of that book in 2006 exposed baseball's dark secret by uncovering a massive steroid scandal in baseball. The book, written by two investigative reporters for the *San Francisco Chronicle*, made BALCO

(Bay Area Laboratory Co-Operative) common parlance in baseball circles and the sporting world.

An excerpt from the book, appearing in *Sports Illustrated*, created a national stir. There were demands for congressional hearings and an independent investigation to look into the allegations of the massive steroid misuse claimed by the authors. The book gave details about the actions of Victor Conte, head of BALCO, and Greg Anderson, personal trainer for home run king Barry Bonds. It portrayed Conte as a big-time steroids dealer whose motto was "Cheat or Lose." The authors claimed Barry Bonds turned to steroids to improve his performance after watching Mark McGuire pass Roger Maris' home run record in 1998. Baseball had a culture of players using performance-enhancing drugs and, as a result, inflated statistics. Baseball wanted to ignore the rumors about Bonds just as it had done about McGuire and Sosa, but being no longer able not to do so, they were forced to act. The BALCO situation also elicited major privacy concerns for professional athletes. In 2002, the U.S. government launched an investigation of BALCO and its alleged distribution of performance-enhancing drugs to professional baseball players. During the investigation, federal agents seized voluminous electronic data that contained the names of hundreds of MLB players and athletes from other professional sports. The baseball players included star players such as Barry Bonds, David Ortiz, Manny Ramirez, Alex Rodriguez, and Sammy Sosa. This information was eventually leaked to the press. The government's "search" in that case dealt with the methods law enforcement officials may use to obtain digital evidence during an investigation.[19]

Eventually, the problem would lead to congressional hearings, criminal indictments, and a detailed investigation by former U.S. Senator George Mitchell. Players and baseball executives were called to testify before Congress to discuss the problems of steroids in baseball.[20]

The Mitchell Report

The Mitchell Report may be the most damning and thorough report ever produced in the history of sports. Former U.S. Senator George Mitchell was requested by the Commissioner of Baseball to investigate drug use in baseball. The commissioner certainly got his money's worth, and maybe even more than for what he bargained. On March 30, 2006, Commissioner Bud Selig requested Senator Mitchell to investigate allegations that many MLB players had used or were currently using steroids or other performance-enhancing drugs. Mitchell's charge from the commissioner was:

> . . . to determine, as a factual matter, whether any Major League players associated with [the Bay Area Laboratory Co-Operative] or otherwise used steroids or other illegal performance-enhancing substances at any point after the substances were banned by the 2002–2006 collective bargaining agreement.[21]

The commissioner gave Senator Mitchell wide latitude to investigate and he was authorized, if necessary, to expand his investigation outside of BALCO and "to follow the evidence wherever it may lead."[22] Senator Mitchell accepted the charge of Commissioner Selig with two caveats: first, he requested that he be given total independence, both during the investigation and in preparing the report; second, Senator Mitchell stated he would only accept the task if he had "full freedom and authority to follow the evidence wherever it might lead."[23] Commissioner Selig agreed to the conditions set by the Senator and the investigation began immediately.

At the outset of the investigation, Mitchell declared he would conduct a "deliberate and unbiased examination of the facts that would comport with American values of fairness."[24] Mitchell's goal in preparing the report was "to provide a thorough, accurate, and fair accounting of what [he] learned in [his] investigation about the illegal use of performance-enhancing substances by players in Major League Baseball."[25] He retained the law firm of DLA Piper US, LLP, to assist him in the investigation.

Mitchell's investigation was extremely thorough. He and his team examined more than 115,000 pages of documents provided to them by a variety of sources, including the Office of the Commissioner of Baseball and all 30 major league teams. Another approximately 20,000 electronic documents provided by the league office and clubs were also reviewed by Senator Mitchell and his investigatory team. More than 700 witnesses were interviewed during the investigation and more than 550 of those witnesses were "current or former club officials, managers, coaches, team physicians, athletic trainers, or resident security agents."[26] Sixteen individuals from the commissioner's office were interviewed, including Commissioner Bud Selig and baseball's Chief Operating Officer Robert DuPuy. Senator Mitchell and his staff attempted to contact almost 500 former players during the investigation but only 68 players agreed to be interviewed. Mitchell also attempted to contact the Players Association but stated in his report that "the Players Association was largely uncooperative."[27]

Senator Mitchell concluded that the use of anabolic steroids and other performance-enhancing substances was "widespread" in the game of baseball and threatened the integrity of the game itself. Senator Mitchell thought MLB was slow to react to the players' use of performance-enhancing drugs and the "steroid era" in general.[28] Mitchell further noted that although baseball's response to the crisis was slow to develop, it did gain momentum after the institution of the joint drug program entered into between the owners and players in 2002. Senator Mitchell found that, at some point, players for all 30 major league teams were involved with performance-enhancing substances. The report named 78 players, most notably baseball's all-time home run leader Barry Bonds, and other notable players such as pitcher Roger Clemens and Clemens's former teammate Andy Pettitte.

The Mitchell Report is hundreds of pages long and lists players that the Senator believed used illegal performance-enhancing drugs. In his report, Senator Mitchell recommended to Commissioner Selig that no disciplinary action be taken against those players named. Why do you think he made that recommendation? Consider that Senator Mitchell had no subpoena power to compel witnesses to testify under oath, thus, his investigation was limited to information that certain individuals voluntarily provided to him. Also, the collective bargaining agreement at the time did not contain mandatory drug testing provisions with proscribed penalties. Under labor law, drug testing is considered a mandatory subject of collective bargaining that must be negotiated and agreed upon between management and labor.

Should professional sports leagues treat recreational drug use such as cocaine and marijuana differently from the use of performance-enhancing drugs? The next case deals with a star pitcher's battle with cocaine. What responsibility, if any, does the league have to help a player overcome a drug addiction?

CASE STUDY 7-1   *Steve Howe and His Addiction*

There was no doubt Steve Howe could play baseball, but he would also test the game's patience. There was also little doubt that he was haunted by personal demons that caused him severe heartache both on and off the diamond throughout his life. He was a two-time all-Big Ten selection at the University of Michigan and a first-round draft pick by the Los Angeles Dodgers in 1979. He paid immediate dividends for the Dodgers, winning the National League Rookie of the Year award in 1980. He saved 17 games in 1980, a record for a rookie, and gave up only one home run in 85 innings. In October, 1981, he won Game 4 and saved Game 6 of the World Series as the Dodgers beat the Yankees to win. In 1982, he was selected to the National League All-Star Team and led the Dodgers in appearances, saves, and earned run average (ERA). At 24 years old, Steve Howe was a baseball star. He had won awards, been an All-Star, and pitched in a World Series. His career was on the rise, but serious trouble was on the horizon. Howe would shuffle in and out of the game of baseball for the next 14 years, at times pitching well and at other times battling personal problems. He would be given multiple chances to redeem himself while trying to shed the personal demons that hounded him throughout his life and his baseball career.

At the 1981 awards ceremony for Rookie of the Year, Howe admitted he used cocaine in an effort to control his nervousness and excitement in receiving the award. His use of cocaine increased and continued throughout his entire baseball career. During the second half of the strike-shortened 1981 baseball season, Howe said he snorted "significant quantities" of cocaine but still managed to pitch pretty well because he had a "system." Beginning in 1982, Howe began to use cocaine during the season. Between the years 1982 and 1988, Howe was hospitalized six times to treat cocaine abuse. During the 1983 season, he was suspended twice by the team, fined $54,000 by the Dodgers, and placed on three years' probation. On May 28, 1983, he was suspended after admitting to drug use and placed in a treatment center until June 29.

Howe was suspended by Commissioner Bowie Kuhn for the entire 1984 season after he tested positive for cocaine during the off-season. Howe agreed not to play in the 1984 season and to continue his probation and treatment for alcohol and drugs. In turn, Commissioner Kuhn removed Howe from baseball's suspended list to an inactive status. The Commissioner's Office issued a statement saying, "Steve continues in treatment, and there is unanimity of feeling among us, including Steve's medical advisers, that a return to baseball this season would not be appropriate. The most important thing for this young man is his long-range recovery." The Dodgers agreed they would forgo the $54,000 fine.

The Dodgers request for repayment would have most likely been an exercise in futility anyway, since Howe had recently filed for bankruptcy. Howe stated that one of the reasons he was forced to file for bankruptcy was his $1500-a-week cocaine habit. The Dodgers agreed to loan Howe $10,000 a month for the remainder of the 1984 season as an advance on his 1985 salary.

Howe returned to the Dodgers for the 1985 season with great enthusiasm. Although he was no longer using cocaine, he was now drinking heavily. After Howe reported late to a game on June 30, 1985, the Dodgers took immediate action, giving him his unconditional release on July 3, 1985. He would once again relapse into cocaine use, and in September 1985, he entered the Chemical Dependency Unit of St. Mary's Hospital in Minneapolis.

The future did not look bright for Steve Howe. Failing to sign on with a Major League club at the beginning of the 1986 season and still wanting to play baseball, he signed a contract with the San Jose Bees of the class-A California League. At 28 years old, Howe, once a National League Rookie of the Year and Major League All-Star, was playing single-A baseball. While with the Bees, Howe was suspended for what was deemed a "drug test discrepancy" but was reinstated by the club in June 1986. He admitted to using cocaine a few weeks later and was suspended for the remainder of the season. As a result of the suspension, Howe's name was placed on baseball's voluntarily-retired list. Howe was seemingly on the bottom, having now been suspended from single-A baseball.

As the 1987 season began, Howe once again got the urge to play baseball. He started the 1987 season playing in Mexico and was surprised and eager when he was picked up by the Texas Rangers in July 1987; however, the Rangers had signed Howe without notifying the Commissioner's Office. When Commissioner Peter Ueberroth learned of the signing, he ordered Howe to play in the minor leagues before playing for the Rangers.

An addendum to Howe's contract with the Texas Rangers contained special provisions dealing with termination for drug use:

> e) The player and the Club ratify, adopt, and incorporate herein . . . all of the terms and conditions of that certain "Texas Rangers After Care Program for Steve Howe" and in the event of a breach, violation, or transgression of any of the covenants contained in the Program, the remedies set out in the Program (including but not limited to suspension and/or termination of this contract) shall be fully enforceable in all respects in accordance with their terms and supersede any and all other covenants or remedies contained in this Contract that relate to the subject matter of the Program.

Howe once again went back down to the minor leagues but was called up by the Rangers on August 6. Former Cleveland Indians great Sam McDowell was a certified alcohol counselor employed by the Rangers and counseled Howe when he pitched for Texas. At the end of the 1987 season, Howe signed a two-year contract with the Rangers, which was to pay him $425,000 for 1988 and $500,000 for 1989, with the opportunity to earn more money through performance bonuses. Notwithstanding the proposed incentives, Howe's demons got the best of him once again. He tested positive for amphetamines in January, 1988 and was given his unconditional release by the Rangers. From 1985 to 1987, Howe pitched for three teams and produced mediocre results. He was now 30 years old and a known drug user in baseball circles. It seemed like Steve Howe had worn out his baseball welcome.

Howe did not play organized baseball in 1988 or 1989, but he still had a burning desire to return to the game he loved. He wrote a letter to the Commissioner on December 12, 1989, asking if he could return to baseball. The Commissioner did not respond to the letter so the Players Association filed a grievance on Howe's behalf, seeking reinstatement. After some negotiations, the parties agreed to have Howe meet with the commissioner and two doctors, Dr. George DeLeon, a psychologist chosen by the Players Association and Dr. Riordan, a psychiatrist chosen by the Commissioner's Office. After meeting with Howe, Dr. DeLeon made several observations about Howe, saying he was aware his recovery was a "lifetime process" and that a return to the game would "not constitute an unacceptable risk to relapse."

Dr. Riordan disagreed with Dr. DeLeon, stating there would be a "high" risk that Howe would turn to substance abuse with therapy alone. He suggested a "very rigid" testing program, saying it was the only guarantee that Howe would not relapse into his previous bad habits. Dr. Riordan reported to the Commissioner:

> We talked about the possibility of Steve giving a supervised urine sample every other day of his life as long as he may remain involved with organized baseball at any level, player, coach, or manager. He acknowledged that he felt that this would be a reasonable strategy. I must emphasize that if this course were chosen and if he had a year or two of success, I would suspect that very likely Steve would come back demanding that this strategy be altered. It is my judgment that any altering of such a strategy, especially if it were successful, would be doomed to clinical failure. I believe that such a strategy must be linked to an absolute statement that a single dirty urine will mean his removal from organized baseball.

After hearing all the evidence, the Commissioner decided to give Howe one more "last chance." On March 10, 1990, the Commissioner's decision to allow Howe to return to the game stated in part:

> Howe will be placed on probation, but permitted to return to Major League Baseball for the 1991 season if he agrees to participate in an aftercare program approved by the Commissioner's Office which includes drug testing, possibly as often as every other day if necessary, through the remainder of his career in Baseball. Howe may sign a Major League contract in the meantime, but he may play only in the minor leagues prior to the 1991 season. This result will afford Howe an opportunity to determine the effects a return to the game will have on his continued sobriety and could lead to a return to the major leagues. As Dr. Riordan recommended, Howe will be immediately removed from Baseball in the event of a positive drug test.

The interpretation of what "one more last chance" meant, would later become an issue of interpretation in arbitration.

Due to Howe's admitted past lies about his drug use, the Commissioner decided that Howe could play one year in the minor leagues and then have a chance to return to MLB with very stringent requirements for drug testing. It was back down to class-A ball where Howe played for Salinas in the Independent California League in 1990, compiling a 0–1 win–loss record with a 2.12 ERA. To the surprise of many, Howe appeared at the New York Yankees spring training camp in 1991 and asked the club for a tryout. He impressed the Yankees so much that they signed him to a contract. Howe pitched for the Yankees from early May until August 10, when he injured his elbow. He went 3–1 appearing in 37 games, saving 3 with a 1.68 ERA in 1991. Steve Howe was back. He had fought his way through the Mexican League, single-A baseball twice, and several years in which he never even played organized baseball. It seemed Howe had finally overcome his personal demons. At the end of the 1991 season, Howe left for his home in Whitefish, Montana to enjoy the great outdoors and to revel in his return to the game he loved. He had just completed a successful season with a good club. On November 7, 1991, Howe signed a new contract with the Yankees for a salary of $600,000 plus incentives that could pay him as much as $2.3 million. Howe's return to baseball was a great comeback story and things were looking positive for Howe; however, once again, his success would be short-lived.

Howe's new contract required that he subject himself to drug testing and if he tested positive, he could be terminated by the Club. Howe's last drug test at the season's end was October 6, 1991. He was contacted by the President of Comprehensive Drug Testing (CDT) on October 30 to arrange for some off-season testing. Howe said he wanted to talk to the Players Association before he agreed to be tested because he had not been tested in the previous off-season. When CDT did not hear back from Howe, the president of CDT called him on November 22, 1991, attempting to arrange for testing. Howe told her that his in-laws were in town and asked if the testing could be postponed again, and it was. He was finally tested on December 4, 6, 12, 13, 17, and 18.

On December 19, 1991, he was arrested for attempted possession of cocaine. Howe was charged with two federal misdemeanor counts for attempted possession of 1 gram of cocaine and possession of 2 grams of cocaine. He pled not guilty to both charges. On November 23, the day after he agreed with CDT that testing would begin on December 4, Howe had made arrangements to buy cocaine. When Commissioner Vincent heard the news about Howe, he stated: "I'm heartbroken. This is terrible news. I'm totally surprised and shocked. It's really disturbing if it's true. If it's true, it's a great tragedy." Eventually, Howe pleaded guilty to attempted possession of cocaine and received three years' probation. He was also required to perform 100 hours of community service and to attend a substance abuse program.

Howe had paid for 2 grams of cocaine but never received it because the man he gave the money to, "J. J." (Jones), dropped the packet of cocaine in a pile of melting slush at the time of the "transaction." Howe later went back to J. J.'s house on several occasions to get the cocaine but discovered J. J. had been arrested. J. J. had told Howe if he was not around, Howe could try to contact Steve Boyd, an employee at a local used car dealership. Howe contacted Boyd about buying cocaine and they met the next day at a car dealership. What Howe did not know was that Boyd was a government informant and was wearing a "wire." They agreed on a price of $100 a gram, and Boyd told Howe to come back later in the day to complete the deal. When Howe returned that same day, Boyd told him the cocaine was located in the visor of a pick-up truck in the car lot. Howe went to the truck and, when he reached for the cocaine in the visor, was surrounded by law enforcement agents and arrested. There was no evidence Howe ever used cocaine, only that he was trying to purchase it. Notwithstanding pending criminal charges, Howe started the 1992 season with the Yankees. On June 8, 1992, he entered a plea of guilty to the criminal charges and on that same day was suspended indefinitely from baseball by Commissioner Faye Vincent. Vincent suspended Howe for life from the game of baseball as a result of Howe's failure to control his cocaine habit. Howe, through the MLB Players Association, appealed the decision of the Commissioner, saying a lifetime ban was unfair even though Howe had previously been given a final warning by Commissioner Vincent. Did Howe overstay his welcome in baseball?

⚖ CASE 7-1   *In the Matter of Arbitration Between Major League Baseball Players Association and the Commissioner of Major League Baseball, Suspension of Steven Howe*

I fully understand Baseball's institutional interest and its need, in so far as possible, to keep its workplaces free of drugs and to deter drug use among players wherever it might occur. I also appreciate the pressures brought to bear on Baseball by those who only see the "athlete-as-hero." But those considerations, as important as they are, must be examined in the light of the just cause standard. Under that standard, Baseball's conduct, as well as Howe's, is subject to review.

In justifying his decision, the Commissioner told the Panel that Baseball had done all that could have been done and that Howe had simply "squandered" the many chances Baseball had given him. If Baseball had, in fact, done all it could, both before Howe's 1990 return to the game and after, the imposition of a lifetime ban would be more understandable. But it is obvious that reality and what the Commissioner perceived to be the case are quite different.

We now know that Howe has an underlying psychiatric disorder that was never diagnosed or treated; that this disorder has been a contributing factor to his use of drugs; and that, absent treatment for the condition, he remains vulnerable to such use.

We also know that in 1990 the Commissioner's medical adviser cautioned against Howe's return unless he was tested every other day of the year throughout his professional career and that Baseball did not heed this clear warning even though the Commissioner suggested in his March 1990 decision that such testing be imposed.

These two factors cast a very different light on the nature of the chance Howe was given in 1990 and, indeed, on the nature of the chances he had been given in earlier years.

It was clear from Dr. Riordan's report that in his expert view continuous testing, including testing in the off-season, was essential if Howe was to succeed in resisting drugs during his career while also seeking to overcome his addiction through therapeutic means. In his decision allowing Howe to return, the Commissioner quoted Dr. Riordan's report at some length. The Commissioner's order that Howe play in the minors for a year, his directions regarding testing and his declaration that Howe would be immediately banned if he tested positive were all based on Dr. Riordan's cautionary advice. But the stringent, year-round testing requirement, as we have seen, was not implemented and Howe was unfortunately set on a course without the strategic safeguard Dr. Riordan considered indispensable to his success.

If that safeguard had been firmly in place and if Howe had never been presented with an opportunity to vary its regularity, an opportunity Dr. Riordan had clearly meant to foreclose, it is not at all likely, given the certainty of detection such a regimen would have imposed, that the events of December 19 would have occurred.

While Howe can certainly be faulted for seeking to delay testing at a time of his admittedly increasing sense of vulnerability, the Office of the Commissioner cannot escape its measure of responsibility for what took place in 1991. Based on medical advice the Commissioner had solicited, the need for continuous testing was obvious. To give Howe "yet another chance" of returning to the game without implementing those conditions was not, in my judgment, a fair shot at success.

The arbitrator overturned the commissioner's decision and allowed Howe back into baseball. Do you believe the arbitrator's decision makes a mockery of baseball's drug policy? Did the commissioner do enough to help Howe overcome his cocaine addiction? What types of rehabilitation programs should sports organizations provide for their players? How rigorous should a players' association be in fighting on behalf of players who use drugs?[29] Should they appeal a suspension of a player if the player confesses to illegal drug use? Could you compare this to a lawyer representing a client he or she knows is guilty of the crime for which they are charged?

Should all professional sports associations and leagues institute drug testing programs and policies? What about sports such as tennis, boxing, baseball, football, badminton, golf, and bowling? In 2007, the Professional Golfers Association (PGA) instituted a drug testing program.[30] In the following case, a professional golfer was denied a therapeutic use exemption (TUE) under the PGA drug testing program and subsequently suspended for one year for failing a drug test.

⚖ *CASE 7-2   Barron v. PGA Tour, Inc.*

670 F.Supp.2d 674 (W.D. Tenn. 2009)

Doug Barron is a professional golfer who joined the PGA Tour in January of 1995. In 1987, when he was eighteen years old, he was diagnosed with mitral valve prolapse and was prescribed a beta blocker, Propranolol, to treat the condition. Without Propranolol, Barron experiences a racing heartbeat and chest pains. In 2005, Barron was found to have low testosterone levels and was prescribed monthly doses of exogenous testosterone in order to maintain his testosterone level within the normal range. Side effects of low testosterone can include fatigue, lethargy, loss of sex drive, and a compromised immune system, resulting in an increased incidence of infection.

The PGA Tour establishes rules and policies that govern the conduct of golfers who participate in PGA and Nationwide Tour events. Golfers must pay dues to the PGA Tour and agree to abide by the rules and policies established by the PGA Tour in order to participate in PGA Tour events.

In 2008, the PGA Tour promulgated its Anti-Doping Program ("the Program"), and on July 3, 2008, the Program went into effect. The Program was developed in conjunction with the major golf tours and governing bodies around the world and incorporated input from leading experts in the field of anti-doping. The Program was modeled on the standards of the World Anti-Doping Agency and its Anti-Doping Code.

The Program contains a list of "Prohibited Substances and Methods," and included on this list of banned substances are Propranolol and exogenous testosterone. The Program allows players to apply for a Therapeutic Use Exemption ("TUE"). If granted, the TUE allows the player to use the substance despite its status on the list of banned substances. In order to obtain a TUE, the player must submit an application and supporting medical information. This information is submitted to a TUE Committee comprised of an independent medical advisor and one or more independent specialists of the medical advisor's choosing with experience in the area relevant to the player's illness or condition. The TUE Committee reviews the medical information and recommends to the PGA Tour whether to grant a TUE. Under the Program, a player may obtain a TUE if four criteria are met:

a. The player would experience a significant impairment to health if the Prohibited Substance or Prohibited Method were to be withheld in the course of treating an acute or chronic medical condition (the use of any Prohibited Substance or Prohibited Method to increase "low-normal" levels of any Endogenous hormone is not considered an acceptable therapeutic intervention); and

b. The therapeutic use of the Prohibited Substance or Prohibited Method would produce no additional enhancement of performance other than that which might be anticipated by a return to a state of normal health following the treatment of a legitimate medical condition; and

c. There is no reasonable therapeutic alternative to the use of the otherwise Prohibited Substance or Prohibited Method; and

d. The necessity for the use of the otherwise Prohibited Substance or Prohibited Method is not a consequence, wholly or in part, of a prior non-therapeutic use of any substance on the PGA Tour Prohibited List.

Prior to the effective date of the Program, on June 23, 2008, Barron submitted two TUE applications to the PGA Tour. The first application sought an exemption for the use of the beta blocker Propranolol. This application was reviewed by a TUE Committee consisting of a panel of doctors, including cardiologists. The application to use Propranolol was denied by the TUE Committee on October 10, 2008. Barron appealed the decision in accordance with the Program and the appeal was denied by the PGA Tour on October 22, 2008. Barron was instructed by the PGA Tour to begin weaning himself off of Propranolol. After his application was denied, Barron began reducing his dosage of Propranolol under a course of treatment prescribed by his medical doctor. He initially started the treatment with 160 milligrams of Propranolol, and by June of 2009, he had reduced his dosage to 40 milligrams.

The second application for a TUE sought an exemption for the use of testosterone. This application was reviewed by a TUE Committee consisting of a panel of doctors, including endocrinologists. At the request of the TUE Committee, Barron was reexamined by an independent endocrinologist. At the request of the independent endocrinologist, Barron stopped receiving monthly testosterone injections in October of 2008. The independent endocrinologist then took Barron's blood samples in November and December of 2008. The November test indicated Barron's Testosterone level was 325, while the December test indicated that it was 296. Both of these levels were within the normal range. The TUE Committee denied his application to use testosterone on January 21, 2009. Barron did not appeal the TUE Committee's decision.

Barron admits that, in early June of 2009, he received a single dose of exogenous testosterone from his medical doctor. Barron then played in the St. Jude Classic golf tournament in Memphis, Tennessee, which began on June 8, 2009. In conjunction with the tournament, he signed a tournament application form, confirming his understanding that he was required to abide by the Program. On June 11, 2009, Barron was tested in connection with his play in the tournament. His sample was found to contain evidence of Propranolol and testosterone. Barron did not dispute the test results and admitted to continued use of both Propranolol and testosterone. Following the positive tests, Barron provided additional medical information to the PGA Tour on July 23, 2009, and August 12, 2009. The TUE Committees reviewed the additional information provided by Barron and found it insufficient to justify TUEs for the use of Propranolol and testosterone.

On October 20, 2009, the Commissioner of the PGA Tour, Timothy W. Finchem, provided Barron with a written decision suspending him for one year from participating in PGA Tour or Nationwide Tour competitions and any related activities ("PGA Tour events"), from September 20, 2009, to September 20, 2010. In that letter, Commissioner Finchem wrote as follows:

> On June 23, 2008, you submitted a Therapeutic Use Exemption (TUE) application under the Program requesting that you be allowed to continue to use exogenous Testosterone and Propranolol. At that time, you were given full opportunity to medically justify your use of both substances. Your Therapeutic Use Exemption Application for Propranolol was denied by the PGA TOUR TUE Committee on October 10, 2008. You appealed that decision and your appeal was denied by Commissioner Finchem on October 22, 2008. Your application to use exogenous Testosterone was denied by the PGA TOUR TUE Committee on January 20, 2009. You did not choose to appeal that decision. As of October 23, 2008, you should have begun weaning off of Propranolol. As of January 21, 2009, you should have totally stopped using exogenous Testosterone. The PGA TOUR heard nothing further from you in 2009 concerning your use of Propranolol and exogenous Testosterone. We assumed, consistent with the denials of your Therapeutic Use Exemption applications, that your use of these Prohibited Substances had been discontinued.

> On June 11, 2009, you provided a doping control sample. That sample was found to contain evidence of both Propranolol and exogenous testosterone. That laboratory finding is not contested, since you have subsequently admitted continuing to use both substances. We invited you to submit any new medical information that might mitigate your continued use of these substances in total disregard of the denial of your TUE applications. You submitted additional information on July 23, 2009, and August 12, 2009. The information that you provided was reviewed by the PGA TOUR TUE Committee and again, no justification for your use of Propranolol or exogenous testosterone was found.

Pursuant to Section H(5) of the Program, Barron could have appealed the PGA Tour's ruling within seven days of receiving the notice of sanction. According to the PGA Tour, Commissioner Finchem told Barron during a telephone call that Barron "was unlikely to prevail in his appeal" and that "the third-party hearing officer would not be bound by the sanction imposed and…could impose a more significant sanction as a result of Mr. Barron's use of two banned substances and as a result of aggravated circumstances." According to Barron, the Commissioner said "in no uncertain terms that he would be wasting his time to appeal and that his punishment could be doubled if he appealed and lost." Barron did not appeal the suspension.

Pursuant to Section 2(M) of the Program, the PGA Tour notified Barron that it would issue a press release regarding his one-year suspension, and invited Barron to participate in the press release by proposing a statement to be read in conjunction with the PGA Tour's statement. On October 30, 2009, counsel for Barron sent a letter to Andrew B. Levinson, Executive Director of the Program, stating that Barron wanted the PGA Tour's press release to include the following statement: "Doug Barron disagrees with the PGA Tour's conclusion that he violated their Anti-Doping policy and the resulting sanction. All of the medications that were taken by Doug Barron were prescribed by his Medical Doctors for diagnosed medical conditions." The PGA Tour declined to release Barron's proposed statement, and instead, the following statement was released: "I would like to apologize for any negative perception of the TOUR or its players resulting from my suspension. I want my fellow TOUR members and the fans to know that I did not intend to gain an unfair competitive advantage or enhance my performance while on TOUR."

As a result of the one-year suspension, Barron alleges that the PGA Tour has violated Title III of the Americans with Disabilities Act, because he suffers from abnormally low testosterone, which causes him to have a reduced sex drive, experience fatigue, and have a compromised immune system, and that by refusing to allow him to take exogenous testosterone and suspending him for using it, the PGA Tour has discriminated against him based on his disability. Barron also alleges in his complaint that the Program is an unconscionable contract and therefore is void; that the PGA Tour has breached its duty of good faith and fair dealing by applying the TUE provisions and imposing the sanction against him in an arbitrary and capricious manner; that by issuing a press release that was misleading, the PGA Tour defamed him and placed him in a false light; and that the PGA Tour tortiously interfered with his prospective business endorsement opportunities.

Barron argues that he qualifies as being "disabled" under the ADA because he has a physical impairment (abnormally low Testosterone) that substantially limits a major life activity (engaging in sexual relations). The Sixth Circuit has not yet found that engaging in sexual activities is "a major life activity."

In addition to sexual relations, Barron also claims that his low testosterone causes fatigue and compromises his immune system. "Since fatigue in and of itself does not constitute an 'activity,' suffering from fatigue cannot qualify as a major life activity." A major bodily function, on the other hand, including functions of the immune system, is considered a major life activity. According to Barron's complaint, "low testosterone can prevent the body from healing at a normal rate and can further compromise a man's immune system, placing him at a higher risk of infection and illness," and Barron "experienced all of these symptoms."

The court held that the PGA Tour did not violate the ADA because Barron's requested accommodation—use of exogenous testosterone and propranolol—was not "necessary" in order for him to continue playing golf.

1. What is the rationale for the PGA to drug test their members?
2. PGA golfers do not have union representation. Should that be a consideration in the implementation of a drug testing program?
3. Under what circumstances should an individual's medical condition excuse him or her from drug testing procedures?
4. If you were the PGA commissioner, how would you make an ethical decision concerning a player's disability and still maintain integrity for the drug testing program?
5. Do you agree with the press release issued by the PGA in this case?

Barron v. PGA Tour, Inc., U.S. Supreme Court.

▶ Ethics of Drug Testing in Amateur Sports

Interscholastic Athletics

Athletes at all levels are willing to use performance-enhancing drugs to gain an advantage, even though it may be against the rules, and amateur athletes are no exception. With college scholarships at stake, high school athletes are facing growing pressure to perform at the highest level possible and hopefully gain an exclusive scholarship.

Amateur athletics has its own set of ethical issues when dealing with drug use and testing. What drug testing procedures should be instituted at the interscholastic level and how should they be implemented? What students should be tested and how often? Is drug testing high school athletes even necessary? Privacy issues are often present with drug testing schemes and procedures but amateur athletes do not have unions who look out for their interests. Union representatives negotiate what they believe to be a fair drug testing program; however, the same is not usually true for the amateur athlete. If a student-athlete in one sport at a high school is tested, should student-athletes in all sports be tested? What about students involved in extracurricular activities that are not sports-related? Should the policy apply to those students as well, to be ethical and fair to all?

In Case 7-3, the parents of a student-athlete challenged a public school district's drug testing program they believed to be unfair and the case made it all the way to the U.S. Supreme Court.

⚖ CASE 7-3 *Vernonia School District v. Acton*

515 U.S. 646 (1995)

… Vernonia School District 47J (District) operates one high school and three grade schools in the logging community of Vernonia, Oregon. As elsewhere in small-town America, school sports play a prominent role in the town's life, and student-athletes are admired in their schools and in the community.

Drugs had not been a major problem in Vernonia schools. In the mid-to-late 1980s, however, teachers and administrators observed a sharp increase in drug use. Students began to speak out about their attraction to the drug culture, and to boast that there was nothing the school could do about it. Along with more drugs came more disciplinary problems. Between 1988 and 1989 the number of disciplinary referrals in Vernonia schools rose to more than twice the number reported in the early 1980s, and several students were suspended. Students became increasingly rude during class; outbursts of profane language became common.

Not only were student-athletes included among the drug users but … athletes were the leaders of the drug culture. This caused the District's administrators particular concern, since drug use increases the risk of sports-related injury…. The high school football and wrestling coach witnessed a severe sternum injury suffered by a wrestler, and various omissions of safety procedures and misexecutions by football players, all attributable in his belief to the effects of drug use.

Initially, the District responded to the drug problem by offering special classes, speakers, and presentations designed to deter drug use.

It even brought in a specially trained dog to detect drugs, but the drug problem persisted …

[T]he administration was at its wits end and … a large segment of the student body, particularly those involved in inter-scholastic athletics, was in a state of rebellion. Disciplinary actions had reached "epidemic proportions." The coincidence of an almost three-fold increase in classroom disruptions and disciplinary reports along with the staff's direct observations of students using drugs or glamorizing drug and alcohol use led the administration to the inescapable conclusion that the rebellion was being fueled by alcohol and drug abuse as well as the student's misperceptions about the drug culture.

At that point, District officials began considering a drug-testing program. They held a parent "input night" to discuss the proposed Student Athlete Drug Policy (Policy), and the parents in attendance gave their unanimous approval. The school board approved the Policy for implementation in the fall of 1989. Its expressed purpose [was] to prevent student-athletes from using drugs, to protect their health and safety, and to provide drug users with assistance programs.

The Policy applie[d] to all students participating in interscholastic athletics. Students wishing to play sports must sign a form consenting to the testing and must obtain the written consent of their parents. Athletes are tested at the beginning of the season for their sport. In addition, once each week of the season the names of the athletes are placed in a "pool" from which a student, with the supervision of two adults, blindly draws the names of 10% of the athletes for random testing. Those selected are notified and tested that same day, if possible.

The student to be tested completes a specimen control form which bears an assigned number. Prescription medications that the student is taking must be identified by providing a copy of the prescription or a doctor's authorization. The student then enters an empty locker room accompanied by an adult monitor of the same sex. Each boy selected produces a sample at a urinal, remaining fully clothed with his back to the monitor, who stands approximately 12 to 15 feet behind the student. Monitors may (though do not always) watch the student while he produces the sample, and they listen for normal sounds of urination. Girls produce samples in an enclosed bathroom stall, so that they can be heard but not observed. After the sample is produced, it is given to the monitor, who checks it for temperature and tampering and then transfers it to a vial.

The samples are sent to an independent laboratory, which routinely tests them for amphetamines, cocaine, and marijuana. Other drugs, such as LSD, may be screened at the request of the District, but the identity of a particular student does not determine which drugs will be tested. The laboratory's procedures are 99.94% accurate. The District follows strict procedures regarding the chain of custody and access to test results. The laboratory does not know the identity of the students whose samples it tests. It is authorized to mail written test reports only to the superintendent and to provide test results to District personnel by telephone only after the requesting official recites a code confirming his authority. Only the superintendent, principals, vice-principals, and athletic directors have access to test results, and the results are not kept for more than one year.

If a sample tests positive, a second test is administered as soon as possible to confirm the result. If the second test is negative, no further action is taken. If the second test is positive, the athlete's parents are notified, and the school principal convenes a meeting with the student and his parents, at which the student is given the option of (1) participating for six weeks in an assistance program that includes weekly urinalysis, or (2) suffering suspension from athletics for the remainder of the current season and the next athletic season. The student is then retested prior to the start of the next athletic season for which he or she is eligible. The Policy states that a second offense results in automatic imposition of option (2); a third offense in suspension for the remainder of the current season and the next two athletic seasons.

In the fall of 1991, James Acton, then a seventh grader, signed up to play football at one of the District's grade schools. He was denied participation, however, because he and his parents refused to sign the testing consent forms.

Vernonia School District v. Acton, U.S. Supreme Court.

The Actons refused to sign the form saying it violated their son's constitutional right to privacy. When a "state actor" such as a public school (or school district) or state high school athletic association takes a bodily fluid sample it constitutes a "search" for purposes of the Fourth Amendment, which essentially provides that we have a privacy right to prevent the state from searching our bodies or property unless it has reasonable cause or suspicion that we committed a crime. Private schools, however, are not state actors.

1. What are primary concerns of a state high school athletic association or public school district when dealing with a drug testing policy? What is the state's interest in drug testing athletes?
2. Were the drug testing procedures in *Vernonia* fair and ethical? How could they be improved?
3. Does high school sports participation actually increase the use of performance-enhancing drugs by young adults?[31]

Drug Testing and the NCAA

Collegiate athletes are one step away from a professional career, although most will not become professional athletes; however, some student-athletes still take performance-enhancing drugs in an attempt to increase their performance on the playing field. The NCAA has a drug testing program applicable to all student-athletes who participate in its member institutions' intercollegiate athletic programs. The program is deemed a "strict liability program" and calls for a one-year suspension from participation in all NCAA sports if a student-athlete tests positive for a banned substance. The NCAA provides a right of appeal to the student-athlete who tests positive.[32]

Consider the following scenario in which a student-athlete objected to drug testing programs from both his university (Northeastern University) and the NCAA. Northeastern University is a private institution and, thus, not a state actor subject to the Fourth Amendment of the Federal Constitution; therefore, the student-athlete brought claims under state law.

⚖ CASE 7-4   *Bally v. Northeastern University*

403 Mass. 713 (1989)

David F. Bally commenced this action … challenging Northeastern University's drug testing program for student athletes on its intercollegiate athletic teams. Bally alleged that Northeastern's policy requiring student athletes to consent to drug testing as a condition of participating in intercollegiate sports violated his civil rights … and his right to privacy …

Bally is a student at Northeastern University … Until January, 1987, Bally was a member of the indoor and outdoor track teams, as well as the cross-country team. Northeastern places numerous conditions on participation in intercollegiate athletics, including signing of a National Collegiate Athletic Association (NCAA) student-athlete statement. The statement includes an NCAA drug testing consent form. In 1986, Northeastern began to require that varsity athletes also sign the university's drug testing consent form authorizing drug testing by urinalysis as a condition of participation in intercollegiate athletics.

In November 1986, Bally signed the NCAA student-athlete statement for the 1986–1987 academic year. He later revoked it by a letter dated March 12, 1987. Bally refused to sign Northeastern's drug testing form, as well as the NCAA's drug testing consent form for the 1987–1988 academic year. Northeastern declared Bally ineligible to participate in the varsity indoor track and cross-country teams. Except for his refusal to sign the NCAA and Northeastern consent forms, Bally has met Northeastern's conditions for eligibility to compete in varsity sports.

Northeastern prohibits the use of those drugs which the NCAA has banned, including certain illicit drugs, some prescribed drugs, and some over-the-counter medications. The parties submitted, as part of their statement of agreed facts, a fifty-five page list of NCAA banned drugs. Northeastern's drug tests do not test for the presence of many of the drugs that the NCAA has banned. Northeastern's program requires that a student-athlete consent to drug testing, through urinalysis, during post-season competition as well as during the regular season. The program requires that student-athletes be tested once annually for certain drugs: viz., amphetamines, barbiturates, benzodiazepine, cannabinoid, cocaine, methaqualone, opiates, and phencyclidine. The program also mandates random testing throughout the academic year, and requires testing of athletes before any NCAA post-season competition. To date, Northeastern has only tested athletes participating in post-season NCAA competition. The random and post-season testing screen for the previously mentioned drugs, anabolic steroids (a substance which sometimes increases muscle mass and may enhance athletic performance), and testosterone. When presenting drug testing forms to student-athletes and asking for their signatures, an athletic director explains that students who refuse to sign the consent form will be ineligible to participate in intercollegiate sports, and may lose any athletic scholarships.

Northeastern cites as its reasons for instituting its drug testing program a desire: (a) to promote the health and physical safety of student athletes; (b) to promote fair intrateam and intercollegiate competition; and (c) to ensure that Northeastern student-athletes, as role models to other students and as representatives of Northeastern to the public, are not perceived as drug users.

The actual testing process requires that a monitor of the same sex as the student-athlete observe the athlete's urination when providing a urine specimen. This is the only means of ensuring that the athlete submits his or her own urine to be tested. Drug-free urine is commercially available and, without a monitor, could be substituted for the athlete's. The urine specimens are labeled by a number code. Only the director of Northeastern's Lane Health Center and Student Health Services has access to the identity of the specimen's donor. A specimen which tests positive will be retested, by using another portion of the same sample. Specimens which test negative on either the initial or second test are not tested further.

If both the initial and second tests are positive, another portion of the same urine sample will be tested by a different method. If this test is positive, the student athlete is notified and requested to confer with the director of the University's Lane Health Center and Student Health Services. The director decides whether to begin counselling the student. The student athlete is given follow-up testing. If a follow-up test is negative, the individualized process ends and the student is simply once again subject to further testing. If a follow-up test is positive, the student is suspended from the team; the athletic director, head coach, and student's parents are notified; and the student athlete is required to attend a formal drug counselling program as a condition of further athletic participation. The student-athlete is then tested at regular intervals and remains suspended from the team until he or she tests negative. If a student tests positive at any time after rejoining a team, he or she will be dismissed from the team for the entire academic year. Thereafter, any positive test result permanently bans the student from participating in intercollegiate athletics at Northeastern. At any point in the process, the student may appeal to the university's drug testing review and appeals committee.

The court held that Northeastern's drug testing program did not violate Massachusetts' civil rights statute, which requires interference by "threats, intimidation, or coercion" (i.e. physical assault).

1. Should NCAA member institutions drug test their student-athletes in addition to complying with the NCAA drug testing program?
2. Do you believe the Northeastern drug testing policy is fair to student-athletes? Why or why not?
3. The Northeastern drug testing policy, like the NCAA policy, requires that a monitor observe the athlete's urination when providing a urine specimen. Do you feel this is too intrusive and violates the athlete's privacy? According to the court, "This is the only means of ensuring that the athlete submits his or her own urine to be tested." Are there other ways to ensure the athlete submits his or her own urine to be tested?

Bally v. Northeastern University, U.S. Supreme Court.

▶ Olympic and International Sports

The World Anti-Doping Code Agency (WADA) code became effective on January 1, 2004. It provides a uniform system of drug-testing procedures and sanctions for violations across all sports and all countries of the world. Although the NCAA and U.S. professional sports leagues are not subject to or bound by the WADA code, all U.S. athletes must agree to comply with the code in order to compete in the Olympic Games and other international sport competitions. Under NCAA rules, a student-athlete serving a drug-testing suspension from a national or international sports governing body that has adopted the WADA code shall not participate in NCAA intercollegiate competition for the duration of the suspension.[33]

The standard sanction imposed for a violation of the WADA code is a two-year ban from competition, four years for deliberately violating anti-doping rules. In an effort to alleviate the sometimes harsh effects of a strict liability standard, the suspension may be reduced in "exceptional circumstances" if the athlete is able to prove that he or she bears "no fault or negligence" (in which case the suspension is eliminated) or "no significant fault or negligence" (in which case the suspension is reduced). Proving "no fault or negligence" is very difficult; in essence, it requires a showing that it was impossible for the athlete, even when exercising the utmost caution, to know that he or she ingested the drug or substance.

The next case study involves tennis star Maria Sharapova's suspension for using a prescribed heart medication and the meaning of "no significant fault or negligence."

🔍 CASE STUDY 7-2 Justice Served?

Maria Sharapova, a five-time Grand Slam champion and former No. 1-ranked player, tested positive for a banned heart medication, meldonium, at the Australian Open in January 2016. The International Tennis Federation (ITF) imposed a two-year doping ban and Sharapova appealed the suspension to the Court of Arbitration for Sport (CAS). CAS reduced the two-year suspension to 15 months because it found the Russian tennis star bore "no significant fault" for her positive drug test and did not intend to cheat.

Why did CAS cut nine months off the suspension imposed on Sharapova? In a 28-page ruling, the arbitration panel found that Sharapova bore "some degree of fault" but "less than significant fault" and decided, "Under the totality of the circumstances, that a sanction of 15 months is appropriate here given her degree of fault." Although Sharapova committed a doping violation, "under no circumstances ... can the player be considered to be an 'intentional doper,'" the panel said.

Sharapova's ban took effect on January 26, 2016 and was originally due to run until January 25, 2018. The CAS ruling allowed her to return to competition on April 26, 2017, one month ahead of the French Open, a Grand Slam tournament she has won twice. Sharapova told the media: "I've gone from one of the toughest days of my career last March when I learned about my suspension to now, one of my happiest days, as I found out I can return to tennis in April. In so many ways, I feel like something I love was taken away from me and it will feel really good to have it back. Tennis is my passion and I have missed it. I am counting the days until I can return to the court."[34]

In 2016, the doping suspension kept then 29-year-old Sharapova out of the French Open, Wimbledon, and U.S. Open, as well as the Olympics in Rio de Janeiro. She would also miss the 2017 Australian Open. Women's Tennis Association CEO Steve Simon told The Associated Press: "Maria is absolutely one of the stars of the game, so she's missed when she's not available to play. We're very much looking forward to seeing her come back to the court next spring."[35]

Sharapova acknowledged taking meldonium before each match at the 2015 Australian Open, where she lost in the quarterfinals to Serena Williams. Sharapova said she was not aware that meldonium, also known as mildronate, had been included on WADA's list of banned substances starting January 1, 2016. According to Sharapova's lawyer, the CAS ruling was a "stunning repudiation" of the International Tennis Federation (ITF), which he said failed to properly notify players of the meldonium ban. "The panel has determined it does not agree with many of the conclusions of the ITF. As we demonstrated before CAS, not only did the tennis anti-doping authorities fail to properly warn Maria, if you compare what the ITF did with how other federations warned athletes of the rule change, it's a night and day difference." WADA acknowledged that CAS "fully scrutinized all available information and evidence" in the case.[36]

Sharapova said her family doctor first prescribed the medication for various medical issues in 2006 and that she took the drug for regular bouts of the flu, possible onset of diabetes and a magnesium deficiency. An independent ITF panel had found that Sharapova did not intend to cheat but bore "sole responsibility" and "very significant fault" for the positive test. The ITF panel also said the case "inevitably led to the conclusion" that she took the substance "for the purpose of enhancing her performance." Meldonium increases blood flow, which improves exercise capacity by carrying more oxygen to the muscles. More than 100 athletes, including many Russians and other eastern Europeans, had tested positive for meldonium early in 2016. Some of them received no suspension because they argued successfully that they stopped taking the drug before January 1, when it officially became a banned substance and that traces had lingered in their system. Sharapova, however, acknowledged that she used meldonium after January 1.

At the appeal hearing before CAS, Sharapova and her legal team argued that she bore no significant fault or negligence and her ban should be reduced to "time served," or about eight months. "I have learned from this, and I hope the ITF has as well," Sharapova said. "I have taken responsibility from the very beginning for not knowing that the over-the-counter supplement I had been taking for the last 10 years was no longer allowed."[37]

Sharapova's racket supplier, Head, hailed the CAS ruling as "justice being served."

"We are very proud to have stood by Maria for the right reasons throughout these difficult and testing times," Head CEO Johan Eliasch said, claiming it was "wholly unfair" that she had been banned at all.[38]

1. By not reducing the suspension, the ITF in effect applied a strict liability standard in finding that Sharapova was responsible for the substance being in her system at the Australian Open and for failing to notice that it had been added to the banned list in January. Which ruling, the ITF or CAS, do you think is the most ethical one? Apply the normative principles to guide your decision.
2. Does the Sharapova case give you a clear indication of what constitutes "no significant fault or negligence" under the WADA code?
3. Should U.S. professional sports leagues and/or the NCAA adopt the same standards for drug use and testing as those adopted at the international level, such as the Olympics?[39]
4. How do advancements in science affect ethical issues in drug testing of athletes?[40]

▶ Summary

Athletes at all levels of sport are motivated to use performance-enhancing drugs by non-moral (or amoral) values of success, money, and fame. The use of performance-enhancing and recreational drugs by athletes will continue to raise ethical dilemmas in the future for the SMP working at all levels of sport. Drug use and testing raises many of the normative principles discussed in Chapter 1: autonomy, harm, honesty, lawfulness, paternalism, social benefit, justice, and right to privacy. As sport leagues and associations continue to heavily regulate drug use and testing, it is imperative that SMPs balance these principles in their actions and decision making in the areas of education, testing procedures, enforcement, and imposition of penalties.

▶ References

1. Jack Scott, "It's Not How You Play the Game, but What Pill You Take," *New York Times*, October 17, 1971.
2. "Meggyesy Charges Drugs Fed to Pros," *Washington Post*, November 3, 1970.
3. "Athletic Drug Use Is Problem," *Chicago Tribune*, November 27, 1973.
4. Jack Scott, "It's Not How You Play the Game, but What Pill You Take," *New York Times*, October 17, 1971.
5. Associated Press, "A-Rod Steroids Report a Baseball Shocker," *CBS News*, February 7, 2009.
6. "A-Rod Admits, Regrets Use of Performance Enhancing Drugs," *ESPN.com*, February 10, 2009.
7. Amy Shipley, "Marion Jones Admits to Steroid Use," *Washington Post*, October 5, 2007.
8. "Clemens' Lawsuit against McNamee Dismissed," *Sporting News*, September 5, 2009.
9. Nathan Jendrick, *Dunks, Doubles, Doping: How Steroids are Killing American Athletics* (Guilford, CT: Lyon Press, 2006); Shaun Assael, "Steroid, Nation: Juiced Home Run Totals, Anti-Aging Miracles, and a Hercules in Every High School: The Secret History of America's True Drug Addiction," *ESPN.com*, 2007.
10. Nicolas Eber, "The Performance-Enhancing Drug Game Reconsidered," *Journal of Sports Economics* (December 21, 2007).
11. Will Dunham, "Steroid Users Seen Twice as Prone to Violence," *Reuters*, October 15, 2008.
12. M. Parssinen and T. Seppala, "Steroid Use and Long-Term Health Risks in Former Athletes," *Sports Medicine* (February 1, 2002).
13. Thomas H. Murray, Willard Gaylin, and Ruth Macklin, *Feeling Good and Doing Better: Ethics and Nontherapeutic Drug Use* (Clifton, NJ: Humana Press, 1984).
14. Arbitration CAS 94/129, Award of May 23, 1995, in Matthieu Reeb, Digest of CAS Awards 1986–1998 (1998) at 187, 193.
15. Mario Thevis, Andreas Thomas, Wilhelm Schänzer, "Mass Spectrometric Determination of Insulins and Their Degradation Products in Sports Drug Testing," *Mass Spectrometry Reviews*, Vol. 27, Issue 1, p. 35–50, 2008.
16. Mario Thevis and Wilhelm Schaenzer, "Mass Spectrometry in Sports Drug Testing: Structure Characterization and Analytical Assays," *Mass Spectrometry Reviews* (August 3, 2006).
17. Nick Cafardo, "Effects of Steroids are Felt," *Boston Globe*, January 6, 2011.
18. "Part I: 1987–1994 Steroids Meets Baseball," *ESPN The Magazine Special Report; Who Knew?*
19. *United States v. Comprehensive Drug Testing, Inc.*, 513 F.3d 1085, 1089 (9th Cir. 2008). Derek Regensburger Bytes, BALCO, and Barry Bonds: An Exploration of the Law Concerning the Search and Seizure of Computer Files and an Analysis of the Ninth Circuit's Decision in *United States v. Comprehensive Drug Testing, Inc.*, Journal of Criminal Law and Criminology (Summer 2007): 1151.
20. Michiko Kakutani, "Game of Shadows: Barry Bonds, BALCO and the Steroids Scandal That Rocked Professional Sports," *New York Times*, March 28, 2006.
21. Major League Baseball. "The Mitchell Report." MLB.com. http://mlb.mlb.com/mlb/news/mitchell /report.jsp?p=49
22. "Report to the Commissioner of Baseball of an Independent Investigation into the Illegal Use of Steroids and Other Performance Enhancing Substances by Players in Major League Baseball," George J. Mitchell, DLA Piper US LLP. December 13, 2007.
23. Ibid.
24. Ibid.
25. Ibid.
26. Ibid.
27. Ibid.
28. "Mitchell Report: Baseball Slow to React to Players' Steroid Use," *ESPN.com*, December 14, 2007.
29. Paul H. Haagen, "Players Have Lost that Argument: Doping, Drug Testing, and Collective Bargaining," *New England Law Review* (2005–2006). David M. Wachutka, "Collective Bargaining Agreements in Professional Sports: The Proper Forum for Establishing Performance-Enhancing Drug Testing Policies," *Pepperdine Dispute Resolution Law Journal* (2007).
30. Bob Harig, "Drug Testing a Necessary Decision by PGA Tour," *ESPN.com*, July 1, 2008. Larry Dorman, "L.P.G.A. to Start Testing for Performance-Enhancing Drugs," *New York Times*, November 15, 2007.
31. Tonya L. Dodge and James J. Jaccard, "The Effect of High School Sports Participation on the Use of Performance-Enhancing Substances in Young Adulthood," *Journal of Adolescent Health* (September 2006).
32. National Collegiate Athletic Association. "NCAA Drug-Testing Program 2018–19." NCAA.org. http:// www.ncaa.org/sites/default/files/SSI2018-19_Drug _Testing_Program_Protocol_20180706.PDF

33. NCAA 2018-19 Division I Manual, Article 18.4.1.4.7.

34. The Associated Press (London), "Maria Sharapova's Doping Ban Cut from Two Years to 15 Months," October 4, 2016.

35. Ibid.

36. Ibid.

37. Ibid.

38. Ibid.

39. Eoin Carolan, "The New WADA Code and the Search for a Policy Justification for Anti-Doping Rules," *Seton Hall Journal of Sports and Entertainment Law* (2006).

40. Angela Jo-Anne Schneider and Theodore Friedmann, *Gene Doping in Sports: The Science and Ethics of Genetically Modified Athletes* (Salt Lake City, UT: Academic Press, 2006).

CHAPTER 8

Ethical Considerations of Race in Sports

▶ Introduction

Racial issues have a long history in both professional and amateur sports.[1] Issues of race, equality, and discrimination are hotly debated in sports. Throughout the history of sports, race relations and discrimination have been topics of much discussion and debate. Racial discrimination in the United States in sports has deep historical roots. At many universities, African American student-athletes were not able to participate in sports until after World War II. Now, however, African American athletes dominate Division I collegiate basketball and football. Although African American athletes dominate the collegiate revenue-producing sports, some argue they are exploited and taken advantage of for financial reasons.[2] In many cases the large revenues produced by African American athletes are then used for purposes other than supporting the educational development of these student-athletes.

Racism has been a part of American sports since long before the beginning of baseball's Negro Leagues.[3] During the first half of the 20th century, all professional athletes were Caucasian. Two noted scholars,

Michael J. Cozillo and Robert L. Hayman, Jr., have summarized the relationship between sports and racial issues,

> . . . how will we explain the unwritten but undeniable rule that governed much of American sports in the first half of the twentieth century: that players—all of them—had to be white? How will we explain vicious reaction to Jackie Robinson when he defied this convention, and how will we account for the iconic status that is—for better but sometimes worse—afforded him today? How will we comprehend the stunning racial disparities in the organization of American sports—where most ballplayers are black or Latino, but nearly all coaches and executives are white—or understand the integrity of the dispute over the treatment of college athletes in the "revenue-producing" sports, where minority ballplayers generate substantial funds for white-dominated educational institutions that not atypically fail even to provide an education in return? Race in American sports: it is all about race in America.[4]

Major League Baseball player Curt Flood, who challenged baseball's reserve clause in the early 1970s, was questioned by other players whether his antitrust lawsuit against baseball was "racially motivated."[5] Flood wrote about the racial hatred and unequal treatment he received while playing minor league baseball in the Deep South in the 1950s. Racial animus continued against Flood even after he became a Major League All-Star for the St. Louis Cardinals.[6] Hall of Fame player Hank Aaron spoke of the hatred he encountered during his chase of Babe Ruth's home run record in 1974:[7]

> **TSN:** The death threats and the letters from bigots are the reasons you didn't enjoy the [home run record] chase, right?

> **Aaron:** The threats and all the controversy. My daughter was in college at Fisk University, and she wasn't able to enjoy it. And I had to put my two boys in private schools, so they weren't there to be bat boys. . . . So I was deprived of a lot of things that really should have belonged to me and my family.[8]

Discriminatory treatment on the basis of race involves intentional discrimination or discrimination on its face; *i.e.,* treatment of one race different from another race. It often involves preconceived ideas (stereotyping, making generalizations, or speculating about the way people think), biases, and/or prejudices. An example of a treatment issue in sports was the "gentlemen's agreement" among the owners of professional baseball teams not to sign any outstanding African American players, which lasted for more than fifty years. Brooklyn Dodgers great Jackie Robinson broke Major League Baseball's color barrier in 1947 with the help of University of Michigan lawyer Branch Rickey.[9] Robinson spoke of his experiences in spring training in 1946: "We had a tough time getting to Daytona Beach . . . So we took a train to Jacksonville, and when we got there we found we'd have to go the rest of the way by bus. We didn't like the bus, and we particularly didn't like the back seat when there were empty seats near the center. Florida law designates where Negroes are to

ride in public conveyances. The law says: 'Black seat.' We rode there."[10] Since baseball's integration in 1947, MLB has made significant efforts to ensure diversity within the American national pastime.

The NFL was integrated from 1920 to 1934, but in 1934 NFL owners entered into a "gentlemen's agreement" banning all African-American players.[11] NBA superstar Bill Russell became the first African-American coach in U.S. major professional sports when he became the head coach of the Boston Celtics in 1966. Since that time, continuing efforts have been made to combat discrimination in the coaching ranks in both professional and amateur sports. Discrimination in professional sports continues today in more subtle ways, oftentimes in the absence of policies or agreements that involve intentional discrimination or discrimination on their face. Thus, a rule, policy, or practice may have a disproportionate impact even if discriminatory treatment is lacking. For example, the opportunities for minority candidates in the front offices of professional sports organizations are still extremely limited and major college football programs continue to hire minority head coach candidates at a very slow pace.

The 1936 Olympics in Berlin, Germany, were supposed to showcase the National Socialist government of Germany and exhibit supremacy of the Aryan Race; however, U.S. Olympian Jesse Owens, an African-American, astounded the world as he won four gold medals. Adolf Hitler refused to shake hands with any black athletes at the 1936 Olympics and did not attend any medal presentations for black athletes.[12]

One event in U.S. history in the 20th century brought race, sports, and culture together in a "perfect storm." The O.J. Simpson criminal trial was viewed by millions across America. A largely African-American jury found Simpson not guilty of killing his wife and her friend, both Caucasians. Simpson was a wildly successful college and professional football player, a popular figure in American culture, and a highly-paid celebrity. He used his charm and fame to achieve movie stardom and a sports broadcasting career. Simpson was the first African-American corporate spokesperson in America. In the 1960s, a Hertz car rental television commercial depicted Simpson dashing through an airport with a briefcase in his hand; however, the night of June 12, 1994, would change Simpson's life and have a major impact on race relations in America. Simpson was charged with the murder of his wife, Nicole Brown Simpson, and her friend, Ronald Goldman. It seemed by many to be a rather "open and shut" case for the prosecution, but celebrity lawyer Johnnie Cochran was able to convince a jury that Simpson was not guilty of all charges levied against him. One of our authors explained in a published journal article how the trial became a metaphor for racial issues in American society.[13] Although Simpson was found not guilty, many believed the jury came to the wrong conclusion and that Simpson was actually guilty of the murders. Because of Simpson's iconic stature in the sports world, the trial and its outcome were topics of discussion for both the African-American and white communities. The verdict in the O.J. Simpson case had a profound effect on race relations in America.

▶ Race and Professional Sports

Organized professional baseball essentially banned African American athletes from participation after 1899; however, many major and minor league baseball players arranged exhibition games against black professional clubs. The Negro Leagues allowed black ballplayers an opportunity to play professional baseball. Many great Negro League baseball players never made it to baseball's major leagues because of discrimination. The Negro League teams stayed in existence until the early 1960s.[14]

In Case 8-1, a program instituted by MLB created an ethical dilemma and a lawsuit relating to benefits provided to former Negro League players. MLB voluntarily decided to provide certain benefits for former Negro League players. Several retired professional baseball players, both Caucasian and Latino, sued MLB claiming a violation of Title VII of the Civil Rights Act of 1964 arguing their exclusion from the medical and supplemental income plans was discriminatory. The Civil Rights Act prohibits discrimination in employment on the basis of race, color, religion, sex, or national origin.

⚖ CASE 8-1 *Moran v. Allan H. Selig, aka "Bud" Selig, as Commissioner of Major League Baseball*

447 F.3d 748 (9th Cir. 2006)

In October 2003, Mike Colbern, a retired Major League Baseball player, brought a class action on behalf of himself and other retired baseball players against Major League Baseball ("MLB") claiming ... that MLB had violated Title VII by excluding them from medical and supplemental income plans devised by MLB for former Negro League players ... [Plaintiffs] are virtually all Caucasian former MLB players who played in the Major Leagues for less than four years between 1947 and 1979 and were accordingly denied MLB pension and medical benefits.

Until 1947, when Jackie Robinson broke the color barrier in the Major Leagues, African-Americans were not allowed to play Major League Baseball and could play only in the so-called "Negro Leagues," associations of professional baseball clubs composed exclusively of black players. These clubs terminated all operations in the early 1960s as a result of the absorption of African-Americans into MLB, and the Negro Leagues ceased to exist. With the coming of racial integration to baseball, the market for a separate league for minority players evaporated.

Having lost their economic base, the former Negro Leagues were unable to offer any pension or medical benefits to their former players. In the 1990s, seeking to make partial amends for its exclusion of African-Americans prior to 1947, MLB voluntarily decided to provide certain benefits to former Negro League players. In 1993, MLB created a plan that provided medical coverage to former Negro League players ("Negro League Medical Plan"). In 1997, it adopted a supplemental income plan that provided an annual payment of $10,000 to eligible players ("Negro League Supplemental Income Plan"). Individuals who had played in the Negro Leagues prior to 1948, i.e., prior to African-Americans being allowed in the Major Leagues, were eligible for such payments ... these two plans are referred to collectively as the "Negro League Plans." Some of the eligible players had subsequently played in the Major Leagues for a period of time too short to qualify them for MLB's regular medical and pension plans and some had never played in the Major Leagues at all.

[Colbern] contends that MLB's provision of medical and supplemental income benefits to certain African-Americans, former Negro League players who played in the Major Leagues between 1947–1979 for too short a period to vest in the MLB medical and pension benefits plans-but not to [him]-constitutes unlawful discrimination on the basis of race.

Although some beneficiaries of the two Negro League Plans may have played MLB baseball for a relatively short period of time, eligibility for benefits is not based on such former employment with MLB or on any employment relationship between MLB and the recipients. Rather, to qualify for the Negro League Plans, a recipient need not be a former MLB player, only a former Negro League player. A former Negro League player who never played for an MLB team is eligible for the benefits even though he was never employed in any way by MLB or one of its clubs. Thus, although they resemble benefits typically conferred on the basis of an employment relationship, the Negro League Plans' benefits are not "part and parcel of the employment relationship" between recipients and MLB nor are they "incidents of employment" of the recipient by MLB. Because the supplemental income payments and medical benefits MLB provides to former Negro League players are not awarded on the basis of an employment relationship with MLB, but rather on the basis of participation in another entity to which MLB had no legal relationship, the receipt of these benefits cannot give rise to a valid Title VII claim. In other words, the fact that [Colbern and other Caucasian and Latino players] do not receive the same or substantially similar benefits as those provided under the Negro League Plans cannot be considered an "adverse employment action" because the provision of these benefits by the MLB is not an "employment action" at all.

. . . Although there are indeed some similarities between [Plaintiff's] circumstances and that of the players to whom they compare themselves, the two groups are not similar in "all material respects." Unlike the beneficiaries of the Negro League Plans, [Colbern and other Caucasian and Latino players] were never prevented from playing for an MLB team, and thus unable to acquire the necessary longevity, for reasons entirely independent of their ability to do the job (i.e., on account of their race). Nor did [Colbern] ever play in the Negro Leagues, a primary requirement for eligibility under the Negro League Plans.

MLB's absolute ban on African-American players before 1947 impeded those players from accumulating the necessary years of service in the Major Leagues to qualify for the medical and pension benefits under the terms of the MLB benefits plans in effect at the time.

. . . we hold that MLB had a legitimate, non-discriminatory and non-pretextual reason for awarding the pension and medical benefits to African-American players who qualified under the Plans . . .

The Negro League Plans were created to remedy specific discrimination that directly affected identifiable individuals and to compensate those individuals for injuries caused by that discrimination, specifically, for the loss of benefits by African-American baseball players-a loss that resulted from their inability to acquire the necessary years of playing time to qualify for MLB's pension and medical benefits. The decision to provide benefits under the Negro League Plans only to individuals, all African-Americans, who were injured by MLB's policy of excluding members of their race from playing MLB baseball does not discriminate against Caucasians. Not only were Caucasians the beneficiaries of the discriminatory policy; they had every opportunity under it to acquire eligibility for the MLB benefits. [Plaintiffs] were never the victims of discrimination and were never deprived, during any portion of their playing years, of an opportunity to acquire the longevity necessary to become eligible for MLB benefits; rather, they simply failed to do so. Although the players who qualify under the Negro League Plans are all African-American, it was African-Americans and not Caucasians who were discriminated against on the basis of their race. It is true that only players who played in the Negro Leagues are eligible to receive benefits under the Plans. It is also true, however, that the Negro Leagues were formed to provide the opportunity to play professional baseball to those who were otherwise excluded because of their race. There is no evidence, and it would strain credulity and one's sense of history, to suggest that [Colbern] or any other Caucasians sought entry to the Negro Leagues or would have been willing to play baseball in that forum. In short, the Plans were adopted for the specific purpose of providing benefits to those who had been discriminated against by being denied the opportunity to play MLB baseball and to qualify for MLB benefits.

To the extent that MLB sought to remedy in part its past discriminatory conduct, it acted honorably and decently and not out of an improper or invidious motive. MLB has thus shown a legitimate, non-discriminatory reason for its decision to provide benefits to former Negro League Players, a reason that is not pretextual in any respect.

1. Apply the normative principles, in particular the justice principle, to the actions of MLB in Case 8-1. "Compensatory justice" is a type of justice that involves the perceived fairness of making good on harm or unfairness that a person (or persons) may have suffered in the past.[15]
2. Were the Negro League players treated fairly under the plan or could have MLB done more for former Negro League players? What about the fact that MLB waited 30–35 years to adopt the plan?
3. How should MLB handle the claims of former players who believed the plan was unethical or unfair?

Moran v. Allan H. Selig, aka "Bud" Selig, as Commissioner of Major League Baseball, U.S. Supreme Court.

🔍 CASE STUDY 8-1 American Football League All-Star Game, 1965

Twenty-one black football players refused to play in the 1965 American Football League (AFL), All-Star Game in New Orleans because of race-related threats and insults they suffered in New Orleans. The 21 black players, more than a third of the players on the team, voted 13–8 not to play in the game. The players issued the following statement: "The AFL is progressing in great strides, and the Negro players feel they are playing a vital role in the league's progression. They are being treated fairly in all cities in the league. . . . However, because of adverse conditions and discriminatory practices experienced by Negro Players while here in New Orleans, the players feel they cannot perform 100 percent as expected in the All-Star Game and be treated differently."[16]

As a result, AFL Commissioner Joe Foss announced that the game would be moved to Houston. The 1965 AFL All-Star Game not only showed the effect of racism on African-American athletes but also displayed the courage of those players who were willing to stand against racism and hatred.[17]

Some would agree that NBA player Craig Hodges did not fit the mold of a typical professional athlete. In the following case, an NBA club terminated his contract. Hodges alleged that the club did so based on the fact that he was African-American and because they did not like his political views. He brought a claim under Section 1981 of the Civil Rights Act, which prohibits intentional racially discriminatory acts in the making or enforcement of a contract. The plaintiff must present sufficient evidence of intentional discrimination by the defendant.

⚖ CASE 8-2 *Hodges v. National Basketball Association*

1998 WL 26183

. . . Craig Hodges is a former professional basketball player who alleges that the National Basketball Association ("NBA") unlawfully discriminated against him because of his race, in violation of § 1981 of the Civil Rights Act, when it conspired to prevent him from acquiring an NBA Player contract.

Hodges, an African-American, was a professional basketball player in the NBA from 1981 until 1992. His career as a professional basketball player was marked with impressive accomplishments: twice he was the NBA three-point field goal champion, he won three consecutive Long Distance Shootout titles in 1989 through 1991. He was a member of the Chicago Bulls when the team won the NBA championship in 1991 and 1992, and at one time, he was the most accurate three-point shooter in NBA history. During his tenure with the NBA, Hodges was also "an outspoken African-American activist," who publicly criticized professional athletes who failed to use their wealth and influence to assist the poor. As a White House guest in 1991, Hodges came garbed in traditional African vestments and presented a letter to President Bush calling for an end to injustice toward the African American community. In 1992, Bulls' representatives conveyed to Hodges that they were embarrassed by these activities. When Hodges' contract with the Bulls expired after the 1992 championship and he became a free agent, the Bulls opted not to re-sign him. Despite his success in the NBA and his efforts to sign with another team, no team has granted Hodges even a try-out or an interview.

Hodges [alleged] that the NBA conspired to keep him from playing on any NBA team because he is black and his political activities were not welcomed by the NBA. Hodges argues that racial discrimination is at the root of the conspiracy, a conclusion supported by the fact that white players with backgrounds similar to his are free to express themselves politically without suffering any retaliation.

The *New York Times* reported the following with regard to the *Hodges* case:

. . . Phil Jackson, the Chicago Bulls' coach . . . [said] "I had the highest regard for Craig, though. He was a great team player, never caused any problems and I respected his views. I'm a spiritual man, and so is he. But I also found it strange that not a single team called to inquire about him. Usually, I get at least one call about a player we've decided not to sign.

And yes, he couldn't play much defense, but a lot of guys in the league can't, but not many can shoot from his range, either."

In the lawsuit, Billy McKinney, the director of player personnel for the SuperSonics, who is black, is quoted as having first voiced interest in Hodges in 1992, and then shortly after backing away, telling Hodges he could do nothing because "brothers have families, if you know what I mean."

"I never heard of any conspiracy whatsoever," said Wayne Embry, the President and Chief Operating Officer of the Cleveland Cavaliers, who is also black. "I'm sure I would have if there was one. And in a league that has about 80 percent black players, it's hard to charge racism." David Stern, the commissioner of the NBA, said that the idea of a conspiracy against Hodges is "ridiculous." "I was even at the White House when Craig wore the dashiki," he said. "I thought it looked great and I told him so."

Perhaps more real than the allegations is the perception of discrimination, especially among some NBA personnel. "It's well known through the League that there may be repercussions if you speak out too strongly on some sensitive issues," said Buck Williams, a forward for the Knicks and the respected head of the Players Association. "I don't know if Hodges lost his

job because of it, but it is a burden when you carry the militant label he has."

Yet such star nonconformists as the bizarre Dennis Rodman and the frequently tasteless Charles Barkley are tolerated and even celebrated. Clearly, then, the dangers of expression in the NBA have less to do with personal stances than with simply being a fringe player.[18]

1. Was Hodge's inability to secure employment based on his wearing traditional African garb to the White House and his expression of his faith or was it a result of his diminished skills?[19]
2. What facts would an SMP need to know to make this determination?
3. Does the fact that Phil Jackson says he usually gets calls about a player and he got none for Hodges, show a conspiracy to keep Hodges out of the league?

⌕ CASE STUDY 8-2   Colin Kaepernick Takes a Stand by Not Standing

In the 2016 NFL pre-season, San Francisco 49ers quarterback Colin Kaepernick immersed himself in controversy when he refused to stand for the playing of the national anthem during the pre-game ceremonies in protest of what he deems are wrongdoings against African-Americans and minorities in the United States. Kaepernick told NFL Media: "I am not going to stand up to show pride in a flag for a country that oppresses black people and people of color. To me, this is bigger than football and it would be selfish on my part to look the other way." Kaepernick's Twitter feed at the time had curated a timeline of events that have found a place in the national discourse about race, politics and police behavior, including a protest by white supremacists in front of a National Association for the Advancement of Colored People (NAACP) headquarters in Houston, an article about how Arizona teenagers were forced by their school to change out of their Black Lives Matters shirts, and the fatal police shooting of an armed black man in Milwaukee. "There are bodies in the street and people getting paid leave and getting away with murder."[20]

The 49ers issued a statement about Kaepernick's refusal to stand: "The national anthem is and always will be a special part of the pre-game ceremony. It is an opportunity to honor our country and reflect on the great liberties we are afforded as its citizens. In respecting such American principles as freedom of religion and freedom of expression, we recognize the right of an individual to choose and participate, or not, in our celebration of the national anthem."[21] Then 49ers coach Chip Kelly told reporters that Kaepernick's decision not to stand during the national anthem is "his right as a citizen [and] it's not my right to tell him not to do something."[22] The NFL responded, "Players are encouraged but not required to stand during the playing of the national anthem."

Kaepernick went from sitting to kneeling during the anthem, and other NFL players around the League soon began taking a knee during the anthem. One month later, a kneeling Kaepernick was featured on the cover of Time magazine. Following the 2016 NFL season, in March 2017, Kaepernick opted out of the final year of his contract with the 49ers amidst speculation that the 49ers were planning to release him.

The 2017 season began without any team signing Kaepernick, but that didn't stop some NFL players from continuing to kneel during the anthem. On September 22, 2017, at a rally speech in Alabama, President Donald Trump told his supporters: "That's a total disrespect of our heritage. That's a total disrespect of everything that we stand for. Wouldn't you love to see one of these NFL owners, when somebody disrespects our flag, you'd say, 'Get that son of a bitch off the field right now. Out! He's fired!'" Two days later, in response to Trump's speech, more than 200 NFL players kneeled during the playing of the anthem before their games. Then, on October 10, Trump tweeted that the NFL should have suspended Kaepernick for kneeling in 2016.

Five days later, on October 15, 2017, Kaepernick filed a grievance against the NFL claiming that he was a victim of collusion, *i.e.*, two or more teams (or the league and at least one team) conspired not to sign him because of the controversy surrounding his kneeling during the playing of the anthem, which would violate the collective bargaining agreement. On August 30, 2018, an arbitrator denied the NFL's request to dismiss Kaepernick's collusion grievance and ruled that enough evidence exists to send the case to an arbitration hearing in which evidence will be presented and attorneys for each side will question witnesses who will testify under oath.

Kaepernick became the recipient of the 2017 *Sports Illustrated* Muhammad Ali Legacy Award. Lonnie Ali, the widow of Muhammad Ali, stated: "I am proud to be able to present this year's *SI* Muhammad Ali Legacy Award to Colin Kaepernick for his passionate defense of social justice and civil rights for all people. Like Muhammad, Colin is a man who stands on his convictions with confidence and courage, undaunted by the personal sacrifices he has had to make to have his message heard. He has used his celebrity and philanthropy to benefit some of our most vulnerable community members."[23] Kaepernick also received Amnesty International's highest honor, the Ambassador of Conscience award.

In May 2018, the NFL attempted to impose a policy that would have barred players from kneeling or sitting while on the sidelines during the anthem while also giving them the option of remaining in the locker room, but the policy was put on hold in July (after the Players Association filed a grievance challenging the NFL policy) to allow the league and Players Association to come to an agreement.

In September 2018, Kaepernick became one of the faces of Nike's 30th anniversary of the "Just Do It" campaign. The advertisement reads in white letters in front of a black-and-white portrait of Kaepernick: "Believe in something. Even if it means sacrificing everything." Nike's Vice President of Brand for North America told the media, "We believe Colin is one of the most inspirational athletes of this generation, who has leveraged the power of sport to help move the World forward. We wanted to energize its meaning and introduce 'Just Do It' to a new generation of athletes."[24]

1. Is it true that 49ers coach Chip Kelly did not have the "right to tell Kaepernick not to do something"? Would Chip Kelly ever say that about one of his college players while coaching at Oregon or UCLA?
2. Case Study 8-2 demonstrates the intersection of business, ethical, and legal issues. Apply the normative principles to the NFL's decision to unilaterally impose its anthem policy. Does it matter that the NFL is a private (non-governmental) employer?
3. If you were the executive director of the Players Association, how would you resolve this issue with the League? Should you investigate how many players in the union believe that it disrespects the flag to sit or kneel during the playing of the anthem?
4. Is Nike's decision to make Kaepernick the face of its anniversary ad campaign an ethical decision? Or was Nike's decision based purely on non-moral (amoral) values?

How could naming a race horse become an issue dealing with race and sports? It became an issue in the following case involving a horse owner who wanted to name his race horse, Sally Hemings.[25]

🔍 CASE STUDY 8-3   "What's in a Name?"

What's in a name? that which we call a rose
By any other name would smell as sweet;
So Romeo would, were he not Romeo call'd,
Retain that dear perfection which he owes
Without that title.
WILLIAM SHAKESPEARE, ROMEO AND JULIET, act 2, sc. 2.

"What's in a name?" To Garrett Redmond, who desired to name his thoroughbred race horse "Sally Hemings," everything is in the name. When the Jockey Club, acting on behalf of the Kentucky Horse Racing Authority (KHRA), denied his request to register his horse under that name, Mr. Redmond protested …

The KHRA is an independent state agency established by statute to "regulate the conduct of horse racing and parimutuel wagering on horse racing, and related activities within the Commonwealth of Kentucky." It has broad power over horse racing activities, including the "full authority to prescribe necessary and reasonable administrative regulations and conditions under which horse racing at a horse race meeting shall be conducted." One such regulation, pertinent to this case, is that "[n]o horse shall be entered or raced in this state unless duly registered and named in the Registry Office of the Jockey Club in New York."

The Jockey Club is the sole organization that registers and maintains records of thoroughbred horses in the United States, Canada, and Puerto Rico. It is a New York–based organization, established in 1894 and offering membership by invitation only, whose principal function is maintaining The American Stud Book Principal Rules and Requirements, which includes the universally-accepted rules and requirements for naming thoroughbred horses. Rule 6(A) states that "names will be assigned based upon availability and compliance with the naming rules as stated herein." Rule 6(F) identifies classes of names that are not eligible for use, including:

…Rule 6(F)(6): Names of persons, unless written permission to use their name is on file with the Jockey Club.
Rule 6(F)(7): Names of "famous" people no longer living, unless approval is granted by the Board of Stewards of the Jockey Club.
Rule 6(F)(8): Names of "notorious" people.
Rule 6(F)(13): Names that are suggestive or have a vulgar or obscene meaning; names considered in poor taste; or names that may be offensive to religious, political, or ethnic groups.

Rule 6(G) gives the Jockey Club Registrar the absolute right to approve all name requests. Rule 20 provides the applicant the right to a hearing, upon payment of a $1,000 non-refundable fee.

When Mr. Redmond submitted the name "Sally Hemings" for his yearling filly in February 2004, the Jockey Club rejected it. A lengthy correspondence ensued, culminating in a telephone call in which the Jockey Club's president, Alan Marzelli, informed Mr. Redmond that the name is "in poor taste and may be offensive to religious, political, or ethnic groups." Ultimately, Marzelli advised Mr. Redmond in writing that:

[T]he name 'Sally Hemings' is not eligible for use under Rule 6(F) of The Principal Rules and Requirements of The American Stud Book as the name is considered by this office to be in poor taste and a name that may be offensive to religious, political, or ethnic groups. . . . Furthermore, and as you are aware, the name of a 'famous' person no longer living is not eligible under Rule 6(F)(7), unless approval is granted by the Board of Stewards of The Jockey Club.

In short, because he has spent three years insisting that he has a constitutional right to name his horse "Sally Hemings" and that no other name will do, Mr. Redmond now finds himself, like the songster of the '70s, having "been through the desert on a horse with no name." If he really wants to race or breed this horse in Kentucky, Mr. Redmond will have to come up with a name that complies with the Jockey Club's rules. A quick look at the Jockey Club's Registry confirms that "Horse With No Name" is no longer available.

Dewey Bunnell, A Horse with No Name, on AMERICA (Warner Brothers 1972).

We note from outside the present record that Mr. Redmond's four-year-old filly made her racing debut on July 1, 2007, under the temporary name "Awaiting Justice," finishing fifth in a nine-horse field. See Churchill Downs Race Results, available at http://www.churchilldowns.com (last visited July 27, 2007); see also Jennie Rees, Filly's Name is Some Affair, Louisville (KY) Courier-Journal, June 30, 2007, available at http:// www.courier-journal. com (quoting Mr. Redmond as saying the name is "strictly temporary") (last visited July 27, 2007). Of course, the term "awaiting justice," being a temporary condition, would appear by its own implication to be necessarily temporary when used as a name.

Mr. Redmond appealed the decision to the Jockey Club Board of Stewards, objecting that it was arbitrary and unwarranted. The board rejected Mr. Redmond's arguments on appeal and concluded that the use of the name "may be offensive to persons of African descent and other ethnic groups, may be offensive to descendants of the specific people involved, may have negative historical implications, may have negative moral implications and may be degrading to ethnic groups and descendants of the people involved." The board also rejected the name based on the prohibition against using the names of "famous person[s] no longer living."[26]

1. Did the Jockey Club make an ethical decision in denying Mr. Redmond the use of his desired name for his race horse?
2. Should an organization such as the Jockey Club be allowed to set its own rules as long as they are legal and ethical?
3. What ethical problems do you see with the implementation of this rule?
4. How many racing fans do you believe know who Sally Hemings was?[27]

🔍 CASE STUDY 8-4 *Banning a Team Owner for Racist Remarks*

On April 25, 2014, *TMZ Sports* released a recording of a conversation between the Los Angeles Clippers owner Donald Sterling and his mistress. In the recording from September 2013, a man confirmed to be Sterling was irritate over a photo his mistress had posted on Instagram, in which she posed with Basketball Hall of Fame player Magic Johnson. Sterling told his mistress: "It bothers me a lot that you want to broadcast that you're associating with black people. Do you have to?"[28]

Sterling's comments promptly attracted substantial outrage. Clippers players protested by wearing their team jerseys inside out so as to obscure any team logo. Several companies terminated their sponsorship agreements with the Clippers. A number of NBA players publicly condemned his remarks and suggested the possibility of boycotting Clippers games.

On April 29, NBA Commissioner Adam Silver fined Sterling $2.5 million, the maximum fine allowed under the NBA constitution, and indefinitely banned him from having any involvement in the management or operation of the club. Sterling was stripped of all of his authority over the Clippers. He was banned from entering any Clippers facility and from attending any NBA games. The punishment was one of the most severe ever imposed on a professional sports team owner.

Do you consider the disciplinary action against Sterling to be a valid exercise of Commissioner Silver's authority to act in the "best interests of the NBA"? Assess whether it was an ethical decision, applying the normative principles.

In 2003, political commentator Rush Limbaugh was hired by ESPN as an NFL analyst. As an analyst he made the following comments regarding NFL quarterback Donovan McNabb:

> Sorry to say this, I don't think he's been that good from the get-go. . . . I think what we've had here is a little social concern in the NFL. The media has been very desirous that a black quarterback do well. There is a little hope invested in McNabb, and he got a lot of credit for the performance of this team that he didn't deserve. The defense carried this team.[29]

Limbaugh was forced to resign from ESPN because of his comments. In 2009, Limbaugh was considering becoming an owner in the St. Louis Rams NFL franchise. Some objected to his ownership because of his comments about McNabb, including the NFL Players Association's Executive Director DeMaurice Smith:

> I've spoken to the Commissioner [Roger Goodell] and I understand that this ownership consideration is in the early stages. But sport in America is at its best when it unifies, gives all of us reason to cheer, and when it transcends. Our sport does exactly that when it overcomes division and rejects discrimination and hatred.[30]

Do you believe it was appropriate for the players association to take a position on ownership of a league franchise?

🔍 CASE STUDY 8-5 *Baseball and Immigration*

Immigration, and specifically illegal immigration, is a tough political issue facing America. Many individuals and groups have differing viewpoints about immigration policy in the U.S. When the state of Arizona passed a controversial immigration bill that made failure to carry immigration documents a crime,[31] the MLB Players Association issued a statement saying the law perpetuated racial profiling.[32] St. Louis Cardinals Manager Tony La Russa, who doubles as an attorney, said he agreed with the law,[33] stating, "I'm actually a supporter of what Arizona is doing . . . If the national government doesn't fix your problem, you've got a problem. You've got to fix it yourself. That's just part of the American way."[34]

1. Should a players association take a stand on immigration or any political issue for that matter, or should it restrict its concerns to issues directly relating to its sport?
2. Were La Russa's comments inappropriate or is he allowed to state his position?

🔍 CASE STUDY 8-6 Interviewing Draft Prospects

In any job interview, an employer will certainly ask the prospective employee about his or her background to determine if the employee is a good fit for the company. The employer is entitled to do so within certain boundaries. The same is true in the sports industry with the same restrictions applicable. When potential draftee Dez Bryant was interviewed before the NFL draft by the Miami Dolphins, general manager Jeff Ireland asked Bryant several questions. One of the questions was whether Bryant's mother was a prostitute. Bryant's mother was only 15 when he was born, and she served time in jail for selling crack cocaine. In his defense, Ireland said, "My job is to find out as much information as possible about a player that I'm considering drafting. Sometimes that leads to asking in-depth questions. . . . Having said that, I talked to Dez Bryant and told him I used poor judgment in one of the questions I asked him. I certainly meant no disrespect and apologized to him."[35]

1. Was the interview "out of bounds" or was it legitimate, considering the amount of money NFL teams have to invest in their newly drafted players?
2. What other questions would you deem inappropriate by NFL teams to players during the interview process?
3. Should NFL teams be able to question players about their family history?
4. As an SMP, how would you handle this situation?
5. What racial overtones are present in case study 8-6?

John Rocker was a left-handed relief pitcher for the Atlanta Braves and became the "poster child" for insensitivity. If not for a *Sports Illustrated* interview, Rocker may have gone into the annals of baseball as just another relatively successful baseball relief pitcher. During the interview, he disparaged multiple races and nationalities and, as a result, was disciplined by the Commissioner of Baseball under the "best interests" clause of the MLB Constitution. Rocker was a fiery left-hander with a 100 mph fastball and a competitive attitude and he quickly developed into a star closer for the Atlanta Braves in the 1999 season. Rocker appeared on the scene very quickly for the Braves and soon developed a "friendly" rivalry with New York Mets fans. The Mets were the chief rival of the Braves in the Eastern Division of the National League. Mets fans jeered Rocker and he gave back as much as he got, sometimes working the crowd into a frenzy. His rivalry with Mets fans was well known throughout the League. Rocker was competitive, and it

showed in his playing style. New York fans are very enthusiastic and Rocker's antics would spur them to greater enthusiasm. Mets fans developed an ongoing feud with Rocker for most of the 1999 season as the Mets and Braves battled for the 1999 National League Championship (NLCS).

The Braves eventually prevailed over the Mets in the NLCS, 4 games to 2. Sports fans began to turn their attention to football, basketball, and hockey while ball players left to play golf and spend time with their families. John Rocker, like many other players, waited in anticipation for the next season to begin. Rocker was asked by *Sports Illustrated* writer Ron Pearlman for an interview and Rocker gave the interview as he drove around in his truck with Pearlman. Rocker was unaware of the impact the interview would have on his career, teammates, and the game of baseball. Rocker's interview with *Sports Illustrated* created a firestorm of controversy and initiated a very public debate about race relations and prejudice in America.

During the interview Rocker was asked a variety of questions and gave uncensored answers on a variety of "hot button" issues, some of which had little to do with baseball. The remarks that were published proved to be extremely controversial. In fairness to Rocker, he was promised by *Sports Illustrated* that some of his answers would be kept off the record, specifically his remarks concerning NBA player Latrell Sprewell.

⚖ CASE 8-3 In the Matter of Arbitration The Major League Baseball Players Association, Panel Decision No. 104, Grievance No. 2000-3, Player: John Rocker

Introduction

On January 31, 2000, Allan H. "Bud" Selig, the Commissioner of Baseball, imposed discipline on John Rocker, a pitcher for the Atlanta Braves, for having engaged in conduct not in the best interests of baseball. Selig specifically referred to "certain profoundly insensitive and arguably racist statements" made by Rocker that were reported in the December 27, 1999 issue of Sports Illustrated. Selig charged that: "Your comments in Sports Illustrated have harmed your reputation, have damaged the image and goodwill of Major League Baseball and the Atlanta Braves and have caused various other harms to the Club and the game."

John Rocker, who now is 25 years old, began his minor league career in the Braves' organization in 1994. During the 1998 season he was called up to the Braves' Major League team as a relief pitcher. In 1999 he became the Braves' closer. His pitching performance during the 1999 regular season and the post-season was outstanding.

During the 1999 season, a mutual and growing antagonism developed between Rocker and the fans at Shea Stadium, the home of the New York Mets, Atlanta's principal rival in the National League East. Mets' fans used abusive and profane language and gestures to taunt Rocker, and he responded in kind. Some, according to Rocker, also threw various objects at him. The ongoing feud received widespread coverage in the media. The situation was exacerbated by critical comments in the press about Rocker and comments he made to the press attacking Mets' fans.

The relationship between Rocker and the Mets' fans intensified after the Braves swept the Mets in a late September series at Shea. The two teams met again in the National League Championship Series. In the third game – the first in that series to be played at Shea – the Braves won 1-0, and Rocker saved the game. Following the game, when Rocker approached the Braves' dugout after doing some interviews, a large group of hostile Mets' fans threatened to surge down onto the field from behind the Braves' dugout. The fans verbally attacked Rocker and he responded in kind. MLB Director of Security Kevin Hallinan was present, and at the hearing he described the situation as being as bad as any he had seen in his fourteen years in baseball. In his view, only quick and effective action by the New York Police Department prevented the fans from physically assaulting Rocker.

Before the start of the fourth game of the NLCS, Hallinan arranged a meeting with Rocker, Braves' Manager Bobby Cox and Braves' General Manager John Schuerholz in which Hallinan expressed his security concerns and asked Rocker to show restraint. Rocker expressed his willingness to do so, and he testified that he did "tone it down" after that meeting. Nonetheless, when Rocker went out onto the field, Hallinan subsequently reported:

His appearance on the field triggered an immediate reaction by the Mets fans who loudly booed, and greeted him with obscenities and verbal abuse. Rocker responded by sticking out his tongue and yelling obscenities at the fans. He departed for the bullpen where he continued to engage in a verbal exchange of hostilities with New York Mets fans.

There were no further meetings or discussions with Rocker regarding his interaction with New York fans, either during the remainder of the NLCS with the Mets or during the World Series, which the Braves lost to the Yankees in four straight games. Rocker testified that he was hit with a battery at Yankee Stadium during the third game of the World Series, but there were no other major incidents with New York fans.

On December 12, 1999, Rocker was interviewed by a reporter for Sports Illustrated. Rocker had agreed to the interview ahead of time, to obtain publicity, and it was conducted in Atlanta where he resides. The reporter spent the better part of the day driving around with Rocker in his vehicle, as he went about his business. He recorded Rocker's comments. Rocker testified that he asked the reporter to keep certain remarks off the record and, with one exception, the reporter complied with his requests.

On December 22, 1999, the Sports Illustrated article first appeared on the magazine's website, and it later appeared in print. It landed like a bombshell, creating a huge nationwide furor, which had not abated by the time of the arbitration hearing in early February 2000. The statements which triggered the Commissioner's decision to discipline Rocker are contained in the following excerpts from the article, and Rocker does not dispute they accurately reflect what he said:

. . . "So many dumb asses don't know how to drive in this town," he says. . . . "They turn from the wrong lane. They go 20 miles per hour. It makes me want – Look! Look at this idiot! I guarantee you she's a Japanese woman." A Beige Toyota is jerking from lane to lane. The woman at the wheel is white. "How bad are Asian women at driving?"

JOHN ROCKER has opinions, and there's no way to sugar-coat them. They are politically incorrect, to say the least, and he likes to express them.

* On ever playing for a New York team: "I would retire first. It's the most hectic, nerve-racking city. Imagine having to take the [Number] 7 train to the ballpark, looking like you're [riding through] Beirut next to some kid with purple hair next to some queer with AIDS right next to some dude who just got out of jail for the fourth time right next to some 20-year-old mom with four kids. It's depressing."

* On New York City itself: "The biggest thing I don't like about New York are the foreigners. I'm not a very big fan of foreigners. You can walk an entire block in Times Square and not hear anybody speaking English. Asians and Koreans and Vietnamese and Indians and Russians and Spanish people and everything up there. How the hell did they get in this country?"

. . . In passing, he calls an overweight black teammate "a fat monkey." Asked if he feels any bond with New York Knicks guard Latrell Sprewell, notorious for choking coach P.J. Carlesimo two years ago, Rocker lets out a snarl of disgust. "That guy should've been arrested, and instead he's playing basketball," he says. "Why do you think that is? Do you think if he was Keith Van Horn – if he was white – they'd let him back? No way." Rocker is rarely tongue-tied when it comes to bashing those of a race or sexual orientation different from his. "I'm not a racist or prejudiced person," he says with apparent conviction. "But certain people bother me."

Immediately after publication of the article, the Braves issued a statement disassociating the Club from the viewpoints attributed to Rocker. In consultation with his agents, Rocker issued a public apology, in which he stated:

While I have evidenced strong competitive feelings about New York fans in the past, and take responsibility for things I have said publicly, including the Sports Illustrated article, I recognize that I have gone way too far in my competitive zeal. I want everybody to understand that my emotions fuel my competitive desire. They are a source of energy for me, however I have let my emotions get the best of my judgment and have said things which, when read with cold, hard logic, are unacceptable to me and to my country. Even though it might appear otherwise from what I've said, I am not a racist. I should not have said what I did because it is not what I believe in my heart.

I was angry and basically firing back at the people of New York. It is time to stop this process.

I fully intend to learn from this experience. Everyone makes mistakes and I hope everyone can put this aside and begin with a fresh start in the 2000 season.

I am contrite.

Commissioner Selig testified that when he read the article he was "stunned" and "shocked". After deliberating with other MLB officials and conferring with the Braves' management, he made the decision to impose the discipline challenged in this grievance. He testified that he based his decision on several factors, including his belief that "all of us in Major League Baseball have a social responsibility". As he stated in his news release announcing the discipline:

Major League Baseball takes seriously its role as an American institution and the important social responsibility that goes with it, said Selig. We will not dodge our responsibility. Mr. Rocker should understand that his remarks offended practically every element of society and brought dishonor to himself, the Atlanta Braves and Major League Baseball.

The terrible example set by Mr. Rocker is not what our great game is about and, in fact, is a profound breach of the social compact we hold in such high regard.

The Commissioner also took into account security concerns and reports from the Atlanta Club that the controversy spawned by Rocker's remarks was affecting its business and the community. On January 5, 2000 the Atlanta City Council unanimously adopted a resolution condemning Rocker's remarks. A coalition of community organizations, many representing groups that were maligned by Rocker's remarks, as well as other individuals (including Jesse Jackson) and groups, demanded swift and decisive action by the Braves and the Commissioner. The Commissioner received literally thousands of communications condemning and, in some instances, defending Rocker's remarks. Many of these communications, while disapproving of Rocker's words, opposed disciplining him on free speech grounds. The Commissioner stressed that the controversy engendered by Rocker's remarks was all that "people want to talk about" with him, and was detracting from his efforts to "move baseball forward".

Matter of Arbitration The Major League Baseball Players Association, Panel Decision No. 104, Grievance No. 2000-3, Player: John RockerSha.

Tested in this case was the extent to which a league commissioner may discipline a player for pure speech, off the field, on the basis that it affects the best interests of baseball. It is undisputed that negative racial comments reinforce racist stereotypes that demean not only the athletes but also the sports they play. In his *Sports Illustrated* interview, John Rocker uttered insensitive and racist statements. The punishment by the Commissioner of Baseball was partially based on the damage that Rocker's statements did to "the image and goodwill of MLB." Is that a sufficient reason for the Commissioner to act? One can argue that Rocker was provoked by fans some three months before the interview. Should this alleged provocation mitigate the punishment he received from the Commissioner? The Commissioner's suspension of Rocker and the amount of the fines were reduced by the arbitrator so that Rocker only lost two weeks of the season and paid only a $500 fine, which was the maximum fine allowed under the League Constitution for off-field behavior deemed not in the best interest of baseball. Was this a just and fair penalty or was it too lenient or too harsh?

Eleven-time NBA All-Star Allen Iverson, a.k.a. "Jewelz," doubled as a rapper and issued a song "40 Bars," which included the following lyrics: "Get murdered in a second in the first degree; / Come to me with faggot tendencies; / You'll be sleeping where the maggots be . . . ; / Die reaching for heat, leave you leaking in the street; / [n-word] screaming he was a good boy ever since he was born; / But fuck it he gone; / Life must go on; / [n-word] don't live that long." After the song's release, many civil rights groups, gay and lesbian groups, as well as NBA Commissioner David Stern, voiced displeasure with Iverson, his musical career, and his controversial lyrics. The commissioner strongly encouraged Iverson to rewrite the song in a less offensive tone, which he did. What actions, if any, should have been taken against Iverson for his controversial lyrics?[36] Does the fact that it happened "off the court" make a difference?

🔍 CASE STUDY 8-7 *Coach Bill Parcels and Secret Plays*

There is no doubt Bill Parcels is an excellent football coach and a motivator of players. He is a proven product in NFL circles. He was always admired for his ability to find unique ways to get the most out of his players. However, he was forced to apologize after making the following statement when talking to reporters during his team's mini-camp in 2007, "No disrespect for the Orientals, but what we call Jap plays. OK. Surprise things."[37] John Tateishi of the Japanese-American Citizens' League, a national civil rights group said "Unfortunately, he [Parcels] is ignorant about racial slurs. I take great offense by what he said. Parcels ought to know better. He sorely needs more education on what is offensive and non-offensive to Japanese-Americans. I am shocked that he would say this."[38]

1. Should the NFL have suspended Parcels for his comments?
2. Should there be a different standard for coaches/owners than players for this type of conduct?

Baseball club owner Marge Schott seemed to say the first thing that popped into her head. She was the first woman to own and operate an MLB team, the Cincinnati Reds. Schott was forced out of baseball temporarily because she embarrassed fellow owners and the game of baseball with her continued use of offensive racial and ethnic slurs. Why Marge Schott was commenting on Adolf Hitler is still a mystery but she did make the following statement about Hitler: "Everything you read, when he came [to power] he was good. . . . They built tremendous highways and got all the factories going. . . . Everybody knows he was good at the beginning but he just went too far."[39] Schott's remarks drew a $25,000 fine and a one-year suspension from baseball. Was the punishment for Schott meted out by the Commissioner appropriate?

🔍 CASE STUDY 8-8 *Stephen Jackson and the NBA Dress Code*

In 2005, the NBA announced the NBA dress code. The NBA excluded certain items:
"The following is a list of items that players are not allowed to wear at any time while on team or league business:
- Sleeveless shirts
- Shorts

- T-shirts, jerseys, or sports apparel (unless appropriate for the event (*e.g.*, a basketball clinic), team-identified, and approved by the team)
- Headgear of any kind while a player is sitting on the bench or in the stands at a game, during media interviews, or during a team or league event or appearance (unless appropriate for the event or appearance, team-identified, and approved by the team)
- Chains, pendants, or medallions worn over the player's clothes
- Sunglasses while indoors
- Headphones (other than on the team bus or plane, or in the team locker room)"[40]

Indiana Pacers guard Stephen Jackson contended that a league ban on chains worn over clothing was a "racist statement" from the NBA. He described the jewellery ban as "attacking young black males." He said, "I think it's a racist statement because a lot of the guys who are wearing chains are my age and are black," said Jackson, 27.

> I wore all my jewellery today to let it be known that I'm upset with it. . . .
>
> I'll wear a suit every day. I think we do need to look more professional because it is a business. A lot of guys have gotten sloppy with the way they dress. But, it's one thing to [enforce a] dress code and it's another thing if you're attacking cultures, and that's what I think they're doing.[41]

> Do you consider the NBA's ban on chains a racist statement from the NBA? While the dress code is not discriminatory on its face because it is race-neutral, one could argue that the ban on chains is drawing a connection between misbehavior and dress culture. One could also argue that the dress code has a discriminatory impact. Certainly, some adornments are associated with young males and are particular to certain ethnic, racial, or religious groups. Should the NBA have negotiated this issue with the Players Association first?[42]

Spike Lee, filmmaker and New York Knicks season ticket holder, supported the dress code 100 percent. Lee said: "If I was employed by an NBA team, I would have on a suit and tie . . . When you work in corporate America, you can't come to work with a do-rag, bling-bling, and what not . . . When you watch the NBA Draft . . . when their name gets called and they come on the stage and they shake David Stern's hand, what are they wearing? Suit and tie. I just think we've got to get back to some of the fundamentals."[43]

▶ Race and Amateur Sports

Many racial issues are prevalent in youth and amateur sports as well[44]—the following cases and case studies explore issues dealing with violence based on race, racial issues in college and high school sports, and ethical dilemmas involving race with coaches.

🔍 CASE STUDY 8-9 *Olympic Protests*

John Carlos and Tommie Smith were exceptional athletes. At the 1968 Olympics in Mexico City, Carlos won the bronze medal in the 200-meter race and Smith took home the gold medal. When they received their medals on the Olympic victory podium, they stood with heads bowed and black gloves thrust skyward, signaling a "Black Power" salute, as the U.S. National Anthem was played. The event created a firestorm of controversy and is one of the more historic moments in Olympic history. "The two said they would make a token gesture . . . to protest racial discrimination in the United States."[45] Smith and Carlos were suspended by the United States Olympic Committee (USOC) for making the black power salute on the victory stand during the playing of the national anthem. And the International Olympic Committee (IOC) banned them for life.

Smith later said he prayed on the victory stand that he would not be shot. Both athletes were booed by the audience and both received over a hundred death threats for their Olympic protest. Smith and Carlos are alumni of San Jose State University. In 2005, a 20-foot sculpture honoring Smith and Carlos was unveiled on campus.

1. Apply the normative principles to the decisions of the USOC and IOC.
2. Consider the manner, place, and time to make such a protest. Is this protest comparable to Colin Kaepernick's protest in Case Study 8-2?

As the next case study demonstrates, regulating non-disruptive speech of college and high school athletes at public institutions raises business, ethical, and legal issues, including First Amendment issues.

🔍 *CASE STUDY 8-10   Banning Displays of Activism While Players Are in Uniform*

In August 2018, after three cheerleaders knelt during the national anthem to protest police brutality, the Southern Illinois University (SIU) Athletics Department quickly decided to ban any kind of displays of activism while players are in their uniforms. The following provision was added to the SIU athletic code of conduct:

It is a privilege and not a right to be a student-athlete, cheerleader, or spirit member at Southern Illinois University (SIU). Members of the department, including student-athletes, cheerleaders and spirit members, must remain neutral on any issue political in nature when wearing SIU official uniforms and when competing/performing in official department of athletics events and activities. Any display (verbal or non-verbal) of activism (either for or against) a political issue will not be tolerated and may result in dismissal from the program.[46]

The Executive Senior Associate Athletics Director at SIU said it doesn't matter what the political issue is; it doesn't belong on the field. "What we're saying is in regard to any political issue—we are taking neither a for or against stance when we are wearing the colors of Saluki Athletics." The Director further said their goal is not to violate players' rights but to create a feeling of inclusion for all people. "This is about unity, forward progress, and respect and dignity for everyone. And we do support all of our student-athletes and whatever their passions."[47]

However, the American Civil Liberties Union (ACLU) viewed it differently. In response to a request for the ACLU's position on the constitutionality of the revised student code of conduct, the ACLU Illinois Director of Communications and Public Policy wrote:

Southern Illinois University's new policy suggesting that players or cheerleaders could be removed from their respective program for peaceful 'displays of activism' falls short of the critical responsibility of a public university to honor and protect free speech rights for their students. It is more troubling that the policy specifically suggests that such displays will not be tolerated on 'a political issue.' A central purpose for any public university is to engage students and the community in the issues of our time.[48]

Within days, the SIU Athletics Department completely reversed course and issued the following statement:

We have heard a great deal of feedback, both positive and negative, on the proposed addition to the SIU Student Athlete Handbook. The purpose of the addition was to display unity and to provide a positive experience for our student-athletes and Saluki fans. However, some have interpreted the language to suggest that our aim was to restrict the free speech rights of our students. That was never our intent. We fully support the free expression of ideas and opinions among our students and the entire Saluki family.

Given the community feedback, it appears that we somewhat missed the mark. We will revisit the language and do not plan to use it as currently written. Instead, we will work with our student-athletes to turn the language into a positive values statement related to the focus and purpose of athletics. We are grateful to all of those who have reached out with constructive feedback. All input helps us to do our best.[49]

In November 2015, dozens of black players on the University of Missouri football team initiated the most high-profile racism protest to date. In response to instances of racism directed at black students and a lack of action from administrators that the students contended had created an intolerable atmosphere on campus, the players announced on a Saturday that they would boycott all football-related activities, including games, until the University President either stepped down or was removed. As outsiders queried whether the players were violating their scholarship terms by refusing to practice and play, the players didn't care; it was clear that they believed it to be a human rights issue and that they were in a position to affect the outcome. On the following Monday, the University President resigned.

Many universities have changed their team names or mascots in response to pressure exerted by the NCAA. Stanford University renamed its team from the Indians to the Cardinals and Marquette University changed from the Warriors to the Golden Eagles. The Washington Wizards in the NBA were originally the Bullets. The Houston Astros were called the Colt .45's from 1962 to 1965. In August 2005,

the NCAA approved a policy that "prohibits NCAA colleges and universities from displaying hostile and abusive racial/ethnic/national origin mascots, nicknames or imagery at any of the 88 NCAA championships" and stated that any school using a Native American mascot would be prevented from hosting future postseason events. Major college football is not affected because there is no official NCAA tournament. The NCAA later announced that approval from American Indian tribes would be a primary factor in giving approval for schools that wanted to use Native American nicknames and mascots in postseason play. Florida State University sought approval from two Seminole groups to use their name for university sports teams. The NCAA subsequently removed these names from the list of banned mascots and team names.[50] What are the ethical issues that arise from the use of Native American mascots?

The next case involves racial taunting and racially stereotypical costumes at a high school basketball game. As you read the court's decision, think about what the school district did right and wrong and how the offending students should be punished.

⚖ CASE 8-4 *Malcom v. Novato United States School District*

2002 WL 31770392

On February 13, 1998, San Marin hosted a basketball game against Tamalpais High School (Tam). Malcolm and Eaton are members of the Tam basketball team. Both are African-American. Prior to the start of the game, a group of approximately 12 to 20 San Marin students arrived at the game dressed in costumes.

Though the exact description of the costumes varies, at least one student was wearing a "black afro wig" and some had on face paint.

While the Tam players were on the gym floor warming up, they heard unknown individuals chanting "[the n-word]." The chant was emanating from the direction of the costumed students. At first the players were unable to discern what was being chanted, but eventually they determined the group was chanting this racial slur. The players reported the chanting to their coach, who instructed them to return to the locker room. The coach reported the incident to Tam Assistant Principal Peg Regan, who reported the incident to San Marin Assistant Principal William Stiveson. Stiveson discussed the chant with the San Marin students and no further group chanting was heard during the game. Later in the game, however, a San Marin fan did yell the same racial slur at an African-American Tam player. The referee heard the shout and spoke with the Tam player and to a San Marin coach about the epithet. The players also saw a swastika drawn in pencil in the boys' bathroom next to the gym, and a San Marin student threatened to kill a Jewish student and his family. The players were also taunted in the parking lot after the game, although the taunts did not include racial slurs.

When Stiveson was told at the game that San Marin fans were chanting the racial slur, he first claimed that the students were chanting "digger, digger digger." Nonetheless, he later confronted the fans sitting in the area from which the slur had emanated and told them of the allegation. The students denied chanting the slur and said that they were chanting "Yanger" for one of San Marin's players, Nick Yang. Yanger was a common chant at San Marin basketball games. Stiveson also inquired of a member of the NUSD Board of Trustees whether he had heard the chant, but the board member said that he had not. Stiveson also told Tassano about the allegation.

The next day, Stiveson and Tassano began their own investigation and received additional information from Tam Principal Ralph Gold. Stiveson and Tassano met with a number of students, including some of the students in the cheering section at the game, other students who attended the game and members of the basketball team, and encouraged them to come forward with any information regarding the chanting of the racial slur at the game. Stiveson and Tassano also discussed the matter with Officer John McCarthy, the school's resource officer who was present at the game, and Phillips and Whitburn, all of whom denied hearing the slur. Tassano held an emergency staff meeting to discuss the allegations and to gather information about the event. On February 25, 1998, Tassano forwarded a letter to Tam in which he apologized on behalf of San Marin for the incidents at the game. He also held two meetings with members of Tam's staff and its basketball team to apologize for the incident. On February 27, 1998, Stiveson issued an announcement to the student body, referencing the February 13th game, in which he reminded all students of the importance of sportsmanship and respect towards opposing teams and their fans. Approximately five weeks later, Whitburn informed Stiveson of a student who had admitted to using a racial slur at the game. Stiveson met with the student and suspended him for five days.

The NUSD received a complaint from Peg Regan about 10 days after the game. A subsequent complaint was received from a parent of a Tam student. Regan's complaint was referred to Michael Watenpaugh, the assistant superintendent, for investigation. Watenpaugh completed his investigation into the allegations and issued his report by March 27, 1998. Watenpaugh's investigation consisted of two interviews with Peg Regan; two interviews with Mike Evans, the Tam coach at the game; two interviews with Ralph Wilson, another Tam coach at the game; individual interviews with eight Tam basketball players who attended the game; an interview with Jeff Stewart, the referee who officiated the game; two interviews with Tassano; two interviews with Stiveson; two interviews with John Baker, the San Marin custodian responsible for removing the graffiti; individual interviews with six San Marin students who were seated in the area from which the slur emanated; an interview with Whitburn; and an interview with Phillips. He also reviewed various photographs and a videotape recording of the game. Based upon this investigation, he made a number of findings, including that the Tam players had heard the racial slur while warming up for the game and that Stiveson had mishandled the complaint once advised by Regan. Watenpaugh made eight recommendations regarding review and revision of the board's policies for workshops for staff and administrators concerning complaints of racial and sexual harassment. Based upon Watenpaugh's findings, [Stivenson was] issued a formal reprimand . . . for having mishandled the situation initially and reminded Stiveson of the procedure by which he was to handle complaints of racial harassment in the future.

Concurrent with Watenpaugh's investigation, Joel Montero, another NUSD employee, met with the staff at San Marin to discuss the February 13th game. He stressed the importance of affording the students, personnel, and any visitors to the district a harassment-free environment and the importance of the staff's role in ensuring such an environment. He also discussed the district's antidiscrimination and harassment policy and conducted a workshop on dealing with discrimination and harassment complaints. Montero conducted a similar meeting with administrators in the district. Montero also planned a meeting between 15 Tam students and 15 San Marin students that was facilitated by a consultant with the Association of California School Administrators. Finally, Montero forwarded to Regan a letter on behalf of the district apologizing for the incident. A letter was also sent to parents in the district to inform them of the district's response to the allegation and to draw them into the efforts to ensure racial sensitivity throughout the district.

At an NUSD board meeting in May 1998, racism within the district was discussed. Members of the community addressed the board and school officials regarding their concerns about the handling of racial issues. The community was informed of a nine-point plan by the district to address racial issues in the future, including a zero-tolerance policy focusing on the responsibility of teachers and administrators to change attitudes within the district and a review of district hiring policies to attract a diverse staff.

Finally, in responding to this incident, the NUSD formed a diversity advisory committee made up of parents, administrators, and members of the community. This group was to provide recommendations on how to address issues of discrimination. In July 1998, the committee held a two-day retreat dealing with issues related to racism and diversity.

In October 1998, the NUSD adopted a policy expressing its expectations of student behavior and the responsibility of the district to protect students' rights to avoid hate crimes and racism. The policy was derived from California Department of Education publications.

In November 1998, the district adopted an equity action plan, designed to stop discrimination before it starts by teaching civility and acceptance. It provides for workshops to train teachers and school employees to confront prejudice. The plan was developed at the retreat of the diversity advisory committee and fine-tuned by the board. Also in November, an all-day diversity training workshop was held for staff and members of the community. In December 1998, the board approved distribution of "respect guidelines" to all students in the district.

1. Was an ethical decision-making process employed by NUSD?
2. Did NUSD perform a satisfactory investigation?
3. What could NUSD have done better to ensure that this situation does not occur again?
4. Did assistant principal William Stiveson do enough to investigate and handle this matter?

Malcolm W. v. Novato Unified School District, U.S. Supreme Court.

In Case 8-5, a collegiate basketball coach had the idea that his use of the n-word during a half-time speech would motivate his players to perform better on the court. He was fired and claimed the termination violated his First Amendment rights to free speech and academic freedom.

⚖ CASE 8-5 Dambrot v. Central Michigan University

55 F.3d 1177 (6th Cir. 1995)

On May 12, 1991, [Keith] Dambrot became the head coach of the Central Michigan University men's basketball team ... This lawsuit arises from events which occurred during the 1992–93 men's basketball season.

The 1992 CMU men's basketball team was made up of eleven African Americans and three Caucasians. The team's full-time coaching staff included two assistant coaches, Derrick McDowell (an African American) and Barry Markwart (a Caucasian). The part-time coaching staff included one voluntary graduate assistant, Chip Wilde (a Caucasian), three managers (all Caucasian), and a professional trainer (a Caucasian).

In January of 1993, Dambrot used the "[n-word]" during a locker room session with his players and coaching staff either during the halftime or at the end of a basketball game in which the team lost to Miami University of Ohio. According to Dambrot's testimony, Dambrot told the players they hadn't been playing very hard and then said "Do you mind if I use the N word?" After one or some of the players apparently indicated it was okay, Dambrot said "you know we need to have more [n-word] on our team ... Coach McDowell is a [n-word],...Sand[er] Scott who's an academic All-American, a Caucasian, I said Sand[er] Scott is a [n-word]. He's hard nose, [sic] he's tough, et cetera." He testified he intended to use the term in a "positive and reinforcing" manner. The players often referred to each other using the N-word during games and around campus and in the locker room. Dambrot stated he used the word in the same manner in which the players used the term amongst themselves, "to connote a person who is fearless, mentally strong and tough."

Prior to the January incident, the record shows Dambrot had used the N-word on at least one other occasion. In November, Dambrot apparently addressed the team after a practice and said he wanted the players to "play like [n-word] on the court" and wished he had more [n-word] on the basketball court. He then said he did not want the team to act like [n-word] in the classroom. When asked why he made these statements Dambrot stated:

Well, that's really a very easy question for me to answer, because we had had an incident early in the year where we had five or six basketball players, some of our bigger kids on our team, in a math class. And our kids were aggressive, tough, you know, a little bit loud, abrasive. And the lady was intimidated, because it was the first year that she ever had taught. And they almost got kicked out of the math class. A matter of fact, Dave Keilitz, myself, Pat Podoll, Doug Nance, who is the faculty rep, and then the head of the department,-I don't remember his name-the math department, met and discussed the situation. And it was my feeling that you can't be aggressive, tough, hard-nosed, abrasive in class, or you're going to get thrown out of classes, especially at a school like Central Michigan where the faculty members don't understand a lot about black people or have many black people in class. And I think our players understood what I meant by, "Don't be [n-word] in the classroom."

The news Dambrot had used the N-word in the locker room incident became known to persons outside the basketball team. In February 1993, Keilitz interviewed members of the men's basketball team at Dambrot's request. Keilitz reported all the African American players he interviewed said they were not offended by the coach's use of the term. At some point after those interviews, a former member of the men's basketball team, Shannon Norris, complained to the university's affirmative action officer, Angela Haddad, regarding Dambrot's use of the N-word during the November incident. The affirmative action officer confronted Dambrot who admitted using the word but stated he used it in a positive manner. The officer viewed Dambrot's use of the word as a violation of the university's discriminatory harassment policy and recommended Dambrot be disciplined. Dambrot accepted the proposed disciplinary action in lieu of a more formal investigation and was suspended without pay for five days.

News of the locker room incident spread through the campus after Dambrot was suspended. An article in the student newspaper was printed in which Dambrot told his side of the story. The statement was characterized by the district court as "considerably more explanatory and defensive than apologetic in tone." Students staged a demonstration and local, regional, and national news media reported accounts of the incident at CMU.

On April 12, 1993, Keilitz, the athletic director, informed Dambrot he would not be retained as head coach for the 1993–94 season. The university stated that it believed Dambrot was no longer capable of effectively leading the men's basketball program.

Dambrot instituted a lawsuit on April 19, 1993, alleging … he was fired because he used the term "[n-word]," and the termination violated his First Amendment rights to free speech and academic freedom. Several members of the basketball team joined the lawsuit …

Dambrot's use of the N-word is even further away from the marketplace of ideas and the concept of academic freedom because his position as coach is somewhat different from that of the average classroom teacher. Unlike the classroom teacher whose primary role is to guide students through the discussion and debate of various viewpoints in a particular discipline, Dambrot's role as a coach is to train his student athletes how to win on the court. The plays and strategies are seldom up for debate. Execution of the coach's will is paramount. Moreover, the coach controls who plays and for how long, placing a disincentive on any debate with the coach's ideas which might have taken place.

While Dambrot argues and we accept as true that he intended to use the term in a positive and reinforcing manner, Dambrot's total message to the players is disturbing. Corey Henderson, one of the players on the 1992–93 team touched on the concern in his deposition testimony.

Question: What did that phrasing that he had wanted you to play like [n-word] on the basketball floor but not be [n-word] in the classroom mean to you as a students? [sic]

Answer: I really am not sure. Because in the context he was trying to use it in, I mean, [n-word] I guess as a-he wanted us-I guess he wanted us to play harder, I suppose, and I didn't understand why if it was good enough on the court then why it wasn't good enough in the classroom.

I mean, I was kind of shocked that he used that word being a coach and all because he-I didn't think that was appropriate for him to use that word, him or any coach, talking to a group of mostly young adult black males. I didn't think it was right for him to use that word.

But then I was kind of disgusted when he said not being one in the classroom. I didn't understand why it was good enough on the court but not good enough in the classroom.

1. How should the Athletic Director at Central Michigan have handled the situation?
2. Does it make any difference that all 11 black players on the team supported the coach and joined him in the lawsuit against Central Michigan?
3. As an SMP, what kind of training would you have implemented for the coach or the team to ensure this never occurs again?

Dambrot v. Central Michigan University, U.S. Supreme Court.

In 1998, Dambrot became the Head Coach at St. Vincent–St. Mary High School in Akron, Ohio. He was there for three seasons and during the last two years, future NBA star LeBron James was on his squad and they won two consecutive state championships. Before playing for Dambrot, James had met with him and followed up on the incident at Central Michigan. In his book, *Shooting Stars*, James said he did not believe Dambrot was a racist. In 2001, Dambrot was hired as an assistant coach by the University of Akron, which competes against Central Michigan in the Mid-American Conference, and became the head coach three years later. Dambrot left Akron after thirteen seasons as the winningest coach in school history with a 305-139 record. At the end of the 2017 season, he left Akron to become the head coach at Duquesne University.

▶ Summary

Distributive justice demands that minorities be hired for coaching and management positions on the basis of their qualifications. To close this chapter, key excerpts are provided from the Executive Summary of the 2016 Report Card produced by the Institute for Diversity and Ethics in Sports at the University of Central Florida. What are your overall impressions of the data?

The 2016 Racial and Gender Report Card: College Sport[51]

Orlando, FL . . . April 6, 2017—The 2016 College Sport Racial and Gender Report Card (CSRGRC) showed the record of the National Collegiate Athletic Association and its member institutions for gender hiring practices, racial hiring practices, and the combined grade.

College Sport received a C+ for racial hiring practices by earning 78.5 points, a decrease from 83.6 points in the 2015 CSRGRC. College sport was the only area covered to have below a B for racial hiring practices.

Lapchick noted, "Opportunities for coaches of color continued to be a significant area of concern in all divisions. For the 2016 season, 86.1 percent of Division I, 88.1 percent of Division II, and 91.7 percent of Division III men's coaches were white. On the women's side, whites held 84.5 percent, 87.5 percent, and 91.6 percent in Divisions I, II, and III, respectively. The lack of opportunity for African-Americans as head coaches increased in 2015-16. African-Americans held 7.7 percent, 4.3 percent, and 4.7 percent of the men's head coaching positions in Divisions I, II, and III, respectively.

Whites made up 84.2 percent, 91.9 percent, and 95.1 percent of basketball, football, and baseball head coaching positions, respectively, in all divisions combined during 2015-2016.

In men's Division I basketball, 20.8 percent of all head coaches were African-American, which was down 1.5 percentage points from the 22.3 percent reported in the 2014–2015 season. Moreover, it is down 4.4 percentage points from the all-time high of 25.2 percent reported in the 2005–2006 season. In all, 23.2 percent of the Division I men's basketball coaches were coaches of color, which is 0.6 percent less than in 2015.

For Division I women's basketball, African-American women head coaches held 10.9 percent of the positions in 2015–2016 and African-American men held 5.9 percent of the positions in 2015–2016 for a combined percentage of 16.8 percent. This was an increase from the 15.1 percent reported in 2014–2015. As in other sports, the 10.9 percent African-American women head coaches stood in stark contrast to the 45.4 percent of the African-American women student-athletes who played basketball.

The number of head football coaches of color at the FBS level remained at 16 in 2016, the same as in the 2015 report. Nearly 88 percent were white.

Whites held the overwhelming percent of the decision-making athletics director positions during the 2015–2016 year at 87.6 percent, 89.4 percent, and 93.6 percent in Divisions I, II, and III, respectively.

Report Highlights for 2016

University Leadership Positions at Football Bowl Subdivision Institutions

- 89.1 percent (114) of FBS university presidents were white. There were six African-American presidents, four Asian presidents, and four Latino presidents. There were no Native-American university presidents.
- The number of athletics directors of color at FBS schools increased from 17 in 2015 to 18 in 2016.

Conference Commissioners

- Nine (90.0 percent) of the ten Football Bowl Subdivisions (FBS), formerly known as Division I-A, conference commissioners were white men. One (ten percent) of the FBS conference commissioners was a white woman. There has never been a person of color who held the commissioner position for an FBS conference.
- Looking at all Division I conferences, excluding Historically Black Conferences, 28 of 30 commissioners were white.

Student-Athletes

- Of all student-athletes in Division I football at the FBS level during the 2016 year, 53.8 percent were African-Americans, 41.3 percent were white, 2.4 percent were Latinos, Asian/Pacific Islanders represented 2.5 percent, and 0.1 percent of male Division I football student-athletes were classified as "other."
- Of the total student-athletes in all of Division I football, 43.8 percent were African-Americans, 42.6 percent were white, Latinos were 2.8 percent, Asian/Pacific Islanders represented 1.8 percent and Native-Americans represented 0.4 percent. Student-athletes identified as two or more races or "other" totaled 8.1 percent.
- Of the total student-athletes in Division I men's basketball, white athletes accounted for 26.8 percent and African-Americans accounted for 54.8 percent.[52]

▶ # References

1. Kenneth Shropshire, *In Black and White: Race and Sports in America*, (NYU Press, 1998).
2. William C. Rhoden, *Forty Million Dollar Slaves* (New York: Three Rivers Press, 2006); Shaun Powell, *Souled Out? How Blacks Are Winning and Losing in Sports* (Champaign, IL; Human Kinetics, 2008).
3. Amy Bass, *In the Game* (New York: Palgrave Macmillan, 2005).
4. Robert L. Hayman and Michael J. Cozzillio, *Sports & Inequality* (Durham, NC: Carolina Academic Press, 2005), 111.
5. Stuart L. Weiss, *The Curt Flood Story: The Man Behind the Myth (Sports and American Culture Series)*, (University of Missouri, 1st ed., 2007).
6. Richard Carter, *Curt Flood: The Way It Is* (New York: Trident Press, 1971).
7. Matt Spetalnick, "Bush: History will Judge if Bonds is True Home-Run King," *Reuters*, August 8, 2007. William C. Rhoden, "In Aaron's View, Bonds is Home Run King," *The New York Times*, February 15, 2009.
8. William Ladson, "Q&A with Hank Aaron," *The Sporting News*, April 8, 1999.
9. J. Gordon Hylton, "American Civil Rights Law and the Legacy of Jackie Robinson," *Marquettte Sports Law Journal* 8, no. 2 (1990): 387–399; Jules Tygiel, *Baseball's Great Experiment: Jackie Robinson* (New York: Oxford University Press, 2008).
10. Steven A. Riess, *Major Problems in American Sport History: Documents and Essays, edited by*, Thomas G. Paterson, Boston, MA: Houghton Mifflin Company, 1974) 373 citing to Jack R. Robinson and Wendell Smith, *Jackie Robinson: My Own Story* (New York: Greenberg, 1948), 65–68, 70–75, 79–80.
11. Craig R. Coenen, *From Sandlots to the Super Bowl: The National Football League, 1920–1967* (University of Tennessee Press, 2005) p. 91.
12. Arnd Kruger and William Murray, *The Nazi Olympics* (Champaign, IL: University of Illinois Press, 2003).
13. Walter T. Champion Jr., "The O.J. Trial as a Metaphor for Racism in Sports," *Thurgood Marshall Law Review* 33 (Fall 2007).
14. Rick Swaine, *The Integration of Major League Baseball* (Jefferson, NC; McFarland & Company, 2006). Lawrence D. Hogan, *Shades of Glory: The Negro Leagues and the Story of African-American Baseball* (Washington, DC: National Geographic Society, January 31, 2006).
15. Angela Lumpkin, Sharon Kay Stoll and Jennifer M. Beller, *Practical Ethics in Sport Management* (Jefferson, NC: McFarland & Company, Inc., 2012) p. 26.
16. Modified from David Barron, "Fighting Against Racial Slights," *Houston Chronicle*, January 16, 2005.
17. "Was This Their Freedom Ride?" *S.I. Vault*, January 18, 1965.
18. Ira Berkow, "The Case of Hodges v. the NBA.," *The New York Times*, December 25, 1996.
19. Ira Berkow, "The Case of Hodges v. the NBA.," *The New York Times*, December 26, 1996.
20. Steve Wyche, "Colin Kaepernick Explains Why He Sat During National Anthem," *NFL.com*, August 27, 2016.
21. Ibid.
22. Ibid.
23. A.J. Perez, "Colin Kaepernick Selected 'Sports Illustrated' Muhammad Ali Legacy Award Winner," *USA Today*, November 30, 2017.
24. Lorenzo Reyes, "Colin Kaepernick Featured in Nike's 'Just Do It' 30th Anniversary Ad," *USA Today*, September 3, 2018.
25. Annette Gordon-Reed, *Thomas Jefferson and Sally Hemings: An American Controversy* (University of Virginia Press, 1998); Redmond v. The Jockey Club, C.A. 6 (Ky.), 2007.
26. Plaintiff-Appellant V THE JOCKEY CLUB; COMMONWEALTH OF KENTUCKY; KENTUCKY HORSE RACING AUTHORITY, U.S. Supreme Court.

27. Peter Nicolaisen, "Thomas Jefferson, Sally Hemings, and the Question of Race: An Ongoing Debate," *Journal of American Studies*, Vol. 37, Issue 01, May 8, 2003, pp. 99–118.
28. John Branch, "NBA Bars Clippers Owner Donald Sterling for Life," *The New York Times*, April 29, 2014.
29. "Limbaugh's Comments Touch off Controversy," *ESPN.com*, October 1, 2003.
30. Chris Mortensen, "Smith Sends E-Mail Detailing Opposition," *ESPN.com*, October 11, 2009.
31. Randal C. Archibold, "Arizona Enacts Stringent Law on Immigration," *The New York Times*, April 23, 2010.
32. Michael O'Keeffe, "MLBPA Statement on Arizona's Immigration Law," *NY Daily News*, April 30, 2010.
33. Patrick Saunders, "Immigration, Race and Baseball Are Inseparable," *Denver Post*, May 3, 2010.
34. Jim McLennon, "Tony La Russa Backs Arizona Immigration Law," *SBNation.com*, July 1, 2010.
35. Modified from Walt Bennett, "Defending the Dolphins: No Question Is Out of Bounds," *New York Times*, May 4, 2010.
36. "Stern: Iverson to Tone Down Lyrics," *CBSnews.com*, October 12, 2000.
37. "Delinquent Bill," *The Dallas Observer*, January 25, 2007.
38. "Parcells Apologized for Making Ethnic Remarks," *ESPN.com*, June 7, 2004.
39. "Marge Schott's Comments on ESPN about Hitler," *Anti Defamation League*, Press Release, May 6, 1996; Richard Goldstein, "Marge Schott, Owner of Cincinnati Reds, Dies," *The New York Times*, March 2, 2004.
40. NBA Player Dress code, www.NBA.com, October 20, 2005.
41. "One-Size-Fits-All Dress Code Draws Divergent Views," *ESPN*, October 19, 2002.
42. Michael Lee, "New Dress Code Draws a Few Threads of Protest," *Washington Post*, October 20, 2005.
43. S. Ronald, "Lee: NBA Dress Code Not 'Racist'" *Chicago Defender*, October 25, 2005.
44. Timothy Davis, "Myth of the Superspade: The Persistence of Racism in College Athletics," *Fordham Urban Law Journal* 22 (1994–1995): 615; R. M. Sellers, "Racial Differences in the Predictors for Academic Achievement of Student-Athletes in Division I Revenue Producing Sports," *Sociology of Sports Journal* (1992); Davis Eitle, "Race, Culture Capital, and the Educational Effects of Participation in Sports," *University of Miami, Sociology of Education* 75 (April 2002): 123–146; Susan Tyler Eastman and Andrew C. Billings, "Biased Voices of Sports: Racial and Gender Stereotyping in College Basketball Announcing," *Howard Journal of Communications* 12, no. 4 (October 2001): 183–201.
45. "2 Accept Medals Wearing Black Gloves," *The New York Times*, October 17, 1968.
46. Logan Gay, "SIU Players Banned from Displays of Activism While in Salukis Uniform," August 29, 2018.
47. Ibid.
48. Ibid.
49. "SIU Athletics Walks Back Policy Change on Activism in Uniform," August 30, 2018, *wpsdlocal6.com*.
50. Aaron Goldstein, "Intentional Infliction of Emotional Distress: Another Attempt at Eliminating Native American Mascots," *Journal of Gender, Race and Justice* (1999–2000): 689; Brian R. Moushegian, "Native American Mascots' Last Stand? Legal Difficulties in Eliminating Public University Use of Native American Mascots," *Villanova Sports & Entertainment Law Journal* 13 (2006): 465; Kenneth B. Franklin, "A Brave Attempt: Can the National Collegiate Athletic Association Sanction Colleges and Universities with Native American Mascots?" *Journal of Intellectual Property Law* 13 (2005–2006): 435.
51. Richard Lapchick, with Saahil Marfatia, Austin Bloom, and Stanley Sylverain, "College Sport," April 6, 2017.
52. Courtesy of Richard Lapchick, National Consortium for Academics and Sports.

CHAPTER 9

Ethical Duties of Sports Agents

▶ Introduction

Long before "show me the money" became a well-worn phrase, ethical dilemmas were present in the sports agent business.[1] The profession of the sports agent is not a new one. Charles C. "Cash and Carry" Pyle represented athletes in the early part of the 19th century,[2] including football star Harold "Red" Grange. Early baseball Hall of Famer and Columbia Law School graduate John Montgomery Ward was the driving force behind the formation of an early baseball players' union, The Brotherhood, in 1890. Ward was the leader of The Brotherhood, which formed the Players League, an organization run solely by the players. Ward represented many early ballplayers in legal matters and in contract disputes with clubs.[3]

Although there have been sports agents throughout the history of sports, agents did not begin to garner national attention until the 1960s and 1970s. The Andy Messersmith and Dave McNally arbitration cases in baseball in 1975 granted all MLB players free agency, and many players began to hire agents to represent their interests after the arbitration decision. Player salaries skyrocketed in sports

in the 1980s, and this trend has continued to the present day, creating a market for sports agents. Player agents stepped in and began to negotiate lucrative player and endorsement contracts. Agents are now a mainstay of the sports industry.

Unfortunately, sports agents have not always had the best reputation. As in any profession, a small group of unethical individuals can make it tough for ethical agents to succeed. Josh Luchs, at the age of twenty, became the youngest contract advisor ever certified by the NFL Players Association (NFLPA). He represented more than 60 NFL players over the course of his career; however, by his own admission, he did it unethically and illegally. In 2010, the NFLPA revoked his agent certification. In that same year, Luchs gave an interview to *Sports Illustrated* in which he detailed his career as an NFL agent. In his confession, Luchs stated:

> Why am I doing this? Why am I telling everything? There are a few small reasons and one big one. People should know how the agent business really works, how widespread the inducements to players are and how players have their hands out. It isn't just the big, bad

agents making them take money. People think the NFLPA is monitoring agents, but it is mostly powerless. People should also be aware of all that an agent does for his clients. Catering to their needs can be an all-consuming job. But those are the small reasons. Recently, my nine-year-old daughter got an iTouch and she has figured out how to get on the Internet. My six-year-old is not far behind. At some point, they are going to Google their daddy's name and before this story they would have found only page after page of stuff saying how I was suspended. I was a good agent and I took care of my players. I don't want my career to be defined by that suspension.[4]

University of Alabama head football coach, Nick Saban, said the following about unethical agents: "I don't think it's anything but greed that's creating it right now on behalf of the agents . . . The agents that do this—and I hate to say this, but how are they any better than a pimp? . . . I have no respect for people who do that to young people. None. How would you feel if they did it to your child?"[5] What do you suppose Saban meant by "it," "this," and "that"? Sports agents can come from many disciplines and industries including business, law, finance, accounting, and engineering. However, many sports agents are lawyers and, well deserved or not, lawyers have suffered from a negative reputation in American society.

If an agent can sign a star player to a representation agreement, the agent could receive a large fee for negotiating just one contract. This can lead to vicious competition between agents attempting to get clients. Unscrupulous, unethical, and cutthroat methods are employed by some sports agents to obtain clients. Steps have been taken by the players associations to clean up unethical activity.

Responsibilities of Agents

Agents owe certain responsibilities and ethical duties to the principal, the athlete. Agents have a duty to perform and carry out their duties in good faith on behalf of the principal and they also must avoid all potential and actual conflicts of interest. Agents have a duty of confidentiality and a duty to account for all funds handled on behalf of the principal. Sports agents act as a fiduciary on behalf of an athlete and should always keep the client's best interests in mind. Agents operate in a position of trust much like the patient-physician relationship, or a stockbroker with a financial client. The primary duties of sports agents are their obligation of undivided loyalty (the duty of loyalty) and their obligation to act in good faith (the duty of care) during the representation process. The duty of care requires agents to perform their job properly, like not missing a deadline to file for free agency. In essence, agents must be honest, credible, trustworthy, and capable of performing the duties of an agent.

An agent may be called upon to perform many duties on behalf of a client. Negotiating a player's contract with a club may just be the beginning of a long-term relationship, with the agent being involved in all aspects of a player's career. An agent also may negotiate endorsement contracts, perform legal work (if a lawyer), arrange for investment counseling, provide career planning advice, protect and promote the public image of the athlete, and counsel the athlete about matters of everyday life, if necessary.

In the following case, a player refused to pay his agent a fee, claiming his agent failed to do his job properly, *i.e.* breached his duty of care, while representing the player.

⚖ CASE 9-1 *Zinn v. Parrish*

644 F.2d 360 (7th Cir. 1981)

For over two decades … Zinn had been engaged in the business of managing professional athletes. He stated that he was a pioneer in bringing to the attention of various pro-football teams the availability of talented players at small black colleges in the South. In the Spring of 1970, Parrish's coach at Lincoln University approached Zinn and informed him that Parrish had been picked by the Cincinnati Bengals in the annual National Football League draft of college seniors, and asked him if he would help Parrish in negotiating the contract. After Zinn contacted Parrish, the latter signed a one-year "Professional Management Contract" with Zinn in the Spring of 1970, pursuant to which Zinn helped Parrish negotiate the terms of his rookie contract with the Bengals, receiving as his commission 10% of Parrish's $16,500 salary. On April 10, 1971 Parrish signed the contract at issue in this case, which differed from the 1970 contract only insofar as it was automatically renewed from year to year unless one of the parties terminated it by 30 days' written notice to the other party. There were no other restrictions placed on the power of either party to terminate the contract.

Under the 1971 contract, Zinn obligated himself to use "reasonable efforts" to procure pro-football employment for Parrish, and, at Parrish's request, to "act" in furtherance of Parrish's interest by: (a) negotiating job contracts; (b) furnishing advice on business investments; (c) securing professional tax advice at no added cost; and (d) obtaining endorsement contracts. It was further provided that Zinn's services would include, "at my request efforts to secure for me gainful off-season employment," for which Zinn would receive no additional compensation, "unless such employment (was) in the line of endorsements, marketing and the like," in which case Zinn would receive a 10% commission on the gross amount. If Parrish failed to pay Zinn amounts due under the contract, Parrish authorized "the club or clubs that are obligated to pay me to pay to you instead all monies and other considerations due me from which you can deduct your 10% and any other monies due you…"

Over the course of Parrish's tenure with the Bengals, Zinn negotiated base salaries for him of $18,500 in 1971; $27,000 in 1972; $35,000 in 1973 (plus a $6,500 signing bonus); and a $250,000 series of contracts covering the four seasons commencing in 1974 (plus a $30,000 signing bonus). The 1974–77 contracts with the Bengals were signed at a time when efforts were being made by the newly-formed World Football League to persuade players in the NFL to "jump" to the WFL to play on one of its teams. By the end of [the] 1973 season Parrish had become recognized as one of the more valuable players in the NFL. He was twice selected for the Pro Bowl game, and named by Sporting News as one of the best cornerbacks in the league. Towards the end of the 1973 season, the Bengals approached Parrish with an offer of better contract terms than he had earlier been receiving. By way of exploring alternatives in the WFL, Zinn entered into preliminary discussions with the Jacksonville Sharks in early 1974, but decided not to pursue the matter once he ascertained that the Sharks were in a shaky financial position. In retrospect, Zinn's and Parrish's decision to continue negotiating and finally sign with the Bengals was a sound one, for the Sharks and the rest of the WFL with them folded in 1975 due to a lack of funds.

Shortly after signing the 1974 series of contracts, Parrish informed Zinn by telephone that he "no longer needed his services." By letter dated October 16, 1975, Parrish reiterated this position, and added that he had no intention of paying Zinn a 10% commission on those contracts … Zinn claims that the total was at least $304,500 including bonus and performance clauses. The 1971 contract by its terms entitled Zinn to 10% of the total amount as each installment was paid, and Zinn claims that he has only received $4,300 of the amounts due him …

In addition to negotiating the Bengals contracts, Zinn performed a number of other services at Parrish's request. In 1972 he assisted him in purchasing a residence as well as a four-unit apartment building to be used for rental income; he also helped to manage the apartment building. That same year Zinn negotiated an endorsement contract for Parrish with All-Pro Graphics, Inc., under which Parrish received a percentage from the sales of "Lemar Parrish" t-shirts, sweatshirts, beach towels, key chains, etc. The record shows that Zinn made a number of unsuccessful efforts at obtaining similar endorsement income from stores with which Parrish did business in Ohio. He also tried, unsuccessfully, to obtain an appearance for Parrish on The Mike Douglas Show. Zinn arranged for Parrish's taxes to be prepared each year by H & R Block.

The evidence showed that, despite his efforts, Zinn was unable to obtain off-season employment for Parrish. In this connection, however, it was Zinn's advice to Parrish that he return to school during the off-season months in order to finish his college degree, against the time when he would no longer be able to play football. With respect to Zinn's obligation to provide Parrish with advice on "business investments," he complied first, by assisting in the purchase of the apartment building; and second, by forwarding to Parrish the stock purchase recommendations of certain other individuals, after screening the suggestions himself. There was no evidence that Zinn ever forwarded such recommendations to any of his other clients; he testified that he only did so for Parrish.

In summing up Zinn's performance under the contract, Parrish testified as follows:

Question: Did you ever ask Zinn to do anything for you, to your knowledge, that he didn't try to do?

Answer: I shall say not, no.

1. Did the agent fulfill his ethical obligations to the client in *Zinn*? What else could he have done on Parrish's behalf? Do you think the 10% commission on player contracts is excessive?
2. The representation agreement contained a provision stating that, if Parrish failed to pay Zinn amounts due under the contract, Parrish authorized his club to pay Zinn directly all money that the club owed Parrish from which Zinn could deduct his 10% and any other monies due Zinn. The union agent regulations now preclude this. Why?
3. What if Zinn had advised Parrish to sign with the Jacksonville Sharks for more money than what the Bengals were offering, knowing that the Sharks were in a shaky financial position?

Fed. Sec. L. Rep. P 97,920leo M. Zinn, Plaintiff and Counter-defendant, Appellant, v. Lemar Parrish, Defendant and Counter-plaintiff, Appellee, 644 F.2d 360 (7th Cir. 1981), U.S. Supreme Court.

🔍 *CASE STUDY 9-1*   *Hiring an Agent*

Major League pitcher Matt Morris fired his agent and negotiated his own contract, a $27 million deal for four years. Morris said the St. Louis Cardinals sent him a deal that was fair, so he signed it. Other well-known players through the years have negotiated their own contracts without an agent.

1. Should players negotiate their own contracts?
2. Should teams negotiate with a player without an agent?
3. Is it fair to the player to be unrepresented when negotiating a multimillion dollar contract?

Len Bias was a great college basketball player and was selected in the first round of the 1986 NBA draft by the Boston Celtics, but Bias would never play a game in the NBA. He died of a cocaine overdose just two days after he was drafted by the Celtics.[6] Prior to the draft, he selected Advantage International Inc., a well-known sports agency, to represent him. After his death, Bias's estate filed a lawsuit against Advantage International saying they had failed to represent Len Bias properly.

⚖️ *CASE 9-2*   *Bias v. Advantage International*

905 F.2d 1558 (D.C. Cir. 1990)

On April 7, 1986, after the close of his college basketball career, [Len] Bias entered into a representation agreement with Advantage whereby Advantage agreed to advise and represent Bias in his affairs.

Fentress was the particular Advantage representative servicing the Bias account. On June 17 of that year Bias was picked by the Boston Celtics in the first round of the National Basketball Association draft. On the morning of June 19, 1986, Bias died of cocaine intoxication. The Estate sued Advantage and Fentress for two separate injuries allegedly arising out of the representation arrangement between Bias and [Advantage].

First, the Estate alleges that, prior to Bias's death, Bias and his parents directed Fentress to obtain a one-million dollar life insurance policy on Bias's life, that Fentress represented to Bias and Bias's parents that he had secured such a policy, and that in reliance on Fentress's assurances, Bias's parents did not independently seek to buy an insurance policy on Bias's life. Although [Advantage] did obtain increased disability coverage for Bias, in a one-million dollar disability insurance policy with an accidental death rider, they did not secure any life insurance coverage for Bias prior to his death.

Second, on June 18, 1986, the day after he was drafted by the Boston Celtics, Bias, through and with Fentress, entered into negotiations with Reebok International, Ltd. ("Reebok") concerning a potential endorsement contract. The Estate alleges that after several hours of negotiations Fentress requested that Bias and his father leave so that Fentress could continue negotiating with Reebok representatives in private. The Estate alleges that Fentress then began negotiating a proposed package deal with Reebok on behalf of not just Bias, but also other players represented by Advantage. The Estate contends that Fentress breached a duty to Bias by negotiating on behalf of other players, and that because Fentress opened up these broader negotiations he was unable to complete the negotiations for Bias on June 18. The Estate claims that as a result of Fentress's actions, on June 19, when Bias died, Bias had no contract with Reebok. The Estate alleges that the contract that Bias would have obtained would have provided for an unconditional lump sum payment which Bias would have received up front.

1. In *Bias*, did the agent fulfill all of his ethical obligations to his client? If not, what else could he have done? Which allegation(s) of the Estate involve the duty of care and which involve the duty of loyalty?
2. Did the agent violate his duty of loyalty to Bias by negotiating on behalf of several clients at one time?
3. The agent told Bias and his parents that he was able to obtain a life insurance policy but actually failed to do so. Even though a court would later rule the agent's failure to obtain the policy was irrelevant because Bias would not have passed a life insurance physical, should the agent still be held accountable because he lied to his client?
4. Should there be a uniform code of ethics for sports agents? If so, what would it include?[7]

Bias v. Advantage International, Inc., 905 F.2d 1558 (D.C. Cir. 1990), U.S. Supreme Court.

⌕ CASE STUDY 9-2   NFL Contract for Ricky Williams

Every NFL first-round draft pick understands the importance of retaining an experienced agent who knows his or her way around the NFL and can negotiate a multimillion dollar contract successfully. Notwithstanding this sound advice, Heisman Trophy winner Ricky Williams chose to hire well-known rapper Master P. (Percy Robert Miller) to represent him. Through Master P., Williams was represented by Leland Hardy for his contract negotiations with the New Orleans Saints. Williams was the lone draft pick of the Saints and instead of securing a contract with guaranteed money up front, his agent negotiated a substantially incentive bonus-based contract which was noted by most experienced NFL agents to be heavily in favor of the team.[8] Hardy constructed a rookie deal for Williams which has subsequently been used in law and business schools as a "model for bad contracts."[9] Two weeks after Williams signed his contract, his agent failed an open-book, take-home exam given to agents by the NFLPA.[10]

The agent was suspended from representing players until he could pass the exam. The contract was a disaster for Williams, and he eventually hired agent Leigh Steinberg to renegotiate his contract.[11]

1. Is this a duty of care issue or a duty of loyalty issue?
2. Does it make a difference if the agent fully informs the player of all the risks associated with signing a contract with little to no guaranteed money, and the player decides to sign it anyway?
3. Is it ever okay to lie during negotiations? Can failing to tell the "whole truth" be part of a negotiating strategy? Should an agent ever represent that he or she has an offer from another club when in fact this is not true, solely to improve the client's negotiating position?[12]
4. Under what circumstances should an agent advise his client to "hold out"? If a player is legally bound under a contract to play, does an agent engage in an unethical act by advising the player to hold out for more money notwithstanding the player's contractual obligations? Would the agent be advising the player to breach his or her contract?

Competition among Agents

Much like other industries, the sports agent business can be unethical at times. There are very few professional athletes to represent; thus, there are many agents seeking just a few clients with very large sums of money at stake for both the player and the agent. This scenario has led to fierce competition among agents. Some agents will do whatever it takes to sign a client, even if that means engaging in unethical conduct to sign a new player, such as stealing clients from other agents and making improper inducements or fraudulent representations. Many unethical agents will try to "persuade" players to sign contracts with them even though the player may already be represented by an agent. Union agent regulations generally prohibit soliciting clients under representation with other agents.

In the following case, one agent sued another for intentional interference with a contract.

⚖ CASE 9-3 Rosenhaus v. Star Sports, Inc.

929 So.2d 40 (3rd Cir. 2006)

Star Sports, Inc. ("Star"), filed a multi-count complaint … against Drew Rosenhaus, Jason Rosenhaus, and Rosenhaus Sports Representation, Inc., alleging intentional interference with an advantageous business relationship and tortious interference with a contractual right. The complaint alleges that Star is in the business of providing marketing and related services to professional football players in the National Football League, and that Drew and Jason Rosenhaus are both certified Contract Advisors with the National Football League Players Association. The complaint alleges that Star entered into a written contract referred to as a "Marketing Agreement" with Anquan Boldin, a professional football player in the NFL, wherein Star was to be Boldin's exclusive agent for marketing and related services. The complaint also alleges that Drew and Jason Rosenhaus intentionally and unjustifiably interfered with this Marketing Agreement by directly soliciting Boldin to have Jason and Drew Rosenhaus and/or Rosenhaus Sports Representation, Inc., represent him in his marketing endeavors and to exclude Star from representing him.

1. How should a court decide *Rosenhaus v. Star Sports, Inc.*? What other factors do you need to know to decide this case?
2. A court eventually found in favor of Rosenhaus. What restrictions should be placed on agents about contacting players who already have an agent?

Rosenhaus v. Star Sports, Inc., U.S. Supreme Court.

Terminating a representation agreement with a sports agent can usually be done by a player by giving proper notice to the agent. Some players skip from agent to agent trying to find the right person to meet their needs. That is what happened in the following case.

⚖ CASE 9-4 *Speakers of Sport, Inc. v. ProServ, Inc.*

178 F.3d 862 (7th Cir. 1999)

... The essential facts, construed as favorably to [Speaker of Sports, Inc., "Speakers"] as the record will permit, are as follows. Ivan Rodriguez, a highly successful catcher with the Texas Rangers baseball team, in 1991 signed the first of several one-year contracts making Speakers his agent. ProServ wanted to expand its representation of baseball players and to this end invited Rodriguez to its office in Washington and there promised that it would get him between $2 and $4 million in endorsements if he signed with ProServ—which he did, terminating his contract (which was terminable at will) with Speakers.

This was in 1995. ProServ failed to obtain significant endorsements for Rodriguez and after just one year he switched to another agent who the following year landed him a five-year $42 million contract with the Rangers. Speakers brought this suit a few months later, charging that the promise of endorsements that ProServ had made to Rodriguez was fraudulent and had induced him to terminate his contract with Speakers.

... Speakers could not sue Rodriguez for breach of contract, because he had not broken their contract, which was, as we said, terminable at will. Nor, therefore, could it accuse ProServ of inducing a breach of contract ... But Speakers did have a contract with Rodriguez, and inducing the termination of a contract, even when the termination is not a breach because the contract is terminable at will, can still be actionable under the tort law of Illinois, either as an interference with prospective economic advantage, or as an interference with the contract at will itself ...

There is in general nothing wrong with one sports agent trying to take a client from another if this can be done without precipitating a breach of contract. That is the process known as competition, which though painful, fierce, frequently ruthless, sometimes Darwinian in its pitilessness, is the cornerstone of our highly successful economic system.

1. Why didn't Speakers of Sport sue Ivan Rodriguez for terminating their representation contract?
2. Did ProServ violate any ethical duty it had to its client, Ivan Rodriguez?
3. If the court is suggesting that client stealing is healthy competition that benefits the players, why do you think the union agent regulations prohibit it?

Speakers of Sport, Inc. v. ProServ, Inc., U.S. Supreme Court.

Leigh Steinberg sued his former employee David Dunn after Dunn left the firm taking multiple clients. After a five-week trial, a jury ordered Dunn and his company to pay Steinberg's firm $44.7 million in damages. The NFLPA had suspended Dunn for two years beginning in 2003 based on evidence revealed at the trial. Dunn filed bankruptcy as a result of the jury's verdict, and his bankruptcy filing suspended the NFLPA's disciplinary action against him. A California appellate court later vacated the award and Dunn eventually agreed to an 18-month suspension from the NFLPA.[13]

▶ # Lawyers as Sports Agents

Attorneys comprise a large percentage of sports agents. Lawyers are trained in many of the skills necessary to be a successful sports agent, including contract interpretation and negotiation. Attorneys are held to a higher standard than agents who are not attorneys because of the Model Rules of Professional Conduct (MRPC), an ethics code that makes attorneys accountable to their clients.[14] If a client is dissatisfied with the representation of a sports agent who is also a lawyer, the client could file a grievance with the state bar association against the sports agent–lawyer, in addition to filing a civil lawsuit for damages. A lawyer who fails to comply with the ethics code for lawyers is subject to discipline, fines, and possibly disbarment from the practice of law; thus, an agent who is not a lawyer is bound by the general principles of agency law (the duty of care and the duty of loyalty), but a lawyer will be governed by both the professional rules of conduct for attorneys and agency law.

There are some advantages to hiring an agent who is also an attorney. Attorneys are more likely to have malpractice insurance coverage in the event of agent negligence, whereas a non-lawyer sports agent may not have liability insurance to cover a judgment if a player sues the non-attorney agent for negligence or breach of contract.

Attorney Discipline

In the following case, an attorney who was working as a sports agent was disciplined by a state bar association for his improper actions.

⚖ CASE 9-5 *In the Matter of Henley*

78 S.E. 2d 134 (1994)

The underlying facts are undisputed. From the fall of 1992 until early 1993 . . . Fredrick J. Henley, Jr., represented Todd Kelly, a 1992 member of the University of Tennessee football team and a 1993 first round draft choice for a National Football League team. In this same time period, Henley entered into an agreement with Bienstock Sports in New York whereby Henley would assist Bienstock in recruiting Kelly as its client. Under the agreement, if Kelly became a client of Bienstock, Henley would receive one-third of any commissions paid by Kelly to Bienstock. Bienstock gave Henley $5,000 in expenses and loaned him an additional $25,000. Following Henley's successful recruitment of Kelly, Bienstock sent Henley a statement crediting him for the kick-back on Kelly's commission payment and deducting the amount Henley owed Bienstock in loans.

Based on the foregoing, the State Bar filed a formal complaint against Henley charging him with violations of various professional standards under Bar Rule 4-102(d), including Standard 30 (representing a client where the attorney has a financial interest, without fully disclosing that interest, and obtaining written consent or giving written notice), and Standard 40 (accepting compensation for legal service from one other than the client without the client's consent after full disclosure).

The record shows Henley violated Standard 30 by failing to give Kelly written notice of the full extent of Henley's own financial interest in Bienstock Sports' obtaining Kelly as its client, or obtaining Kelly's written consent to Henley's representation notwithstanding Henley's financial interests. We find unpersuasive Henley's contention that no discipline is appropriate because his client requested that Henley represent him, and was aware of the loans and expenses provided by Bienstock Sports to Henley. There is no evidence that Henley disclosed the kickback arrangement between him and Bienstock Sports which is the very essence of Henley's conflict in this case. Neither is there evidence of either written notice to Kelly, nor written consent by Kelly following Henley's full disclosure of his financial interest as required by Standard 30. These requirements are not mere formalities. Rather, they are crucial safeguards. A lawyer's representation of a client where the lawyer has a financial or personal interest which will or reasonably may affect the lawyer's professional judgment illustrates one of the most blatant appearances of impropriety. The requirements of full disclosure and written notice to or consent from the client are intended to insure to some extent both that a client will receive professional legal services, and that a lawyer may be protected should he or she choose the risky course of representing a client despite the lawyer's potentially conflicting personal or financial interest. By failing to meet these requirements, Henley violated Standard 30. Likewise, Henley violated Standard 40, precluding a lawyer's acceptance of compensation or anything of value from one other than the client relating to the representation of the client, without obtaining the client's consent after the lawyer's full disclosure.

In mitigation we note that at the time of the conduct involved in this disciplinary matter, Henley was a relatively recent member of the State Bar, having been admitted to practice in 1990. While not a mitigating factor per se, we note that the client states he was not harmed by Henley's conduct. Contrary to Henley's arguments, the fact that the client is a close friend of Henley's and does not object to Henley's conduct does not negate Henley's violations of professional standards. In aggravation, we note that Henley has been previously disciplined and suspended from the practice of law, for failing to provide discovery to the Bar in another proceeding. In this proceeding also, Henley has obstructed the disciplinary proceedings by intentionally failing to comply with the special master's order on discovery, resulting in the sanction of striking his answer. Henley has consistently refused to acknowledge the wrongful nature of his conduct. In light of Henley's violations in this matter, and having considered the mitigating and aggravating factors above, a 90-day suspension from the practice of law is appropriate.

1. What was Henley's conflict of interest in this case? How does the conflict impact Kelly's interest?
2. What was Henley's ethical obligation to Kelly?
3. Was Henley's penalty sufficient for his wrongful actions? Should Henley be disbarred for his actions?

Matter of Henley, 478 S.E.2d 134 (1996), U.S. Supreme Court.

One of the glaring ethical issues that has been raised in the agent business is the advantage a non-attorney has over an attorney in attempting to sign new clients. The non-attorney is not bound by the MRPC's client solicitation restrictions as attorneys are, and therefore, would seem to have an advantage over the attorney–agent in the recruitment of new clients. Attorney ethics rules prohibit solicitation of new clients and state: "A lawyer shall not by in-person or live telephone contact or solicit professional employment from a prospective client with whom the lawyer has no family or prior professional relationship when a significant motive for the lawyer's doing so is the lawyer's pecuniary gain."[15] This ethical rule could make it more difficult for the lawyer to compete with the non-lawyer in the recruiting of new athlete clients. If a lawyer has to wait for the potential client to contact him or her, the lawyer will most likely not get as many new clients as a non-lawyer. Some lawyers have attempted to maneuver around the rule by operating a sports management company in addition to a law firm and performing the recruiting aspects of the business through the sports management company.

In the following case, an attorney sought an opinion from the bar association regarding his dual role as an attorney and sports agent.

⚖ CASE 9-6 Illinois State Bar Association-ISBA Advisory Opinion on Professional Conduct

IL. Adv. Op. 700, 1980 WL 130464

ISBA Advisory Opinions on Professional Conduct are prepared as an educational service to members of the ISBA. While the Opinions express the ISBA interpretation of the Illinois Rules of Professional Conduct and other relevant materials in response to a specific hypothesized fact situation, they do not have the weight of law and should not be relied upon as a substitute for individual legal advice.

Digest: It is professionally improper for an attorney to initiate private communications with coaches and athletic directors to inform them that he engages in the practice of "sports law" and is available to represent clients.

It is professionally proper to handle "player representation" from the attorney's law office.

Ref: Rule 2-103(a)ABA EC 2-8

Facts

Attorney has a "sports law" practice and represents athletes in contract negotiations. The athletes he represents are handled through his law office from which he conducts a private law practice.

Question

May the attorney advise college athletic directors and coaches of his "sports law" practice and representation of athletes without naming any specific athletes that he represents, and inform the athletic directors and coaches that he is "available"? Secondly, may the "player representation" be carried on in the attorney's law office?

Opinion

Rule 2-103(a) of the Illinois Code of Professional Responsibility … provides:

> "A lawyer shall not by private communication … directly or through a representative, recommend or solicit employment of himself, his partner or his associate for pecuniary gain or other benefit and shall not for that purpose initiate contact with a prospective client." …

EC 2-8 of Canon 2 of the Code of Professional Responsibility of the American Bar Association provides in part as follows:

> "Selection of a lawyer by a lay person should be made on an informed basis. Advice and recommendation of their parties—relative, friends, acquaintances, business associates, or other lawyers—and disclosure of relevant information about the lawyer and his practice may be helpful. A lay person is best served if the recommendation is disinterested and informed. In order that the recommendation be disinterested, a lawyer should not seek to influence another to recommend his employment."

Advising coaches and athletic directors that one practices "sports law" and represents athletes in contract negotiations and is "available" would appear to be designed to encourage the coaches and directors to recommend the attorney to the athletes under their charge. The committee is of the opinion, therefore, that the initiation of communications by an attorney to coaches and athletic directors to inform them of the attorney's availability to represent athletes would be professionally improper.

The second question presented deals with whether an attorney may handle "player representation" from the same office in which he engages in the general practice of law. It would appear, therefore, that the attorney making this inquiry questions whether the representation of athletes is actually the practice of law in that it may include a wide range of business counselling, as well as contract negotiation. This doubt could be prompted by the fact that no lawyers frequently engage in these activities.

The committee is of the opinion that, when an attorney engaged in the private practice of law represents a client in contract negotiations and general business counselling, these activities constitute the practice of law and it would be professionally proper to handle them from the same office in which he engages in the general practice of law.

Illinois State Bar Association-ISBA Advisory Opinion on Professional Conduct IL. Adv. Op. 700, 1980 WL 130464.

▶ Conflict of Interest

One example of an ethical dilemma for an agent deals with handling conflicts of interest. The following is the quintessential case in sports ethics dealing with conflict of interest. It is rudimentary that a team owner should not also be working as an agent, much less on the same deal.

⚖ CASE 9-7 *The Detroit Lions, Inc. v. Argovitz*

580 F.Supp. 542 (6th Cir. Mich. 1984)

The plot for this Saturday afternoon serial began when Billy Sims, having signed a contract with the Houston Gamblers on July 1, 1983, signed a second contract with the Detroit Lions on December 16, 1983. On December 18, 1983, the Detroit Lions, Inc. (Lions) and Billy R. Sims filed a complaint in the Oakland County Circuit Court seeking a judicial determination that the July 1, 1983, contract between Sims and the Houston Gamblers, Inc. (Gamblers) is invalid because Jerry Argovitz (Argovitz) breached his fiduciary duty when negotiating the Gamblers' contract and because the contract was otherwise tainted by fraud and misrepresentation …

Sometime in February or March 1983, Argovitz told Sims that he had applied for a Houston franchise in the newly formed United States Football League (USFL). In May 1983, Sims attended a press conference in Houston at which Argovitz announced that his application for a franchise had been approved. The evidence persuades us that Sims did not know the extent of Argovitz's interest in the Gamblers. He did not know the amount of Argovitz's original investment, or that Argovitz was obligated for 29 percent of a $1.5 million letter of credit, or that Argovitz was the president of the Gamblers' Corporation at an annual salary of $275,000 and 5 percent the yearly cash flow. [Argovitz] could not justifiably expect Sims to comprehend the ramifications of Argovitz's interest in the Gamblers or the manner in which that interest would create an untenable conflict of interest, a conflict that would inevitably breach Argovitz's fiduciary duty to Sims. Argovitz knew, or should have known, that he could not act as Sims' agent under any circumstances when dealing with the Gamblers. Even the USFL Constitution itself prohibits a holder of any interest in a member club from acting "as the contracting agent or representative for any player."

Pending the approval of his application for a USFL franchise in Houston, Argovitz continued his negotiations with the Lions on behalf of Sims.

On April 5, 1983, Argovitz offered Sims' services to the Lions for $6 million over a four-year period. The offer included a demand for a $1 million interest-free loan to be repaid over 10 years, and for skill and injury guarantees for three years. The Lions quickly responded with a counter offer on April 7, 1983, in the face amount of $1.5 million over a five-year period with additional incentives not relevant here. The negotiating process was working. The Lions were trying to determine what Argovitz really believed the market value for Sims really was. On May 3, 1983, with his Gamblers franchise assured, Argovitz significantly reduced his offer to the Lions. He now offered Sims to the Lions for $3 million over a four-year period, one-half of the amount of his April 5, 1983, offer. Argovitz's May 3rd offer included a demand for $50,000 to permit Sims to purchase an annuity. Argovitz also dropped his previous demand for skill guarantees. The May 10, 1983, offer submitted by the Lions brought the parties much closer.

On May 30, 1983, Argovitz asked for $3.5 million over a five-year period. This offer included an interest-free loan and injury protection insurance but made no demand for skill guarantees. The May 30 offer now requested $400,000 to allow Sims to purchase an annuity. On June 1, 1983, Argovitz and the Lions were only $500,000 apart. We find that the negotiations between the Lions and Argovitz were progressing normally, not laterally as Argovitz represented to Sims. The Lions were not "dragging their feet." Throughout the entire month of June 1983, Mr. Frederick Nash, the Lions' skilled negotiator and a fastidious lawyer, was involved in investigating the possibility of providing an attractive annuity for Sims and at the same time doing his best to avoid the granting of either skill or injury guarantees. The evidence establishes that on June 22, 1983, the Lions and Argovitz were very close to reaching an agreement on the value of Sims' services.

Apparently, in the midst of his negotiations with the Lions and with his Gamblers franchise in hand, Argovitz decided that he would seek an offer from the Gamblers. Mr. Bernard Lerner, one of Argovitz's partners in the Gamblers agreed to negotiate a contract with Sims. Since Lerner admitted that he had no knowledge whatsoever about football, we must infer that Argovitz at the very least told Lerner the amount of money required to sign Sims and further pressed upon Lerner the Gamblers' absolute need to obtain Sims' services. In the Gamblers' organization, only Argovitz knew the value of Sims' services and how critical it was for the Gamblers to obtain Sims. In Argovitz's words, Sims would make the Gamblers' franchise.

On June 29, 1983, at Lerner's behest, Sims and his wife went to Houston to negotiate with a team that was partially owned by his own agent. When Sims arrived in Houston, he believed that the Lions organization was not negotiating in good faith; that it was not really interested in his services. His ego was bruised and his emotional outlook toward the Lions was visible to Burrough and Argovitz. Clearly, virtually all the information that Sims had up to that date came from Argovitz. Sims and the Gamblers did not discuss a future contract on the night of June 29th. The negotiations began on the morning of June 30, 1983, and ended that afternoon. At the morning meeting, Lerner offered Sims a $3.5 million five-year contract, which included three years of skill and injury guarantees. The offer included a $500,000 loan at an interest rate of 1 percent over prime. It was from this loan that Argovitz planned to receive the $100,000 balance of his fee for acting as an agent in negotiating a contract with his own team. Burrough testified that Sims would have accepted that offer on the spot because he was finally receiving the guarantee that he had been requesting from the Lions, guarantees that Argovitz dropped without too much quarrel. Argovitz and Burrough took Sims and his wife into another room to discuss the offer. Argovitz did tell Sims that he thought the Lions would match the Gamblers financial package and asked Sims whether he (Argovitz) should telephone the Lions. But, it is clear from the evidence that neither Sims nor Burrough believed that the Lions would match the offer. We find that Sims told Argovitz not to call the Lions for purely emotional reasons. As we have noted, Sims believed that the Lions' organization was not that interested in him and his pride was wounded. Burrough clearly admitted that he was aware of the emotional basis for Sims' decision not to have Argovitz phone the Lions, and we must conclude from the extremely close relationship between Argovitz and Sims that Argovitz knew it as well. When Sims went back to Lerner's office, he agreed to become a Gambler on the terms offered. At that moment, Argovitz irreparably breached his fiduciary duty. As agent for Sims he had the duty to telephone the Lions, receive its final offer, and present the terms of both offers to Sims. Then and only then could it be said that Sims made an intelligent and knowing decision to accept the Gamblers' offer.

During these negotiations at the Gamblers' office, Mr. Nash of the Lions telephoned Argovitz, but even though Argovitz was at his office, he declined to accept the telephone call. Argovitz tried to return

Nash's call after Sims had accepted the Gamblers' offer, but it was after 5 p.m. and Nash had left for the July 4th weekend. When he declined to accept Mr. Nash's call, Argovitz's breach of his fiduciary duty became even more pronounced. Following Nash's example, Argovitz left for his weekend trip, leaving his principal to sign the contracts with the Gamblers the next day, July 1, 1983. [Argovitz], assert[s] that neither Argovitz nor Burrough can be held responsible for following Sims' instruction not to contact the Lions on June 30, 1983. Although it is generally true that an agent is not liable for losses occurring as a result of following his principal's instructions, the rule of law is not applicable when the agent has placed himself in a position adverse to that of his principal.

During the evening of June 30, 1983, Burrough struggled with the fact that they had not presented the Gamblers' offer to the Lions. He knew, as does the court, that Argovitz now had the wedge that he needed to bring finality to the Lions' negotiations. Burrough was acutely aware of the fact that Sims' actions were emotionally motivated and realized that the responsibility for Sims' future rested with him. We view with some disdain the fact that Argovitz had, in effect, delegated his entire fiduciary responsibility on the eve of his principal's most important career decision. On July 1, 1983, it was Lerner who gave lip service to Argovitz's conspicuous conflict of interest. It was Lerner, not Argovitz, who advised Sims that Argovitz's position with the Gamblers presented a conflict of interest and that Sims could, if he wished, obtain an attorney or another agent. Argovitz, upon whom Sims had relied for the past four years, was not even there. Burrough, conscious of Sims' emotional responses, never advised Sims to wait until he had talked with the Lions before making a final decision. Argovitz's conflict of interest and self-dealing put him in the position where he would not even use the wedge he now had to negotiate with the Lions, a wedge that is the dream of every agent. Two expert witnesses testified that an agent should telephone a team that he has been negotiating with once he has an offer in hand. Mr. Woolf, [expert for Detroit club], testified that an offer from another team is probably the most important factor in negotiations. Mr. Lustig, [expert for Argovitz], believed that it was prudent for him to telephone the Buffalo Bills and inform that organization of the Gamblers' offer to Jim Kelly, despite the fact that he believed the Bills had already made its best offer to his principal. The evidence here convinces us that Argovitz's negotiations with the Lions were ongoing and it had not made its final offer. Argovitz did not follow the common practice described by both expert witnesses. He did not do this because he knew that the Lions would not leave Sims without a contract and he further knew that if he made that type of call Sims would be lost to the Gamblers, a team he owned.

On November 12, 1983, when Sims was in Houston for the Lions game with the Houston Oilers, Argovitz asked Sims to come to his home and sign certain papers. He represented to Sims that certain papers of his contract had been mistakenly overlooked and now needed to be signed. Included among those papers he asked Sims to sign was a waiver of any claim that Sims might have against Argovitz for his blatant breach of his fiduciary duty brought on by his glaring conflict of interest. Sims did not receive independent advice with regard to the wisdom of signing such a waiver. Despite having sold his agency business in September, Argovitz did not even tell Sims' new agent of his intention to have Sims sign a waiver. Nevertheless, Sims, an unsophisticated young man, signed the waiver. This is another example of the questionable conduct on the part of Argovitz who still had business management obligations to Sims. In spite of his fiduciary relationship he had Sims sign a waiver without advising him to obtain independent counseling.

The parties submitted a great deal of evidence and argued a number of peripheral issues. Although most of the issues were not determinative factors in our decision, they do demonstrate that Argovitz had a history of fulfilling his fiduciary duties in an irresponsible manner. One cannot help but wonder whether Argovitz took his fiduciary duty seriously. For example, after investing approximately $76,000 of Sims' money, Argovitz, with or without the prior knowledge of his principal, received a finder's fee. Despite the fact that Sims paid Argovitz a 2 percent fee, Argovitz accepted $3800 from a person with whom he invested Sims' money. In March 1983, Argovitz had all of his veteran players, including Sims, sign a new agency contract with less favorable payment terms for the players even though they already had an ongoing agency agreement with him. He did this after he sold his entire agency business to Career Sports. Finally, Argovitz was prepared to take the remainder of his 5 percent agency fee for negotiating Sims' contract with the Gamblers from monies the Gamblers loaned to Sims at an interest rate of 1 percent over prime. It mattered little to Argovitz that Sims would have to pay interest on the $100,000 that Argovitz was ready to accept. While these practices by Argovitz are troublesome, we do not find them decisive in examining Argovitz's conduct while negotiating the Gamblers' contract on June 30 and July 1, 1983. We find this circumstantial evidence useful only insofar as it has aided the court in understanding the manner in which these parties conducted business.

We are mindful that Sims was less than forthright when testifying before the court … We remain persuaded that on balance, Argovitz's breach of his fiduciary duty was so egregious that a court of equity cannot permit him to benefit by his own wrongful breach. We conclude that Argovitz's conduct in negotiating Sims' contract with the Gamblers rendered it invalid.

The relationship between a principal and agent is fiduciary in nature, and as such imposes a duty of loyalty, good faith, and fair and honest dealing on the agent.

A fiduciary relationship arises not only from a formal principal-agent relationship, but also from informal relationships of trust and confidence.

In light of the express agency agreement, and the relationship between Sims and Argovitz, Argovitz clearly owed Sims the fiduciary duties of an agent …

An agent's duty of loyalty requires that he not have a personal stake that conflicts with the principal's interest in a transaction in which he represents his principal.

(T)he principal is entitled to the best efforts and unbiased judgment of his agent …

A fiduciary violates the prohibition against self-dealing not only by dealing with himself on his principal's behalf, but also by dealing on his principal's behalf with a third party in which he has an interest, such as a partnership in which he is a member.

Where an agent has an interest adverse to that of his principal in a transaction in which he purports to act on behalf of his principal, the transaction is voidable by the principal unless the agent disclosed all material facts within the agent's knowledge that might affect the principal's judgment.

The mere fact that the contract is fair to the principal does not deny the principal the right to rescind the contract when it was negotiated by an agent in violation of the prohibition against self-dealing …

Once it has been shown that an agent had an interest in a transaction involving his principal antagonistic to the principal's interest, fraud on the part of the agent is presumed. The burden of proof then rests upon the agent to show that his principal had full knowledge, not only of the fact that the agent was interested, but also of every material fact known to the agent which might affect the principal and that having such knowledge, the principal freely consented to the transaction.

It is not sufficient for the agent merely to inform the principal that he has an interest that conflicts with the principal's interest. Rather, he must inform the principal "of all facts that come to his knowledge that are or may be material or which might affect his principal's rights or interests or influence the action he takes."

Argovitz clearly had a personal interest in signing Sims with the Gamblers that was adverse to Sims' interest—he had an ownership interest in the Gamblers and thus would profit if the Gamblers were profitable, and would incur substantial personal liabilities should the Gamblers not be financially successful. Since this showing has been made, fraud on Argovitz's … part is presumed, and the Gamblers' contract must be rescinded unless Argovitz has shown by a preponderance of the evidence that he informed Sims of every material fact that might have influenced Sims' decision whether or not to sign the Gamblers' contract.

We conclude that Argovitz has failed to show … either: (1) that he informed Sims of the following facts, or (2) that these facts would not have influenced Sims' decision whether to sign the Gamblers' contract:

   a. The relative values of the Gamblers' contract and the Lions' offer that Argovitz knew could be obtained.

   b. That there was significant financial differences between the USFL and the NFL not only in terms of the relative financial stability of the Leagues, but also in terms of the fringe benefits available to Sims.

   c. Argovitz's 29 percent ownership in the Gamblers; Argovitz's $275,000 annual salary with the Gamblers; Argovitz's five percent interest in the cash flow of the Gamblers.

   d. That both Argovitz and Burrough failed to even attempt to obtain for Sims valuable contract clauses which they had given to [NFL player Jim] Kelly on behalf of the Gamblers.

   e. That Sims had great leverage, and Argovitz was not encouraging a bidding war that could have advantageous results for Sims.

… We are dismayed by Argovitz's egregious conduct. The careless fashion in which Argovitz went about ascertaining the highest price for Sims' service convinces us of the wisdom of the maxim: no man can faithfully serve two masters whose interests are in conflict.

Detroit Lions, Inc. v. Argovitz, 580 F. Supp. 542 (E.D. Mich. 1984), U.S. Supreme Court.

In *Detroit Lions, Inc. v. Argovitz*, the court found that Argovitz had breached his duty to his client regarding conflict of interest. Why was there a conflict of interest? What was the agent required to do under the circumstances? Would it be a conflict of interest for an agent to represent a coach and a player on the same team?

🔍 CASE STUDY 9-3 *Representing Multiple Players*

Assume an agent represents two NBA players who play the same position and are both unrestricted free agents and are able to sign with any NBA club. During negotiations with an NBA club, the agent is told by the general manager of the club that salary cap considerations only allow the signing of one star player. Does the agent have an irreconcilable conflict of interest in this scenario? What are the agent's ethical duties in this case?

What about an agent who is told by a team that his client, Player A, needs to take a salary cut to make room for Player B on the squad and the agent represents both players? What conflict of interest issues arise under those circumstances? Can the agent continue to represent both players under the circumstances?

▶ Agent Fees

The topic of agent fees can raise many ethical and legal concerns amongst players, unions, and agents. Agent fees can be determined by the players associations pursuant to their agent regulations or left to the marketplace. Most of the players associations set fees for agents. For example, the maximum NFL contract advisor fee is 3% of the player contract. A player's "juice" sometimes allows a player to negotiate a lower agent's fee. Some NFL star players have been able to reduce the agent's fee to as low as 1%.

The following case deals with the always sticky situation of agent fees, prior to the adoption of agent regulations by the players associations. Well-known sports agent Bob Woolf was sued after a professional hockey player claimed Woolf took more of a fee than to which he was entitled.

⚖ CASE 9-8 *Brown v. Woolf*

554 F.Supp. 1206 (7th Cir. 1983)

[Brown] seeks compensatory and punitive damages and the imposition of a trust on a fee [Woolf] allegedly received, all stemming from [Woolf]'s alleged constructive fraud and breach of fiduciary duty in the negotiation of a contract for the 1974–75 hockey season for [Brown] who was a professional hockey player. [Brown] alleges that prior to the 1973–74 season he had engaged the services of [Woolf], a well known sports attorney and agent, who represents many professional athletes, has authored a book, and has appeared in the media in connection with such representation, to negotiate a contract for him with the Pittsburgh Penguins of the National Hockey League. [Brown] had a professionally successful season that year under the contract [Woolf] negotiated for him and accordingly again engaged [Woolf]'s services prior to the 1974–75 season. During the negotiations in July 1974, the Penguins offered [Brown] a two-year contract at $80,000.00 per year but [Brown] rejected the offer allegedly because [Woolf] asserted that he could obtain a better, long-term, no-cut contract with a deferred compensation feature with the Indianapolis Racers, which at the time was a new team in a new league. On July 31, 1974, [Brown] signed a five-year contract with the Racers. Thereafter, it is alleged the Racers began having financial difficulties. [Brown] avers that Woolf continued to represent [Brown] and negotiated two reductions in [Brown]'s compensation including the loss of a retirement fund at the same time [Woolf] was attempting to get his own fee payment from the Racers. Ultimately the Racers' assets were seized and the organizers defaulted on their obligations to [Brown]. He avers that he received only $185,000.00 of the total $800,000.00 compensation under the Racer contract but that [Woolf] received his full $40,000.00 fee (5% of the contract) from the Racers.

[Brown] alleges that [Woolf] made numerous material misrepresentations upon which he relied both during the negotiation of the Racer contract and at the time of the subsequent modifications. [Brown] further avers that [Woolf] breached his fiduciary duty to [Brown] by failing to conduct any investigation into the financial stability of the Racers, failing to investigate possible consequences of the deferred compensation package in the Racers' contract, failing to obtain guarantees or collateral, and by negotiating reductions in [Brown]'s compensation from the Racers while insisting on receiving all of his own. [Brown] theorizes that such conduct amounts to a prima facie case of constructive fraud for which he should receive compensatory and punitive damages and have a trust impressed on the $40,000.00 fee [Woolf] received from the Racers.

1. Was Woolf's fee excessive? How much money should Woolf be entitled to?
2. Did the agent breach his fiduciary duty to his client? Which of Brown's claims relate to the duty of care and which relate to the duty of loyalty?
3. The agent took his entire fee even though the player did not receive the full amount of the contract. Should an agent only get paid when and if the player gets paid?

Brown v. Woolf, 554 F. Supp. 1206 (S.D. Ind. 1983), U.S. Supreme Court.

▶ Regulation of Sports Agents

Numerous entities have attempted to keep unethical and criminal conduct of agents out of the sports industry. Agents are now regulated and monitored from a variety of sources. Although the NCAA lacks jurisdiction and legal authority to regulate agents, as they are not members of the NCAA, the NCAA can sanction a university if one of its players violates the NCAA's rules pertaining to the use of agents. Players associations, legislative bodies, state attorney generals, and universities have all attempted to curb the unethical conduct of agents.[16]

Union Regulations

Players associations regulate and monitor the activities and conduct of sports agents. Pursuant to federal labor law, unions are the "exclusive representative" of the players, which gives them jurisdiction and legal authority to regulate agents. The unions also have an interest in making sure that union members are being adequately and properly represented. Unions have taken a myriad of actions to ensure that agents are properly prepared to represent professional athletes. Unions can require agents to have a certain education level or possess comparable business experience to be a certified agent. They can perform criminal background checks on agents, require agents to pass an exam to become a certified agent, and also set desirable fee structures. Unions have a lot of input about who can be an agent, as unions also possess the power to certify agents and decertify them for improper conduct.

The NFLPA has by far been the most aggressive organization in regulating the conduct of agents. The suspensions of contract advisors David Dunn and Carl Poston provide examples of the NFLPA's regulatory power. In 2006, the NFLPA suspended Poston after his client LaVar Arrington signed a contract that failed to include a $6.5 million bonus that Poston and the Redskins had negotiated and was supposed to be included in the contract. Poston was not present when Arrington signed the contract in Washington. According to Poston, the Redskins represented to him that they added language to the contract to include the bonus, when in fact they did not. Both Poston and Arrington blamed the Redskins for excluding the bonus from the contract, and Arrington opposed the NFLPA's suspension of his agent. Poston sued the NFLPA, challenging the fairness of the NFLPA's arbitration process to resolve an agent's appeal of the union's disciplinary action.[17] The matter became the subject of congressional activity and one of the authors of this book testified at the hearing.[18]

In the following case study, a former lawyer for MLB sought to be a player-agent but was turned down by the Players Association.

🔎 CASE STUDY 9-4 *Barry Rona and Collusion in Major League Baseball, 1985–1989*

In *Barry Rona and Major League Baseball Players' Association* (Arbitration 1993), the Major League Baseball Players Association rejected Barry Rona's application under section 2(c) of its regulations, which allowed the union to refuse certification to anyone whose conduct "may adversely affect his credibility [or] integrity . . . to serve in a representative and/or fiduciary capacity on behalf of players." The arbitrator stated:

[T]he Arbitrator finds that the Players Association acted arbitrarily and capriciously in rejecting Rona's application.

The Players Association's conclusion that Rona was part of the collusion in the 1985 and 1986 free agent markets because he was a leading figure in the PRC [Player Relations Committee] is fundamentally at odds with the Code's very clear position that lawyers do not act unethically merely because they represent individuals or institutions that are found to have engaged in wrongful activities. And there is no evidence, nor any finding by Chairman Roberts or Chairman Nicholau that it was or should have been obvious to Rona that his clients were acting "merely for the purpose of harassing or maliciously injuring any person." . . . On the contrary, he expressed his "concerns" to his clients, asked them directly whether they were involved in collusion to destroy the free agent markets in 1985 and 1986 and, when they replied negatively, allowed them to so testify under oath before the Roberts and Nicholau Panels. Rona acted entirely properly . . . in allowing his clients to have their day in court to attempt under oath to refute the circumstantial evidence that they were engaged in collusion can hardly be termed taking a "frivolous legal position." . . . This Arbitrator believes that these are not even close questions. For the foregoing reasons the Arbitrator concludes that the Players Association's rejection of Rona's application because of his alleged involvement in the 1985 and 1986 collusion was arbitrary and capricious.

The union rejected the application of Barry Rona, stating he was an integral part of the collusion by baseball owners in the 1980s to keep player salaries down in MLB. Rona was able to convince an arbitrator otherwise. Do you believe the arbitrator was correct in this decision? Could a former general manager of a team become an agent? What about a sports agent who leaves the players' side to go to the management side of sports? What ethical and legal ramifications does this pose? What issues of confidentiality do these scenarios present?

In the following arbitration case, an agent had his license revoked by the players' union after he publicly criticized the National Basketball Players Association during a two-month lockout in the 1998–99 NBA season.

⚖ CASE 9-9 *In the Matter of the Agent Certification Application of Stephen M. Woods (Opinion and Award)*

On January 5, 1999, two days before an agreement was reached to end the lockout imposed by the NBA, the NBPA Committee on Agent Regulation, acting under the "emergency circumstance" clause of Section 2E of the Regulations, invalidated the certification of Agent Stephen Woods. That action was grounded in Section 3 B(m), which provides that discipline, ranging from a reprimand to decertification, may be imposed for conduct "which reflects adversely on [an individual's] fitness as a player agent or jeopardizes the effective representation of player agents."

In a 19-page specification Woods was charged with a number of acts which, in the Committee's estimation, harmed the Union's bargaining position in the negotiations that occurred during the long lockout. Included were such acts as publicly seeking to undermine the Union's bargaining position after being warned to desist; repeatedly issuing misleading statements, both to the press and in a sports column of which he was the author; publicly and offensively attacking NBA players, including the Union leadership; engaging in activity that created an actual or potential conflict of interest with the effective representation of NBA players by revealing as a columnist confidential information he had obtained as an agent; billing the NBPA for a hotel room at a meeting of players to which he was not invited; and making misrepresentations in his 1994 application for certification.

Woods denied all the charges and appealed his decertification.

Modified from the Matter of the Agent Certification Application of Stephen M. Woods (Opinion and Award).

🔍 CASE STUDY 9-5 *Agent Exam*

Should a sports agent be required to pass a written exam to be able to represent players in a professional league? If the agent does not pass on the first try, how many times should he or she be able to re-take the exam? On what should a potential agent be tested? Should there be a minimum passing score for certification?

In the following case, a player-agent challenged the NBPA's agent certification system.

⚖ CASE 9-10   *Collins v. National Basketball Players Association*

850 F. Supp 1468 (D. Col. 1992)

Like other sports and entertainment unions, the NBPA believes that the collective good of the entire represented group is maximized when individualized salary negotiations occur within a framework that permits players to exert leverage based on their unique skills and personal contributions. The NBPA therefore has authorized the players or their individually selected agents to negotiate individual compensation packages. This delegation of representational authority to individual players and their agents has always been limited solely to the authority to negotiate individual compensation packages, and to enforce them through the grievance-arbitration procedure established by the NBPA-NBA Agreement.

Player agents were unregulated by the NBPA before 1986. By the mid-1980s, a substantial number of players had complained to the officers of the NBPA about agent abuses. Specifically, players complained that the agents imposed high and non-uniform fees for negotiation services, insisted on the execution of open-ended powers of attorney giving the agents broad powers over players' professional and financial decisions, failed to keep players apprised of the status of negotiations with NBA teams, failed to submit itemized bills for fees and services, and, in some cases, had conflicts of interest arising out of representing coaches and/or general managers of NBA teams as well as players. Many players believed they were bound by contract not to dismiss their agents regardless of dissatisfaction with their services and fees, because the agents had insisted on the execution of long-term agreements. Some agents offered money and other inducements to players, their families and coaches to obtain player clients.

In response to these abuses, the NBPA established the Regulations, a comprehensive system of agent certification and regulation, to insure that players would receive agent services that meet minimum standards of quality at uniform rates. First, the Regulations provide that a player agent may not conduct individual contract negotiations unless he signs the "Standard Player Agent Contract" promulgated by the Committee. The "Standard Player Agent Contract" limits player agent fees by prohibiting any fee or commission on any contract which entitles the player to the minimum salary and by limiting agent fees on all contracts. Second, the Regulations contain a "code of conduct" which specifically prohibits an agent from providing or offering money or anything of value to a player, a member of a player's family or a player's high school or college coach for the purpose of inducing the player to use that agent's services. The code also prohibits agents from engaging in conduct that constitutes an actual or apparent conflict of interest (such as serving as an agent for a player while also representing an NBA team, general manager or head coach), engaging in any unlawful conduct involving dishonesty, fraud, deceit, misrepresentation, or engaging in any other conduct that reflects adversely on his fitness to serve in a fiduciary capacity as a player agent or jeopardizes the effective representation of NBA players.

Third, the Regulations restrict the representation of players to individuals who are certified player agents, and set up a program for the certification of agents who are then bound by the Regulations' fee restrictions and code of conduct. Prospective player agents must file the "Applications for Certification as an NBPA Player Agent" with the Committee. The Committee is authorized to conduct any informal investigation that it deems appropriate to determine whether to issue certification and may deny certification to any applicant:

1. Upon . . . determining that the applicant has made false or misleading statements of a material nature in the Application;
2. Upon . . . determining that the applicant has ever misappropriated funds, or engaged in other specific fraud, which would render him unfit to serve in a fiduciary capacity on behalf of players;

3. Upon . . . determining that the applicant has engaged in any other conduct that significantly impacts adversely on his credibility, integrity, or competence to serve in a fiduciary capacity on behalf of players; or

4. Upon . . . determining that the applicant is unwilling to swear or affirm that he will comply with these Regulations and any amendments thereto and that he will abide by the fee structure contained in the standard form player-agent contract incorporated into these Regulations.

Regulations, Section 2C.

Any prospective agent whose application for certification is denied may appeal that denial by filing a timely demand for arbitration. The arbitration procedure incorporates by reference the Voluntary Labor Arbitration Rules of the American Arbitration Association, and includes the right to be represented by counsel, to cross-examine the Committee's witnesses, to present testimonial and documentary evidence and to receive a transcript. The arbitrator is empowered to order certification if he determines, based on the evidence, that the Committee did not meet its burden of establishing a basis for denying certification. The arbitrator's decision is final and binding on all parties and is not subject to judicial review. The NBPA's selected arbitrator, George Nicolau, is experienced and highly qualified in handling labor relations in the sports industry. He is currently the chairman of the arbitration panel for the Major League Baseball and the Major League Baseball Players Association and the contract arbitrator for the Major Indoor Soccer League and Major Indoor Soccer League Players Association. The NBPA player representatives of each NBA team approved the Regulations which became effective on March 7, 1986.

After unilaterally promulgating the Regulations, the NBPA obtained, in arms length collective bargaining, the NBA's agreement to prohibit all member teams from negotiating individual player salary contracts with any agent who was not certified by the NBPA.

Collins was an agent for several NBA players from 1974 until 1986. Collins applied for and received certification in 1986 soon after the Regulations took effect. In late 1986 or early 1987, he voluntarily ceased functioning as a player agent because of a lawsuit filed against him by a former NBA player client, Kareem Abdul-Jabbar, the former center of the Los Angeles Lakers, but retained his certification. Collins said he would not resume agent activities until he was exonerated of all charges in the pending lawsuit. In that case, Abdul-Jabbar, together with Ain Jeem, Inc. a corporation Abdul-Jabbar had established, alleged that Collins had committed numerous serious breaches of the fiduciary duty he owed as an agent to Abdul-Jabbar.

The alleged breaches included mishandling of Abdul-Jabbar's federal and state income tax returns which caused Abdul-Jabbar to pay approximately $300,000 in interest charges and late penalties; improvidently investing Abdul-Jabbar's money; mismanaging Abdul-Jabbar's assets; and transferring funds from Abdul-Jabbar's accounts without permission to the accounts of other players who were also Collins' clients. Collins' certification was revoked because he failed to pay agent dues and failed to attend at least one agent seminar as required by the Regulations.

Collins submitted an application to be recertified as a player agent. His application noted that there was still pending against him another lawsuit filed by another NBA player, Lucius Allen, and that eight of his former player clients—Abdul-Jabbar, Alex English, Lucius Allen, Rickey Sobers, Terry Cummings, Ralph Sampson, Rudy Hackett and Brad Davis—had discharged him by the end of 1986.

By letter dated December 14, 1990, the Committee issued its decision denying Collins certification as a player agent. The letter explained that based on the allegations against him by Abdul-Jabbar and the information gathered by the Committee, the Committee concluded that Collins was unfit to serve in a fiduciary capacity on behalf of NBA players and that he made false or misleading statements to the Committee concerning a relevant subject in connection with the investigation into his application. Specifically, the Committee found: (1) Collins violated fiduciary duties to his former client Kareem Abdul-Jabbar and Ain Jeem, Inc. in his preparation and filing of federal and state tax returns, causing penalties and interest in excess of $300,000 to be imposed on Mr. Abdul-Jabbar and the corporation. (2) In handling the financial and business affairs of Mr. Abdul-Jabbar and other players, Collins acknowledged commingling funds from one account to another without authorization and resulting in losses of over $200,000 to

Mr. Abdul-Jabbar. (3) Collins ignored requests by Mr. Abdul-Jabbar to invest money in safe investments, and invested in speculative ventures, many of which produced negative investment results. (4) In December 1985, Collins converted a corporate indebtedness of approximately $290,000 into a personal obligation of Mr. Abdul-Jabbar's without his approval. He also caused Mr. Abdul-Jabbar to execute loan documents relating to several investments making him jointly and severally liable for repaying loans. (5) Collins told the Committee that he had not filed his own Federal income taxes for the four year period 1986 through 1989 (even though he admitted earning over $300,000 in 1986). (6) Collins falsely represented to the Committee that Mr. Abdul-Jabbar paid $300,000 of Collins indebtedness to the Bank of California in connection with settling a lawsuit filed by Mr. Abdul-Jabbar and Ain-Jeem against Collins.

1. Were the NBPA actions against Collins ethical and fair?
2. What were the agent abuses that lead to the NBPA's adoption of agent regulations in 1986?
3. Should unions require agents to carry malpractice insurance during the representation process with a player?
4. Why do unions require Standard Representation Agreements (SRAs) between a player and an agent? Why not allow each player to negotiate whatever agreement he or she can with an agent? Why would a union want all agreements to be uniform?

Collins v. National Basketball Players Ass'n, 850 F. Supp. 1468 (D. Colo. 1991).

Most unions can decertify an agent for misconduct. What type of misconduct would require union intervention? What about an agent who files for personal bankruptcy? What about an agent who is charged with or convicted of drunk driving or domestic violence? Should a union be able to regulate an agent's conduct "off the field"?

Former NBA star Scottie Pippen prevailed against his former financial advisor Robert Lunn and won a judgment of $11.8 million. Pippen never recovered any of the money because his former advisor filed for bankruptcy after the judgment.[19] Baseball great Sandy Koufax lost a substantial amount of money due to the fraudulent actions of Bernard Madoff.[20] Should a players association be able to regulate the financial advisors of players as well as agents? The NFLPA publishes guidelines on the regulations of financial advisors.[21]

State Agent Legislation

The states that currently have agent legislation, for the most part, have adopted the Uniform Athlete Agents Act (2000) (UAAA), which was drafted by a commission made mostly of university and NCAA representatives. The UAAA, which protects primarily the interests of colleges and universities, only applies to an agent's dealings and transactions with amateur athletes and requires an agent to be registered before initiating contact with an amateur athlete. If an agent enters into an agency contract with an amateur athlete, the UAAA requires the agent to immediately notify the athletic director of the educational institution at which the athlete is enrolled (or intends to enroll).

The UAAA directs each state to determine the criminal sanctions and civil penalties (fines) that will result from violations of the UAAA. It also gives an educational institution a right of action against (the ability to sue) an agent or a former student-athlete for damages caused by losses and expenses incurred as a result of the institution being penalized, disqualified, or suspended from participation in athletics by the NCAA, by an athletic conference, or by self-imposed disciplinary action. In your view, is it a good use of state resources to enforce a private association's (the NCAA's) bylaws against agents because the association has no jurisdiction over agents?

In the states that have adopted legislation, athlete agents must register with the state where they reside and with each state where they do business. States provide a list of eligible sports agents to universities who in turn allow the agent on campus to interview student-athletes. If the agent's name does not appear on the certified state list, the agent cannot recruit student-athletes in that state.

In many states an application must be completed by the potential athlete agent before he or she can become certified. The application sometimes requires a fee, and renewal of the license also requires a fee. In addition, some states require agents to obtain a surety bond. The athlete agent registration typically requires the applicant to provide information relating to the following before the applicant can be considered for certification by the state:

- Entity name and type
- Background and employment experience
- References
- Athlete representation experience
- Additional persons who recruit or solicit athletes
- Financially interested parties

University Regulations

What ethical duties do universities have to assist student-athletes in the proper selection of an agent? Many universities hold an agent day on campus so registered agents can come to the university campus and be interviewed by student-athletes who are contemplating a professional career. How should colleges and universities go about regulating agents, if at all? Some universities and colleges have established rules and regulations for agents who desire to interview college athletes on campus. The following is a sample university policy dealing with agents and student-athletes:

The University requires that all agents and their interactions with the University's student-athletes comply with the following policies:

1. Any contact with a University student-athlete with eligibility remaining must be arranged through the University's Athletic Director for Compliance and Eligibility.

2. The Athletic Director for Compliance and Eligibility will advise the agent in the event a student-athlete requests an interview with that player agent. The location and time of the interview program will also be communicated to the player agent by a representative of the Office of Compliance.

3. Agents and their runners and/or representatives are prohibited from any type or form of contact (including but not limited to phone calls, letters, email messages, fax messages, text, Twitter, and communications in person) not made under the supervision and assistance of the Athletic Director for Compliance and Eligibility with a student-athlete, their spouse, parents, or legal guardian while that student-athlete remains eligible for intercollegiate competition.

4. All agents are required to direct all correspondence to the University's Athletic Director for Compliance and Eligibility where each student-athlete has a file.

5. In the event a student-athlete, their parents, or legal guardians contact an agent to arrange a discussion of that agent's qualification or proficiency in the marketing of the student-athlete's athletic ability or reputation, that agent is not permitted to discuss that agent's services until after the agent has given notice of the proposed discussion to the University's Associate Athletic Director for Compliance and Eligibility.

6. All agents interested in representing a student-athlete from the University are required to register with the University Athletic Director for Compliance and Eligibility.

The University will establish dates on which interviews may be held with University student-athletes during the academic year.

Why do you suppose a university or college would want to have a policy like this? If you were an athletic director for compliance, would you want to have such a policy? What are the pros and cons? NCAA bylaws do not prohibit contact or communications between agents and student-athletes. The University of Southern California sued sports agent Robert Caron for what they deemed to be improper contact with student-athletes. He allegedly gave student-athletes airline tickets, rent money, and phone cards for promises of future representation. The case was eventually settled for $50,000.[22]

National Collegiate Athletic Association (NCAA)

What role should the NCAA play in regulating sports agents? The NCAA's "no agent" rule declares an athlete ineligible if a lawyer represents the athlete in contract negotiations with a professional team. NCAA Bylaw 12.3.2 states: "Securing advice from a lawyer concerning a proposed professional sports contract shall not be considered contracting for representation by an agent under this rule, unless the lawyer also represents the individual in negotiations for such a contract." NCAA Bylaw 12.3.2.1 states: "A lawyer may not be present during discussions of a contract offer with a professional organization or have any direct contact (in person, by telephone or by mail) with a professional sports organization on behalf of the individual. A lawyer's presence during such discussions is considered representation by an agent."

What are the ethical dilemmas in hindering a lawyer-agent from representing an individual's best interest by negotiating a contract with a professional team? In Case 9-11, a college baseball player successfully obtained a court order that struck down the NCAA's "no agent" rule.

⚖ CASE 9-11　*Andrew Oliver v. National Collegiate Athletic Association*

920 N.E.2d 203 (Ohio Ct. Com. Pl. 2009)

…. [T]he defendant, and for that matter OSU, was required to deal honestly and reasonably with the plaintiff as a third-party beneficiary of its contractual relationship. Surely each party is entitled to the benefit of its bargain. With that stated, if this court determines that Bylaw 12.3.2.1 is void because it is against the public policy of Ohio or because it is arbitrary and capricious, and Bylaw 19.7 interferes with the delegation of judicial power to the courts of this state, then the defendant has not dealt with the plaintiff honestly or reasonably and the defendant has breached the contract.

…. [T]he crux of this case falls under Bylaw 12.3.2, which carves out an exception to the no-agent rule by allowing a student-athlete to retain a lawyer (not even the defendant can circumvent an individual's right to counsel).

…. The process advanced by the NCAA hinders representation by legal counsel, creating an atmosphere fraught with ethical dilemmas and pitfalls that an attorney consulting a student-athlete must encounter. Will the attorney be able to advance what is best for the client or will a neutral party, the NCAA, tie his hands? What harm could possibly befall the student-athlete if such a rule were not found?

…. If the defendant intends to deal with this athlete or any athlete in good faith, the student-athlete should have the opportunity to have the tools present (in this case an attorney) that would allow him to make a wise decision without automatically being deemed a professional, especially when such contractual negotiations can be overwhelming even to those who are skilled in their implementation.

Andrew Oliver v. National Collegiate Athletic Association, U.S. Supreme Court.

What purpose does the NCAA's "no agent" rule serve? Professor Karcher served as an expert in the case on behalf of Andy Oliver and testified that the rule has no relation to the stated purpose of preserving "amateurism." He also testified about the necessity for an MLB draft prospect to have an agent and that a substantial majority of prospects have an agent. Is the rule unethical? What ethical normative principles guided the judge in his ruling that declared the NCAA's rule void as against public policy? Rather than appeal the court's ruling, the NCAA settled with Oliver by paying him $750,000. The court's order was vacated as part of the settlement.

▶ Criminal Acts of Agents

The criminal acts of sports agents have become widely known through media reports. Reports of agents mismanaging and misappropriating the fortunes of players have become headline news, as have reports of agents who pay amateur players and bestow gifts on potential clients who are still amateur athletes. All this activity creates ethical issues in the sports agent business, and some agents have even been prosecuted for criminal behavior.

Norby Walters and Lloyd Bloom were able to sign 58 college football players to representation agreements. They also "loaned" money to amateur players. All but two of their clients fired them after the players graduated from college. Walters and Bloom were eventually found guilty of criminal charges arising out of their activities. In the following case, Walters and Bloom filed a civil lawsuit to enforce a "postdated" agency agreement they entered with a football player at Auburn before or during the football season of his senior year.

⚖ CASE 9-12 *Walters v. Fullwood*

675 F.Supp. 155 (S.D.N.Y. 1987)

Brent Fullwood … was an outstanding running back with the University of Auburn football team in Alabama. His success in the highly competitive Southeastern Athletic Conference marked him as a top professional prospect. At an unspecified time during his senior year at Auburn, Fullwood entered into an agreement with W.S. & E., a New York corporation ("the W.S. & E. agreement"). The agreement was dated January 2, 1987, the day after the last game of Fullwood's college football career, and the first day he could sign such a contract without forfeiting his amateur status under sec. 3-1-(c) of the N.C.A.A. Constitution … The contract was arranged and signed for the corporation by [Lloyd] Bloom, and granted W.S. & E. the exclusive right to represent Fullwood as agent to negotiate with professional football teams after the spring draft of the National Football League ("N.F.L."). [Norby] Walters and Bloom were the corporate officers and sole shareholders of W.S. & E. As a provisionally certified N.F.L. Players' Association ("N.F.L.P.A.") contract advisor, Bloom was subject to the regulations of that body governing agents ("N.F.L.P.A. Agents' Regulations"), which require the arbitration of most disputes between players and contract advisors.

On August 20, 1986, W.S. & E. paid $4,000 to Fullwood, who then executed a promissory note [for Walters and Bloom] for that amount … At various times throughout the 1986 season, [Walters and Bloom] sent to Fullwood or his family further payments that totaled $4,038.

… While neither [Walters and Bloom] nor [Fullwood] have specifically admitted that the W.S. & E. agency agreement was postdated, they have conspicuously avoided identifying the actual date it was signed. There is a powerful inference that the agreement was actually signed before or during the college football season, perhaps contemporaneously with the August 20 promissory note, and unethically postdated as in other cases involving [Walters and Bloom]. No argument or evidence has been presented to dispel this inference, and the Court believes the parties deliberately postdated the contract January 2. Even if this likelihood is not accepted, it is conceded by all parties and proven by documentary evidence that a security interest was granted on Fullwood's future earnings from professional football, by the express terms of the promissory note of August 20, 1986.

At some point prior to the N.F.L. spring 1987 draft, Fullwood repudiated his agreement with W.S. & E., and chose to be represented by [agent] George Kickliter, an attorney in Auburn, Alabama. As anticipated,

Fullwood was taken early in the N.F.L. draft. The Green Bay Packers selected him as the fourth player in the first round; he signed a contract with them, and currently is playing in his rookie season in the N.F.L.

Walters v. Fullwood, 675 F. Supp. 155 (S.D.N.Y. 1987), U.S. Supreme Court.

According to the court, there was a powerful inference that the agency agreement was "unethically postdated." Is it unethical to postdate a contract? If so, why?

In the following case, the U.S. government sued an agent for his unethical and illegal acts over his dealing with amateur athletes.

⚖ CASE 9-13   *United States v. Piggie*

303 F.3d 923 (8th Cir. 2002)

In the mid to late 1990's, Myron Piggie (Piggie) created and pursued a secret scheme to pay talented high school athletes to play basketball for his "amateur" summer team. Because the athletes intended to play college basketball, the scheme produced multiple violations of National Collegiate Athletic Association (NCAA) rules which require college athletes to be amateurs. Piggie pled guilty to one count of conspiracy to commit mail and wire fraud and one count of failure to file an income tax return.

Between 1995 and 1999, Myron Piggie devised a scheme to assemble elite high school basketball players and compensate them for their participation on his traveling Amateur Athletic Union (AAU) basketball team, known first as the Children's Mercy Hospital 76ers and later as the KC Rebels. The payments were designed to retain top athletes on his team, gain access to sports agents, obtain profitable sponsorship contracts, and forge ongoing relationships with players to his benefit when the athletes joined the National Basketball Association (NBA).

The pre-sentence report shows Piggie realized at least $677,760 in income through his scheme. In the plea agreement, Piggie concedes that, as a result of his fraud, he received a total of $420,401 between 1995 and 1998. Piggie received at least $184,435 from team owner Tom Grant, $159,866 from team sponsor Nike, and $76,100 from sports agents Jerome Stanley and Kevin Poston. He further planned on receiving a portion of his players' compensation when they became professional athletes.

Piggie received a gross income of approximately $99,100 from these sources during the 1998 calendar year, and he knowingly and willfully failed to file a tax return by April 15, 1999. Piggie also failed to file income tax returns in 1995, 1996, and 1997. In the plea agreement, the parties stipulated to a total tax loss of $67,662.69 for the period of 1995 to 1998.

Piggie took portions of the money he was receiving as the coach of this elite AAU team and made payments to the high school athletes in a clandestine manner, frequently hiding the money in Nike shoe boxes. All of the parties intended to keep the payments a secret from authorities. During the conspiracy, Piggie paid Jaron Rush $17,000, Korleone Young (Young) $14,000, Corey Maggette (Maggette) $2,000, Kareem Rush $2,300, and Andre Williams (Williams) $200.

After accepting Piggie's payments to play AAU basketball, Jaron Rush, Maggette, Kareem Rush, and Williams submitted false and fraudulent Student-Athlete Statements to the universities where they were to play intercollegiate basketball. These four athletes falsely certified that they had not previously received payments to play basketball. The athletes delivered through the U.S. Postal Service signed letters of intent asserting their eligibility. Based upon the false assertions that these athletes were eligible amateurs, the University of California, Los Angeles (UCLA); Duke University (Duke); the University of Missouri-Columbia (Missouri); and Oklahoma State University (OSU) (collectively Universities) awarded scholarships to these athletes, enrolled them in classes, and allowed them to play on NCAA basketball teams.

NCAA regulations permit universities to award only thirteen basketball scholarships per year. When Piggie's payments to these players were discovered, the Universities became subject to NCAA penalties. Each school lost the use of one of the thirteen scholarships and lost the value of each player's participation due to the player's NCAA-required suspension. The scholarships were forfeited, and the Universities lost the opportunity to award the scholarships to other top amateur athletes, who had actual eligibility to play intercollegiate basketball. In 1999 and 2000, UCLA lost the benefit of playing Jaron Rush, the $44,862.88 scholarship awarded to him, and also forfeited $42,339 in tournament revenue; Missouri lost the benefit of playing Kareem Rush, and the $9,388.92 scholarship awarded to him; and OSU lost the benefit of playing Williams and the $12,180 scholarship awarded to him. Duke provided Maggette with a $32,696 scholarship for the 1998-1999 season based upon the false assertion that he was an eligible amateur. As a result of the ineligible athlete's participation, the validity of Duke's entire 1998-1999 season was called into question.

NCAA regulations also required each of the four Universities involved to conduct costly internal investigations after Piggie's scheme was discovered. UCLA spent $59,225.36 on the NCAA-mandated investigation of Jaron Rush, Duke spent $12,704.39 on the NCAA-mandated investigation of Maggette, Missouri spent $10,609 on the NCAA-mandated investigation of Kareem Rush, and OSU spent $21,877.24 on the NCAA-mandated investigation of Williams. The total monetary loss to the Universities was $245,882.79. The scandal following the disclosure of Piggie's scheme caused further intangible harms to the Universities including adverse publicity, diminished alumni support, merchandise sales losses, and other revenue losses.

Pembroke Hill High School (Pembroke), where Jaron and Kareem Rush played high school basketball, sustained a loss of $10,733.89 in investigative costs and forfeiture of property as a result of the conspiracy. Pembroke was placed on probation by the State of Missouri after the violations of Jaron and Kareem Rush were discovered and a mandatory investigation of the matter was concluded.

After Piggie's guilty plea, the district court sentenced him to 37 months imprisonment, three years supervised release, and $324,279.87 in restitution.

1. Was Piggie's conduct unethical? Why or why not?
2. Do you believe the penalty fits the crime? What exactly was the crime?
3. Did Piggie cause damage to the universities? Or was the damage self-inflicted by the universities as a result of their own voluntary association's "amateurism" rules? Could Piggie assert that but for the rules they created, they wouldn't have been damaged?

United State v. Piggie, U.S. Supreme Court.

In the next case, an uncertified sports agent sued Marcus Camby and his agent ProServ (the same agency sued in Case 9-4 for stealing Ivan Rodriguez from Speakers of Sport), claiming the player "took him for a ride" and promised the uncertified agent that he could represent him when he began his professional career.

⚖ CASE 9-14 *Lounsbury v. Camby*

2003 WL 22792348

… John Lounsbury initiated an action against Camby and ProServ, Inc. ("ProServ"). Lounsbury alleges that, while a student at the University of Massachusetts and a member of its basketball team, Camby promised that he would sign an exclusive agency contract with [Lounsbury] when he ended his collegiate career if Lounsbury provided Camby, his friends and family with money, gifts, gratuities and services. At the time of the alleged agreement, Lounsbury was not a certified agent and therefore was not authorized, in accordance with the collective bargaining agreement between the Players Association and the National Basketball Association (NBA), to represent Camby in contract negotiations with any NBA team. In 1996 Camby signed an exclusive agency contract with ProServ to represent him in contract negotiations with the NBA team that drafted Camby … Lounsbury alleges that Camby breached his oral contract with him by signing with ProServ and that ProServ tortuously interfered with his agreement with Camby.

ProServ states that Lounsbury is basing his action … on conduct that violates Connecticut civil and criminal law with respect to prohibited acts of athlete agents. In Connecticut General Statutes § 20-555, Prohibited Acts are defined as:

An [athlete-agent] shall not:

1. Publish or cause to be published any false, fraudulent or misleading information, representation, notice or advertisement or give any false information or make any false promises or representations to any person concerning any employment;
2. Divide fees with or receive compensation from a professional sports league or franchise or its representative or employee;
3. Enter into any agreement, written or oral, by which the athlete agent offers anything of value to any employee of an institution of higher education located in this state in return for the referral of any athlete by that employee;
4. Enter into an oral or written agent contract or professional sport services contract with an athlete before the athlete's eligibility for collegiate athletics expires; or
5. Give, offer or promise anything of value to an athlete, his guardian or to any member of the athlete's immediate family before the athlete's eligibility for collegiate athletics expires.

The statutory civil and criminal penalties for failing to comply with § 20-555 include,

a. 1. The Commissioner of Consumer Protection may, after notice and conducting a hearing … revoke or suspend any certificate of registration.
    2. The commissioner shall revoke any such certificate of registration held by any person.
b. The Commissioner of Consumer Protection may, after notice and conducting a hearing … order restitution or impose a civil penalty, or both … Any civil penalty imposed by the commissioner under this subsection shall not exceed one thousand dollars plus the amount of profits derived as a result of the violation minus any amount paid as restitution.
c. In addition to any other remedy provided any person who violates any provision shall [also] be guilty of a class B misdemeanor.

Modified from Lounsbury v. Camby.

Marcus Camby later admitted to having taken thousands of dollars in cash from agents in violation of NCAA rules while at the University of Massachusetts (UMass). Agents supplied him with "money, jewelry, rental cars, and prostitutes," which he accepted and sometimes even requested. He left UMass after his junior year of college and, with the help of ProServ, negotiated a 3-year $8 million contract as the number 2 pick in the 1996 NBA draft. Camby admitted that while at an electronics store with John Lounsbury in March 1995, he asked the agent to buy him a stereo for his birthday which Lounsbury bought on the spot for $1,066.00.[23] To what extent should Marcus Camby be held responsible for his actions? Is Camby as culpable as his uncertified agent for what transpired?

▶ Summary

Because of a few bad apples, sports agents have not always had the best reputation. Although "unscrupulous," "unethical," and "cutthroat" qualities are synonymous with the profession, the reality is that most agents look after the best interest of their clients and serve as zealous advocates on their behalf. The sport management professional must understand the nature of the fiduciary relationship that exists between the agent and athlete, including the agent's responsibilities imposed by the duties of loyalty and care under state law agency principles. The sport management professional must also be familiar with the web of agent regulations that players' associations, legislative bodies, state attorney generals, and universities have adopted in an attempt to curb the unethical conduct of agents.

▶ References

1. In the 1990s sport agents were given a Hollywood spotlight when Tom Cruise starred as *Jerry McGuire*, the fictional NFL agent representing an Arizona Cardinals wide receiver who possessed a good dose of talent, confidence, and attitude.
2. Jim Reisler, *Cash and Carry: The Spectacular Rise and Hard Fall of C.C. Pyle, America's First Sports Agent*, McFarland Publishing, 2008.
3. David Stevens, *Baseball's Radical for All Seasons: A Biography of John Montgomery Ward*, The Scarecrow Press, Inc., 1998.
4. George Dohrmann, "Confessions of an Agent," *Sports Illustrated*, October 18, 2010.
5. Associated Press, "Alabama Coach Nick Saban Compares Unscrupulous Agents to a 'Pimp,'" *ESPN. com*, July 22, 2010.
6. Lori K. Miller, "A Uniform Code to Regulate Athlete Agents," *Journal of Sports & Social Issues* 16, no. 2 (1992): 93, 102.
7. Keith Harriston and Sally Jenkins, "Maryland Basketball Star Len Bias is Dead at 22," *Washington Post*, June 20, 1986.
8. Jason Cole, "Williams Should Have Gotten Better Deal," *Yahoo! Sports*, September 5, 2008.
9. Ibid.
10. Kenneth L. Shropshire, Timothy Davis, *The Business of Sports Agents*, 2nd Edition, University of Pennsylvania Press, 2nd Edition, May 28, 2008.
11. Karen Crouse, "Pro Football, Ricky Williams Steps Carefully Toward Return," *New York Times*, July 11, 2005; Jason Cole, "Williams Should Have Gotten Better Deal," *Yahoo! Sports*, September 5, 2008. "In the Replay Booth: Looking at Appeals of Arbitration Decision in Sports Through Miami Dolphins v. Williams," *Harvard Negotiation Law Review* (Spring 2007).
12. Ron Simon, *The Game Behind the Game, Negotiating in the Big Leagues* (Stillwater, MN: Voyageur Press, 1993).
13. *Steinberg Moorad & Dunn Inc. v. Dunn*, 136 Fed App 6 (9th Cir 2005); Liz Mullen, "David Dunn Agrees to 18-Month Suspension," *Sports Business Daily*, November 22, 2006.
14. Ronald D. Rotunda, *Legal Ethics in a Nutshell, 3rd Ed.*, Thomson West, 2007.
15. Model Rules of Professional Conduct, Rule 7.3.
16. Kenneth L. Shropshire and Timothy Davis, *The Business of Sports Agents* (Philadelphia, PA; University of Pennsylvania Press, 2008).
17. *Carl Poston v. NFL Players Association*, United States District Court Southern District of New York, 06 Civ. 2249 (BSJ).
18. Letter to the Honorable Henry Hyde and the Honorable Sheila Jackson Lee dated July 14, 2006, from NFLPA president, Eugene Upshaw. "Testimony of Richard A. Berthelsen, General Counsel, NFLPA" and "Testimony of Professor Richard Karcher" before the Administrative and Commercial Law Subcommittee of the Judiciary Committee, U.S. House of Representatives, December 7, 2006. Richard T. Karcher, "Fundamental Fairness in Union Regulation of Sports Agents," *Connecticut Law Review* 40, no. 2 (2007): 357.
19. Geoff Dougherty, "Chicago Bulls' Scottie Pippen Wins Judgment over Investment Advice," *Chicago Tribune*, November 24, 2004, B1.
20. Thomas Zambino and Larry Mcshane, "Sandy Koufax, John Malkovich Among Bernie Madoff Victims as Court Filings Are Released," *New York Daily News*, February 5, 2009.
21. "Securities and Exchange Commission, No-Action Letter under: Investment Advisers Act of 1940-Sections 202(a)(11); 206(4) and Rule 206(4)-3, National Football League Players Association," January 25, 2002, Response of the Office of Chief Counsel Division of Investment Manager, No. 2002-1251421, National Football League Players Association.
22. "College Football; Agent Agrees to Settle Suit," *New York Times*, October 14, 1995.
23. Phil Taylor, "Tangled Web: Marcus was Both Victim and Villain in his Illicit Dealings with Agents While at UMass," *Sports Illustrated*, September 15, 1997.

CHAPTER 10

Gender Discrimination and Title IX

▶ Introduction

American women have faced many historical challenges. A discriminatory attitude toward women has permeated virtually every aspect of American society, from business to politics, to the sports world; however, in the past few decades, women have seen many changes to the roles they play in society. Women have held a variety of leadership positions in all aspects of society and have become major political figures, leading business executives, attorneys, and educators. In the sports world, women have become announcers, participants, sports lawyers, team executives, and sports agents. Notwithstanding the substantial progress that has been made, women executives in sports still face many hurdles and a glass ceiling still exists at certain levels of sport. Few women hold the position of vice president or higher in professional sports franchises.

Fortunately, the role of women in sports has increased in recent years. Girls are participating more than ever in sports at the amateur level and colleges and universities are promoting women's sports at an increasing rate. In 1972, only 1 in 27 girls in secondary schools

participated in sports, or about 300,000 girls; by 2008, almost 3 million girls were participating in high school athletics, or about 1 in 3. Nonetheless, women today continue to face many obstacles and barriers in the sports field. Women and girls are still subjected to sexual harassment and discrimination, whether as a team executive or a professional or amateur athlete.

Prior to the 1970s, women had very few opportunities to participate in athletics and there were virtually no opportunities for women in the coaching or administrative ranks of sport. Historically, several arguments were offered in support of the spurious theory that women were not suited for or capable of successfully competing athletically with or against men. Women were falsely stereotyped as being too delicate, frail, or weak to participate in sports. Because of this traditional, but obviously misguided perspective, females of all ages have historically been denied athletic opportunities. In 1972, virtually no colleges offered women's sports scholarships, and women's participation in sports was restricted many times to being a mere bystander.

It has also long been asserted that men consistently outperform women and that they are physiologically superior to women. Although it is true that the anatomical composition of males and females is quite different, studies have shown that each has advantages and disadvantages.[1] One study, in particular, described the differences between the sexes in relation to athletics and concluded that due to the structure of the male body, a man has an advantage over a woman in throwing, striking, and physically explosive types of events; whereas the proportions of the female body allow advantages in balance, stability, and flexibility. It is undisputed that women can participate in competitive sports at the highest levels.

Some have argued that segregation of the sexes is necessary to prevent physical and psychological injury to girls and women; unfortunately, this outdated argument perpetuates the stereotype of the "weak woman" who is unable to cope with the competitive nature associated with athletics.[2] Furthermore, it has been argued that "tradition" in sports requires separate teams. Finally, unfortunately, many have clung to the stereotype that girls should not be involved in sports in any manner on a competitive level with boys. Schools have not historically allocated an equal amount of funding for female athletic programs and have discriminated against girls by providing better schedules, better fields, and better equipment for boys. Boys also traditionally have been given a wider selection of sports to play than girls.

Nonetheless, in the past two decades, the number of women participating in sports programs and the amount of money expended in support of women's athletics have increased dramatically; furthermore, women's professional sports leagues have become very popular. There are several reasons for this development in athletics for women, one of which is the changing societal attitude towards women in general. This has included women's own perceptions about their athletic capabilities and participation.

One helpful hand has come from the NCAA, which is committed to providing equal athletic opportunities without regard to gender, and they have remained true to this goal over a long period of time.

There has been a growing interest in female sports by spectators and fans at both the professional and amateur levels. Local and national media coverage of female athletic events has also greatly increased. The women's NCAA "Final Four" in basketball is very popular, as is the "Frozen Four" in women's hockey. Media coverage for the women's NCAA Final Four in basketball has increased greatly. The number of media credentials issued for the women's NCAA Final Four in 1982 was only 37. That number grew to 557 for the women's NCAA Final Four in St. Louis in 2009.

Although girls in amateur sports have achieved some success, many have been treated like "second class" citizens during their athletic careers. Progress has been made in recent years, and increased funding for women's athletics at the high school and collegiate levels has expanded athletic opportunities for women and girls. All of these issues are encouraging and indicate a positive movement towards more female involvement in sports at all levels. Still, some significant considerations need to be addressed. As women reach higher competitive levels, they will begin to face the same pressures to succeed that men face and will experience the same pressures to prevail in the competitive world of sports.[3]

▶ Ethics of Opportunities for Girls and Women in Sports

On December 26, 1974, the Federal Little League Baseball Charter was amended by Pub. L. No. 93–551 (December 26, 1974, 88 Stat. 1744, 93 Congress). The amended charter deleted the word "boys" from each place it appeared in the original charter and replaced it with "young people." The phrase "citizenship, sportsmanship and manhood" was replaced with "citizenship and sportsmanship." The stated purpose of the amendment was to indicate that Little League "shall be open to girls as well as boys." Approximately 5 million girls have participated in Little League Baseball and Softball since 1970.

Case 10-1 involves a fierce baseball player and a Little League All-Star. Her high school had a girls' softball team, but she wanted to play baseball. If her school maintained a separate girls' team in the same or a related sport, the rules said that a girl could not play on the boys' team. The question presented was whether baseball and softball were "substantial equivalents."

⚖ CASE 10-1 Israel v. West Virginia Secondary Schools Activities Commission

388 S.E.2d 480 (1989)

Ms. Israel has a great deal of experience playing baseball. She began playing baseball at the age of six in the local park and recreation league where she learned the basic fundamentals of the game. At the age of nine, Ms. Israel progressed into the Little League system. Her Little League coach testified that Ms. Israel's skills were always above average. He stated that "[s]he was very aggressive, understood the game, its concepts, and its technique." While playing Little League, Ms. Israel was nominated for every all-star team. At the age of thirteen, she became the first female to ever play on a Pony League team in Pleasants County. When Ms. Israel was a freshman at St. Marys High School, and expressed a desire to play on the all-male baseball team, the high school baseball coach told her he had no objections to her playing for him and promised to give her a fair tryout. In February, 1984, Ms. Israel tried out for the all-male high school baseball team. She was prohibited from playing on the team because of a regulation promulgated by the Secondary Schools Activities Commission (SSAC).

Rule No. 3.9, which provides:

"If a school maintains separate teams in the same or related sports (example: baseball or softball) for girls and boys during the school year, regardless of the sports season, girls may not participate on boys' teams and boys may not participate on girls' teams. However, should a school not maintain separate teams in the same or related sports for boys and girls, then boys and girls may participate on the same team except in contact sports such as football and wrestling."

Shortly after Ms. Israel tried out to play on the baseball team, she was informed by St. Marys' assistant principal that she was ineligible to play on the baseball team because St. Marys had a girls' softball team. The assistant principal explained that if the school allowed Ms. Israel to play baseball, it would be in violation of Rule 3.9 and would be barred from playing in state tournaments. After numerous futile efforts to have the rule changed through the internal mechanisms provided by the SSAC, Ms. Israel filed a complaint with the Human Rights Commission.

From the record in this case, we find that the games of baseball and softball are not substantially equivalent. There is, of course, a superficial similarity between the games because both utilize a similar format. However, when the rules are analyzed, there is a substantial disparity in the equipment used and in the skill level required.

> The difference begins with the size of the ball and its delivery, and differences continue throughout. The softball is larger and must be thrown underhanded, which forecloses the different types of pitching that can be accomplished in the overhand throw of a baseball.
>
> 1. Should Ms. Israel be allowed to play on the boys' team?
> 2. Rule 3.9 essentially tracks the requirements under Title IX (but it does not say "related"). Is the rule discriminatory and reflective of outdated stereotypes?
> 3. Do you consider any rule that discriminates based on gender as opposed to skill unethical?
> 4. Is there a legitimate reason for the "contact sport" exception in Rule 3.9 and Title IX?
>
> Israel v. West Virginia Secondary Schools Activities Commission, U.S. Supreme Court.

Gender Discrimination

Historically, discrimination against women and girls has taken many forms. Gender discrimination is both unethical and illegal and can be remedied through the court system in attempts to prevent future discriminatory behavior. Historically, girls' sports teams have typically suffered inequalities in the following areas and more, at all levels of sports:

- Publicity for sports teams or individual athletes
- Medical services provided to the team or athlete (trainers, etc.)
- Travel expenses
- Scheduling
- Operating expenses and funds for athletic competition
- Recruiting budgets
- Provision of equipment and facilities
- Number of coaches
- Payment to coaches
- Access to facilities and quality of facilities

The general rule in both contact and non-contact sports is that when only one team is available, both sexes must be allowed to try out for and play on the team. In the majority of cases involving non-contact sports in which no women's team is available, the trend is to allow women to participate on the men's team. If there is ample opportunity for women to compete on their own, courts appear less apt to allow women to compete with men in contact sports.

The HEW regulations under Title IX permit an athletic department that receives federal funds to maintain separate teams for each sex if selection for the teams is based on competitive skill or if the sport involved is a contact sport. The competitive skill exception applies to most programs because athletics, by their very nature, are based on individual skill; therefore, separate teams are permissible for most sports. If no team is sponsored for one gender in a particular sport, the excluded sex must be permitted to try out for that team, unless it is a contact sport. Contact sports include boxing, wrestling, rugby, ice hockey, football, basketball, and other sports in which the purpose or major activity involves bodily contact. In some cases, baseball and soccer have also been determined to be contact sports.

Women and girls have had to overcome many obstacles in their quest to achieve equality in the sporting world at all levels. In the following case, the issue was whether a woman could play on a college football team. Why not? Many women have done it and have been successful at it.[4] Placekicker Heather Sue Mercer was "kicked off" the Duke University football team. She then sued the University based on discrimination for their actions. The jury awarded $2 million in punitive damages to Mercer for her claim of discrimination against Duke University. The U.S. Court of Appeals overturned the award.

⚖ CASE 10-2 *Mercer v. Duke University*

190 F.3d 643 (1999)

... Duke University operates a Division I college football team. During the period ... (1994–98), ... Fred Goldsmith was head coach of the Duke Football team and ... Heather Sue Mercer was a student at the school.

Before attending Duke, Mercer was an all-state kicker at Yorktown Heights High School in Yorktown Heights, New York. Upon enrolling at Duke in the fall of 1994, Mercer tried out for the Duke football team as a walk-on kicker. Mercer was the first—and to date, only—woman to try out for the team. Mercer did not initially make the team, and instead served as a manager during the 1994 season; however, she regularly attended practices in the fall of 1994 and participated in conditioning drills the following spring.

In April 1995, the seniors on the team selected Mercer to participate in the Blue-White Game, an intrasquad scrimmage played each spring. In that game, Mercer kicked the winning 28-yard field goal, giving the Blue team a 24–22 victory. The kick was subsequently shown on ESPN, the cable television sports network. Soon after the game, Goldsmith told the news media that Mercer was on the Duke football team, and Fred Chatham, the Duke kicking coach, told Mercer herself that she had made the team. Also, Mike Cragg, the Duke sports information director, asked Mercer to participate in a number of interviews with newspaper, radio, and television reporters, including one with representatives from "The Tonight Show."

Although Mercer did not play in any games during the 1995 season, she again regularly attended practices in the fall and participated in conditioning drills the following spring. Mercer was also officially listed by Duke as a member of the Duke football team on the team roster filed with the NCAA and was pictured in the Duke football yearbook.

During this latter period, Mercer alleges that she was the subject of discriminatory treatment by Duke. Specifically, she claims that Goldsmith did not permit her to attend summer camp, refused to allow her to dress for games or sit on the sidelines during games, and gave her fewer opportunities to participate in practices than other walk-on kickers. In addition, Mercer claims that Goldsmith made a number of offensive comments to her, including asking her why she was interested in football, wondering why she did not prefer to participate in beauty pageants rather than football, and suggesting that she sit in the stands with her boyfriend rather than on the sidelines.

At the beginning of the 1996 season, Goldsmith informed Mercer that he was dropping her from the team. Mercer alleges that Goldsmith's decision to exclude her from the team was on the basis of her sex because Goldsmith allowed other, less qualified walk-on kickers to remain on the team. Mercer attempted to participate in conditioning drills the following spring, but Goldsmith asked her to leave because the drills were only for members of the team. Goldsmith told Mercer, however, that she could try out for the team again in the fall.

On September 16, 1997, rather than try out for the team again, Mercer filed suit against Duke and Goldsmith, alleging sex discrimination.

The court ruled in favor of Mercer. Under Title IX, Duke did not need to give Mercer a tryout because football is a "contact sport", but once they did and she made the team, the antidiscrimination provisions apply. Answer the following questions:

1. Were Coach Goldsmith's actions unethical?
2. Describe Coach Goldsmith's ethical decision-making process.
3. What actions should Duke University have taken against Coach Goldsmith, if any?

Mercer v. Duke University, U.S. Supreme Court.

Why are there not any women umpires in MLB? If women are able to perform the tasks of an umpire and are good enough to compete, shouldn't MLB allow them on the field as an umpire? Unbeknownst to many, baseball has a history of women umpires. The Baseball Hall of Fame recognizes Amanda Clement as the first woman to umpire a baseball game. She umpired for six years at the semi-pro level, umpiring her first game in 1904 when she was only 16 years old. Clement worked her way through Yankton College and The University of Nebraska earning $15 to $25 for umpiring games.[5] Her solid reputation as an umpire spread and she became a huge gate attraction. It was reported she received more than 60 marriage offers from players, but never married. Clement was regarded as an umpire who was fair, knew the rules, and was multi-talented. She later worked as a justice of the peace, a newspaper reporter, a social worker, and taught at the University of Wyoming.

No woman has yet made it as an umpire in the major leagues. Although many have tried, Pam Postema gave it her best shot. She encountered a glass ceiling and had to fight it out in court with MLB. They eventually settled the case with her on a confidential basis.

⚖ CASE 10-3 *Postema v. National League of Professional Baseball Clubs (MLB)*

799 F.Supp. 1475 (S.D. New York 1992)

Pamela Postema, a California resident, is a former professional baseball umpire.

After graduating from umpiring school with the rank of 17th in a class of 130 students, [Postema] began work in 1977 as a professional baseball umpire in the Gulf Coast League, a rookie league. At that time, she was the fourth woman ever to umpire a professional baseball game. [Postema] worked in the Gulf Coast League during 1977 and 1978. In 1979, she was promoted to the Class A Florida State League, where she umpired during the 1979 and 1980 seasons. In 1981, [Postema] was promoted to the AA Texas League, and she umpired there in 1981 and 1982. She was the first woman to ever umpire a professional baseball game above the Class A level.

In 1983, [Postema] was promoted to the AAA Pacific Coast League, where she umpired from 1983 to 1986. In 1987, her contract was acquired by Triple-A, and she umpired in that league from 1987 until her discharge in 1989.

[Postema] alleges that during her employment as a Triple-A umpire, [MLB] conferred on her significant duties and responsibilities, including the following:

- In 1987, [Postema] was the home plate umpire for the Hall of Fame exhibition game between the New York Yankees and the Atlanta Braves.
- In 1988, [Postema] was selected to umpire the Venezuela All Star game.
- In 1988 and 1989, [Postema] was the chief of her umpiring crew, with ultimate responsibility for its umpiring calls and performance.
- In 1988 and 1989, [Postema] was appointed to umpire Major League spring training games.
- In 1989, [Postema] was the home plate umpire for the first Triple-A Minor League All Star Game.
- In 1989, [Postema] was asked by Triple-A to become a supervisor for umpires in the minor league system.
- From 1987 to 1989, [Postema] received high praise from qualified and experienced baseball people, including Chuck Tanner, Tom Trebelhorn, Hal Lanier, and Roger Craig, all current or former managers of Major League teams.

Notwithstanding these responsibilities and honors, [Postema] alleges that throughout her career as a minor league umpire she was subjected to continual, repeated, and offensive acts of sexual harassment and gender discrimination. Such acts included the following:

- On numerous occasions, players and managers addressed her with a four-letter word beginning with the letter "c" that refers to female genitalia.
- Players and managers repeatedly told [Postema] that her proper role was cooking, cleaning, keeping house, or some other form of "women's work," rather than umpiring.
- Bob Knepper, a pitcher with the Houston Astros, told the press that although [Postema] was a good umpire, to have her as a major league umpire would be an affront to God and contrary to the teachings of the Bible.
- During arguments with players and managers, [Postema] was spat upon and was subjected to verbal and physical abuse to a greater degree than male umpires.
- In 1987, the manager of the Nashville Hounds kissed [Postema] on the lips when he handed her his lineup card.
- At a Major League spring training game in 1988, Chuck Tanner, then the manager of the Pittsburgh Pirates, asked [Postema] if she would like a kiss when he gave her his lineup card.
- Although [Postema] was well known throughout baseball as an excellent ball and strike umpire, she was directed and required by Ed Vargo, the Supervisor of Umpiring for the National League, to change her stance and technique to resemble those used by him during his career. No such requirement was placed on male umpires.

[Postema] continually took action against such conduct through warnings, ejections, and reports. Although the existence of such conduct was well known throughout baseball, no one in a position of authority, including [MLB], took action to correct, stop, or prevent such conduct.

[Postema] alleges that at the time she began her service with Triple-A, she was fully qualified to be a Major League umpire, and she had repeatedly made known to [MLB] her desire for employment in the Major Leagues. While she was not promoted to or hired by the National League or American League, male umpires having inferior experience, qualifications, and abilities were repeatedly and frequently promoted and hired by the National and American Leagues.

[Postema] alleges that in 1988 and 1989, "events came to a head" in her effort to become a Major League umpire. Specifically, in July 1987, Dick Butler, then Special Assistant to the President of the American League and the former supervisor of umpires for the American League, told Newsday that for [Postema] to become a Major League umpire:

"She realizes that she has to be better than the fellow next to her. She's got to be better because of the fact that she's a girl. I'm not saying it's fair, but it exists and she's not going to change it."

These comments were widely reported in the media, including in the *Los Angeles Times*. [MLB] neither issued any statements contradicting, retracting, or correcting Butler's statements, took any remedial or disciplinary action with respect to Butler, nor otherwise said or did anything to communicate that Butler had not stated the true position of professional baseball …

On May 14, 1989, Larry Napp, Assistant Supervisor of Umpires for the American League, told the *Richmond Times-Dispatch* that [Postema] would never become a Major League umpire. He stated:

"She's a nice person, and she knows the rules. But the thing is, she's got to do the job twice as good as the guy. …"

[MLB] neither issued any statements contradicting, retracting, or correcting Napp's statements, took any remedial or disciplinary action with respect to Napp, nor otherwise said or did anything to communicate that Napp had not stated the true position of professional baseball. …

During the 1989 season, Ed Vargo required [Postema] to adopt the above mentioned changes in her umpiring technique.

[Postema] alleges that during the 1989 season, [MLB] either ignored or criticized her. She and her partner were the only two of the nine minor league umpires invited to 1989 spring training who were not given the opportunity to fill in for ill or vacationing Major League umpires, an opportunity which was given to male umpires with inferior abilities, experience, and qualifications. At the end of the 1989 season, [Postema] received an unfairly negative written performance evaluation which alleged that she had a "bad attitude." Prior to 1989, [Postema] had never received a written performance evaluation.

On November 6, 1989, Triple-A discharged and unconditionally released [Postema] from her employment as an umpire. The reason for [Postema's] discharge was that the National League and American League were not interested in considering her for employment as a Major League umpire. [Postema] alleges that the sole reason for her discharge, for her inability to obtain a job in the Major Leagues [is] intentional discrimination on the basis of gender [by MLB].

1. Do you believe Postema was discriminated against?
2. Would training women at the high school level to become umpires assist in creating more of an interest in the umpire position for women?
3. Is MLB doing enough to encourage women to become umpires? If not, what more could be done?

Postema v. NATIONAL LEAGUE OF PRO. BASEBALL CLUBS, 799 F. Supp. 1475 (S.D.N.Y. 1992), U.S. Supreme Court.

A jury found that the NBA discriminated against a woman referee, Sandra Ortiz-Del Valle, when they failed to hire her as a referee. Even though the NBA had a woman referee at the time, Ortiz-Del Valle was able to prevail in front of a jury. In 1998, a jury awarded her $7.85 million after she had been passed over several times for an NBA referee position. The jury awarded her $100,000 for lost wages, $750,000 in mental pain and emotional distress, and $7 million in punitive damages. A federal judge reduced the award to $350,000. The NBA took a giant step forward when they hired Dee Kanter and Violet Palmer as NBA referees in 1997. Palmer said, "When I started my fourth season, I could kind of see the heads not turn anymore. . . . I could see players come up to me and just talk."[6] Palmer has proven that she can referee at the highest level of the sport and is one of the best in the world at what she does.

Sarah Thomas was a major college football referee. Thomas was the first woman to officiate a major college football game, the first to officiate a bowl game, and the first to officiate in a Big Ten stadium. She commented on her position, "Most of the time they are so focused on what they are doing, they don't notice me . . . and that is what every other official strives for. Our best games are the ones that no one knows we're there."[7] On April 8, 2015, the NFL officially announced that Thomas would become the first permanent female official in NFL history. On September 13, 2015, Thomas made her NFL regular season debut in a game between the Kansas City Chiefs and the Houston Texans.

Discrimination against women has historically permeated every aspect of the sports business, including the coaching ranks. There have been many successful women coaches, but historically most sports programs have been controlled and administered by men. Women have been under-represented at the highest levels of power in sports. Many reasons have been given for this, including that men have well-established connections to assist them in job searches, professional development opportunities are minimal for women, and many sports organizations are insensitive to the family responsibilities of coaches and administrators. Furthermore, most of the hiring at the highest levels of education is done by men, and, for a variety of reasons, many times men are hesitant to hire a woman in a position such as athletic director or coach. This has led to discrimination against women in the coaching ranks. In Case 10-4, a woman basketball coach claims she was discriminated against.

⚖ *CASE 10-4* *Bowers v. Baylor University*

862 F.Supp. 142 (W.D. Texas 1994)

Pam Bowers ("Bowers") was hired by Baylor University ("Baylor") to coach its women's basketball team in 1979. In 1989, Bowers began to complain about the disparate allocation of resources in the men's and women's basketball programs, including but not limited to the disparate terms and conditions of her employment versus the terms and conditions of employment by and between Baylor and the men's basketball coach. Her first contact with the Office of Civil Rights of the Department of Education was in March of 1989, and Baylor was aware of [Bowers] complaints at or about the same time. Bowers' employment was initially terminated by Baylor in 1993. Bowers alleges that the termination was premised on alleged violations of NCAA and Southwest Conference rules, and that her win-loss record was not even mentioned. After her termination, Bowers filed a complaint with the Office of Civil Rights and the Equal Employment Opportunity Commission. Immediately after filing the complaint, Bowers was notified that she would be reinstated (1) on the same terms under which she had been employed the previous 14 years, or (2) on a two-year written contract. Bowers alleges that she was forced to accept the first offer because the terms of the written contract were vague and ambiguous and Baylor refused to discuss them.

Despite her reinstatement, Bowers continued to pursue her employment complaints with the federal agencies. In an employment evaluation of August 30, 1993, Bowers' win-loss record was mentioned, and she was informed that she needed to achieve a winning season. On or about March 28, 1994, Bowers was notified in writing that her employment would be terminated as of May 31, 1994, because of her unsuccessful win-loss record throughout her employment at Baylor.

1. Do you believe Bowers was discriminated against?
2. What other information would you need to make this determination?

Bowers v. Baylor University, 862 F. Supp. 142 (W.D. Tex. 1994), U.S. Supreme Court.

In *Ludtke v. Kuhn*, 461 F.Supp. 86 (S.D.N.Y. 1978), Melissa Ludtke brought a civil rights lawsuit to prevent the New York Yankees from enforcing a policy by then baseball Commissioner Bowie Kuhn that prevented women from entering the clubhouse after a game. Ludtke worked for *Sports Illustrated* as a reporter and was assigned to cover the 1977 World Series between the Yankees and the Dodgers. Before the series began, the Dodgers told Ludtke she was free to enter the clubhouse after the game; however, the commissioner said she was not allowed to immediately enter the clubhouse, even though her male counterparts were. The Commissioner did make special arrangements for Ludtke to interview players after the game. Some ballplayers were offended by the policy and supported Ludtke, particularly Yankees slugger Reggie Jackson.

Sexual Harassment in Sports

Sexual harassment consists of unwelcomed sexual advances, requests for sexual favors, and other physical and verbal conduct. Sexual harassment is prevalent throughout society and in the workplace. It is a violation of the law and in some cases can be criminally prosecuted. Unfortunately, sexual harassment is present in the sports world as well, with little doubt deterring girls and women from participating and developing as athletes. The development of sexual harassment policies by organizations helps to deter this behavior. SMPs should take a leadership role in establishing policies that clearly indicate that sexual harassment will not be tolerated in the workplace in any manner, under any circumstances.

It is clear that consensual sex or a romantic relationship between a coach and a student-athlete compromises the professional integrity of the coach and harms the student-athlete. It can result in termination of employment for the coach and may subject the coach and the university to penalties from an athletic association or other governing body. It could also lead to legal action against the university, high school, or coach. Coaches are in the position of authority over student-athletes, including making recommendations that further an athlete's goals. Opportunities for a coach to abuse his or her power and sexually exploit an athlete are inherent in this relationship. These types of relationships also create unworkable conflict of interest situations; thus, even if the athlete consents to sexual relations with his or her coach, consent is not truly "voluntary" for the following reasons: (1) the coach-athlete relationship is one of "trust," similar to a fiduciary relationship, pursuant to which the coach is responsible for looking after the athlete's best interest; (2) the coach can "influence" the athlete's career in a variety of ways, either positively or negatively; (3) the coach has "control" over the athlete, similar to a boss, in regard to what the athlete is required to do on a daily basis, both on and off the field; (4) the coach is in a position of "authority" such that the athlete is not supposed to question the coach's directives; and (5) coaches should be viewed as "role models" and sexual relationships with athletes under their charge calls the coach's moral judgment into question.

Legal and administrative remedies are available to those who have been harassed and a coach may be subject to criminal charges depending on the age of the athlete. Sexual harassment has severe consequences for its victims and for the sports organization: it lowers the self-esteem of girls and women, impairs the functioning capacity of its victims to experience full athletic participation, destroys the atmosphere of mutual respect and trust between a coach and the athlete, and it may make girls and women reluctant to accept employment or a leadership role in sports. Administrators responsible for the oversight of coaches and athletic programs should take charges of sexual harassment seriously and educate and address all instances that may occur within the sports organization.

Examples of sexual harassment in a sports context include the following:

- A coach who sexually intimidates an athlete. For example, when a coach unnecessarily and continually holds an athlete in the process of explaining a correct technique.
- An athlete's selection on a team becomes dependent on compliance with an implied sexual proposition.
- A team whose acceptance or initiation rituals require the athlete to perform demeaning physical acts of a sexual nature.
- A coach who requests or requires sexual favors as a way of influencing decision making.

In Case 10-5, a woman employee sued, saying she was sexually harassed by members of the Detroit Tigers baseball team while on the Club's private jet.

⚖ CASE 10-5 Kesner v. Little Caesars Enterprises, Inc.

2002 WL 1480800 (2002)

[Kesner] alleges that she was harassed by members of the Detroit Tigers. [Kesner] alleges that the harassment started on her first flight with the Tigers in April 2000, when a group of players were looking at pornographic material on one of the player's laptop computer. She alleges that the computer was positioned in a way that allowed [Kesner], as well as at least one other flight attendant, Jenifer Campbell, to witness it. [Kesner] alleges that the harassment was thereafter continued. For instance, she alleges that some of the players repeatedly called her pejorative and profane names, such as "bitch," "cunt," and "hide." She alleges that some players would make comments with sexual innuendos. For example, [Kesner] alleges that when she would ask players if they wanted a dessert, players would occasionally reply by asking whether she had any "cooter pie" or "hair pie." Or else, she alleges that two players, Doug Brocail and Gregg Jefferies, asked her whether she would give her husband a "blowjob in a van?" [Kesner] also alleges that some of the players would touch or rub against her breasts and buttocks in a manner that she thought was inappropriate, and that made her uncomfortable.

[Kesner] alleges that the harassment from the players culminated in July 2000. Before the airplane took off, [Kesner] alleges that she noticed a player, Jeff Weaver, walk out of the lavatory. She saw a smoke cloud and smelled burnt marijuana following him out of the lavatory, and saw ashes inside the lavatory. [Kesner] alleges that she approached Weaver and Matt Anderson, who were sitting next to each other, and told them that smoking marijuana was not permitted on the flight. She alleges that Anderson responded by barking profanities at her, and calling her a "stupid bitch." Later that flight, she alleges that another player, Bobby Higginson, confronted and chastised her for reporting the marijuana smoking. A third player, Brad Ausmus, also confronted [Kesner], and allegedly called her a "dumb bitch" for reporting the marijuana smoking incident. [Kesner] alleges that she was treated this way by the players because of her gender, and that she had never seen the players treat her male counterparts on the flight crew in the same manner.

[Kesner's] complaints extend beyond the treatment she received from the players; she alleges that she was mistreated by other members of the flight crew as well. [Kesner] alleges that two pilots, Al Long and Pat White, repeatedly touched her in a manner that she thought was "inappropriate," including repeatedly touching her breasts with their hands, and that a third pilot, Rob Mintari, touched her buttocks with his hands on three separate occasions.

[Kesner] had many difficulties with Mintari, who was the chief pilot. [Kesner] alleges that Mintari personally disliked [Kesner], and stated that he would fire her if he had the chance.

What actions should the club take against its players for their highly inappropriate and illegal conduct?

Kesner v. Little Caesars Enterprises, Inc., U.S. Supreme Court.

⌕ CASE STUDY 10-1   *Erin Andrews*

This post previously contained a video showing the USC linebacker and ESPN sideline reporter Erin Andrews. A reference in the post described his actions on the Rose Bowl sideline as "dancing" with Andrews. Maualuga later apologized to Andrews. The video has since been removed once it was deemed inappropriate based on *Times* standards and practices and should not have been posted.[8]

What can be done to stop this type of offensive and unethical behavior in the future by athletes?

ESPN commentator Tony Kornheiser is known for his sarcastic approach to sports reporting. He created a media "storm" when he commented on one of his colleagues, Hannah Storm's, wardrobe on his radio show. He said about Storm: "I know she's very good, and I'm not supposed to be critical of ESPN people, so I won't but Hannah Storm, come on plaid skirt. Way too short for somebody in her 40s—or maybe early 50s by now. She's got on her typically very, very tight skirt. She looks like she has a sausage casing wrapping around her upper body."[9]

He later apologized: "I'm a troll; look at me. . . . I have no right to insult what anyone else looks like, what anyone else wears."[10] He was suspended by the network for his comments. His comments were certainly inappropriate and degrading to his colleague.

Abuse and Violence against Women in Sports

Abuse in any form harms and prevents women and girls from participating and developing as athletes and as individuals. Cases of extreme abuse can psychologically damage girls and women athletes and keep them from ever participating. Organizations that set policies dealing with abuse against women in sports are likely to decrease the frequency of such abuse. Coaches are in a position of authority over women athletes in interscholastic athletics and can affect their performance. They hold a position of power over the student-athlete. If this power is abused, it can lead to the abuse of the woman athlete.

Any abuse whatsoever by a coach demeans and devalues the woman athlete and should not be tolerated. Abuse has dire consequences for both the coach and the victim. Sports organizations and bodies should formulate and enforce policies dealing with all types of abuse. Issues dealing with abuse of women

athletes also apply to athletic trainers, school administrators, sports officials, and sports information personnel.

A variety of different types of abuse can occur in sports against girls and women that include sexual abuse, physical abuse, mental or emotional abuse, and verbal abuse.

The most common types of verbal abuse are name calling, making disparaging comments about a player's performance, swearing at players or officials, or making any comments that demean or devalue a woman athlete. Examples of verbal abuse can include the following:

- Referring to a woman athlete's body parts. This can also constitute sexual harassment.
- Comparing women's teams to the men's teams and insinuating that the men's teams are better or have more skill.
- Using derogatory terms for women athletes such as "chicks," "hotties," "sweetie," "babes," "bitches," or any other term which demeans or diminishes a female athlete.

Emotional abuse can be as simple as having unrealistic expectations for a woman or girl athlete, preventing women athletes from playing in games because of assumed limits or underdeveloped skills, issuing threats against players, or violating the privacy rights of women athletes.

Physical abuse occurs when a coach or other individual touches a player in a way that causes physical pain, including excessive exercise, denial of fluids, or using unreasonable requests as a form of punishment. "Bullying" can take many forms and can be verbal, physical, or psychological.[11] Hazing is another kind of physical abuse that can take a variety of forms against women. Examples of physical abuse include the following:

- A coach putting the success of a team on the shoulders of one "superstar."
- Slapping, grabbing, spitting, shoving, hitting, or throwing equipment.

- A coach demanding that players run around the track until they vomit or pass out.
- "Punishment type" practices for losing games after playing poorly.
- Instances in which coaches or other players know about or are participants in any harmful or degrading initiation rituals involving new players. Examples of these rituals include running through a line of players who assault the player, performing lewd acts, being forced to drink excessive amounts of alcohol, or any act that demeans or devalues a player.

A coach can play an important role in the development of young athletes, especially young women. A coach must be trustworthy. Most coaches work hard to develop young athletes' self-worth, confidence, and athletic ability; however, a few individuals abuse their position of power and look for a chance to take sexual advantage of women or girl athletes. Criminal penalties are in place for such sexual abuse. A civil lawsuit can also be brought against a coach or a school for damages in cases of sexual abuse.

Sexual abuse falls into two categories:

1. *Noncontact*: "Flashing or exposing sexual body parts to a young athlete, watching intrusively as a young athlete changes or showers, speaking or communicating sexually/seductively with a young athlete, showing pornographic films, magazines or photographs to young athletes; having young athletes participate in the creation of pornographic materials, forcing a young athlete to watch a sexual act performed by others; objectifying or ridiculing a young athlete's body parts."

2. *Contact*: "Kissing or holding a young athlete in a sexual manner; touching a young athlete's sexual body parts or forcing a young athlete to touch another person's sexual parts; penetrating a young athlete anally or vaginally with objects or fingers; having vaginal, anal, or oral intercourse with a young athlete."[12]

In Case 10-6, a coach was criminally charged for sexual harassment and for engaging in sexual intercourse with a female athlete.

CASE 10-6 State of Montana v. Thompson

243 Mont. 28, 792 P.2d 1103 (1990)

On May 25, 1989, Gerald Roy Thompson was charged with two counts of sexual intercourse without consent and one count of sexual assault.

Gerald Roy Thompson, the principal and boys basketball coach at Hobson High School, was accused of two counts of sexual intercourse without consent, and one count of sexual assault.

Count I
On or between September, 1986 and January, 1987 in Judith Basin County, Montana, [Thompson] knowingly had sexual intercourse without consent with a person of the opposite sex; namely Jane Doe, by threatening Jane Doe that she would not graduate from high school and forced Jane Doe to engage in an act of oral sexual intercourse.

Count II
On or between February, 1987 and June, 1987 in Judith Basin County, Montana, [Thompson] knowingly had sexual intercourse without consent with a person of the opposite sex; namely Jane Doe, by threatening Jane Doe that she would not graduate from high school and forced Jane Doe to engage in an act of oral sexual intercourse.

The affidavits filed in support … contained facts and allegations supporting the two counts of sexual intercourse without consent. In essence, they alleged that the threats "caused Jane Doe great psychological pain and fear."

The State contended that fear of the power of Thompson and his authority to keep her from graduating forced Jane Doe into silence until after she graduated from high school in June of 1987. On November 25, 1988, Jane Doe filed a letter with the Hobson School Board describing the activities against her by Thompson. After investigations by both the school board and the Judith Basin County prosecutor's office, the prosecutor filed an information on May 25, 1989. The information charged Thompson with two counts of sexual intercourse without consent, both felonies, and with one count of attempted sexual assault, a felony.

The State in its information and accompanying affidavit complain that Thompson deprived Jane Doe of consent to the sexual act by threatening that he would prevent her from graduating from high school. The threat required, is "a threat of imminent death, bodily injury, or kidnapping to be inflicted on anyone …" A threat one will not graduate from high school is not one of the threats listed … The State argues that the definition "threat of bodily injury" includes psychological impairment. Unfortunately, the statute sets forth bodily injury, not psychological impairment. A threat that eventually leads to psychological impairment is not sufficient. The statute only addresses the results of three specific kinds of threats, and psychological impairment is not one of them.

State of Montana v. Thompson (1990), U.S. Supreme Court.

Case 10-6 demonstrates how clearly unethical sexual behavior does not always result in a criminal conviction against the abuser. Organizations and institutions have a responsibility to protect their athletes from being victimized by sexual abuse committed under their watch. Following Larry Nassar's conviction in 2017, more than 150 federal and state lawsuits were filed against him, Michigan State University (MSU), the United States Olympic Committee, USA Gymnastics, and the Twistars Gymnastics Club. The entire 18-member board of USA Gymnastics resigned. MSU President Lou Anna Simon and the athletic director both resigned. Nassar's crimes at Michigan State and USA Gymnastics drew comparisons to Jerry Sandusky's pedophilic activity at Penn State University. In both cases, individuals in charge "turned a blind eye" or tried to hide the activities of a child molester instead of immediately contacting law enforcement. MSU settled lawsuits filed by 332 alleged victims of Nassar by agreeing to pay them $500 million, which is the largest amount of money in history settled by a university for a sexual abuse case.

⚖ CASE 10-7 *Special Olympics Florida, Inc. v. Showalter*

6 So.3d 662 (2009)

The central question in this case is whether [The Special Olympics] may be found liable for the acts of one of its volunteers who molested … two developmentally disabled adults, in a bowling center parking lot.

[The Special Olympics] is a nonprofit organization that "[p]rovide[s] sports training and competition for persons with … disabilities, [and] ongoing opportunities to participate with their families and the community." All of [Special Olympics]'s activities are run by county coordinators, who are volunteers, as are the coaches and others who assist in operating the programs. [Special Olympics] has approximately 34 paid staff members throughout Florida and as many as 17,000 volunteers. Margaret Showalter and

Nancy Vasil, are both developmentally disabled adults who participate as athletes in [Special Olympics]'s events. Ms. Showalter is apparently somewhat self-reliant, although a social worker resides with her. Ms. Vasil lives with her father, who is her guardian.

One of [Special Olympics]'s organized activities, in which [Showalter and Vasil] participate, is an annual bowling competition. The athletes practice between August and November each year and then participate in county, regional, and state competitions. [Special Olympics] arranged with Colonial Lanes, a public bowling center in Orange County, to conduct much of its bowling activity there. Practices were scheduled to begin every Saturday at 1:30 p.m. and the athletes were instructed to arrive no earlier than 1:00 p.m. However, the athletes widely ignored this instruction. As a consequence, volunteers routinely arrived at practices early because they anticipated that the athletes would arrive early and need supervision.

On October 25, 2003, the day of the molestations, bowling practice was scheduled for 1:30 p.m. On the same day and at the same facility, [Special Olympics] also scheduled physicals for some of the athletes, beginning at 10:00 a.m. [Special Olympics] had announced the physicals at a prior event via loudspeaker … [Showalter and Vasil] knew they were not scheduled for physicals, but they both arrived early to socialize before practice. Ms. Showalter travelled to the bowling center using public transportation. Ms. Vasil's father dropped her off at the bowling alley at 10:00 a.m. Although Ms. Vasil's father was aware that practice started at 1:30 p.m., he assumed, based on past experience that someone from Special Olympics would be there to supervise.

Another early arriver to the October 25 practice was the accused molester, 79-year-old James McDonald, who had been involved with [Special Olympics] for many years in several capacities. As his son was an athlete, Mr. McDonald participated in events as a parent. He was also a registered volunteer. In this capacity, he had been head bowling coach from the 1980s until 1994, at which time he stepped down as head coach due to accusations that he had molested another athlete and her sister. The incidents were investigated by the police, but the charges were dropped two years later.

Evidence was presented that Mr. McDonald's volunteer application remained on file until after the molestations involved in this case. According to routine practice, this suggested that Mr. McDonald's volunteer status had not been terminated. He continued to attend practices and events regularly, even arriving early to help all the athletes, not just his son. Louise Newton, the successor bowling coach, admitted that Mr. McDonald was still there every week acting like he was in charge. As she stated:"I guess it was hard [for Mr. McDonald] to let go." After the instant molestations, [Special Olympics] sent a letter to Mr. McDonald banning him from attendance at events, but stating that "there will be an investigation and [Special Olympics] shall either reinstate your volunteer duties and opportunities or we shall have to determine an appropriate course of action … depending on the outcome of the investigation." Mr. McDonald apparently heeded the directive as he did not attend any of [Special Olympics] events up to the date of trial in 2007.

In addition to the accusations that Mr. McDonald had previously molested an athlete and her sister in 1994, other allegations against Mr. McDonald were brought to [Special Olympics] attention prior to October 25, 2003. Between 1994 and 2003, one of the [Special Olympics athletes] reported to Ms. Newton that Mr. McDonald had molested her on more than one occasion, albeit not in connection with any of [Special Olympics] events. During this same time period, Ms. Newton was also informed that Mr. McDonald attended dances conducted for developmentally disabled adults (not associated with [Special Olympics] activities) where he escorted attendees to and from his van. Ms. Newton discussed these issues with Mr. McDonald but accepted his denial of claims of wrongdoing. She did, however, caution him to avoid taking developmentally disadvantaged people to his van because it appeared inappropriate. At some point in the year 2000 or 2001, Ms. Newton began keeping a "closer eye" on Mr. McDonald and had a discussion with Charlotte Day, [Special Olympics] county coordinator, about whether he was a liability. Ms. Newton did not, however, warn anyone else associated with [Special Olympics] or the athletes' parents or guardians about any suspicions concerning Mr. McDonald.

Other than to accept Mr. McDonald's resignation as head bowling coach, [Special Olympics] did nothing to limit his involvement with its activities. In fact, most people within the [Special Olympics] organization gave no apparent credit to the accusations against Mr. McDonald. For example, the county coordinator in 1994, Jane Fournier, did nothing to investigate the 1994 incident, assuming that because prosecutors dropped the charges two years later, Mr. McDonald was cleared of wrongdoing.

When Charlotte Day took over as county coordinator in 1998, Ms. Fournier told her that the 1994 incident had been unfounded. Consequently, Ms. Day did not investigate the charges in any way. The county co-coordinator, Patricia Webb, although aware of many of the allegations against Mr. McDonald, concluded that he was "completely harmless."

On the day of the instant molestations, Ms. Webb arrived at the bowling center shortly after 10 a.m. to assist a volunteer physician with performing the physicals. Meanwhile, Mr. McDonald lured [Showalter and Vasil] outside to his van where he subsequently molested them, one after the other, either in or near his van. At some point in time, Ms. Webb looked out the window into the parking lot and saw Mr. McDonald molesting [Showalter and Vasil]. While she was summoning police to report the incident, Mr. McDonald molested the other [Showalter and Vasil]. He was subsequently arrested, and his culpability is not herein disputed.

… [Showalter and Vasil] assert that [Special Olympics] was under a duty to protect them or control Mr. McDonald, or both, so as to prevent the foreseeable conduct of Mr. McDonald, and [Special Olympics] failure to do so amounted to negligence. The jury returned a verdict for each [Showalter and Vasil] …

1. To what extent was the Special Olympics at fault in this case? What specifically should the individuals working for the organization have done, or not have done, that could have prevented the sexual abuse in this case?
2. What policies should have been in force to prevent these tragic circumstances?

Special Olympics Florida, Inc. v. Showalter, U.S. Supreme Court.

🔍 CASE STUDY 10-2   Jets Fans

In 2007, it was reported that rowdy New York Jets fans would gather at halftime on a pedestrian ramp at the stadium and "chant obscenities" at women to encourage them to expose their breasts.[13] The team issued a statement saying:

> "We expect our fans to comply with all rules at the stadium, and the vast majority do. For those who don't, we expect and encourage N.J.S.E.A. security to take appropriate action."[14]

1. What actions should the league take against the fans? The New York Jets football club?
2. How should the club or league enforce a fan code of conduct when dealing with these issues?

🔍 CASE STUDY 10-3   Elizabeth

Elizabeth plays in a mixed sports team in a lower grade competition. In a particular match Elizabeth believed she was subjected to sexual harassment by way of a touch on the genital area that she claimed was premeditated by two male players. What should she do? What action should league officials take?

⌕ *CASE STUDY 10-4* **Jennifer**

Jennifer volunteered to be an official for an upcoming athletic event with her local athletic club. She was sexually harassed by the male volunteer coordinator at the club. The behavior included sex-based insults and innuendos, intrusive questions about her personal life, and repeated requests to go out on a date. Jennifer asked that the behavior cease as she felt intimidated and humiliated and stated that she would complain to a member of the club's board should the behavior continue. The next day, Jennifer was informed that her services as a volunteer were no longer needed. What should she do?

▶ **Title IX**

Proponents of women's rights sought a federal legislative remedy to reverse sex discrimination in education. The Title IX statute provides in part the following remedy:

> No person in the United States shall, on the basis of sex, be excluded from participation in, be denied the benefits of, or be subjected to discrimination under any education program or activity receiving federal financial assistance.[15]

The act prohibits any federally-funded education program from discriminating on the basis of gender. It forbids discrimination in any program, including athletic programs, organizations, or agencies that receive federal funds. Title IX applies to primary and secondary schools as well, and it applies to private colleges and universities because they receive funds from federally-funded student loans. The objective of the statute was to give women an equal opportunity to develop their skills and to apply those skills. This act, as enforced by the Department of Health, Education, and Welfare, is limited to discrimination against participants of federally-funded educational programs. Exceptions to Title IX include educational institutions that traditionally admit members of only one sex, institutions that train individuals for military service, and institutions whose compliance with Title IX would violate religious benefits.

A normative principle that supports the passing and implementation of Title IX is justice. Distributive justice involves the fair and equitable distribution of benefits and burdens relative to outcomes. Equitable does not mean equal or the same treatment in the sense that distribution of money, success, winning, etc. is the same or equal; rather, equitable means that each of us has the same or equal *chance or opportunity* to achieve it. Thus, if one gender is provided more athletic opportunities than the other gender, the distribution is not equitable.

Many problems have arisen in regard to the scope of the statute's application and have led to extensive debates about the application of Title IX. The following case discusses how Title IX has greatly increased the opportunities for women in sports. Brown University women student-athletes sued the university, arguing Brown violated Title IX.

⚖ *CASE 10-8* **Cohen v. Brown University**

101 F.3d 155 (1st Cir. 1996)

This is a class action lawsuit charging Brown University, and its athletics director with discrimination against women in the operation of its intercollegiate athletics program, in violation of Title IX. The … class comprises all present, future, and potential Brown University women students who participate, seek to participate, and/or are deterred from participating in intercollegiate athletics funded by Brown.

This suit was initiated in response to the demotion in May 1991 of Brown's women's gymnastics and volleyball teams from university-funded varsity status to donor-funded varsity status. Contemporaneously, Brown demoted two men's teams, water polo and golf, from university-funded to donor-funded varsity status. As a consequence of these demotions, all four teams lost, not only their university funding, but most of the support and privileges that accompany university-funded varsity status at Brown ...

There can be no doubt that Title IX has changed the face of women's sports as well as our society's interest in and attitude toward women athletes and women's sports. In addition, there is ample evidence that increased athletics participation opportunities for women and young girls, available as a result of Title IX enforcement, have had salutary effects in other areas of societal concern.

One need look no further than the impressive performances of our country's women athletes in the 1996 Olympic Summer Games to see that Title IX has had a dramatic and positive impact on the capabilities of our women athletes, particularly in team sports. These Olympians represent the first full generation of women to grow up under the aegis of Title IX. The unprecedented success of these athletes is due, in no small measure, to Title IX's beneficent effects on women's sports, as the athletes themselves have acknowledged time and again. What stimulated this remarkable change in the quality of women's athletic competition was not a sudden, anomalous upsurge in women's interest in sports, but the enforcement of Title IX's mandate of gender equity in sports.

Cohen v. Brown University, 879 F. Supp. 185 (D.R.I. 1995), U.S. Supreme Court.

In the following case, individuals claimed Temple University engaged in unlawful gender discrimination.

⚖ CASE 10-9 *Haffer v. Temple University of the Commonwealth System of Higher Education*

678 F. Supp. 517, 1987

This is a class action alleging unlawful gender discrimination in Temple University's intercollegiate athletic program. The class consists of "[a]ll current women students at Temple University who participate, or who are or have been deterred from participating because of sex discrimination in Temple's intercollegiate athletic program." [The plaintiffs'] claims focus on three basic areas: (a) the extent to which Temple affords women students fewer "opportunities to compete" in intercollegiate athletics; (b) the alleged disparity in resources allocated to the men's and women's intercollegiate athletic programs; and (c) the alleged disparity in the allocation of financial aid to male and female student athletes.

The plaintiffs' complaint is that, despite the fact that Temple's student body is approximately fifty percent female, approximately one-third of the participants in Temple's intercollegiate athletic program are women. Figures produced by [Temple] reveal that approximately 450 men and 200 women participate in Temple's intercollegiate athletic program. That is, by sponsoring more women's teams and/or fewer men's teams, Temple could increase the participation rate of females in the University's athletic program to 50, 75, or even 100%.

Plaintiffs claim that the differences in expenditures for the men's and women's intercollegiate athletic programs violate [the law]. Temple presently spends approximately $2,100 more per male student athlete than per female student athlete.

In addition, some evidence suggests that each of the women's teams engages in fund raising, while only the men's crew and baseball teams raise funds ... There is conflicting evidence regarding which teams find it necessary to engage in fund raising. A finding that substantially all of the women's teams and few of the men's teams engage in fund raising would support plaintiffs' claim of disparate impact in the area of expenditures.

[Temple] argue[s] that there is no gender discrimination because the women student athletes outperform the men student athletes and the "expenditure patterns reflect Temple's policy of operating a unified athletics program while promoting at a higher level its three revenue producing teams."

Plaintiffs claim that [Temple] discriminate[s] against women student athletes regarding team travel. In 1985-86, Temple spent $423,908 on team travel for men's teams, and $162,110 on team travel for women's teams. In 1984-85, the relevant figures were $349,492 for the men's teams and $145,297 for the women's teams. The per capita figures also favor the men. Plaintiffs have produced evidence that when a men's and a women's team travel to the same destination, the men's team receives superior treatment. For example, during the 1984-85 season, the men's and women's basketball teams played at the University of Rhode Island. The men's team flew to their game; the women's team took a bus. There is also evidence that various women's teams must raise funds to travel to certain competitions. Temple argues that the mode of travel depends on distance, the size of the team, and the coach's preference.

There are also factual disputes over the accommodations [Temple] offers student athletes on team trips. . . . Temple's "policy is to house 3 players in a room, 1 to a bed, except for the football and 2 basketball teams." Players on these teams are housed 2 to a room, 1 to a bed. There is also evidence that "Temple's policy is one student per bed and two students per room" and that some coaches deviate from this policy. Plaintiffs have presented evidence that the women's badminton and softball teams have been housed 4 to a room, and that the women's swim team was housed 5 to a room. The present record provides conflicting accounts of Temple's policy and is unclear regarding the actual room assignments.

Plaintiffs allege that [Temple] provide[s] male athletes with superior support in the areas of uniforms, equipment, including locker rooms, and supplies. In 1985-86, Temple spent $100,669 on uniforms, equipment and supplies for men's teams, and $33,318 on the women's teams. In 1984–85, the figures were $85,491 on men's teams, and $43,735 on the women's teams. However, as average expenditures vary widely from team to team and year to year, it is difficult to interpret the significance of the figures introduced. However, it seems clear that, assuming male student athletes receive adequate uniforms, equipment and supplies, the female student athletes must likewise receive adequate uniforms, equipment and supplies.

Plaintiffs allege that [Temple] provide[s] superior housing and dining facilities to male student athletes. As to dining facilities, plaintiffs point to evidence that the men's football team has a training table, but that no women's team has a training table. The un-contradicted record establishes that the head coaches of the men's football team, women's field hockey, and the women's volleyball teams select the menu to be served to their players during preseason camp. There is no evidence that any women's team requested, but did not receive, a training table.

Temple provides off-campus housing for student athletes who practice or compete during school vacation periods. This is called "holiday living." Plaintiffs allege that holiday living expenditures favor male student athletes. [Temple has] introduced evidence that the average expenditure for holiday living for the women's teams was higher than the comparable figure for the men's program.

Plaintiffs allege that [Temple] provide[s] superior publicity to the men's athletic teams. There is evidence that, in 1985-86, [Temple] spent $189,688 on the football and men's basketball teams, and $0 on the women's teams. Over the last three years, [Temple] spent $410,672 to publicize the football and men's basketball teams, $1,580 to promote sports generally, and $945 to promote the women's lacrosse team. There is evidence that men's teams receive more publicity than do the women's teams.

[Temple] attempt[s] to justify these spending disparities on the grounds that they "represent an outgrowth of Temple's aim to promote the three revenue producing sports," and that Temple supports the teams with the greatest spectator interest. In the context of the expenditures claim, Temple argued that it treated the women's basketball team as a revenue sport . . .

Haffer v. Temple University, 678 F. Supp. 517 (E.D. Pa. 1988), U.S. Supreme Court.

Is it fair to disband men's teams in favor of women's teams for Title IX purposes? What place should the generation of revenue and spectator interest play in Title IX? If women's sports are not generating as much revenue as men's sports, how should that be viewed under Title IX?

The next case addresses Eastern Michigan University's (EMU) decision in 2018 to cut four teams—two men's teams and two women's teams—for budgetary reasons. The United States District Court for the Eastern District of Michigan ruled that EMU couldn't satisfy the "effective accommodation" three-prong test under Title IX and, therefore, entered an order granting the plaintiffs' motion for preliminary injunction to reinstate the two women's teams.

⚖ CASE 10-10 *Marie Mayerova and Ariana Chretien v. Eastern Michigan University, et al.*

Case 2:18-cv-11909-GCS-RSW (September 27, 2018)

.... This lawsuit was filed following EMU's decision to eliminate four teams: men's wrestling, men's swimming and diving, women's tennis, and women's softball. Plaintiffs seek to represent a class of every impacted woman student-athlete, recruit, and future recruit/student-athlete. Count I of the complaint alleges a violation of Title IX. Count II, brought pursuant to 42 U.S.C. § 1983, alleges a violation of the Equal Protection Clause of the Fourteenth Amendment.

.... Approximately 12,700 undergraduates attend EMU, which is a member of the Mid-American Conference. Defendants assert that 59.5% of undergraduates for the 2017–2018 school year were women, and 40.5% were men. At that time, EMU had 729 undergraduate student-athletes participating in varsity athletics on twenty-one teams. Four hundred and six men, or 55.7% of EMU student-athletes, participated on nine teams: baseball, basketball, cross country, football, golf, swimming and diving, track and field (indoor and outdoor), and wrestling. Three hundred twenty-three women, or 44.3% of EMU student-athletes, participated on twelve teams: basketball, cross country, golf, gymnastics, rowing, soccer, softball, swimming and diving, tennis, track and field (indoor and outdoor), and volleyball.

EMU has operated with a budget deficit for the last seven years. The university attributes its financial struggles to declining state support and shifts in population and enrollment. Because EMU's athletic department is not self-sufficient, the university's financial problems have impacted athletic funding. In March 2018, EMU decided to reduce athletic spending by $2 million by eliminating four teams: men's wrestling, men's swimming and diving, women's tennis, and women's softball. Eighty-three student-athletes participated on these teams during the 2017-2018 school year – fifty-eight men and twenty-five women.

In making the decision to eliminate teams, EMU sought to retain NCAA Division 1 standing and remain in the Mid-American Conference. This required maintaining sixteen sports, including football, men's and women's basketball, and volleyball, as well as at least six male sports. EMU avers that remaining in the Mid-American Conference "adds value to EMU degrees and provides a financial benefit to the University," which would incur substantial costs if it were to exit the conference. EMU also considered the costs associated with each sport, including the cost per athlete. Although EMU tried "to be as least impactful . . . as possible" to female athletic participation, it claims that it could not achieve its budgetary goals by eliminating men's teams alone. Tr. at 84-85, 92.

EMU announced the teams' elimination on March 20, 2018. Student-athletes could choose to transfer without sacrificing any period of their NCAA eligibility or remain at EMU and continue to receive their athletic and academic scholarship aid.

.... Plaintiffs' claim seeks effective accommodation – the equal opportunity to participate in athletics – pursuant to § 106.41(c)(1).

In 1979, the administering agency issued a Policy Interpretation to "clarif[y] the obligations which recipients of Federal aid have under Title IX to provide equal opportunities in athletic programs. In particular, the Policy Interpretation provides a means to assess an institution's compliance with equal opportunity requirements of the regulation which are set forth at [34 C.F.R. §§ 106.37(c) and 106.41(c)]." *Cohen v. Brown Univ.*, 809 F. Supp. 978, 983 (D. R.I.1992) (citing 44 Fed. Reg. at 71415 (Dec. 11, 1979)) (*Cohen I*).

The Policy Interpretation includes a three-part test to determine compliance in the area of accommodation:

1. Whether intercollegiate level participation opportunities for male and female students are provided in numbers substantially proportionate to the respective enrollments; or
2. Where the members of one sex have been and are underrepresented among intercollegiate athletes, whether the institution can show a history and continuing practice of program expansion which is demonstrably responsive to the developing interest and abilities of the members of that sex; or
3. Where the members of one sex are underrepresented among intercollegiate athletes, and the institution cannot show a continuing practice of program expansion such as cited above, whether it can be demonstrated that the interests and abilities of the members of the sex have been fully and effectively accommodated by the present program.

44 Fed. Reg. 71413, 71418 (Dec. 11, 1979) ("Three-Part Test"). Since the issuance of the Policy Interpretation, the Department of Education has provided further clarification that educational institutions need to comply only with one part of the Three-Part Test to provide nondiscriminatory athletic opportunities. Office of Civil Rights, U.S. Department of Education, *Clarification of Intercollegiate Athletics Policy Guidance: The Three-Part Test* (Jan. 15, 1996) ("1996 Clarification").

In assessing whether the first part of the Three-Part Test is satisfied, the court must determine whether EMU provides intercollegiate level participation opportunities for male and female students in numbers substantially proportionate to the respective enrollments. This analysis "begins with a determination of the number of participation opportunities afforded to male and female athletes in the intercollegiate athletic program." *Biediger*, 691 F.3d at 93 (quoting 1996 Clarification at 2-3). "[A]n athlete who participates in more than one sport will be counted as a participant in each sport in which he or she participates." *Id.* The court then considers whether "the numbers are substantially proportionate to each sex's enrollment." *Id.* at 94.

For the 2017-2018 school year, women comprised 59.5% of EMU's undergraduate enrollment and 44.3% of its athletes. Of 729 athletes, 406 or 55.7% were male, and 323 or 44.3% were female. Given this clear disparity, EMU does not claim to provide "substantially proportionate" athletic opportunities to its female student-athletes. *See, e.g., Cohen I*, 809 F. Supp. at 991 (university failed substantial proportionality prong when women were 48.2% of undergraduates but only 36.6% of athletes); *Favia v. Indiana Univ. of Pa.*, 812 F. Supp. 578, 584-85 (W.D. Pa. 1993) (no substantial proportionality when 55.61% of students and 37.77% of athletes were women). EMU correctly notes that a failure to achieve substantial proportionality does not, in itself, constitute a Title IX violation. *See Roberts v. Colorado State Bd. of Agriculture*, 998 F.2d 824, 831 (10th Cir. 1993). Rather, EMU finds a "safe harbor" if it satisfies the second or third parts of the Three-Part Test.

.... Based upon this record, the court is unable to conclude that Defendants have met their burden of demonstrating a history and continuing practice of expansion. The actual numbers reveal a participation disparity that has lingered for at least fifteen years, with no evidence of a serious effort to address it. In light of this history, it is difficult for the court to credit EMU's 2018 roster management plan as anything more than "mere promises to expand its program . . . at some time in the future," which is insufficient to satisfy part two of the Three-Part Test. *See* 1996 Clarification at 4.

. . . . Under part three, the court considers whether women's "interests and abilities have been fully and effectively accommodated by the present program." Defendants do not argue that EMU satisfies this part of the test. Indeed, Plaintiffs, as members of eliminated teams, represent interests and abilities that are not effectively accommodated by the present program. Accordingly, part three of the Three-Part Test does not provide safe harbor for Defendants.

. . . . Defendants have failed to meet their burden to establish compliance with either the second or third prong of the Three-Part Test. Plaintiffs are therefore likely to succeed on the merits of their Title IX claim.

. . . . Defendants assert that reinstating the softball and tennis teams would cost approximately $1 million, forcing EMU to divert resources from other programs and harming other EMU students. The court recognizes this financial burden, as the cost to reinstate the teams is not insignificant. The court notes, however, that Defendants have not provided information regarding EMU's entire athletic budget, precluding a complete assessment of whether the reinstatement of the teams would present an undue burden on EMU. *See Barrett*, 2003 WL 22803477 at *14 ("In examining this fact, courts generally look to the school's athletic budget and consider the overall expense of reinstating the program[s] as compared with the entire athletic budget."); *Favia*, 812 F. Supp. at 854 (no undue harm to defendants where the "budget, while shrinking, has space for reallocation and cutbacks in other areas").

Moreover, the court finds that the financial burden on EMU is outweighed by the harm to Plaintiffs if the teams are not reinstated. Indeed, financial hardship is not a defense to a Title IX violation. *See Horner v. Kentucky High Sch. Athletic Ass'n*, 43 F.3d 265, 275 (6th Cir. 1994) (an institution "may not simply plead limited resources to excuse the fact that there are fewer opportunities for girls than for boys"). Although it is mindful of and sympathetic to EMU's need to cut costs, the court concludes that the balance of equities favors Plaintiffs.

Defendants assert that the public interest strongly favors deferring to EMU's budgetary decision. Defendants rely upon *Equity in Athletics I*, which determined that the public interest "weighs in favor of permitting colleges and universities to chart their own course in providing athletic opportunities without judicial interference or oversight, *absent a clear showing that they are in violation of the law*." 504 F. Supp. 2d at 112 (quoting *Gonyo*, 837 F. Supp. at 996) (emphasis added). The court acknowledges that the public interest is generally served by allowing public universities to determine how to allocate financial resources, but, as stated above, there is a clear showing that Defendants are in violation of Title IX. Moreover, "the public interest demands that [EMU] comply with federal law and in this instance that means compliance with Title IX." *Barrett*, 2003 WL 22803477 at *15. *See also Cohen I*, 809 F. Supp. at 1001 (stating that "the public interest will be served by vindicating a legal interest that Congress has determined to be an important one"); *Favia*, 812 F. Supp. at 585 ("The public has a strong interest in prevention of any violation of constitutional rights."). "Title IX does not purport to override financial necessity. Yet, the pruning of athletic budgets cannot take place solely in comptrollers' offices, isolated from the legislative and regulatory imperatives that Title IX imposes." *Cohen II*, 991 F.2d at 905. For these reasons, the court finds that the public interest is best served by upholding the goals of Title IX.

1. Should there be a Title IX exception when a school cuts certain sports for "budgetary reasons"? In other words, should financial hardship be a defense to a Title IX violation?
2. Which normative ethical principles seem to support the holding of the court? Apply those normative principles to specific statements made by the court in the opinion.

Marie Mayerova and Ariana Chretien v. Eastern Michigan University, et al., U.S. Supreme Court.

Disparity in Pay Between Men and Women in Sports

More than 60 percent of head coaching positions for women's teams in intercollegiate athletics are held by men. The "2016 College Sport Racial and Gender Report Card" revealed these shocking statistics:

> Forty-five years after the passage of Title IX, women still did not hold the majority of coaching opportunities in women's sports. Women only held 38.8 percent of the head coaching jobs for women's sports in Division I, which was a 0.1 percentage point decrease from 2014–2015. Women held 35.3 percent of the head coaching jobs for women's sports in Division II, which was a 0.1 percentage point decrease from 2014–2015. Women held 43.9 percent of the head coaching jobs for women's sports in Division III, which was a 0.1 percentage point increase from 2014–2015.[16]

In addition, there is a huge disparity in pay between men and women coaches, even in the same sport. Is it unethical to pay a women's basketball coach at a major university less than the men's basketball coach? What if the women's basketball program is more popular on campus? Should the women's coach make more than the men's coach?

The gender pay disparity exists with professional athletes too. Is it unethical to pay women athletes less than their male counterparts? On March 29, 2016, five members of the U.S women's national soccer team,

including Hope Solo, filed a charge of discrimination against the U.S. Soccer Federation with the Equal Employment Opportunity Commission (EEOC), alleging disparity in pay between male and female U.S. soccer players. They argue that women's national team players earn as little as 40% of what players on the men's national team earn, despite outperforming them on the international stage. All five of these players were on the 2015 World Cup-winning roster. Their attorney Jeffrey Kessler said: "[I]t is time for the USSF to stop playing games and provide equal pay for equal work. If the USSF truly supports the women's game, it should not have to be dragged into legal compliance by the EEOC."[17] In August 2018, Solo filed her own civil lawsuit against U.S. Soccer Federation in federal district court in Northern California, alleging a violation of the Equal Pay Act.

Summary

More than 45 years since the passing of Title IX, women and girls continue to face many obstacles and barriers in the sports field. They are still subjected to sexual harassment and discrimination and have not been provided the same opportunities as their male counterparts. Progress has been made in recent years, and increased funding for girls and women's athletics at the high school and collegiate levels has expanded athletic opportunities for girls and women. The progress is encouraging and indicates a positive movement toward more female involvement in sports at all levels. Distributive justice demands it.

References

1. M. Barnekow-Bergkvist, G. Hedberg, U. Janlert, and E. Jansson, "Physical Activity Patterns in Men and Women at the Ages of 16 and 34 and Development of Physical Activity from Adolescence to Adulthood," *Scandinavian Journal of Medicine & Science in Sports*, Vol. 6, Issue 6, pp. 359–370, December 1996.

2. Jennifer L. Knight and Traci A. Giulano, "He's a Laker; She's a 'Looker': The Consequences of Gender-Stereotypical Portrayals of Male and Female Athletes by the Printed Media," *Behavioral Science, Sex Roles*, Volume 45, Number 3–4, 217–229.

3. Mary Lou Sheffer and Brad Schultz, "Double Standard: Why Women Have Trouble Getting Jobs in Local Television Sports," *Journal of Sports Media*, Volume 2, 2007, pp. 77–101.

4. Katie Hnida, *Still Kicking: My Dramatic Journey as the First Woman to Play Division One College Football* (New York: Scribner, 2006).

5. Sharon L. Roan, "No One Yelled 'Kill the Ump' When Amanda Clement was a Man in Blue," *Sports Illustrated*, April 5, 1982.

6. Benjamin Weiser, "Pro Basketball, Jury Tells N.B.A. to Pay Female Referee $7.85 Million," *New York Times*, April 10, 1998.

7. Joe Drape, "Earning Her Stripes in College Football," *New York Times*, September 19, 2009.

8. Adam Rose, "All Things Trojan: Rey Maualuga Dances with Erin Andrews," *Los Angeles Times*, January 3, 2009.

9. Helen Kennedy, "ESPN Suspends Tony Kornheiser for Comments about SportsCenter Anchor Hannah Storm's Wardrobe," *My Daily News*, February 23, 2010.

10. Ibid.

11. Kayan Brown, "Crunch Time: Confronting Coaching Bullying," *Women's Sports Foundation*, August 13, 2008.

12. "Coach Notes: Preventing Sexual Abuse of Children in Sport, Making It Safer," www.mhp.gov.on.ca.

13. "Zero Tolerance on Harassment," *New York Times*, December 16, 2007; Associated Press, "Lawmaker Wants to Rein in Jets Fans," *CNNSI.com*, November 20, 2007.

14. David Picker, "At Jets Game, a Halftime Ritual of Harassment," *The New York Times*, November 20, 2007.

15. Title IX and Sex Discrimination, U.S. Department of Education, Office for Civil Rights. https://www2.ed.gov/about/offices/list/ocr/docs/tix_dis.html

16. Richard Lapchick, with Saahil Marfatia, Austin Bloom, and Stanley Sylverain, "College Sport," April 6, 2017.

17. Ahiza Garcia, "Hope Solo on 'Equal Play Equal Pay' T-Shirts: We'll Keep Pushing," *CNNMoney*, July 12, 2016.

CHAPTER 11

Ethical Considerations in Sports Media

▶ Sports and the Media

Sports and the media have always been interrelated. Individuals have been reading and writing about sporting events for over a century.[1] Whether a fan is checking the box score of his or her favorite team or gathering news about a favorite sports star, individuals are interested in getting information about the sporting life and those who play sports.

Historically, fans only followed their local teams; however, technology has made sports a global business. Fans all over the world follow a variety of sporting events, teams, players, and coaches. The NFL is popular in other countries and football (soccer) is a global sport. With the explosion of coverage by the sports media on an international basis, teams such as Real Madrid, the New York Yankees, Manchester United, and the New England Patriots have become international franchises followed by millions of fans around the globe.

Before cable television, sports programming consisted of a relatively few sporting events on the weekend with MLB's game of the week operating as the cornerstone of sports programming. Now, sports fans can proudly sit in front of a big screen television for hours on end and watch a myriad of sporting events, 24 hours a day, seven days a week. Cable television, and more specifically ESPN, has transformed sports reporting, production, and the viewing of sports in the last three decades. Sports fans now have multiple channels exclusively dedicated to sports programming and offering many different sports from around the world. Who would want to watch sports 24 hours a day, seven days a week? Evidently, millions of people, because that is exactly what has transpired in today's sports media bonanza. ESPN now has multiple channels showing sports from many different countries. Television, radio, Internet, print, and other forms of media are able to deliver sports programming to rabid fans. All of these various forms of media deliver a constant stream of sporting events, news, and information to viewers. The wide range of sports they broadcast includes the traditional four major U.S. professional league sports of baseball, hockey, football (American), and basketball, and also includes many other sports such as golf, weightlifting, competitive cheerleading, lumberjacking, spelling bees, bowling, track and field, poker tournaments, tennis, volleyball, and hunting and fishing. Media outlets not only deliver the games and the events themselves, but also ancillary programming such as pre- and postgame shows, fantasy game shows, coaches' shows, and draft programs, all exploring every conceivable angle of a particular sporting event.

Drafts for professional leagues used to be something a fan would read about in the newspaper days or even weeks later, but ESPN has turned the NFL draft and other sports drafts into a "must see" event for sports fans. Radio shows abound with sports talk and sports news. Callers and hosts discuss every conceivable angle of the sport and players. Professional sports leagues understand that fans want to view the games so they developed their own broadcast venues. MLB "Extra Innings," NHL "Center Ice," MLS "Direct Kick," NBA "League Pass," and the NFL Network are all exclusively dedicated to showing programming from each particular league. Collegiate athletic conferences have quickly followed by establishing their own programming networks. The University of Texas at Austin was the first university to develop its own television network dedicated exclusively to showing Longhorn athletic events.[2]

Sports programming and news are now delivered through a variety of forms of media. Fewer fans are getting their news from the daily newspaper, instead choosing the Internet and other nontraditional media sources to gather their sports information. Sports fans are retrieving their sports, news, scores, and information from Internet websites, blogs, Twitter, YouTube, Facebook, text messages, and cable television. Print media now takes a backseat to other forms of media that can deliver the sports news much more quickly to the fan. At one time, only the local sportswriter was able to express opinions about local sports teams and players, but a variety of individuals are now involved in the media process and have the ability to have input on a variety of issues. Fans have always had their own opinions on what a team or professional player should do to improve their skills or chances of winning, this

is not new; however, technological advances have provided fans with easier access to voice comments, concerns, and recommendations to general managers, coaches, and players. Players have blogs and send out tweets and coaches do the same. Call-in radio shows and local television programs also offer access to sports fans. University athletic directors make themselves available to alumni and students on the web or through a blog. Fans (some who have nothing intelligent to say whatsoever) have also gained access to the sports forum through the Internet, text messaging, and via a variety of handheld devices. In short, if a sports fan wants to watch, listen, comment, or follow sports, numerous media platforms are now available.

"Journalism" involves the gathering, processing, and dissemination of news. The advent of technology has resulted in numerous sources competing with each other for the consumer's eyeballs, transforming the sports journalism business model into one in which the revenue generation is based primarily on advertising. Content and articles that attract the most eyeballs will generate the most advertising dollars—it's that simple; therefore, it is important for the SMP to be more critical of sports media and journalism and recognize issues that can influence the way the news is presented.

The Society of Professional Journalists (SPJ) Code of Ethics declares these four principles as the foundation of ethical journalism and encourages their use in its practice by all people in all media:

1. *Seek truth and report it.* Take responsibility for the accuracy of their work. Verify information before releasing it. Use original sources whenever possible. Identify sources clearly.
2. *Minimize harm.* Balance the public's need for information against potential harm or discomfort. Pursuit of the news is not a license for arrogance or undue intrusiveness. Show compassion for those who may be affected by news coverage.
3. *Act independently.* Avoid conflicts of interest and disclose unavoidable conflicts. Refuse gifts, favors, fees, free

travel and special treatment, and avoid political and other outside activities that may compromise integrity or impartiality, or may damage credibility. Be wary of sources offering information for favors or money; do not pay for access to news. Identify content provided by outside sources, whether paid or not.

4. *Be accountable and transparent.* Respond quickly to questions about accuracy, clarity and fairness. Acknowledge mistakes and correct them promptly and prominently. Explain corrections and clarifications carefully and clearly.[3]

Ethical dilemmas exist for all people involved in the sports media process. In 2010, ESPN faced an ethical dilemma when dealing with basketball's biggest star.

🔎 CASE STUDY 11-1 The Decision

When NBA star LeBron James became a free agent, his decision to join the NBA's Miami Heat became a media circus. ESPN aired a one-hour special about James, called "The Decision," and James used the program to announce that he was joining the NBA's Miami Heat. James's sports marketing company suggested to ESPN that the show's advertisers would donate money to the Boys and Girls Clubs of America, a favorite charity of Mr. James.[4] In addition, James selected the person to interview, who did not even work for ESPN. *The Washington Post* reported:

The most troubling aspect of the whole ill-conceived mess was ESPN's willingness to hand over an hour of prime-time television to an egomaniacal athlete the network should be covering as a news story. After all, James's final choice of teams already had previously been reported and confirmed by several other news outlets, including ESPN's own man, Chris Broussard. Wasn't that enough?[5]

1. Was ESPN's agreement to air "The Decision" a violation of media ethics?
2. How do you view the donation by the show's advertisers to a charity chosen by James?
3. Did ESPN lose its editorial independence by airing the program?[6]

🔎 CASE STUDY 11-2 2010 Olympic Luge Controversy

Deciding what should be shown to the viewing public can be a difficult task. Media outlets are showered with images and, with technological advances, are able to capture a moment in time that not too long ago would have been impossible. Controversy sells and the media clearly understands that concept. Money and ratings are important to media outlets and exploiting a controversy could bring more viewers to that outlet.

In the 2010 Olympics, a Georgian Luger was tragically killed during an Olympic training run. NBC decided to show the footage of the death of the athlete. NBC News anchor Brian Williams gave the following warning before showing the footage: "We owe folks a warning here . . . these pictures are very tough for some people to watch." Could the story have been told just as well without showing the fatal accident of the athlete? *USA Today* stated:

News organizations frequently weigh the imperative of depicting the reality of the world they cover with concerns about whether images would be too disturbing for the public. In this case, the network warned viewers and used the video. NBC, in a departure from its usual policy of holding onto video because it is the U.S. Olympics rightsholder, let other networks use it.[7]

1. Should such a tragic event be shown on television? Was it a breach of journalistic ethics on behalf of NBC to show such an event?
2. What considerations should be given to the viewing public before showing the event?

3. What considerations should be given to the family of the athlete before showing the event?
4. Was it a necessary part of the story to show an athlete being killed on television? What is the point in this particular instance?

▶ **Media Ethics**

Ethics, in particular journalistic ethics, is not a new field. Ethics in journalism has been a subject of debate for many years.[8] In 1967, the Supreme Court, for the first time, grappled with the question of what role professional standards of journalism and a publisher's departure from those standards, should have in determining liability for defamation involving statements made about an athletic director of a large university. In *Curtis Publishing Co. v. Butts*, the evidence showed that the *Saturday Evening Post* had published an accurate account of an unreliable informant's false description of the University of Georgia athletic director's purported agreement to "fix" a college football game. Although there was reason to question the informant's veracity, the editors did not interview a witness who had the same access to the facts as the informant and did not look at films that revealed what actually happened at the game in question. This evidence of the publisher's intent to avoid the truth most certainly violated journalism ethics principles.

Reporters don't always get it right. Reporting the facts of a story can sometimes be difficult as writers and reporters try to determine the truth. Reporters and writers wield a great deal of power and can, with just a few words, reveal a devastating truth or a bold-faced lie. The First Amendment gives the press a remarkable degree of freedom in the United States. The media can control the fate of nations and important people in society. Along with that power, the media also has ethical duties and responsibilities to fulfill. Media outlets have a responsibility to perform journalism in accordance with the highest standards.[9]

Integrity is an essential quality for any journalist or media outlet. Simply put, media outlets and their employees must produce accurate information. A journalist must be trusted to produce a quality product. Reporters, editors, and producers who prepare stories, graphics, and interactive media must do so in a manner consistent with ethical standards.

The cornerstone of any reporting is accuracy—seeking the truth. If the news and stories produced are not accurate, a media outlet will lose credibility with the viewing public and may be out of business due to multiple lawsuits. Any interpretation from the facts of a story must be reasonable and fair, not merely the opinion of a writer or producer. Reporters, editors, and writers must be committed to the concept of fairness in the pursuit of any story.

No individual can be totally objective; everyone brings their own experiences, background, and education to a situation and this may influence their viewpoint of a story; however, some basic principles of fairness do exist. Fairness translates to completeness. No story is fair if it is incomplete or fails to attempt to present both sides of an issue. No story should omit significant facts that would shed light on the truthfulness of the story; furthermore, news reporting should never exclude important facts at the expense of irrelevant information. If a story misleads or deceives a reader, it should not be told. The concept of fairness means being straightforward with the reader. Certain essential questions should be asked before a news story is released:

1. Does the story present both sides of the issue?
2. Were both sides of the dispute given a chance for equal input in the story?

3. Does the story show bias in any way?
4. Does the story deceive the reader or viewer in any way?
5. Was every reasonable effort made to determine the truth of the matter?

Recognizing and avoiding conflicts of interest are essential to the integrity of any media outlet. Writers, producers, and employees of media outlets should not accept gifts or any form of preferential treatment when covering a story. It is the essence of journalistic integrity to show independence. Reporters must fully understand their role and the trust they have been given to report a story fairly and accurately.

In our technological age, a news story can be transmitted instantaneously. Media outlets have immense power to tell a story and persuade. It is essential they get it right to avoid damage to their own reputation or to those who are the subject of the story.

It is also essential that reporters not make the news, only report the news. Writers should be able to distinguish between advocacy and news reporting; furthermore, during the news gathering process, reporters must be careful not to misrepresent their identity. They should be truthful and forthright with all individuals they interview while investigating a story.

How can a media outlet ensure that it is publishing a true and accurate version of the facts of every newsworthy story? Accuracy should be the major goal of any media outlet. Any significant errors in facts, or omission of facts, should be promptly corrected in a responsible and an ethical manner, making it clear that the media outlet was at fault in reporting the story. Media outlets should publish, in an acceptable manner to all parties involved, a proper retraction to set the record straight, accepting responsibility for their actions.

A recent example of failed reporting occurred in the sport of baseball. Because of the suspicion of steroid use by players, Commissioner Bud Selig solicited former U.S. Senator George Mitchell to investigate and issue a report about drug use in America's national pastime. The Mitchell Report contained the names of many MLB players that former Senator Mitchell said used performance-enhancing drugs (PEDs). When the report was released, St. Louis Cardinals star Albert Pujols was not named in the report as a player who used PEDs; however, that did not prevent WNBC-TV in New York from reporting on its website that Pujols was listed in the Mitchell Report as a user of PEDs. KTVU, a St. Louis television station, picked up the story and also reported that Pujols appeared in the report as a user of PEDs. It was also incorrectly reported that MLB player Johnny Damon was listed in the Mitchell Report. After being named in the report, many MLB players confessed that they did, in fact, use illegal drugs. Reporting that players were in the report, when in fact they were not, could cause major legal problems for the media outlets who engaged in false reporting and rumors as well as creating substantial ethical dilemmas. Pujols's agent issued the following statement on his behalf:

> [S]everal national and local news outlets have published false reports that associated my name with the Mitchell Report. . . . I would like to express how upset and disappointed I am over the reckless reporting that took place this morning. . . . What concerns me, is the effect that this has had on my family and that my character and values have now been questioned due to the media's lack of accuracy in their reporting.[10]

The New York station issued an apology to Pujols.[11] What other actions should they have taken to correct their mistake? If making an apology is all the station has to do, is that a sufficient deterrent for breaches of journalism ethics?

🔍 CASE STUDY 11-3 A Proper Retraction

A si.com report posted earlier this month incorrectly stated that Boston College defensive tackle B.J. Raji's name would appear on the NFL's list of players who tested positive for drugs at the NFL Scouting Combine in February. We regret the error.[12]

1. Do you consider the retraction satisfactory? Does it matter where it is posted?
2. How could *Sports Illustrated* have made the retraction more effective?
3. Should they have issued a formal apology directly to the Boston College player?
4. How do you think the publication error impacted Raji both personally and professionally? Could it have any influence on Raji's potential employers, all 30 NFL teams?

The *New York Times* reported that James Stewart, a former star running back for the University of Miami, had failed a drug test given by the NFL. His attorney stated: "It's libel to take a young man about to start a pro career to have his name go forward as a marijuana user, when in fact he is not."[13] Stewart played in the NFL for the Minnesota Vikings.

Superstar David Beckham demanded a front page retraction from a U.S. celebrity gossip magazine after it was reported that he allegedly slept with a prostitute. His agent said: "The allegations that have been made are completely untrue and totally ridiculous as the magazine was clearly told before publication . . . sadly we live in a world where a magazine can print lies and believe they can get away with it. We are taking legal action against the magazine."[14]

Certainly news outlets should make sure they have the correct information before publishing it. A story needs to be investigated, vetted, and verified. Media ethics require a retraction when a story is wrong or misleading. The law can also address this issue; for example, Florida law states the following with regard to a retraction:

(1) If it appears upon the trial that said article or broadcast was published in good faith; that its falsity was due to an honest mistake of the facts; that there were reasonable grounds for believing that the statements in said article or broadcast were true; and that, within the period of time specified in subsection (2), a full

and fair correction, apology, or retraction was, in the case of a newspaper or periodical, published in the same editions or corresponding issues of the newspaper or periodical in which said article appeared and in as conspicuous place and type as said original article or, in the case of a broadcast, the correction, apology, or retraction was broadcast at a comparable time, then the plaintiff in such case shall recover only actual damages. (2) Full and fair correction, apology, or retraction shall be made:

(a) In the case of a broadcast or a daily or weekly newspaper or periodical, within 10 days after service of notice;

(b) In the case of a newspaper or periodical published semimonthly, within 20 days after service of notice;

(c) In the case of a newspaper or periodical published monthly, within 45 days after service of notice; and

(d) In the case of a newspaper or periodical published less frequently than monthly, in the next issue, provided notice is served no later than 45 days prior to such publication.[15]

Plagiarism is one of the unforgivable sins of the journalist. All producers, reporters, and writers should fully understand the concepts and principles surrounding plagiarism. Materials taken from other sources must be given their proper attribution. No work should be passed off as original if it has been copied from another source. Plagiarism can lead to lawsuits and possibly even a criminal conviction. Taking another individual's idea without giving proper credit can devastate the credibility of a journalist, reporter, or media outlet and is clearly an ethical violation.

Media sources should make every effort to disclose the source of their information whenever possible. Relying on "unnamed sources" relates to a journalist's ethical obligation to seek the truth and report it; however, if a journalist promises to protect the identity of an informant, then every effort should be made to keep the identity of that source confidential.

When producing and delivering a story, every effort should be made to abstain from showing profanity, violence, or indecent behavior unless it can be shown to be an essential part of the story that needs to be told.

The first and primary goal of any news media outlet should be to tell the truth. Sometimes the truth is hard to define and even tougher to find. Reporters may discover competing versions of the truth and the versions must be reconciled whenever possible. Images are a major part of reporting and of truth-seeking, particularly in light of advanced technology in reporting. People remember what they see long after what they hear. A media outlet's depiction of images must always be genuine and truthful. No objects or pictures should ever be rearranged, distorted, or removed from a scene in an attempt to tell a story. It is essential that images surrounding the story never be staged or posed. The use of a picture, image, or video must be done in a manner that advances the fairness of the story being told. Enhancing an image for technical clarity is permissible if done fairly and when consistent with the overall objective of the story being told.

When reporting a story, writers should always refrain from stereotyping based on age, gender, national origin, religion, sexual orientation, geography, disability, physical appearance, or social status. It is essential that media outlets treat every individual with respect and dignity. Unfortunately, they don't always do that, particularly when reporting on sports.

🔎 CASE STUDY 11-4 *"Broadway Joe" in Primetime*

Joe Namath was a showman and a great football player in the AFL and NFL. In December 2003, Namath was being interviewed by ESPN's Suzy Kolber during a Monday night football game. As the interview progressed, it was clear that Namath was intoxicated. The interview was paused while the camera went back to the action on the field. After the next play, the interview continued with Namath still clearly intoxicated. He then asked Kolber if he could kiss her. Kolber did the best she could under the circumstances to deal with the situation, saying she would take Namath's statement as a compliment. ESPN executive Jeff Drake stated, "If we had known definitively (Namath) was in that kind of state, we wouldn't have conducted the interview." Namath later apologized to Kolber and ESPN, and the apology was accepted.[16, 17]

Once the broadcaster determined Namath was drunk, did the broadcaster have an ethical obligation to terminate the interview and not place Namath back on camera?

Does the sports media community as a whole focus too much on the athletes who market themselves rather than those who don't seek the limelight? Should the sports media focus on the overwhelming majority of athletes who never have any personal problems and are contributing to their community rather than the few who engage in bad behavior? There is a lack of media stories about the good things athletes do in the community because those don't sell as well. Is the media just giving sports fans what they want? What ethical obligations do media professionals have to supply the public with stories that are wholesome and good?

It has been argued that one of the dominant messages in sports programming is that many aggressive athletes are praised and rewarded. Sports highlights are always shown for the "toughest hits" or "best fights." Sports commentators will commonly use phrases such as the following:

- The players are doing "battle."
- A player is "killing" his opponent.
- A team is going on the "attack mode."
- An offensive is "explosive."
- "Battle lines" have been drawn.

Are these types of references suitable for younger viewers? What kind of messages are they sending to the kids who are watching about how they should play sports? Is there any correlation between athletes who engage in aggressive behavior off the field and violent play on the field?

🔍 CASE STUDY 11-5 Reporter Reports on Golfer Michelle Wie

A simple proposition in the media industry is that a reporter should never become the story or even part of the story. In 2005, golfer Michelle Wie was disqualified from the Samsung World Championship when a *Sports Illustrated* reporter alerted an LPGA official that Wie had allegedly violated tournament rules by taking an illegal drop during the event. The reporter was *Sports Illustrated* senior writer Michael Bamberger. Bamberger had spent a year caddying on the PGA tour. He said, "I don't think she cheated. I think she was simply hasty." Before reporting her, he first went to Wie and discussed the situation with her. He said, "I felt the correct thing was to go to Michelle first. I wanted to hear what she had to say. That's a reporter's first obligation."[18]

1. Did Bamberger act ethically in reporting Wie's actions on the golf course?
2. Should Bamberger have merely written a story about Wie's alleged violation of the rules instead of turning her in?
3. Is it ever proper for a reporter to step out of his or her role as a reporter and become a "self-appointed referee" as Bamberger did?

▶ Ethics of Fair Reporting

Many times a story will reveal facts and circumstances that are not flattering to the individual who is the subject of the story. A media outlet must make a decision about what stories should be told and which ones are not newsworthy. In the sporting world, a newsworthy story could be an injury to a star athlete, the gambling problems of an owner, the negotiation of a new collective bargaining agreement for a professional league, corruption or scandal involving sporting events and organizations, or any other relevant or significant news about a sport and those who play it.

Rumors run rampant in the sports industry and journalists should never issue a report solely based on rumors. They have an important investigative responsibility to separate fact from fiction and "seek the truth." They must be more concerned with reporting an accurate story and less concerned with ratings and getting the "scoop." The *New York*

Times had addressed this issue when a judging corruption scandal occurred in Olympic figure skating:[19]

> When a sprightly Canadian figure-skating pair perform flawlessly in their Olympic event, only to be judged inferior to an elegant but wobbly Russian pair, the journalists' task was clear: find out if the fix was in. The French judge in the competition was dismissed for failure to rule impartially. The sources that reporters used to look into vote-trading accusations seemed, at times, obscure. Among them were:
>
> - "Unsubstantiated reports"
> - "Various reports, citing unnamed sources"
> - "Speculation"
> - "Rumors"

A close call for a media outlet is whether to cover a story that may be more personal in nature, but still concerns a sports star, team, or event. Media professionals should be concerned with the privacy rights of those people who are the subject of their reporting and furthermore, must ensure that their rights are respected while they are investigating and reporting on a newsworthy story.

Coaching and leading a major college football program can be a high-profile job, especially if that job is at the University of Alabama. Historically, Alabama has been one of college football's winningest programs. Mike Price was hired as the new football coach at the university but would never coach a game for the Crimson Tide. Price's antics at a local establishment created a media frenzy and eventually cost him his head coaching job. Price sued Time, Inc. for a story that appeared in *Sports Illustrated* magazine. The issue was to what extent could *Sports Illustrated* and their writer be forced to reveal a confidential source for an article that was published about Coach Price and his activities at a Florida night club.

⚖ CASE 11-1 *Price v. Time, Inc.*

416 F.3d 1327 (11th Cir. 2005)

In the Spring of 2003, Mike Price was head coach of the University of Alabama's Crimson Tide football team. Given the near-fanatical following that college football has in the South, the head coach at a major university is a powerful figure. However, as Archbishop Tillotson observed three centuries ago, "they, who are in highest places, and have the most power . . . have the least liberty, because they are most observed."[1] If Price was unaware of that paradox when he became the Crimson Tide's coach, he learned it the hard way a few months later in the aftermath of a trip he took to Pensacola, Florida.

While in Pensacola to participate in a pro-am golf tournament, Price, a married man, visited an establishment known as "Artey's Angels." The name is more than a little ironic because the women who dance there are not angels in the religious sense and, when he went, Price was not following the better angels of his nature in any sense. Scandal ensued, and as often happens in our society, litigation followed closely on the heels of scandal.

[The issue in the case is] whether *Sports Illustrated* magazine and one of its writers are protected under Alabama law or by the federal Constitution from being compelled to reveal the confidential source for an article they published about Price and his activities in Pensacola.

. . . The federal constitutional question involves application of the First Amendment qualified reporter's privilege, which in this case comes down to one factor: whether Price has made all reasonable

[1]Thomas Birch, The Life of Dr. John Tillotson Compiled Chiefly from His Original Papers and Letters, in 1 The Works of the Most Reverend Dr. John Tillotson, Lord Archbishop of Canterbury lxxix (London, J. & R. Tonson et al. 1752).

efforts to discover the identity of the confidential source in ways other than by forcing *Sports Illustrated* and its writer to divulge it . . . we conclude that *Sports Illustrated* is not a newspaper for purposes of Alabama's shield law, but we also conclude that Price has not yet exhausted all reasonable efforts to discover through other means the identity of the confidential source.

Don Yaeger is a reporter for *Sports Illustrated*, a weekly magazine published by Time, Inc., which contains sports-related features, reports, opinions, and advertisements. The issue of *Sports Illustrated* that hit the newsstands on May 8, 2003 (but actually bore the date of May 12, 2003) contained an article written by Yaeger entitled, "Bad Behavior: How He Met His Destiny At A Strip Club." The "he" in the title refers to Price, and the "Destiny" reference is a double-entendre playing off the stage name of one of the strippers at Artey's Angels. The *Sports Illustrated* article itself recounts allegations of boorish behavior and sexual misconduct by Price in the months following his ascension to the position of head football coach at the University of Alabama. The article indicates that it relies on confidential sources for the most salacious parts of its content.

One of the incidents described in the article involves sexual advances Price allegedly made, shortly after he was hired in late 2002, towards some unnamed female students in a bar and at an apartment complex in Tuscaloosa, Alabama, where the University is located. The parties refer to this as "the Tuscaloosa incident." . . . Price's counsel informed us that since . . . he has uncovered by other means the identity of the confidential sources for the reporting about the Tuscaloosa incident . . .

Price has not yet discovered the identity of the confidential source for the article's reporting on "the Pensacola incident," . . . The article states that shortly after arriving in Pensacola, Florida, on the afternoon of April 16, 2003, Price went to a strip club called "Artey's Angels." It says that he spent most of his time with a dancer named Lori "Destiny" Boudreaux, who is quoted in the article as saying that Price bought her drinks, tipped her $60 for "semiprivate" dances, and touched her inappropriately during those dances, which was against the house rules. Price told Destiny that he had a room at a hotel in town and that he wanted her to meet him there later that night.

The article also alleges that Price visited Artey's a second time, later on the same day, after he had left the golf tournament's sponsor dinner early. The article says that while sitting at the bar in Artey's, Price was "kissing and fondling a waitress until a reminder from the deejay prompted him to stop." It describes how he continued to buy several hundred dollars' worth of drinks and dances until about midnight, and finally invited two dancers back to his hotel room where the three of them supposedly had sex. The article includes this description of what allegedly occurred at Price's hotel room:

> At about midnight [after leaving the club] Price headed back to the hotel. He eventually met up with two women, both of whom he had earlier propositioned for sex, according to one of the women, who agreed to speak to *SI* about the hotel-room liaison on the condition that her name not be used. The woman, who declined comment when asked if she was paid for the evening, said that the threesome engaged "in some pretty aggressive sex." She said that at one point she and her female companion decided to add a little levity to the activity: "We started screaming 'Roll Tide!' and he was yelling back, 'It's rolling baby, it's rolling.'"

On May 3, 2003, five days before the article was published, Yaeger called Price to get his response to the allegations about the Pensacola incident. Yaeger asked Price if it was true that "both Jennifer (Eaton) and 'Destiny,'" two exotic dancers from Artey's Angels, "met [him] back at the hotel" after he left the club. Price expressed surprise at the allegations and asked Yaeger who had told him that. Price denied having sex with any woman in his hotel room that night. He said the allegations were "[c]ompletely not true." When asked if he had invited anyone back to his hotel room, Price said "[a]bsolutely not." Although Price initially declined to comment when Yaeger asked if he had awakened the next morning with "at least one woman," Price did tell Yaeger "[t]hat story you heard is completely false." When told by Yaeger that Jennifer and Destiny claimed he had paid them $500 plus a "healthy" tip for sex, Price responded: "Well, someone bought 'em, bought 'em off because it's a lie. A flat lie."

On May 6, 2003, only two days before the magazine appeared on the newsstands, Yaeger went on the popular radio show of Paul Finebaum, a sportswriter in Birmingham, Alabama, to discuss the upcoming article. Yaeger told listeners about Price's alleged hijinks in Tuscaloosa and Pensacola. The parties agree that the statements Yaeger made on the radio show are not materially different from what he said in the article.

Based on Yaeger's comments on the Finebaum show and the published article, Price sued Yaeger and Time, which is *Sports Illustrated's* publisher and parent company [for] . . . libel, slander, and outrageous conduct . . .

. . . Price labels as "false and defamatory" most of the allegations in the *Sports Illustrated* article. He does admit visiting Artey's Angels once while in Pensacola for the golf tournament, but he denies everything else . . . Price vehemently denies having sex with anyone mentioned in the article.

Price [says *Sports Illustrated*] "knew or had reason to know" of the "falsity and lack of verified or factual support" for Yaeger's story, and that they published the account of the incidents in Tuscaloosa and Pensacola "knowing of its sensationalizing sting and falsity with malice by intent and/or reckless disregard for the truth in an effort to increase sales and profit to the[ir] benefit." Price [says *Sports Illustrated*] "created this sensational and provocative article in a malicious effort to publish untruths that were assigned to purported anonymous sources and without a full and fair investigation into the truth or veracity of the [facts in the article] in an effort to get the story to press as quickly as possible regardless of its truth and defamatory content so it would explode into the newsstands." . . . Price claims that [*Sports Illustrated*] maliciously defamed him either by lying about having a confidential source, or by relying exclusively on a confidential source that they knew, or should have known, to be untrustworthy.

1. What is the reasoning behind allowing reporters to use materials in a news story that are gathered from confidential sources?[20]
2. Should a media outlet be forced to reveal the confidential sources of a story under any circumstances?
3. Do you think *Sports Illustrated* and writer Don Yaeger treated Coach Price ethically and fairly in their reporting?
4. Do you think Coach Price's "activities" were newsworthy because of his position at the university or do you consider them a private matter not worthy of reporting?
5. If Coach Price's contract contained a morals clause, would that change your answer?
6. Would your decision about whether the matter was newsworthy change if the university was a private institution rather than a state university?

Michael B. PRICE, Plaintiff-Appellee, v. TIME, INC., Don Yaeger, Defendants-Appellants, U.S. Supreme Court.

What is the definition of "newsworthy"? Does it mean any information that an individual has been unable to keep secret and for which the press seeks to publish? Thus, if it's in the public domain, then it's fair game? According to one of the authors of this book,

This definition of newsworthiness contains no privacy parameters whatsoever and provides the media with unfettered discretion to determine whether the information is of sufficient public interest or significance, which, in essence, amounts to coverage that most effectively sells papers or boosts ratings. The

public domain view neglects to take into consideration whether the matter is highly offensive to the ordinary person . . . . Moreover, the public domain view is inconsistent with journalism ethical duties of (1) providing not only information that citizens want but information citizens "*need* to function in a free society" and (2) considering harm to individual privacy interests such that "[o]nly an overriding public need can justify intrusion into anyone's privacy."[21]

In the following case, an NBA player sued Time, Inc., a famous sports writer, and a legendary coach about an article that appeared in *Sports Illustrated*. The player, Neil Johnston, claimed he was defamed by the article. The writer, George Plimpton, claimed Johnston had been destroyed

"psychologically" by NBA great Bill Russell. For further study, read the entire *Sports Illustrated* article[22] and determine if what George Plimpton wrote was a fair and accurate recording of the events.

⚖ CASE 11-2 *Johnston v. Time, Inc., et al.*

321 F.Supp. 837 (M.D.N.C. 1970)

This is an action for libel brought against Time, Inc., Arnold 'Red' Auerbach and George Plimpton, to recover damages resulting from an article appearing in the December 23, 1968, issue of *Sports Illustrated*. The allegedly libelous statements were printed in connection with a cover story on Bill Russell, star center for the Boston Celtics professional basketball team. George Plimpton, the author of the article, chose a format which included interviews with various people in the sporting world who had come into contact with Russell. Among those he selected was 'Red' Auerbach, coach of the Boston Celtics, to whom is attributed the following statement upon which [Johnston] bases this action:

'* * * That's a word you can use about him (Russell)—he 'destroyed' players. You take Neil Johnston—a good set shot and a great sweeping hook shot, a big long-armed guy who played for Philly and was the leading scorer in the NBA the year before. Russell destroyed him. He destroyed him psychologically as well, so that he practically ran him out of organized basketball. He blocked so many shots that Johnston began throwing his hook farther and farther from the basket. It was ludicrous, and the guys along the bench began to laugh, maybe in relief that they didn't have to worry about such a guy themselves.'

1. Do you think the *Sports Illustrated* article falls under the category of fair reporting?
2. Do you consider what coach Auerbach said or what George Plimpton wrote unethical?
3. This case was filed in 1970. Would this case be brought today?
4. Bill Russell was arguably one of the greatest NBA defensive players of all time. Does this justify the article and the comments made about Johnston?[23]

Johnston v. Time, Inc., 321 F. Supp. 837 (M.D.N.C. 1970), U.S. Supreme Court.

Is Robert Dee the worst tennis player in the world? Evidently several media outlets thought so, publishing articles calling him the "world's worst player" after the 21-year-old professional tennis player lost 54 consecutive matches. Dee sued them for libel, saying his reputation was damaged and the newspapers should issue a retraction.[24]

Crime dominates the lead story on many news broadcasts. When an athlete is charged with a crime, media outlets should be careful about how they report the story. How they

portray the athlete can be significant for both ethical and legal reasons. Under the U.S. legal system, an individual is presumed innocent until proven guilty, but unfortunately, media outlets tend to presume guilt until innocence is proven. Former Major Leaguer John Montefusco was irate about how he was portrayed by ESPN after he was charged with criminal conduct toward his wife. He sued the media behemoth claiming they unfairly compared him to another athlete who had been charged with a crime, O.J. Simpson.

⚖ CASE 11-3   Montefusco v. ESPN, Inc.

2002 WL 31108927

John Montefusco, formerly a Major League Baseball pitcher for the San Francisco Giants, the Atlanta Braves, and the New York Yankees, and once the National League's "Rookie of the Year," was the subject of a telecast by the ESPN sports news show, "SportsCenter." In the SportsCenter telecast, ESPN described criminal proceedings in New Jersey concerning charges against Montefusco by his ex-wife, Doris Montefusco, of sexual and physical violence. Doris Montefusco charged Montefusco with rape, threatened murder, and three attempts to seriously injure her with extreme indifference to human life. The ESPN broadcast noted that a jury found Montefusco not guilty of eighteen felony counts, but convicted him of assault and criminal trespass. Several times throughout the telecast, Montefusco's case was analogized to that of O.J. Simpson, "another ex-athlete accused of domestic violence." Montefusco sued ESPN for defamation and made a claim for false light invasion of privacy. Both the defamation claim and the false light claim were based on identical grounds. Montefusco argues that the comparison with Simpson implies that Montefusco is guilty of the crimes of which he was acquitted.

In holding in favor of ESPN, the court stated:

> In the instant case, none of the statements made in the sports news broadcast were defamatory: all of the statements related to the criminal charges were factually accurate, as was the comparison of Montefusco's case to Simpson's...

> Pursuant to New Jersey's "fair report privilege," ESPN's presentation was "accurate and complete," and did not mislead viewers as to the Simpson case or Montefusco's circumstances.

1. Was ESPN's comparison of Montefusco to O.J. Simpson fair?
2. Do you consider this a newsworthy story?
3. Are all alleged criminal activities of athletes "fair game" for the media? Under what circumstances would they not be?
4. Is an athlete's paternity case a newsworthy story? What about a divorce case or a lawsuit involving sexual harassment of an owner, player, or sportscaster?

Montefusco v. ESPN, Inc., U.S. Supreme Court.

In Case 11-4, a famous surfer was dissatisfied with the way he was portrayed in a *Sports Illustrated* article so he sued the magazine for false light.

⚖ CASE 11-4   Virgil v. Sports Illustrated

424 F.Supp. 1286, (S.D. 1976)

The facts themselves, putting out cigarettes in his mouth and diving off stairs to impress women, hurting himself in order to collect unemployment so as to have time for bodysurfing at the Wedge during summer, fighting in gang fights as a youngster, and eating insects are not sufficiently offensive to reach the very high level of offensiveness necessary . . . to lose newsworthiness protection. . . . The above facts are generally unflattering and perhaps embarrassing, but they are simply not offensive to the degree of morbidity or sensationalism. In fact they connote nearly as strong a positive image as they do a negative one. On the one hand Mr. Virgil can be seen as a juvenile exhibitionist, but on the other hand he also comes across as the tough, aggressive maverick, an archetypal character occupying a respected place in the American consciousness. Given this ambiguity as to whether or not the facts disclosed are offensive at all, no reasonable juror could conclude that they were highly offensive.

... Along with the facts complained of *Sports Illustrated* included directly therewith Mr. Virgil's retrospective, more mature, perception and explanation of them. Mr. Virgil was quoted as saying:

"I guess I used to live a pretty reckless life. I think I might have been drunk most of the time. ... I'm not sure a lot of the things I've done weren't pure lunacy."

Any negative impression a reader might have of Mike Virgil would be tempered considerably by Virgil's own admissions that in hindsight he may have been acting a bit crazily.

... For highly offensive facts, *i.e.* those having a degree of offensiveness equivalent to "morbid and sensational," to be denied protection as newsworthy, the revelation of them must be "for its own sake." Both parties agree that body surfing at the Wedge is a matter of legitimate public interest, and it cannot be doubted that Mike Virgil's unique prowess at the same is also of legitimate public interest. Any reasonable person reading the *Sports Illustrated* article would have to conclude that the personal facts concerning Mike Virgil were included as a legitimate journalistic attempt to explain Virgil's extremely daring and dangerous style of body surfing at the Wedge.

1. Do you agree that "body surfing at the Wedge" or Mr. Virgil's "unique prowess" is a matter of legitimate public interest? What standards should be employed to make such a decision?
2. Is it inconsistent for the court to say that the facts revealed in the article are "unflattering and perhaps embarrassing" but not "highly offensive"?
3. Can and should a matter of public interest be defined differently in sports reporting than elsewhere?

Virgil v. Sports Illustrated (S.D. 1976), U.S. Supreme Court.

Sports talk radio is very popular. Sports fans call and debate everything from a player's performance on the field to his or her personal life. At times, the topics seem to have no boundaries. Many times, what is said can be highly inappropriate, even bordering on defamation. Talk show hosts sometimes go too far in commenting on a team or player. It is clear that fans and sports broadcasters alike have varying opinions on the skill levels of players. Many times, fans' comments about a sports star's abilities can be very cruel and harsh.

In Case 11-5, a well-known radio talk show host was sued by an owner of an NBA team after the broadcaster continuously took the owner to task over his operation of the NBA's Cleveland Cavaliers.

⚖ CASE 11-5 *Stepien v. Franklin*

528 N.E.2d 1324 (1988)

The area of sports is a traditional haven for cajoling, invective, and hyperbole; therefore, a reasonable listener to a sports talk program is on notice that the host's descriptions of a sports public figure as, inter alia, "stupid," "dumb," "buffoon," "nincompoop," "scum," "a cancer," "an obscenity," "gutless liar," "unmitigated liar," "pathological liar," "egomaniac," "nuts," "crazy," "irrational," "suicidal," and "lunatic" are statements of opinion which are constitutionally protected.

Public figures, having thrust themselves into the public eye, cannot prevent others from criticizing or insulting them for their acts or deeds.

Theodore J. Stepien ("Stepien") is the former President of the Cleveland Professional Basketball Company, more commonly known as the Cleveland Cavaliers. The Cleveland Cavaliers is a professional basketball franchise operated under the auspices of the National Basketball Association ("NBA"). [Stepien's] tenure as President of the Cavaliers began in June 1980 and he remained in that position until the team was sold to George and Gordon Gund in May 1983.

Peter J. Franklin ("Franklin") is the host of a radio sports talk show known as "Sportsline." During the period in question, Sportsline was regularly broadcast Monday through Friday, 7:00 p.m. to midnight, unless it was pre-empted by a live sports event. Franklin principally employed an audience call-in format—listeners are encouraged to call in and give their opinions and/or solicit Franklin's opinion about sports. Sportsline is entertainment, designed to encourage and capitalize on the considerable public interest in professional sports.

The style of radio and television personalities who host talk shows such as Sportsline varies widely, from the erudite analysis of William F. Buckley to the insults of Joan Rivers. Franklin's style, which is immediately apparent from listening to his show, is an extreme version of the "insult" genre of entertainment. Franklin is often loud, opinionated, rude, abrasive, obnoxious, and insulting. In a manner reminiscent of the popular comedian Don Rickles, Franklin frequently hangs up on his callers and/or calls them insulting names.

The period when Stepien was the President of the Cavaliers, June 1980 to May 1983, is also the time period in which the alleged slander and emotional distress took place.

[Stepien], after becoming President of the Cavaliers, immediately began an aggressive style of management that involved making numerous player transactions and staff appointments. [Stepien] went through more than fifty players and six coaches in two and one-half years, including the hiring and firing of one coach twice. This aggressive style of management and the lack of the Cavaliers' success thereafter resulted in [Stepien] receiving a great deal of unfavorable criticism in the press, nationally and locally.

The factual background specifically relevant to the alleged defamatory statements can be broken down into three general topics:

1. National Basketball Association's moratoriums on trading;
2. The finances of the Cavaliers; and
3. The proposed sale of the team and move to Toronto.

Many of Franklin's alleged defamatory statements complained of herein consisted of those that challenged [Stepien's] ability to manage an NBA team. These remarks by Franklin involved Cavaliers' player transactions and the league's subsequent reaction to them. In November 1980, the Cavaliers engaged in the above-stated trades that resulted in the team's trading away several first-round draft choices. These trades were criticized by most observers and fans as being detrimental to the Cavaliers. In response, the NBA Commissioner imposed a restriction referred to as a "moratorium on trades" involving the Cavaliers. The restriction permitted the team to make trades, but only upon consulting with the league office and obtaining final approval. After a short while, the moratorium was lifted, but in February 1983, a second moratorium occurred. This restriction required the Cavaliers to give the NBA twenty-four hours to consider any trade and was apparently motivated by the NBA's concern that the Cavaliers' troubles might lead them to make unwise player transactions in order to raise operating capital. The Cavaliers' financial problems were acute. [Stepien] considered many options to alleviate this problem. Between January and April 1983, [Stepien] explored several possibilities including selling the team to out-of-town buyers, selling the team to a local buyer, or retaining ownership and moving the team to Toronto. During this period, the media harshly criticized [Stepien] for not completing the sale and for proposing that the team move away from Cleveland.

There is no question that during [Stepien's] three-year period of ownership of the Cavaliers, Franklin was a harsh and critical commentator. His descriptions of [Stepien], extracted from tapes of the show provided to this court, include: "stupid," "dumb," "buffoon," "nincompoop," "scum," "a cancer," "an obscenity," "gutless liar," "unmitigated liar," "pathological liar," "egomaniac," "nuts," "crazy," "irrational," "suicidal," "lunatic," etc.

1. Do you consider Franklin's remarks fair reporting of the facts?
2. Does the fact that Franklin said them over a three-year period make any difference?
3. Is this just a situation of a sports commentator giving his honest opinion about the running of a local franchise, or did he cross the line?

Stepien v. Franklin, 528 N.E.2d 1324 (Ohio Ct. App. 1988), U.S. Supreme Court.

One scholar noted the following about sports commentator Pete Franklin and his opinions on the Cleveland Indians Major League Baseball team:

Franklin's attacks on the Indians franchise could be merciless, though to be fair, were often quite accurate. The team was mired in mismanagement and presented itself more often than not as being a player or two away from winning it all. In actuality, the team was mortgaging its future by selling out its player development system at an astonishing rate in favor of young players with questionable skills and a bevy of well-known but past-their-prime veterans who offered little on the field.[25]

He also said,

[A]lthough Franklin could be brusque as well as childlike, those who knew him off-mike would also maintain that he could be positively charming. . . . When pressed on the subject, Nick Mileti—the Cleveland sports magnate of the 1970s who targeted Franklin specifically to anchor his newly purchased 50,000 watt station—said that off-air Franklin was "the sweetest man who ever lived," . . . noting well that "[he] turned into a killer" once the microphones were turned on, a refrain heard time and again by peers and associates.[26]

🔍 CASE STUDY 11-6 *Media Accuracy and Ethics*

Assume a media outlet has been producing a story about a university's athletic program and the lack of academic success achieved by its student-athletes. The athletic director for the university calls the media outlet and wants to see the final product before it goes on the air, citing concerns over accuracy and wanting to ensure that the university and its student-athletes are portrayed accurately and fairly. Should the media outlet allow the athletic director access? If not, what alternatives could be offered to be fair?

Sometimes the target of a story will go on the offensive. In 2009, ESPN's show *Outside the Lines* did a segment on Florida State 's academic scandal among its student-athletes. FSU denied all the charges made by ESPN. FSU e-mailed a letter to its supporters, stating in part:

Dear Florida State Supporters:

I want to let you know about an upcoming ESPN "Outside the Lines" television program that we know will portray the academic profile of student-athletes and the admissions and retention process at the Florida State University in a negative way. The promotions for this program already have shown that it contains false information.

Therefore, I and other top administrators have called and e-mailed Vince Doria, vice president of News at ESPN who has oversight of "Outside the Lines," to report our concerns and urge the network not to air this program. That e-mail follows, and we encourage you to read it."[27]

If someone believes he, she, or the organization they work for is unjustly depicted in a story, should that person go on the offensive as FSU did? What are the pros and cons? When is that not a good course of action to take?

▶ Ethics and Social Media in Sports

The term *social media* is now a common phrase in the business community. Social media is essentially a platform that enables the dissemination of information through Internet tools such as Twitter, Facebook, LinkedIn, Instagram, and Snapchat. Social media can include news and information that is posted by the user and can take many different forms, including: forums, blogs, web sites, podcasts, and message boards. How information is gathered, transcribed, and reported has changed immensely with advancing technologies.

Social media has affected the reporting of sports in a variety of ways. The first way is the speed of information. Information that may have taken weeks or even months to gather, verify, and distribute can now be compiled and distributed instantaneously. A second way is that information moves through a myriad of modern communication devices available to millions of viewers or readers on a global basis. Advanced technologies can be used for both good and bad applications. Fair and accurate reporting is essential to any story, and with information moving quickly along the information highway, verifying the truth of a story and fact-checking can become a much more difficult task, which is a third way that social media has affected sports reporting. One wrong statement or impression can be transmitted to numerous individuals who in turn can transmit that information to others,

and this can lead to unfair damage to the reputation of an innocent person.

Do ethics for reporters and writers in traditional media differ from those for reporters in the social media area? Many media outlets have social media policies in an effort to ensure that journalistic ethics are also upheld in the social media environment. Broadcasting giant ESPN issues its own social media guidelines and Rob King, editor-in-chief of ESPN.com, made the following comments about the policy:

> It's an important opportunity to reiterate to folks that this technology is the equivalent of a live microphone. . . . There's a lot of education that goes along with it. Anyone who's ever had a tweet re-tweeted to an audience knows that it can be presented in ways that you might never have understood or intended when you originally articulated those 140 characters.[28]

Technological advances have enabled more sports fans and participants to participate and contribute to the discourse, which is a fourth way that social media has affected sports reporting, but, unfortunately, the comments of many individuals can go unchecked. A media professional must abide by ethical rules when reporting on a story. The same standard is not always applicable to those who may have a variety of social media applications at their fingertips. An individual fan or player can distribute information instantaneously but is not held to the same standard as a media professional. They are, of course, still subject to the law and its requirements, but with so many individuals having access to information, it is inevitable that damaging information will go unchecked and eventually be transmitted. Newspapers and other traditional forms of publishing have editors who review and analyze a story before it is published; the same cannot be said for many nontraditional forms of media – hence, a fifth way that social media has affected sports reporting.

Sports teams and players are using social media just like any other business or celebrity.[29] Leagues, teams, and players understand the value of connecting with fans and many have used social media platforms to further promote their brands, sell tickets, and provide more exposure to star players; however, along with that exposure comes responsibility. Professional sports leagues have issued social media guidelines in an attempt to regulate social media use by players and management. Not surprisingly, NBA Dallas Mavericks owner Mark Cuban was issued the NBA's first fine under the NBA social media policy when he tweeted a complaint about NBA referees.[30]

Miami Heat star Dwyane Wade has more than 100,000 followers on Twitter. He said:

> When you come to work, you come to work . . . you can tweet before, you can tweet after. It's not addicting like where I'm going to take a bathroom break, go downstairs and tweet. I think people take it a little too far with that. But I think it's very good to have communication with your fans personally. A lot of people, you can see them in a different light.[31]

Many teams ban Twitter from their practices because of the distraction it brings to the team, thus imposing a stricter ban on social networking than the league requires, calling it "team time." Players see the social media world as a way to promote themselves, some call it marketing, but as a team member and employee of the club, a player must abide by all team rules and keep the team's interest ahead of the player's interest. It is never a good idea to say the first thing that comes

to mind. A tweet in the hands of the wrong person can lead to disaster. For example, former Kansas City Chiefs running back Larry Johnson tweeted a gay slur when referring to his head coach.[32] He was suspended and fined for his actions.

Should universities and high schools be able to limit and monitor what student-athletes post on social networking websites or do you consider that too overreaching and an invasion of privacy? What about free speech rights for student-athletes? Should amateur athletic associations have social networking policies?[33] What should be contained in a professional sports league's Twitter policy? Should professional teams have social networking policies as well? Is it overly paternalistic to regulate the speech of college and professional players, who are all adults?

▶ Ethics and Athlete Privacy

In today's media-driven world, it is clear that star professional athletes are public figures. Millions of fans follow sports teams and their players on the field, the Internet, on television, and a variety of other places, both on and off the field. They seem to want to know every excruciating detail, both professionally and personally, about their sports stars. American society loves celebrities, and athletes are celebrities. An issue that arises is at what point is an athlete's private life off-limits to the media and fans? Certainly, the private life of Tiger Woods was exposed to the entire world when he engaged in extra-marital affairs. His actions and their repercussions received worldwide attention. They were debated endlessly by "talking heads" in all forms of media. What did his actions have to do with his ability to play golf?

There are many questions to be answered in this context. Is the media overstepping its bounds by reporting such behavior? Should the private lives of athletes, coaches and administrators be off-limits to reporters if their actions have nothing to do with the sport? A stated justification for digging into their private lives is that, as "role models" and "public figures," they have voluntarily thrust themselves into the public eye and thus, have assumed the risk that others will criticize or insult them for their acts or misdeeds. Should the "assumption of risk" be limited to actions that relate to the sport they play? Sports journalists are relentless in their efforts to uncover incidents of misconduct involving professional and amateur athletes, whether it involves (1) alleged felony or misdemeanor criminal behavior before the formal filing of charges, (2) allegations of non-criminal behavior that may impact competition on the field or the integrity of the game, such as alleged use of performance-enhancing drugs and other forms of "cheating," or (3) a failure to exercise "good moral character and judgment" that does not constitute a crime and has no connection whatsoever with performance on the field.[34]

Is every professional and amateur athlete, coach, and administrator a public figure? The public figure status, in essence, shields journalists and media outlets from defamation lawsuits because, in order to prevail, the public figure must show that the statements about the public figure were published with knowledge of their falsity or with reckless disregard for their falsity.

Which of the following would you argue are not "newsworthy" events of an athlete and should not be reported?

1. A professional or amateur athlete is charged with domestic violence.
2. A professional or amateur athlete takes an illegal drug.
3. A professional or amateur athlete engages in an extramarital affair.
4. A professional or amateur athlete gets a divorce from their spouse.
5. A professional or amateur athlete is charged with driving under the influence of alcohol.
6. A professional or amateur athlete donates no money to charity.
7. A professional or amateur athlete gambles in Las Vegas as a "hobby."
8. A professional or amateur athlete's religious views.
9. A professional or amateur athlete's family member has a serious disease.
10. A professional or amateur athlete fails to pay taxes.

Should big-time college athletes be considered public figures and give up their privacy for reporting purposes? Isn't it inconsistent to treat them like professionals in relation to their privacy rights but then not treat them like professionals in relation to their compensation rights? College athletes involved in revenue-generating sports get the worst of both worlds. One justification for public figure status is that the public has a right to know when those who profit from their public status are alleged to have committed a misdeed; however, college athletes do not profit from their public status (at least not as of the time of this writing).

Consider how former UCLA basketball player Reeves Nelson was portrayed in the media. *Sports Illustrated* published an article in 2012 titled, "Not the UCLA Way," in which an *SI* reporter described Nelson as a chronic troublemaker. The article cited "more than a dozen players and staff members from the past four Bruins teams" who had alleged numerous misdeeds in the UCLA program over the past few seasons and singled out Nelson for boorish behavior, including: urinating on a teammate's clothes, routinely getting in physical altercations with teammates, and intentionally injuring other players. Nelson sued the media outlet, denying each of the reported incidents. Nelson had obtained signed declarations from 18 current or former UCLA players stating that Nelson did not do any of the acts to them as alleged in *SI*'s report. Only two of those 18 players said they had spoken with the reporter before the article was published and, in their signed declarations, both players said they even told the reporter that he had incorrect information regarding Nelson's behavior.[35]

Brett Favre was one of the greatest quarterbacks in NFL history. He has thrown more than 500 touchdown passes. In 2010, Favre became the subject of an NFL investigation after it was alleged he sent pictures of his private anatomy to a New York Jets female employee when Favre played for the Jets in 2008. The sports website deadspin.com posted photos, text messages, and voice mails it had obtained by paying an undisclosed party $3.2 million. People viewed the photos and listened to the calls. This represented a five-fold increase in the website's usual weekly traffic.[36] *The New York Times* writer David Carr stated the issue well:

> While we were not the first people to use the Internet to look at another person's privates,

something more pernicious and tawdry was underway. Deadspin violated a promise to a source, then paid for the photos and voice mails that it asserted were from Favre. But the "news" spread throughout other media organizations despite a lack of information about the provenance of the photos or the motivations of the source.[37]

Favre refused to cooperate with the NFL during the investigation and was subsequently fined $50,000 by the league for failing to cooperate with the Commissioner's office.[38] Favre was later sued for sexual harassment by former Jets employees.[39]

1. Did Deadspin act ethically in obtaining the information and reporting the story?
2. If it is a newsworthy story, is it only newsworthy because it involves a famous NFL quarterback?
3. Does it change your viewpoint if it is determined that Favre's actions constituted sexual harassment under New York law?

⌕ CASE STUDY 11-7   More LeBron James and ESPN

Evidently, it is true, what happens in Vegas, stays in Vegas! ESPN chose to remove from its website a story detailing LeBron James's visit to Las Vegas with his friends. Reporter Arash Markazi wrote a story about James and his friends; however, ESPN pulled the story saying:

> We looked into the situation thoroughly and found that Arash did not properly identify himself as a reporter or clearly state his intentions to write a story.[40]

⌕ CASE STUDY 11-8   Fair or Foul Questions?

Reporters ask questions, it's what they do. Some questions are well thought out and some are not. There is no doubt Tiger Woods has had his personal struggles, as all individuals do. The media has been "on the case," keeping the public updated on Tiger's activities with every excruciating detail. Before the 2010 Ryder Cup, a British reporter asked him: "You don't win majors anymore. . . . You don't win regular tournaments anymore. And you are about to be deposed by Europeans as the world No. 1, or [by] Phil Mickelson. Where is the Ryder Cup now that you're an ordinary golfer?" Tiger's response was: "I remember you're the same one at the British Open who asked me that, too. . . . I hope you're having a good week."[41]

1. Did the reporter draw too much attention to himself by asking the questions?
2. Do you consider the questions insulting or just part of the sports landscape in today's sports media-driven world?
3. From the viewpoint of a journalist, what is the point or desired result of the question posed by the reporter?

In Case 11-6, media outlets reported on a story involving the sexual molestation of members of a Little League Baseball team. Privacy issues became a major concern for coaches and team members because of the reporting of the story.

⚖ CASE 11-6 *M.G. v. Time Warner, Inc.*

89 Cal.App.4th 623 (2001)

In September 1999, *Sports Illustrated* and an HBO television program, *Real Sports*, used the 1997 team photograph of a Little League team to illustrate stories about adult coaches who sexually molest youths playing team sports. [Plaintiffs], all of whom appear in the photograph, were formerly players or coaches on the Little League team. The team's manager, Norman Watson, pleaded guilty to molesting five children he had coached in Little League. [Plaintiffs] have sued Time Warner [Parent company of HBO].

The 10 [Plaintiffs] were eight players and two coaches for a Little League team in Highland, California. Norman Watson was the team's manager in 1996 and 1997, until it was discovered in September 1997 that he had a long history of sexually abusing children, beginning with a molestation conviction in 1971. Watson pleaded guilty in April 1998.

In September 1999, *Sports Illustrated* published a cover story, *Every Parent's Nightmare*, on incidents of child molestation in youth sports. Using Watson as one example, the article reported Watson had "pleaded guilty to 39 counts of lewd acts with children, four boys and a girl, that had occurred between 1990 and 1996, when Watson was a San Bernardino Little League coach and umpire and the five kids were all playing in the league." Watson was further described as having "spent most of his 54 years sexually preying on children . . . [m]ost of . . . whom he first met through his work in Little League."

Accompanying the article was a team photograph of 18 people, including the 10 [Plaintiffs] in this case. The photograph featured a sign board reading: "East Baseline S P 1997." (We use only the team's initials to preserve its members from further notoriety.) The photograph also bore a caption: "A fixture, Watson (center, in black) coached for years not far from a hospital where he'd been incarcerated as a molester."

Also in September 1999, HBO broadcast a similar report on child molesters in youth sports. The story discussed Watson and his involvement with [Plaintiffs'] team. The story employed a fleeting shot of the team photograph.

The *Sports Illustrated* article and the HBO program did not name any of the people shown in the team photograph except Watson. The article did not identify any of Watson's victims by his or her real name. Two victims were identified by pseudonyms. One player, who is not a [Plaintiff] was interviewed on the HBO program, apparently using his real name . . . four of the eight [Plaintiffs] had been molested by Watson and four had not.

First, [Plaintiffs] themselves are of three different types: the four players who were Watson's victims, four players who escaped being molested, and two adult assistant coaches who also appeared in the team photograph. Second, two different publications are involved, the *Sports Illustrated* article and the television program. Depending on which category of [Plaintiffs] and which publication are involved, a different theory of liability may apply.

The parties seem to agree that disclosure of information connecting a person with sexual molestation potentially may offend a reasonable person. But Time Warner argues that the photograph of [Plaintiffs] was not private and its publication met the test of newsworthiness. [Plaintiffs] of course, assert the photograph was private and was not newsworthy.

As to what constitutes a private fact, Time Warner asserts the information was not private because plaintiffs had played a public sport and the team photograph had been taken on a public baseball field. Furthermore, during the two years after Watson was found out, it had been widely reported that Watson had coached a Little League team, occasionally identified as the S P, and that Watson had admitted molesting Little League players. Time Warner maintains that [their] use of the team photographs disclosed only information that was already publicly known: ". . . Norman Watson, a convicted child molester, had coached the East Baseline S P."

[Plaintiffs] counter that their identities, as coaches or players on Watson's team, were not revealed in any of the coverage of the Watson case until the publication of the team photograph, an event which publicly linked [Plaintiffs] with child molestation as either victims, perpetrators, or collaborators. [Plaintiffs] stated that, immediately after the article and the program appeared, they were teased and harassed at school and called "gay," "faggot," "queer," and one of "Norm's boys." As a consequence, the [Plaintiffs'] academic performances suffered. Some of them were forced to quit school, to transfer, or to be home-schooled. The two coaches have stated they were "ridiculed, questioned, and harassed" and received crank phone calls accusing them of being molesters or of condoning molestation.

Time Warner apparently equates "private" with "secret" and urges any information not concealed has been made public. But the claim of a right of privacy is not "'so much one of total secrecy as it is of the right to define one's circle of intimacy—to choose who shall see beneath the quotidian mask.'" Information disclosed to a few people may remain private.

In the present case, none of the previous media coverage specifically identified [Plaintiffs] as team members. Nor, as the trial court observed, is there evidence in the record that the team photograph was ever widely circulated. . . . But [Plaintiffs] maintain the photograph was intended to be private, only for dissemination among family and friends. Although [Plaintiffs] do not know how Time Warner acquired the photograph, they never consented to its use.

"An analysis measuring newsworthiness of facts about an otherwise private person involuntarily involved in an event of public interest by their relevance to a newsworthy subject matter incorporates considerable deference to reporters and editors, avoiding the likelihood of unconstitutional interference with the freedom of the press to report truthfully on matters of legitimate public interest. In general, it is not for a court or jury to say how a particular story is best covered. The constitutional privilege to publish truthful material 'ceases to operate only when an editor abuses his broad discretion to publish matters that are of legitimate public interest.' By confining our interference to extreme cases, the courts 'avoid unduly limiting . . . the exercise of effective editorial judgment.'

"On the other hand, no mode of analyzing newsworthiness can be applied mechanically or without consideration of its proper boundaries. To observe that the newsworthiness of private facts about a person involuntarily thrust into the public eye depends, in the ordinary case, on the existence of a logical nexus between the newsworthy event or activity and the facts revealed is not to deny that the balance of free press and privacy interests may require a different conclusion when the intrusiveness of the revelation is greatly disproportionate to its relevance. Intensely personal or intimate revelations might not, in a given case, be considered newsworthy, especially where they bear only slight relevance to a topic of legitimate public concern."

Furthermore, the article and the program in themselves demonstrate the team members' faces should have been concealed. Although the program showed footage of boys playing baseball, it did not show their faces but photographed them without their faces showing. In the program and the article, the victims were given pseudonyms unless they consented to using their real names. Nor is this case analogous to one in which a news documentary used the first name of a rape victim and a picture of her house. The intrusion here, in which the children's faces were revealed, is far greater and outweighs the values of journalistic impact and credibility.

1. Was the privacy of the coaches or players properly protected in this case?
2. Do you agree with the court's definition of newsworthy?
3. How should a media professional treat individuals who are thrust into the spotlight?
4. How should a media professional approach a story involving children, such as in this case?

M.G., a minor, et al., Plaintiffs and Respondents, v. TIME WARNER, INC. et al., U.S. Supreme Court.

▶ Summary

Sports programming and news are delivered through a variety of media forms – *e.g.*, Internet websites, blogs, Twitter, YouTube, Facebook, and cable television. The consumer's ability to obtain sports content and information from all of these media platforms results in numerous sources competing for the consumer's attention. The SMP plays a critical role in the process and should recognize issues that can influence the way media outlets and journalists gather, process and disseminate sports news. Given the public figure status of athletes, coaches, and administrators, it is important for the SMP to be critical of sports media and journalism and be mindful of their primary ethical obligations: seek the truth, minimize harm, act independently, and be accountable and transparent.

▶ References

1. David Remnick, *The Only Game in Town: Sportswriting from the New Yorker* (New York: Random House, 2010).
2. Chris Duncan, "Longhorns Get Own TV Network," theeagle.com, Bryan-College Station Texas, February 20, 2011.
3. Society of Professional Journalists, "SPJ Code of Ethics," September 6, 2014.
4. "ESPN's Internal Watchdog Slams Network's LeBron James Special," *Wall Street Journal*, July 21, 2010. Richard Deitsch, "MEDIA CIRCUS," *Sports Illustrated*, July 9, 2010.
5. Leonard Shapiro, "Coverage of LeBron James's Decision Brings ESPN's Integrity into Question Yet Again," *The Washington Post*, July 13, 2010.
6. Ibid.
7. David Bauder, "Networks Criticized for Video of Fatal Luge Accident at Olympics," *USA Today*, February 13, 2010.
8. Cooper Rollow, "Sportscasters Debate TV Sports' Ethics, Style," *Chicago Tribune*, June 9, 1977.
9. Lawrence A. Wenner, *MediaSport* (New York: Routledge, 1998). Lee Witkins and Clifford G. Christians, *The Handbook of Mass Media Ethics* (New York: Routledge, 2008).
10. "Pujols Reacts upon Hearing Name on Rumored List," ESPN.com, December 14, 2007.
11. Associated Press, "Pujols Bans TV Station That Erred Naming Him in Mitchell Report," *ESPN.com*, January 21, 2008.
12. "Correction: BC's Raji not on NFL's Drug List," *Sports Illustrated*, April 21, 2009.
13. Alan Goldfarb. "Ex-Miami Player Sues Times for Libel," *The New York Times*, March 30, 1995.
14. John Plunkett, "David Beckham to Demand Front-Page Retraction from In Touch Magazine," *Guardian.co.uk*, September 23, 2010.
15. Fla. Stat. Ann. § 770.02 (West).
16. Rudy Martzke, "Embarrassed Namath Apologizes to Kolber," *USA Today*, December 23, 2003; Associated Press, "Still Broadway Joe," *SI.com*, December 21, 2003.

17. Modified from David Pincus, *Today in Sports History: December 20th*, 2010.

18. Modified from Alan Shipnuck, "Steep Drop," *SI Vault*, October 24, 2005.

19. Felicity Barringer, "The News Media; Sports Reporting: Rules on Rumors," *The New York Times*, January 3, 2008. Robert E. Cooper, "Libel and the Reporting of Rumor," *Yale Law Journal* (1982).

20. Jane Kirtley, "A Magazine Is Not a Newspaper," *American Journalism Review* (October/November 2005).

21. Modified from Richard T. Karcher, "Tort Law and Journalism Ethics," *Loyola University Chicago Law Journal*, Volume 40, 781, 827-28 (2009). Brett Hutchins and David Rowe, "Reconfiguring Media Sports for the Online World: An Inquiry into 'Sports News and Digital Media,'" *International Journal of Communication* 4 (2010): 696–718; Benjamin T. Hickman, "Old Law, New Technology: The First Amendment's Application When Sports Teams and Leagues Attempt to Regulate New Media," *Communications Lawyer* (July, 2010). Arthur A. Raney and Jennings Bryant, *Handbook of Sports and Media* (Mahwah, NJ: Earlbaum Associates, 2006); K. Tim Wulfemeyer, "Ethics in Sports Journalism: Tightening Up the Code," *Journal of Mass Media Ethics* 1, no. 1 (Autumn 1985); Sarah K. Fleish, "The Ethics of Legal Commentary: A Reconsideration of the Need for an Ethical Code in Light of the Duke Lacrosse Matter," *Georgetown Journal of Legal Ethics* (Summer, 2007); Thomas P. Oates and John Pauly, "Sports Journalism as Moral and Ethical Discourse," *Journal of Mass Media Ethics* 22, no. 4 (2007): 332–347; Brad Schultz, *Sports Media, Second Edition: Reporting, Producing, and Planning* (Boston, MA: Focal Press, 2005).

22. George Plimpton, "Sportsman of the Year Bill Russell," *SI Vault*, December 23, 1968.

23. "ESPN and Bill Bradley," ESPN College Basketball Encyclopedia: The Complete History of the Men's Game (ESPN, 2009): 75; Frank Deford, "The Ring Leader," *SI Vault*, May 10, 1999.

24. Ben Dowell, "British Tennis Player Sues Three Papers," *Guardian.co.uk.*, June 11, 2008.

25. Joel Nathan Rosen, "The Mouth Roars No Longer: Pete Franklin, Sports Talk, and Cleveland Indians Baseball, 1967–1987," NINE: *A Journal of Baseball History and Culture* 15, no. 1 (Fall 2006): 13–26.

26. Ibid.

27. Modified from "Florida State Tries to Pre-Empt ESPN's 'Outside the Lines,'" *Tampabay.com*, December 2009.

28. "ESPN.com's Rob King Discusses Guidelines for Use of Social Media," *Sports Business Daily*, August 5, 2009.

29. Lon Safko, *The Social Media Bible: Tactics, Tools, and Strategies for Business Success* (Hoboken, NJ: Wiley, 2010).

30. Marc Stein, "NBA Social Media Guidelines Out," *ESPN.com*, September 30, 2009.

31. Associated Press, "Heat ban Twitter During 'Office Hours,'" *ESPN.com*, September 28, 2009.

32. "Johnson Uses Slurs for Haley, Reporters," *ESPN.com*, October 26, 2009.

33. Allegra M. Richards, "NCAA Clarifies Facebook Policy," *The Harvard Crimson*, March 14, 2007.

34. Richard T. Karcher, "Tort Law and Journalism Ethics," *Loyola University Chicago Law Journal*, Volume 40, 781, 800 (2009).

35. Peter Yoon, "Reeves Nelson Files Lawsuit," *ESPN.com*, May 23, 2012.

36. David Carr, "When Salacious Is Irresistible," *The New York Times*, October 17, 2010.

37. Ibid.

38. "Favre Fined $50,000, not Suspended in Sterger Case," *CBSSports.com*, December 29, 2010.

39. Andrea Canning, Jessica Hopper and Katie Morison, "Brett Favre Sexual Harassment Suit the 'Tip of the Iceberg'?" *ABC News*, January 4, 2010.

40. ESPN Killed That LeBron Story Because Reporter "Did Not Properly Identify Himself", July 29, 2010, Retrieved from https://deadspin.com/espn-killed-that-lebron-story-because-reporter-did-not-30884183

41. Gene Wojciechowski, "For Once, Tiger Needs the Ryder Cup," *ESPN.com*, September 28, 2010.

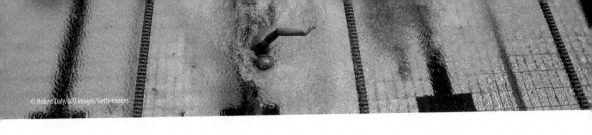

CHAPTER 12

Commercialization of College Sports

▶ Introduction

After teaching Sports Law for many years, the authors are very aware of key issues that stimulate discussion, including: (1) some college coaches earn up to $10,000,000 per year, but college-athletes earn nothing, and (2) 80% of all professional athletes are broke in six years. The overriding question is whether universities are about education or sports? In Europe, there is no question that universities are all about education and that sports are usually relegated to the club level. In England, talented soccer players join premier teams at age 16; whereas in the United States, football players must stay in college for three years and basketball players for one year.

"Art for Art's Sake Money for God's Sake"[1] captures the theme of former USC defensive end Bobby Demars' documentary, *The Business of Amateurs*.[2] The entire crew of the film consisted of former collegiate athletes. In the titles, there was a Coach Max Cash. Bobby Demars' point was that "revenue athletes are accountable to coaches, athletic directors, the financial department, accounting, students,

and alumni. Athletics is a priority, not academics—some athletes come in at a third grade reading level and leave that way. The "Business of Amateurs" is about the financial exploitation of athletes and a parallel failure to protect their physical health. The NCAA says it was founded for two reasons: to protect the athlete's health and to protect athletes from commercial exploitation; however, when it comes to the second goal, what they really mean is to prevent others from exploiting the athletic talent that they are commercially exploiting.[3] The NCAA neither reaps nor do they sow. The concept of equitable sharing is unknown to the NCAA, which is especially egregious since the athletes are the cash cow, but they reap little from their efforts.

Arrington v. NCAA is an ongoing class action concussion lawsuit against the NCAA. Basically, it seeks to assist the NCAA in readjusting their priorities from money-making to safekeeping their young student-athletes from premature dementia. The lawsuit takes particular delight in emphasizing the many reputable concussion studies that the NCAA has ignored. The chief contentions of the original class action complaint as explained in their "Nature of the Action" are as follows:

1. For over 30 years, the NCAA has failed its student-athletes—choosing instead to sacrifice them on an altar of money and profits. The NCAA has engaged in a long-established pattern of negligence and inaction with respect to concussions and concussion-related maladies sustained by its student-athletes, all the while profiting immensely from those same student-athletes.

2. Specifically, the NCAA has failed to address and/or correct the coaching of tackling methodologies that cause head injuries; the NCAA has failed to implement system-wide "return to play" guidelines for student-athletes who have sustained concussions; the NCAA has failed to implement system-wide guidelines for the screening and detection of head injuries; the NCAA has failed to implement legislation addressing the treatment and eligibility of student-athletes who have sustained multiple concussions in the course of play; and the NCAA has failed to implement a support system for student-athletes who, after sustaining concussions, are left unable to either play football or even lead a normal life.

3. On average, the NCAA makes over $740 million in revenue each year. Unlike a professional sports organization, the NCAA does not use revenues to pay its athletes, nor does the money go towards pension or medical benefits for post-collegiate athletes. The NCAA gives no medical or financial support to post-collegiate student-athletes who sustained concussions while playing an NCAA sport and who then cope with the costs and care needed resulting from their injuries.

4. The NCAA's conduct is particularly egregious in light of the fact that its policies and procedures—or lack thereof—leave student-athletes like Plaintiff and members of the below-defined Classes inadequately protected from sustaining, monitoring, and recovering brain injuries at a particularly early and vulnerable point in their lives. Unlike professional athletes, who at least have resources to pay for medical care necessitated by head injuries caused during their professional careers, collegiate players typically range in age from 18–23 and are just beginning their adult lives. For each NCAA student-athlete, including Plaintiff and the putative Classes, these injuries have long-term, debilitating effects, ranging from an inability to finish their education, to loss of memory, to depression, and early-onset dementia.

5. Accordingly, this nationwide class action seeks medical monitoring and financial recovery for the long-term and chronic injuries, financial losses, expenses and intangible losses suffered by the Plaintiff and members of the Classes as a result of the NCAA's carelessness, negligence, and concealment of information.[4]

In an ongoing antitrust lawsuit. *Jenkins v. NCAA,* attorney Jeffrey Kessler is suing the NCAA for gross violations of the Sherman Act:

1. The defendant in this action—the National Collegiate Athletics Association ("NCAA") and five major NCAA conferences that have agreed to apply NCAA restrictions (the "Power Conferences")—earn billions of dollars in revenues each year through the hard work, sweat, and sometimes broken bodies of top-tier college football and men's basketball athletes who perform services for Defendants' member institutions in the big business of college sports. However, instead of allowing their member institutions to compete for the services of those players while operating their businesses, Defendants have entered into what amounts to cartel agreements with the avowed purpose and effect of placing a ceiling on the compensation that may be paid to these athletes for their services. Those restrictions are pernicious, a blatant violation of the antitrust laws, have no legitimate pro-competitive justification, and should now be struck down and enjoined.

2. The plaintiffs—four current top-tier college football and men's basketball players, along with the class members whom the players

seek to represent—are exploited by Defendants and their member institution infer false claims of amateurism. The Defendants and their billon dollar contracts wholly disconnected from the interests of "student athletes," who are barred from receiving the benefits of competitive markets for their services even though their services generate these massive revenues. As a result of these illegal restrictions, market forces have been shoved aside and substantial damages have been inflicted upon a host of college athletes whose services have yielded riches only for others. This class action is necessary to end the NCAA's unlawful cartel, which is inconsistent with the most fundamental principles of antitrust law.

3. This class action is brought to permanently enjoin violations by each Defendants of the federal antitrust laws. Moreover, the named Plaintiffs seek to recover individual damages resulting from those violations.

4. Plaintiffs, and the classes of football and basketball player whom the player plaintiffs seek to represent, are athletes who have performed services for Defendants' member institutions in top-tier college football and men's basketball competitions. Those classes of athletes have entered into financial agreements with Defendants' member institutions that sponsor and operates football and men's basketball programs subject to the rules of the NCAA and the members conferences that have all agreed to apply NCAA restrictions.

5. Defendants have jointly and conspired with their members institution to deny Plaintiffs the ability to provide and/or market their services as football and men's basketball

players to top-tier college football and men's basketball markets through a patently unlawful price-fixing and group boycott arrangement.

6. The Defendants' agreed-upon rules impose an artificial and unlawful ceiling on the remuneration that players may receive for their services as football and men's basketball players in the multi-billion dollar college sports industry. Under NCAA and Power Conference rules, players may receive only tuition, required institutional fees, room and board, and required course-related books in exchange for their services as college football and men's basketball players. This amount is defined by the NCAA as a "full grant-in-aid" and commonly referred to as an "athletic scholarship."

7. These arguments to price-fix players' compensation, and to boycott any institution or players who refuse to comply with the price fixing agreement, are per se illegal acts under Section 1 of the Sherman Act, 15 U.S.C. § 1. They also constitute an unreasonable restraint of trade under rule of reason, whether under a "quick look" or full-blown rule of reason analysis.

8. As a result of Defendants' anticompetitive agreements, Plaintiffs and other similarly situated current and future college football and men's basketball players in the relevant markets described ... have received and/or will receive less remuneration for their playing services than they would receive in a competitive market. A permanent injunction, on behalf of the proposed injunctive class, is the only relief that can bring these unlawful restrictions to an end.[5]

1. The title of Bobby Demars' documentary, "The Business of Amateurs" is an oxymoron. Do you agree with him?
2. Bobby argues that the commercial exploitation of the college athlete is connected to the physical exploitation of the athletes who suffer concussions. Do you agree with him?
3. The Arrington case contends that "for over 30 years, the NCAA had failed its student-athletes – choosing instead to sacrifice then on an altar of money and profits." What is your response to the charge that the NCAA, as a fiduciary to the athletes, failed to keep them safe?

⚖ CASE 12-1 Board of Regents v. NCAA

546 F.Supp. (W.D. Okla. 1982)

BURCIAGA, District Judge, Sitting by Designation.

THIS MATTER came on for trial to the Court on the merits on June 7 through 15, 1982. At issue is the legality of the controls exercised by the National Collegiate Athletic Association over the televising of college football games. The plaintiffs, both members of NCAA, allege that these controls violate the Sherman Antitrust Act, 15 U.S.C. ss 1-2 (1980). The Court holds as follows:

1. The television football controls exercised by NCAA constitute a horizontal agreement among competitors to fix prices and restrict output, in violation of 15 U.S.C. s 1;
2. The controls constitute a group boycott, in violation of 15 U.S.C. s 1;
3. The NCAA exercises monopoly power over the market of college football television, in violation of 15 U.S.C. s 2; and
4. The plaintiffs are entitled to injunctive relief under the Clayton Act, 15 U.S.C. s 26 (1980).

This memorandum opinion shall constitute the Court's findings of fact and conclusions of law.

I. Findings of Fact

The parties to this case are the Board of Regents of the University of Oklahoma, the University of Georgia Athletic Association, and the National Collegiate Athletic Association. Defendant National Collegiate Athletic Association (hereinafter, "NCAA") is a private non-profit association organized in 1905. NCAA consists of approximately 900 members. Membership is open to four-year institutions which meet certain academic standards. Oklahoma's intercollegiate football program has, over the years, produced many outstanding and highly-ranked teams. Oklahoma is capable of attracting large national television audiences for its televised games. Oklahoma now seeks to maximize its revenues from football television. Like Oklahoma, Georgia has compiled a record of outstanding success with its intercollegiate football program, and football is the major revenue-producing sport for Georgia. Budgetary pressures have forced cuts in Georgia's athletic program, including the elimination of its intercollegiate wrestling program. Georgia also seeks to maximize the revenues generated from the televising of its football games ...

Until 1982, the contracts were always made with a single network, although all three of the major networks competed for the rights, and each has held those rights at one time or another. The length of the contracts was always either one or two years until 1977, when NCAA contracted with American Broadcasting Companies for a four-year term covering the 1978 to 1981 seasons. ABC held the exclusive right to broadcast NCAA football at the network level from the year 1965 to 1981. The basic concepts of the original controls have survived to the present. The Plan is reviewed and changes in the Plan are made periodically to reflect the concerns of the membership ... In addition to the controls exercised by the NCAA over football television, NCAA legislates on a number of other aspects of college football. Playing rules, standards of amateurism, regulation of the recruitment of athletes, standards for academic eligibility, and certification of bowl games involving NCAA members have long been a part of the regulatory scheme developed by NCAA to govern college football. NCAA also regulates other college sports. Significantly, however, football is the only sport in which NCAA has taken unto itself the power to regulate the televising of college athletic events. The schools are free to make whatever arrangements they desire for televising regular season games in all sports except football, subject only to some restraints imposed by the various athletic conferences ...

Partly out of dissatisfaction with different aspects of the NCAA regulations governing college football, a number of major football conferences and independent schools, all members of NCAA, banded together to form the College Football Association (hereinafter, "CFA"). Both Oklahoma and

Georgia are members of CFA. CFA consists of five of the major football-playing conferences-the Big 8, Southeastern, Southwestern, Atlantic Coast and Western Athletic Conferences-and major football-playing independents such as Notre Dame, Penn State, Pittsburgh, and the service academies …

The original purpose of the CFA, which is itself a member of NCAA, was to lobby and promote the interests of major football playing schools within the NCAA structure …

CFA then began investigating the possibility of negotiating an agreement of its own with the networks for the broadcast rights to games involving CFA members …

NCAA, having learned of the CFA effort to negotiate football television rights on behalf of its members, was not long in responding …

It is true that membership is voluntary in the sense that a member institution may withdraw from NCAA at any time. However, it is clear from the evidence that an institution which withdraws or is expelled from the NCAA could no longer operate a fully-rounded intercollegiate athletic program. Non-member institutions could not compete in the prestigious NCAA championship events in such sports as baseball, basketball, track, swimming, wrestling and gymnastics. They would therefore be unable to recruit quality athletes into their programs. Its football team could not play on television against members of the NCAA. As a practical matter, membership in the NCAA is a prerequisite for institutions wishing to sponsor a major, well-rounded athletic program …

Under the NCAA's plan for the 1978 through 1981 seasons, ABC held the exclusive right to televise college football on the network level. For this right, ABC paid a so-called "minimum aggregate fee." A part of this fee, some 8% of the total, went directly to the NCAA to help fund certain of its activities …

Once ABC had decided to televise any particular game, it would notify the host team of its decision. Up through the 1980 season, ABC would send a telegram and "require" confirmation of the school's acceptance of the rights fee which had been established. Beginning in 1981, ABC would only "request" confirmation. However, it is clear that negotiation of the rights fee was not anticipated, nor would it have been tolerated …

The NCAA makes much of the fact that under the terms of the contract with ABC, member schools were allowed to negotiate with ABC for the rights fee to be paid for any particular game. This so-called right to negotiate was clearly illusory, however. The practical effect of granting exclusive rights to ABC was to create a monopsony; that is, a situation in which there is only one eligible buyer in a product market. The school could not sell the rights to CBS or NBC, unless it was willing to flaunt the NCAA plan. Such a course would violate NCAA rules and subject the school to the disciplinary proceedings which would certainly follow …

In addition to the broadcast network contracts, NCAA entered into a contract with Turner Broadcasting System, Inc., for the exclusive live cablecasting of NCAA football games. TBS will pay a minimum aggregate fee of $17,696,000 over the next two years. NCAA argues that because it invited bids from all three of the major broadcast networks, it has met the Sherman Act's requirement of open competition. However, the evidence supports the opposite conclusion. The fact that both ABC and CBS will pay an identical price for identical packages leads the Court to conclude that there was no true negotiation. NCAA substantially dictated the terms under which both networks could televise NCAA football. The networks were offered a take-it-or-leave-it proposition. A truly free market would not have yielded the identical prices and packages which result from the contracts …

Each network must broadcast a college football game on at least 14 different dates, and a minimum of 35 games must be shown per year by each network. At least seven of the broadcasts must be national, and a minimum of six must be regional broadcasts. At least one of the networks must broadcast a game on each Saturday of the fall season. No one school can appear any more than six times during any two-year period, and no school can appear nationally more than four times over two years. At least 82 different teams must appear on each network over a two-year period. The number of times any one school may appear during the two-year period must be divided equally between ABC and CBS …

However, the greatest flaw in the NCAA's argument is that it is manifest that the new plan for football television does not limit televised football in order to protect gate attendance ...

If the NCAA is seeking to improve competition on the football field, it has chosen a much too far-reaching manner of doing so. The NCAA regulations on recruitment, the limitations on the number of scholarships each team may award, and the other standards for preserving amateurism found in NCAA legislation are sufficient to achieve this goal. Rather than relying on the NCAA to improve their competitive position by restraining competition, the schools can and should compete on their own and improve their position in that way ...

Similarly, it is clear that the sellers in this market are the schools whose teams play the games. NCAA insists that the sellers are the networks which sell commercial time to the advertisers. This analysis is flawed ...

It is clear that these sellers are unique in the television business. The primary business of these sellers is not television, but education. This fact alone distinguishes these sellers from others. Moreover, there are no other entities which can produce the product. Only the colleges of the nation are able to produce high quality amateur football. High school football does not have the appeal of college football and is never televised at the network level ... The evidence is also clear that there is no other product readily substitutable for college football. The most logical substitute, professional football, is not available on Saturday afternoons during the college football season ...

Second, when college football is available on one network, other networks are hard pressed to find competitive programming other than Major League Baseball. This is evident from the fact that in recent seasons, CBS often "went dark" when ABC was broadcasting college football. Third, both ABC and CBS were willing to pay a great deal more for the right to broadcast college football for the years 1982 through 1985 than ABC paid for the years 1978 through 1981 ...

NCAA urges that the controls were adopted because of a genuine concern among NCAA members that college football television would reduce gate attendance ...

In summary, the Court concludes that the NCAA controls over college football make NCAA a classic cartel. This cartel has an almost absolute control over the supply of college football which is made available to the networks, to television advertisers, and ultimately to the viewing public. Like all other cartels, NCAA members have sought and achieved a price for their product which is, in most instances, artificially high. The NCAA cartel imposes production limits on its members and maintains mechanisms for punishing cartel members who seek to stray from these production quotas. The cartel has established a uniform price for the products of each of the member producers, with no regard for the differing quality of these products or the consumer demand for these various products. Like all cartels, NCAA seeks to regulate the distribution of revenues to the cartel members. The distribution of football television revenues under the NCAA program in no way resembles the distribution to be expected in a free market. Like all cartels, NCAA, the umbrella under which the cartel has formed, takes for itself a sizable cut of the revenues from the cartelized product. Finally, the internal wranglings among NCAA members strongly resemble classic cartel infighting. The many less prominent schools seek to expand their football revenues beyond what they would receive in a non-cartelized market. As in all cartels, these artificially high revenues must, at some point, be derived at the expense of more prominent cartel members. The NCAA's attempts to placate the prominent producers, such as Georgia and Oklahoma, have failed. These plaintiffs and others whose superior competitive practices have earned them prominence in the sport of college football wish to no longer suffer the economic injury visited upon them by the less prominent members of the cartel. Most cartels ultimately fall because of a healthy self-interest among the producers whose competitive ability has earned them prominence in the market. The NCAA football television cartel is no different.

1. This is the district court version of *Board of Regents* that granted injunctive relief on the grounds that the NCAA's TV package of collegiate football was a classic cartel (*NCAA v. Board of Regents,*

546 F.Supp. 1276 (W.D. Okla. 1982), aff'd 707 F.2d 1147 (10th Cir. 1983), aff'd 468 U.S. 85 (1984). Was the NCAA inherently unethical since it knew that major fan bases could attract more lucrative TV deals if given the opportunity?

2. The District Court realizes that NCAA membership is not really voluntary since it is clear that withdrawal or suspension would ensure that the institution "could no longer operate a fully-rounded intercollegiate athletic program" and, if not a member, you cannot compete in lucrative NCAA championship events in basketball, baseball, track and field, wrestling, swimming, and gymnastics. Is this a form of economic blackmail?

3. Should there be a difference between revenue-providing football programs and those that are less blessed?

⚖ CASE 12-2 *Bloom v. NCAA*

93 P.3d 621 (Colo. App. 2004)

Opinion by Judge DAILEY.

In this dispute concerning eligibility to play college football, plaintiff, Jeremy Bloom, appeals the trial court's order denying his request for a preliminary injunction against defendants, the National Collegiate Athletic Association (NCAA) and the University of Colorado (CU). We affirm.

I. Background

The NCAA is a voluntary unincorporated association that regulates intercollegiate amateur athletics among its more than 1200-member colleges and universities. Its rules are established by representatives of member institutions and are carried out by its Council. Among other things, it maintains rules of eligibility for student participation in intercollegiate athletic events. Bloom, a high school football and track star, was recruited to play football at CU. Before enrolling there, however, he competed in Olympic and professional World Cup skiing events, becoming the World Cup champion in freestyle moguls. During the Olympics, Bloom appeared on MTV, and thereafter was offered various paid entertainment opportunities, including a chance to host a show on Nickelodeon. Bloom also agreed to endorse commercially certain ski equipment, and he contracted to model clothing for Tommy Hilfiger. Bloom became concerned that his endorsements and entertainment activities might interfere with his eligibility to compete in intercollegiate football. On Bloom's behalf, CU first requested waivers of NCAA rules restricting student-athlete endorsement and media activities and, then, a favorable interpretation of the NCAA rule restricting media activities. The NCAA denied CU's requests, and Bloom discontinued his endorsement, modeling, and media activities to play football for CU during the 2002 fall season. However, Bloom instituted this action against the NCAA for declaratory and injunctive relief, asserting that his endorsement, modeling, and media activities were necessary to support his professional skiing career, something which the NCAA rules permitted. In his complaint, Bloom alleged: (1) as a third-party beneficiary of the contract between the NCAA and its members, he was entitled to enforce NCAA bylaws permitting him to engage in and receive remuneration from a professional sport different from his amateur sport; (2) as applied to the facts of this case, the NCAA's restrictions on endorsements and media appearances were arbitrary and capricious; and (3) those restrictions constituted improper and unconscionable restraints of trade. For these reasons, Bloom requested that the NCAA restrictions be declared inapplicable, and that the NCAA and CU be enjoined from applying them, to activities originating prior to his enrollment at CU or wholly unrelated to his prowess as a football player. The trial court ordered CU joined as an indispensable party in the case, and CU aligned with the NCAA as an involuntary defendant. After an evidentiary hearing, the trial court determined that, although Bloom was a third-party beneficiary of NCAA bylaws, he was not entitled to preliminary injunctive relief ...

Here, the trial court found, and we agree, that the NCAA's constitution, bylaws, and regulations evidence a clear intent to benefit student-athletes. And because each student-athlete's eligibility to compete is determined by the NCAA, we conclude that Bloom had standing in a preliminary injunction hearing to contest the meaning or applicability of NCAA eligibility restrictions. *See Hall v. NCAA*, 985 F.Supp. 782, 796–97 (N.D.Ill.1997) (given importance of NCAA's function to benefit student-athletes, and NCAA's role in determining eligibility of student-athletes, court assumed student-athlete was likely to succeed in proving third-party beneficiary standing vis-a-vis the contract between the NCAA and its members) ...

Here, Bloom is not a member of the NCAA, and he does not have a constitutional right to engage in amateur intercollegiate athletics at CU. *See, e.g., Graham v. NCAA*, 804 F.2d 953, 955 (6th Cir.1986); *Colo. Seminary (Univ. of Denver) v. NCAA*, 570 F.2d 320, 321 (10th Cir.1978); *Hart v. NCAA*, 209 W.Va. 543, 550 S.E.2d 79, 86 (2001). Nor does he assert any property interest in playing football for CU ...

In sum, we conclude that Bloom has third-party beneficiary standing to pursue what in essence are two claims for violation of his contractual rights ...

Bloom relies on NCAA Bylaw 12.1.2, which states that "[a] professional athlete in one sport may represent a member institution in a different sport." He asserts that, because a professional is one who "gets paid" for a sport, a student-athlete is entitled to earn whatever income is customary for his or her professional sport, which, in the case of professional skiers, primarily comes from endorsements and paid media opportunities. We recognize that, like many others involved in individual professional sports such as golf, tennis, and boxing, professional skiers obtain much of their income from sponsors. We note, however, that none of the NCAA's bylaws mentions, much less explicitly establishes, a right to receive "customary income" for a sport. To the contrary, the NCAA bylaws prohibit every student-athlete from receiving money for advertisements and endorsements. In this regard, NCAA Bylaw 12.5.2.1 states:

> Subsequent to becoming a student-athlete, an individual shall not be eligible for participation in intercollegiate athletics if the individual: (a) Accepts any remuneration for or permits the use of his or her name or picture to advertise, recommend or promote directly the sale or use of a commercial product or service of any kind, or (b) Receives remuneration for endorsing a commercial product or service through the individual's use of such product or service.

Additionally, while NCAA Bylaw 12.5.1.3 permits a student-athlete to continue to receive remuneration for activity initiated prior to enrollment in which his or her name or picture is used, this remuneration is only allowed, if, as pertinent here, "the individual became involved in such activities for reasons independent of athletics ability; ... no reference is made in these activities to the individual's name or involvement in intercollegiate athletics; [and] ... the individual does not endorse the commercial product." Further, NCAA Bylaw 12.4.1.1 prohibits a student-athlete from receiving "any remuneration for value or utility that the student-athlete may have for the employer because of the publicity, reputation, fame or personal following that he or she has obtained because of athletics ability." Unlike other NCAA bylaws, the endorsements and media appearance bylaws do not contain any sport-specific qualifiers. *See, e.g.,* NCAA Bylaw 12.3.l (ineligibility of student-athlete to compete in intercollegiate sport based on agreement with agent to market athlete's athletic ability or reputation "in that sport"). In our view, when read together, the NCAA bylaws express a clear and unambiguous intent to prohibit student-athletes from engaging in endorsements and paid media appearances, without regard to: (1) when the opportunity for such activities originated; (2) whether the opportunity arose or exists for reasons unrelated to participation in an amateur sport; and (3) whether income derived from the opportunity is customary for any particular professional sport. The clear import of the bylaws is that, although student-athletes have the right to be professional athletes, they do not have the right to simultaneously engage in endorsement or paid media activity and maintain their eligibility to participate in amateur competition. And we may not disregard the clear meaning of the bylaws simply because they may disproportionately affect those who participate in individual professional sports. Further, the record contains ample evidence supporting the trial court's conclusion that this interpretation is consistent with both the NCAA's and its member institutions' construction of the bylaws. An NCAA official testified that both the endorsement and media appearance provisions have been consistently applied and interpreted in a non-sport-specific manner. Indeed, another NCAA official related that association members had resisted efforts to change the endorsement rule to be sport-specific. Although the evidence is conflicting, the record supports the trial court's conclusion that, from the beginning, CU understood that the endorsement and media activity rules were nonsport-specific in scope. Thus, even if the bylaws were viewed as ambiguous, the record supports the trial court's conclusion that the bylaws would ultimately be interpreted in accordance with the NCAA's and its member institutions' construction of those bylaws ...

Under that tradition, "college sports provided an important opportunity for teaching people about character, motivation, endurance, loyalty, and the attainment of one's personal best—all qualities of great value in citizens. In this sense, competitive athletics were viewed as an extracurricular activity, justified by the university as part of its ideal objective of educating the whole person." The NCAA's "Principle of Amateurism" states:

> Student-athletes shall be amateurs in an intercollegiate sport, and their participation should be motivated primarily by education and by the physical, mental and social benefits to be derived. Student participation in intercollegiate athletics is an avocation, and student-athletes should be protected from exploitation by professional and commercial enterprises.

NCAA Const. art. 2.9.

The NCAA's purpose, in this regard, is not only "to maintain intercollegiate athletics as an integral part of the educational program," but also to "retain a clear line of demarcation between intercollegiate athletics and professional sports." NCAA Const. art. 1, § 1.3.1. Here, the trial court found that application of the endorsement and media appearance rules in Bloom's case was rationally related to the legitimate purpose of retaining the "clear line of demarcation between intercollegiate athletics and professional sports." The trial court noted that salaries and bonuses are an acceptable means for attaining income from professional sports, but endorsement income is not acceptable if a student-athlete wishes to preserve amateur eligibility. According to NCAA officials: (1) endorsements invoke concerns about "the commercial exploitation of student-athletes and the promotion of commercial products"; and (2) it is not possible to distinguish the precise capacity in which endorsements are made. A CU official related that generally, the endorsement rule prevents students from becoming billboards for commercialism, and in Bloom's case, there would "be no way to tell whether he is receiving pay commensurate with his ... football ability or skiing ability." ...

Similar concerns underlie the NCAA's prohibition on paid entertainment activity. Paid entertainment activity may impinge upon the amateur ideal if the opportunity were obtained or advanced because of the student's athletic ability or prestige, even though that activity may further the education of student-athletes such as Bloom, a communications major. As the trial court noted, there are "various shades of gray within which such events could fall." And, as should be evident, the NCAA does not prohibit *unpaid* internships, externships, or other educational opportunities in the entertainment field. In this case, Bloom presented evidence that some of his acting opportunities arose not as a result of his athletic ability but because of his good looks and on-camera presence. However, the record contains evidence that Bloom's agent and the Tommy Hilfiger Company marketed Bloom as a talented multi-sport athlete, and a representative from a talent agency intimated that Bloom's reputation as an athlete would be advantageous in obtaining auditions for various entertainment opportunities. Further, the NCAA indicated, when asked to interpret its rules, that it was unable, due to insufficient information, to determine which of Bloom's requested media activities were, in fact, unrelated to his athletic ability or prestige. Under these circumstances, we perceive no abuse of the trial court's discretion in failing to fault the NCAA for refusing to waive its rules, as requested by CU, to permit Bloom "to pursue any television and film opportunities while he is a student-athlete at CU." *See Cole v. NCAA,*120 F.Supp.2d 1060, 1071–72 (N.D.Ga.2000)(NCAA decisions regarding "challenges of student-athletes are entitled to considerable deference," and courts are reluctant to replace the NCAA as the "decision-maker on private waiver applications"); *see also NCAA v. Lasege, supra,* 53 S.W.3d at 83 (voluntary athletic associations "should be allowed to 'paddle their own canoe' without unwarranted interference from the courts"). Bloom also asserts that the NCAA is arbitrary in its application of the endorsement and media bylaws. He notes that, while the NCAA would bar him from accepting commercial endorsements, it will allow colleges to commercially endorse athletic equipment by having students wear the equipment, with identifying logos and insignias, while engaged in intercollegiate competition. But the trial court determined, and we agree, that this application of the bylaws has a rational basis in economic necessity: financial benefits inure not to any single student-athlete but to member schools and thus to all student-athletes, including those who participate in programs that generate no revenue. Bloom further argues that the NCAA is arbitrary in the way it applies its bylaws among individual students. Bloom presented evidence that, in one instance, a student-athlete was permitted to make an unpaid, minor appearance in a single film. But the NCAA could rationally conclude that this situation was different: Bloom did not seek permission to make an unpaid appearance in one specific instance; he wanted to take advantage of any number of television and film opportunities, and he wanted to be paid. Bloom also presented evidence that a second student-athlete was permitted to appear on television while he participated in his professional sport. But Bloom did not show that the NCAA would prohibit him from appearing on television while participating in his professional sport …

1. The NCAA stopped Jeremy Bloom, who now is an inspirational speaker, from making money in endorsement from skiing which he intended to use to offset the lack of money, other than scholarship, for playing college football. Should the NCAA have that much power?
2. The NCAA has modified its rules so that *Bloom* would probably not be decided this way if the case was filed today. But then again how many two-sport phenomena like Jeremy Bloom are there?
3. Should there be a difference between skiing endorsements and, let's say, advertisements and endorsements based on his singing abilities?

Bloom v. NCAA, 93 P.3d 621 (Colo. App. 2004), U.S. Supreme Court.

⚖ *CASE 12-3 O'Bannon v. NCAA*

7 F.Supp.3d 955 (N.D. Cal. 2014)

FINDINGS OF FACT AND CONCLUSIONS OF LAW INTRODUCTION

Competition takes many forms. Although this case raises questions about athletic competition on the football field and the basketball court, it is principally about the rules governing competition in a different arena – namely, the marketplace.

Plaintiffs are a group of current and former college student-athletes. They brought this antitrust class action against the National Collegiate Athletic Association (NCAA) in 2009 to challenge the association's rules restricting compensation for elite men's football and basketball players. In particular, Plaintiffs seek to challenge the set of rules that bar student-athletes from receiving a share of the revenue that the NCAA and its member schools earn from the sale of licenses to use the student-athletes' names, images, and likenesses in videogames, live game telecasts, and other footage. Plaintiffs contend that these rules violate the Sherman Antitrust Act. The NCAA denies this charge and asserts that its restrictions on student-athlete compensation are necessary to uphold its educational mission and to protect the popularity of collegiate sports.

A non-jury trial on Plaintiffs' claims was held between June 9, 2014 and June 27, 2014. After considering all of the testimony, documentary evidence, and arguments of counsel presented during and after trial, the Court finds that the challenged NCAA rules unreasonably restrain trade in the market for certain educational and athletic opportunities offered by NCAA Division I schools. The procompetitive justifications that the NCAA offers do not justify this restraint and could be achieved through less restrictive means. The Court makes the following findings of fact and conclusions of law and will enter as a remedy a permanent injunction prohibiting certain overly restrictive restraints.

FINDINGS OF FACT

I. Background

A. The NCAA

The NCAA was founded in 1905 by the presidents of sixty-two colleges and universities in order to create a uniform set of rules to regulate intercollegiate football. Today, the association has roughly eleven hundred member schools and regulates intercollegiate athletic competitions in roughly two dozen sports. According to its current constitution, the association seeks to "initiate, stimulate and improve intercollegiate athletics programs for student-athletes and to promote and develop educational leadership, physical fitness, athletics excellence and athletics participation as a recreational pursuit."

To achieve these goals, the NCAA issues and enforces rules governing athletic competitions among its member schools. These rules are outlined in the association's constitution and bylaws and cover a broad range of subjects. Among other things, the rules establish academic eligibility requirements for student-athletes, set forth guidelines and restrictions for recruiting high school athletes, and impose limits on the number and size of athletic scholarships that each school may provide …

Division I itself further is divided, for the purposes of football competition, into two subdivisions: the Football Bowl Subdivision (FBS) and the Football Championship Subdivision (FCS). FBS schools are allowed to offer up to eighty-five full scholarships to members of their football teams. In contrast, FCS schools are permitted to offer only a smaller number of full scholarships to members of their teams. Because FBS schools are able to offer more football scholarships than FCS schools, the level of football competition within FBS is generally higher than within FCS. The rules governing participation and competition in Division I are enacted by an eighteen-member body known as the Division I Board of Directors, which typically receives proposals from the division's member schools and conferences. The Board is made up of university presidents and chancellors from eighteen different colleges or universities.

1. The case enclosed is the district court version of *O'Bannon v. NCAA*, 7 F.Supp.3d 955 (M.D. Cal. 2014), aff'd in part and vacated in part, 802 F.3d 1049 (9th Cir. 2015). Judge Claudia Wilkins' decision was a bombshell which stated that NCAA rules banning payment to college athletes violate antitrust laws, which was affirmed on appeal. Will this open up the alleged Pandora's Box?
2. The district court's injunction allows the NCAA to cap payments, but if it does, the minimum amount is $5,000 per year for particular collegiate football and basketball players. The Appeals Court disagreed with this remedy and stated that allowing cash compensation of $5,000 per year was erroneous. Was the baby thrown out with the bathwater?
3. *O'Bannon*, 2009 WL 4899217 (N.D. Cal.), began when former UCLA basketball player, Ed O'Bannon, who currently sells Toyotas in Henderson, NV, sued the NCAA and the Collegiate Licensing Co. (CLC) for violating antitrust laws by conspiring to prevent him from reaping monetary benefits from the use of his image in video games. Does this sound fair?

▶ Knight Commission Report on Restoring the Balance: Dollars, Values, and the Future of College Sports

The Knight Commission on Intercollegiate Athletics issued its third report in June of 2010, "Restoring the Balance: Dollars, Values, and the Future of College Sports." The Knight Commission suggested a variety of changes to control unsavory college athletic spending; key reforms include:

- Compile annual reports on athletic revenues and expenditures
- Reinstate "financial integrity" in NCAA certification process
- Require at least 50 percent of players to be on track for graduation for teams to qualify for postseason championships
- Redistribute revenue for postseason basketball and football play to reward academic improvement efforts
- Reduce length of seasons and number of sporting events
- Limit the number of non-coaching personnel
- Consider reducing scholarship levels

"The report sets forth reforms that are achievable and that, if implemented, will create a foundation upon which future reforms can build. Our blueprint for restoring educational values and priorities begins with strengthening accountability for intercollegiate athletics in three ways:

1. Requiring greater transparency and the reporting of better measures to compare athletics spending to academic spending
2. Rewarding practices that make academic values a priority
3. Treating college athletes as students first and foremost—not as professionals."[6]

1. The Knight Commission has been the "John the Baptist" of college athletics; of course, you know what happened to John the Baptist. Their point is to treat college athletes as students first and foremost and not as objects of commercial exploitation as pseudo-professionals. The NCAA has apparently ignored the Knight Commission's sage advice. Why?
2. In an earlier report in March 1991, the Knight Foundation published "Keeping Faith with the Student-Athlete: A New Model for Intercollegiate Athletics." The Commission expressed a concern that the abuse of athletics has reached proportions that threaten the very integrity of higher education. Is the Commission being realist or alarmist?
3. Unlike the vague NCAA's "Collegiate Model of Athletics," the Commission specifically cited the need for reforms in Presidential Control, Academic Integrity, Financial Integrity, and Certification. What approach is the most effective?

▶ The NCAA's "Collegiate Model of Athletics"

The Templar for ethical interaction in collegiate sports was formulated by then NCAA President Myles Brand, who, as President of Indiana, fired Coach Bobby Knight under a zero-tolerance regime. This model for ethical behavior is known as the "Collegiate Model for Intercollegiate Athletics." In this Magna Carta, all college sports "[c]ontribute to the overall college experience; they play a lasting role for alumni; they attract millions of fans and, at times, large television audiences; and, most significantly, each year they help thousands of people pursue a college education."[7] Professor Richard M. Southhall and Richard T. Karcher in their excellent article "Distributive Injustice: an ethical analysis of the NCAA's 'collegiate model of athletics and its jurisprudence'" took umbrage to Brand's Utopian view of college sports:

> However, while the NCAA contends US college sports is an integral part of college campuses nationwide, many college students do not have a college-sport spectator experience. Furthermore, if they do attend a game it is likely one of a narrow range of sports (e.g., football, men's basketball, baseball). Significantly, most college sports do not play a lasting role for alumni or attract large number of fans or television audiences. In addition, while the number of NCAA athletes (approximately 460,000) seems large, as a percent of students, it is no more than 2% of the full-time student population (National Center for Education Statistics 2013).[8]

However, the NCAA persists in insisting that its modus operandi, as espoused in their "collegiate model of athletics," is to fully integrate athletics with academics.[9]

In his State of the Association speech on January 19, 2004, Myles Brand urged the delegates to fortify the bond between academics. He did admit though that intercollegiate athletics is at a crossroads. However, "collegiate athletics is valuable both for student-athletes and their home universities and colleges. That value is diminished or lost entirely if intercollegiate athletics fails to respect and embrace the educational mission of the university or fails to meet the academic and social, as well as the athletic, needs of student-athletes. When athletics programs are integrated into the university's mission and when student-athletes are afforded genuine academic opportunities, there are enormous benefits for all."[10] The collegiate model is a product of "a strategic-planning process . . . The initiative under way to create a more flexible, "student-athlete friendly" Association, and our collective commitment to act on the highest ethical standards of integrity and inclusiveness will be, of course, included in our strategic plan. The plan as a whole

represents a recommitment to the collegiate model of athletics ... The collegiate model is a value-based template for intercollegiate athletics. It is a vision for the future that must guide us."[11]

Myles Brand did not want collegiate athletics to slip into the nefarious morass of the professional model.

> There is a real threat that the collegiate model will be transported into a system that more closely resembles the professional sports approach. If this movement continues, college sports as we know it will disappear, and with it, the educational value to student-athletes and the institutional good will and support from alumni and fans . . . The threat is real, and the consequences devastating. I want to go on record as calling attention to this potential disaster.[12]

Myles Brand saw the "collegiate model of athletics" as the preeminent step in his goal of reform and advocacy.

In his 2009 State of the Association speech, Brand speculated on the role of commercial activity in economies that constrain university and college budgets. "Our ability to understand both the necessity of monetalizing the assets of college sports and the potential damages of commercialization gone wild . . . and to find a proper balance of opportunities as possible without swamping the principle of amateurism . . . may either ensure the place of intercollegiate athletics in higher education and the American culture or relegate it in many instances to third-rate professional sports."[13]

> Some believe that college sports should be totally devoid of commercial interest . . . Some level of commercial activity—from nominal levels of local sponsorships to huge media and corporate contracts—touches every NCAA athletics program in the country regardless of division. Without commercial activity, intercollegiate athletics as we know it could not exist.[14]

Brand's 2006 State of the Association speech is entitled, "The Principles of Intercollegiate Athletics," – in the speech he indicated:

> Three key principles that constitute the collegiate model, namely ones that pertain to participants, the contests, and the enterprise as a whole. Principle No. 1—Those who participate

in intercollegiate athletics are students attending a university or college. Principle No. 2—Intercollegiate athletics contests are to be fair, conducted with integrity, and the safety and well-being of those who participate are paramount. Principle No. 3—Intercollegiate athletics is wholly embedded into universities and colleges.[15]

1. As previously mentioned, the NCAA's "Collegiate Model of Athletics" appears to be a locker room pep talk as opposed to specific directives for change. What is the better approach?
2. The Model espouses the goal to fully integrate athletics with academics. Is this just nice talk, or, are there any teeth to their goal? Do their actions speak louder than words? What is the impression of the college-athlete?
3. The NCAA claims to be "student-friendly." Is there any basis to this assertion?
4. The NCAA's collegiate model is never actually defined in the NCAA's bylaws. Was that done purposefully?
5. With this lack of clear definition, can the NCAA use this uncertainty to continue increasing the revenues of the power schools?
6. One of the NCAA's core values is the pursuit of excellence in both academics and athletics. Is that possible? Judge Miles Lord does not think so; athletes are given few chances to be scholars "and few persons care how the student athletes perform academically" *Hall v. Univ. of Minn.*, 532 F.Supp. 104, 109 (D. Minn. 1982).

▶ Ethical Justification for "Collegiate Model of Athletics"

The NCCA believes that they are morally justified to maintain the "collegiate model of athletics" under a classic utilitarianism ethos on the grounds that the system maximizes "good" results. The NCAA's model is based on "core values" that are presented as self-evident axioms.[16] In "the collegiate model of athletics, amateurism is the student-participation model that guides the relationship between students and institutions."[17] "Within this ethical framework, college-sport issues (*e.g.*, economic exploitation of profit-athletes, lack of meaningful educational opportunities for "special admission" athletes, etc.) are consistently discussed as regrettable, but acceptable, by-products of

a system that overwhelmingly provides educational and athletics benefits (*e.g.*, goodness) to the vast majority of college athletics"[18] Brand also used a social-benefit justification for the NCAA's amateurism rules that denies profit-athletes access to a market that is unavailable to all college athletes.[19]

In his 2006 State of the Association speech, Brand noted that:

> [t]he NCAA, of course, does not have the luxury to redesign the enterprise from scratch. We inherit the history of college sports. . . . We must all be singularly aware that college sports do not exist in vacuum, a Platonic heaven, so to speak, uninfluenced by the dynamics of the real world. The popularity of college sports, with its attendant serious financial interest, affects what we can and should do.[20]

The NCAA seeks "[t]o be the voice and conscience of college sports, to be true to the intent of those in our universities who founded our organization and continue to provide leadership, and yet to be appropriately pragmatic, we need a conceptual framework for college sports that is aspirational and value-based, but realistic."

This framework is "The Collegiate Model of Athletics."[21]

Brand continues,

[t]he fundamental reason we do not pay student-athletes to play is because they are students. This commitment is captured in the first principle of the collegiate model. The participants in intercollegiate athletics are students. They are not, in their roles as athletes, employees of the university. They are students who participate in athletics as part of their educational experience. This is the heart of the enterprise.[22]

Brand returned to the

Despite differences among the divisions in grant-in-aid, fan bases and expenditure levels, and despite variations within divisions among conferences and institutions within conferences, the underlying business plan at all athletic programs are basically the same . . . Universities attempt to maximize

their revenues and redistribute those resources according to their educational mission. . . . they do have an obligation to generate significant amounts of revenue to pursue their mission.[23]

Brand speaks of the "obligation" of the revenue-producing schools in football and basketball:

Commercial activity, meaning, for example, the sale of broadcast rights and logo licensing, is not only acceptable, but mandated by the business plan, provided that it is done so in a way that fully respects the underlying principles of the university. Instances in which advertising is offensive, in which it is crass or overwhelming, are incompatible with these values. But commercialism per se is not. . . . "Amateur" defines the participants, not the enterprise.[24]

The core of the ethical justification of the NCAA's "collegiate model of athletics" and their embrace of commercialization is this: "[T]he controlling factor in all that is undertaken to enhance revenue is that decisions and actions are informed by these values most important to higher education."[25]

1. It has been said that core values of the Collegiate Model of Athletics "are consistent with a strict interpretation of *consequentialism* most often referred to as *classical utilitarianism*, in which benefits that accrue to the many are offered as a justification for the collegiate model" (Southall & Karcher "Distributive injustice," 15 Int'l Sports L. J. 210, 212). Do "benefits that accrue to the many" include African-American athletes?
2. The NCAA also espouses a social-benefit justification for its rules on amateurism. Again, who does this benefit?
3. In *Banks v. NCAA*. 977 F.2d 1081 (7th Cir. 1992), the Court found that the NCAA's no-agent rule did not violate the antitrust laws. It has been said in the "Business of Amateurs" that in any other profession one can receive counseling or guidance before entering into an employment contract or a first career, but not with college athletes. Is this rule consistent with the NCAA's Collegiate Model?
4. Similarly, in *Gaines v. NCAA*, 764 F.Supp. 738 (M.D. Tenn.), the Court held that a college athlete who was denied eligibility to return to school once he tested the waters to ascertain his worth in the professional football market, did not violate antitrust laws. The alleged agency connection was the agent for the player's older brother, who briefly discussed a free agency contract with a team who had already contacted the player. Is this counter-productive?

⚖ CASE 12-4 *Vernonia Sch. Dist. v. Acton*

515 U.S. 646 (1995)

Opinion

Justice SCALIA delivered the opinion of the Court.

The Student Athlete Drug Policy adopted by School District 47J in the town of Vernonia, Oregon, authorizes random urinalysis drug testing of students who participate in the District's school athletics programs. We granted certiorari to decide whether this violates the Fourth and Fourteenth Amendments to the United States Constitution. Petitioner Vernonia School District 47J (District) operates one high school and three grade schools in the logging community of Vernonia, Oregon. As elsewhere in small-town America, school sports play a prominent role in the town's life, and student athletes are admired in their schools and in the community. Drugs had not been a major problem in Vernonia schools. In the mid-to-late 1980's, however, teachers and administrators observed a sharp increase in drug use. Students began to speak out about their attraction to the drug culture, and to boast that there was nothing the school could do about it …

Not only were student athletes included among the drug users but, as the District Court found, athletes were the leaders of the drug culture. 796 F.Supp. 1354, 1357 (Ore.1992). This caused the District's administrators particular concern, since drug use increases the risk of sports-related injury …

Initially, the District responded to the drug problem by offering special classes, speakers, and presentations designed to deter drug use. It even brought in a specially trained dog to detect drugs, but the drug problem persisted … At that point, District officials began considering a drug-testing program …

The Policy applies to all students participating in interscholastic athletics. Students wishing to play sports must sign a form consenting to the testing and must obtain the written consent of their parents. Athletes are tested at the beginning of the season for their sport.

As to the efficacy of this means for addressing the problem: It seems to us self-evident that a drug problem largely fueled by the "role model" effect of athletes' drug use, and of particular danger to athletes, is effectively addressed by making sure that athletes do not use drugs …

Taking into account all the factors we have considered above—the decreased expectation of privacy, the relative unobtrusiveness of the search, and the severity of the need met by the search—we conclude Vernonia's Policy is reasonable and hence constitutional …

Justice O'CONNOR, with whom Justice STEVENS and Justice SOUTER join, dissenting.

The population of our Nation's public schools, grades 7 through 12, numbers around 18 million. By the reasoning of today's decision, the millions of these students who participate in interscholastic sports, an overwhelming majority of whom have given school officials no reason whatsoever to suspect they use drugs at school, are open to an intrusive bodily search. In justifying this result, the Court dispenses with a requirement of individualized suspicion on considered policy grounds.

[The key to the NCAA's ethical justification of their "collegiate model of athletics" is that the system maximizes good results – or, smooth sailing. *Acton* deals with high schools but the school district's policy is comparable to the NCAA's policy. But, Justice O'Connor nails what's wrong with the school district's policy, and the problem with the collegiate model – namely, that Constitutional rights are being swept away in the name of "good results."]

1. Do you agree with the majority or dissenting opinion?
2. Do you think the athletes that are chosen for testing are really blindly selected?
3. Is Justice Scalia's locker room mentality argument defensible?

Vernonia School Dist. 47J v. Acton, 515 U.S. 646 (1995), U.S. Supreme Court.

⚖ CASE 12-5 Univ. of Colo. v. Derdeyn

863 P.2d 929 (Colo. 1993)

Opinion
Justice LOHR delivered the Opinion of the Court.

We granted certiorari in order to determine whether random, suspicionless urinalysis-drug-testing of intercollegiate student athletes by the University of Colorado, Boulder (CU), violates the Fourth Amendment to the United States Constitution or Article II, Section 7, of the Colorado Constitution. Following a bench trial conducted in August of 1989 in which a class of current and prospective CU athletes challenged the constitutionality of CU's drug-testing program, the Boulder County District Court permanently enjoined CU from continuing its program. The trial court found that CU had not obtained voluntary consent from its athletes for such testing, and it declared such testing unconstitutional under both the federal and state constitutions. The Colorado Court of Appeals generally affirmed. *See Derdeyn v. University of Colorado*, 832 P.2d 1031 (Colo.App.1991). We agree with the court of appeals, that in the absence of voluntary consents, CU's random, suspicionless urinalysis-drug-testing of student athletes violates the Fourth Amendment to the United States Constitution and Article II, Section 7, of the Colorado Constitution. We further agree, that the record supports the finding of the trial court that CU failed to show that consents to such testing given by CU's athletes are voluntary for the purposes of those same constitutional provisions. Accordingly, we affirm the judgment of the court of appeals. CU began a drug-testing program in the fall of 1984 for its intercollegiate student athletes. CU has since amended its program in various ways, but throughout the existence of the program participation was mandatory in the sense that if an athlete did not sign a form consenting to random urinalysis pursuant to the program, the student was prohibited from participating in intercollegiate athletics at CU …

1. If an athlete is prohibited from participating in intercollegiate athletics if they do not sign the consent form, is the consent still voluntary?
2. In *Derdeyn*, the Supreme Court of Colorado found that the University's random, suspiciousless urinalysis drug testing of student-athletes was an unconstitutional search, the University's programs were similar and based on the NCAA's policy. Colorado, of course, is the poster child for state's rights – *e.g.*, smoking pot at the black jack table. Does legally (and ethically) supporting state's rights initiatives run afoul of the NCAA's ethical justification of their "collegiate model of athletics"?

Univ. of Colo. v. Derdeyn, 863 P.2d 929 (Colo. 1993), U.S. Supreme Court.

⚖ CASE 12-6 Agnew v. NCAA

683 F.2d 3289 (7th Cir. 2012)

Opinion
FLAUM, Circuit Judge.

Joseph Agnew and Patrick Courtney ("plaintiffs") have at least two things in common: they were both highly successful high school football players that earned scholarships to play for National Collegiate Athletic Association ("NCAA") Division I football programs, and they both suffered career-ending football injuries during their college tenures. The athletic scholarships held by plaintiffs at the time of their injuries were good for one year only and needed to be renewed to be valid for any subsequent seasons. When plaintiffs' injuries prevented them from playing football, their scholarships were not renewed. Plaintiffs claim that two NCAA regulations—the cap on the number of scholarships given per team and the prohibition of multi-year scholarships—prevented them from obtaining scholarships that covered the entire cost of their college education. These regulations, according to plaintiffs, have an anticompetitive effect on the market for student-athletes, and therefore violate § 1 of the Sherman Act. 15 U.S.C. § 1. The NCAA filed a motion to dismiss and the district court granted that motion, finding that plaintiffs failed to allege a relevant market on which the NCAA's Bylaws had an anticompetitive effect. Plaintiffs appealed the dismissal. While we depart from some of the district court's reasoning, we ultimately conclude that plaintiffs' complaint did not sufficiently identify a commercial market—an obvious necessity for Sherman Act violations—and thus we affirm the district court's dismissal of plaintiffs' suit.

I. Background

In 2006, after receiving several offers from a number of college football teams, Agnew enrolled at Rice University on an athletic scholarship. In exchange for agreeing to play football at Rice, Agnew received a year of education, room, and board at no charge. That scholarship was renewed for Agnew's second year at Rice. During his sophomore year, Agnew suffered a series of football-related injuries. The injuries, along with a coaching change at Rice, resulted in the school's decision not to renew Agnew's scholarship for his junior year. Agnew successfully appealed this decision and received one more year-long scholarship, but he was unable to acquire a scholarship for his senior year. As a result, he was forced to pay full price for the last year of his undergraduate education. Courtney endured a similar experience. In 2009, Courtney decided to attend North Carolina A & T on full athletic scholarship to play football. As with Agnew, the scholarship was only a year long. During training camp Courtney was injured, and as a result, his scholarship was not renewed. Due to his financial circumstances and the high cost of out-of-state tuition, Courtney was forced to transfer to a different school and pay tuition out-of-pocket. Plaintiffs allege that their failure to acquire a scholarship equal to the full cost of obtaining a bachelor's degree is the result of the NCAA's regulation of participating schools' athletic scholarships. Plaintiffs specifically cite two NCAA bylaws (the "Bylaws") as the source of their injury: (1) the one-year scholarship limit, which prohibits NCAA member schools from offering student-athletes multi-year scholarships, 2009–10 NCAA DIVISION I MANUAL, Bylaw 15.3.3.1 (2009–10); and (2) the cap on the number of athletic scholarships a school can offer for each team in a given year, see, e.g., 2009–10 NCAA DIVISION I MANUAL, Bylaw 15.5.4. According to plaintiffs, NCAA member schools compete intensely over the premier student-athletes in the country, and if the Bylaws had not been passed, schools would need to offer multi-year scholarships to stay competitive in the market for elite athletes. They assert that multi-year scholarships used to be the norm before the Bylaws went into effect. The current ban on such scholarships, they claim, forces student-athletes who do not have their scholarships renewed to pay more for their undergraduate education. Plaintiffs further contend that the limit on the number of athletic scholarships a school can offer reduces the total number of athletic scholarships offered, thus preventing some students—perhaps those that are injured but would have been offered a multi-year scholarship but for the Bylaws—from obtaining a bargained for education. Plaintiffs therefore maintain that the Bylaws violate § 1 of the Sherman Act. 15 U.S.C. § 1 ...

The Sherman Act clearly applies to at least some of the NCAA's behavior. See Bd. of Regents, 468 U.S. 85, 104 S.Ct. 2948; see also Law, 134 F.3d 1010 (holding that the Sherman Act applies to the NCAA's regulation of the salaries of coaches). The question for us, however, is whether and when the Sherman Act applies to the NCAA and its member schools in relation to their interaction with student-athletes. The Supreme Court has not weighed in on this issue directly, but Board of Regents, the seminal case on the interaction between the NCAA and the Sherman Act, implies that all regulations passed by the NCAA are subject to the Sherman Act. 468 U.S. at 117, 104 S.Ct. 2948. In Board of Regents, the Supreme

Court ruled that the NCAA's restrictions on televising football games were a violation of § 1of the Sherman Act …

This presumes the applicability of the Sherman Act to NCAA bylaws, since no procompetitive justifications would be necessary for noncommercial activity to which the Sherman Act does not apply. Nonetheless, courts have struggled with the applicability of the Sherman Act to NCAA regulations …

The Bylaws at issue in this case, however, are not eligibility rules, nor do we conclude that they "fit into the same mold" as eligibility rules. *See In re NCAA I–A Walk-on Football Players Litigation,* 398 F.Supp.2d 1144, 1149 (W.D.Wash.2005) (finding that the cap on the number of scholarships a college team can grant does not implicate student-athlete eligibility "in the same manner as rules requiring students to attend class or rules revoking eligibility for entering a professional draft"). These Bylaws—a one-year limit to scholarships and a limit on scholarships per team—are not inherently or obviously necessary for the preservation of amateurism, the student-athlete, or the general product of college football. Issuing more scholarships (thus creating more amateur players) and issuing longer scholarships cannot be said to have an obviously negative impact on amateurism. Nor is there an obvious effect on the ability of college football to survive without the Bylaws in question. The NCAA argues that multi-year scholarships would make it too difficult for less wealthy schools to compete in the recruiting market, but this claim is weakened by the fact that the restriction on multi-year scholarships was only instituted in 1973 …

It is true that the prohibition against multi-year scholarships is, in a sense, a rule concerning the amount of payment a player receives for his labor, and thus may seem to implicate the split between amateur and pay-for-play sports. After all, student-athletes are paid, but their payment is limited to reimbursement for costs attendant to receiving an education. For the purposes of college sports, and in the name of amateurism, we consider players who receive nothing more than educational costs in return for their services to be "unpaid athletes." It is for this reason, though, that the prohibition against multi-year scholarships does not implicate the preservation of amateurism, for whether or not a player receives four years of educational expenses or one year of educational expenses, he is still an amateur. It is not until payment above and beyond educational costs is received that a player is considered a "paid athlete." …

1. Is the plaintiff a proper plaintiff? It appears that Joseph Agnew and Patrick Courtney were elite athletes who were offered scholarships. Should the NCAA make four-year scholarships mandatory?

Joseph AGNEW, et al., Plaintiffs–Appellants, v. National Collegiate Athletic Association, U.S. Supreme Court.

⚖ *CASE 12-7   In re NCAA 1-A Walk-On Football Players Litig.*

398 F.Supp. 2d 1144 (W.D. Wa. 2005)

Defendant, the National Collegiate Athletic Association, is a voluntary, non-profit standard-setting association that promulgates the rules of competition for and operates annual national championships in 22 sports across three divisions. Plaintiffs are walk-on football players at Division I-A schools who allege that they would have received full grant-in-aid scholarships but for the anti-competitive agreement between the Division I-A members of the NCAA to save money by artificially restricting the number of football scholarships awarded by each school to 85 …

The NCAA now moves the Court for judgment on the pleadings on the basis of the following arguments: (1) NCAA rules, preserving amateurism and protecting fair competition have been uniformly upheld under the Sherman Act; (2) Plaintiffs have not alleged a legally cognizable relevant market; (3) Plaintiffs have not alleged injury to competition; and (4) Plaintiffs' Section 2 claim fails as a matter of law because the Amended Complaint contains insufficient factual allegations showing that the NCAA has monopoly power in any relevant market ...

The NCAA also argues that Plaintiffs have failed to allege facts showing that the challenged football scholarship limits substantially injure economic competition as a whole in any relevant market. They seek some reference to economic injury to consumer welfare ...

Plaintiffs allege that the NCAA "operates as a classic cartel" because it is "a combination of producers of a product joined together to control its production, sale, and price." They also allege that the NCAA "exercises an almost absolute control over intercollegiate athletics," including the input market of Division I-A football players. Indeed, the NCAA's power to control intercollegiate athletics has been noted by other courts. In light of the monopsony discussion above, the Court finds that Plaintiffs have alleged sufficient facts that the NCAA has monopoly power over the alleged market. Plaintiffs should have the opportunity to demonstrate that this monopoly caused antitrust injury.

1. Do walk-on football players have the standing to sue?
2. Does it make a difference that these players were "preferred and requested" walk-ons?

In re NCAA 1-A Walk-On Football Players Litig., 398 F.Supp. 2d 1144 (W.D. Wa. 2005), U.S. Supreme Court.

⚖ *CASE 12-8* *Justice v. NCAA*

577 F.Supp. 356 (D. Ariz. 1983)

MEMORANDUM OF DECISION AND ORDER
KELLEHER, District Judge.

The plaintiffs in this action, student-athlete players at the University of Arizona, request that a preliminary injunction be issued against the National Collegiate Athletic Association (NCAA) to prevent enforcement of NCAA sanctions which render the University of Arizona football team ineligible to participate in post-season competition in the 1983 and 1984 seasons or to make television appearances in the 1984 and 1985 seasons ...

I. FACTS

The pertinent facts on this record are without significant dispute. The four plaintiffs in this action are members of the University of Arizona varsity football team. Plaintiff Lesnik is a senior undergraduate in his last year of eligibility. Plaintiff Wood is a junior undergraduate. Plaintiffs Vesling and Justice are sophomore undergraduates, although Justice is classified as a "freshman red shirt" for purposes of athletic eligibility. Plaintiffs Lesnik, Wood, and Vesling are members of the first-string football team. All four of the plaintiffs were awarded an athletic scholarship to play football at the University of Arizona and were recruited by the University prior to the imposition and announcement of the sanctions. The NCAA is an unincorporated association that regulates a substantial part of the nation's intercollegiate athletics ...

The University of Arizona is a public institution and at all pertinent times has been a member of the NCAA. The NCAA publishes annually a manual which contains the NCAA constitution, bylaws, executive regulations, enforcement procedures, recommended policies, and rules of order. The NCAA constitution states in Article 2, Section 2, that "[a] basic purpose of the Association is to maintain intercollegiate athletics as an integral part of the educational program and the athlete as an integral part of the student body and, by so doing, retain a clear line of demarcation between college athletics and professional sports." The constitution also sets forth certain principles for the conduct of intercollegiate athletics. The section entitled the "Principle of Amateurism and Student Participation" defines an amateur student-athlete as "one who engages in a particular sport for the educational, physical, mental and social benefits derived therefrom and to whom participation in that sport is an avocation." *Id.* at Article 3, Section 1. This section also provides that a student-athlete shall not be eligible for participation in an intercollegiate sport if the individual: "(1) Takes or has taken pay, or has accepted the promise of pay, in any form, for participation in that sport . . . ." *Id.* Section 3-1-(g) of the constitution details the types of practices that constitute "pay" for participation in intercollegiate athletics, and the NCAA bylaws contain numerous provisions concerning recruitment of and financial aid to student athletes by member universities. On May 17, 1983, the Committee on Infractions of the NCAA issued Confidential Report No. 183(107). The report contained the results of the NCAA's investigation of the University of Arizona's football program, and detailed numerous violations of the NCAA constitution and bylaws by the University during the years 1975 through 1979. The Committee on Infractions proposed that disciplinary action be imposed upon the University of Arizona, including loss to the University football program of its eligibility both to participate in post-season competition following the 1983 and 1984 seasons and to appear on television during the 1984 and 1985 seasons. Ineligibility for post-season competition and for television appearances are among the disciplinary measures which Section 7-(b) of the NCAA Enforcement Procedure Program allows the Infractions Committee or Council to impose against member institutions. The Committee notified the University of its right to appeal any of the findings or penalties to the NCAA Council. No appeal was taken. The Infractions Committee's report documented numerous occasions on which staff members and representatives of the University football program – including the then head coach of the football team – provided compensation or extra benefits to student athletes who are either in the University's football program or being recruited for the program. Specifically, the football staff was found to have provided the student athletes with benefits such as free airline transportation between school and their homes, free lodging, and cash and bank loans for the athletes' car payments, rental payments, and personal use. The University of Arizona has at no time denied that these violations occurred. Neither do the plaintiffs in this action dispute the fact that the violations did occur ...

The plaintiffs in this case have been deprived neither of their scholarships nor their right to participate in intercollegiate athletics ... The plaintiffs' second argument is that they have a constitutionally protected right to participate in intercollegiate athletics – including televised and post-season bowl game competition – that has been infringed upon without due process of law ...

The sanctions imposed by the NCAA in this case are not arbitrary or irrational. The protection and fostering of amateurism in intercollegiate athletics is a legitimate objective of the NCAA. The NCAA rules which provide for sanctions when member universities compensate athletes directly or indirectly for participation in intercollegiate competition are rationally related to the NCAA's stated objective of promoting amateurism. The sanctions imposed in this case were directed against specific misconduct by the University of Arizona. They serve to deter the University and other member institutions from engaging in similar misconduct in the future and are meant to deny the University the benefits derived from its improper practices. The plaintiffs' interests in participating in post-season and televised football contests and remaining free of punishment absent guilt must give way to the NCAA's broader interests in maintaining intercollegiate athletics as an integral part of the educational program and preserving the amateur nature of the college sport ...

In sum, there are simply too many factors other than the NCAA sanctions and the alleged injury for this Court to find that a proximate relationship exists ... The Court concludes that there is little more than a remote possibility that the plaintiffs' "value" in the professional football trade would be substantially different but for the sanctions or would improve were this Court to grant the injunctive relief.

1. *Justice* deals with NCAA punishment. The standard is that sanctions must not be arbitrary or intentional. One of the sanctions was a ban on post-season competition, which certainly can affect your potential draft status.

Justice v. National Collegiate Athletic Ass'n, 577 F. Supp. 356 (D. Ariz. 1983), U.S. Supreme Court.

⚖ *CASE 12-9 Jones v. NCAA*

392 F.Supp. 295 (D. Mass. 1975)

OPINION AND ORDER
TAURO, D. J.

This is an action brought by a Northeastern University (Northeastern) hockey player against the National Collegiate Athletic Association … The plaintiff seeks to enjoin the defendants from declaring him ineligible to play intercollegiate ice hockey. He also asks this court to restrain the N.C.A.A. and Byers from imposing sanctions upon Northeastern for either permitting him to participate in intercollegiate hockey, or for providing him with financial assistance on the same basis that it provides such aid to other student-athletes with demonstrable financial need …

The plaintiff is an American citizen and a resident of Melrose, Massachusetts. He is currently a full-time student at Northeastern's Boston campus, and receives no financial aid from the University. He is in good academic standing …

In April 1974, the plaintiff enrolled in Northeastern's College of Business Administration. Upon matriculation, the plaintiff informed Northeastern officials of his desire to participate in the school's intercollegiate ice hockey program. Plaintiff was then asked to complete both an "Intercollegiate Ice Hockey Affidavit" prepared by the E.C.A.C. and an "Ice Hockey Questionnaire" from the N.C.A.A. The completed documents revealed that during the last three years of high school, and for the two hockey seasons between his high school graduation and admission to college, the plaintiff had played for a succession of Canadian and American "amateur" hockey teams. Plaintiff received compensation from these teams not only while he was attending school, but also during the two years that he was not pursuing his education. On the basis of this information, Gallagher concluded that plaintiff was in violation of the N.C.A.A. rules of amateurism and therefore ineligible for intercollegiate hockey. Nevertheless, Gallagher sought "waivers" from both organizations. If granted, these waivers would have allowed Northeastern to permit plaintiff to represent the school in intercollegiate competition without fear of sanctions by either association. On September 11, 1974, the E.C.A.C. granted such a "waiver," but on November 18, 1974, the N.C.A.A. denied Northeastern's request. Following the N.C.A.A.'s decision, Northeastern declared that the plaintiff was ineligible to represent the University in intercollegiate hockey games for the 1974-75 season. The plaintiff then brought this action …

The plaintiff was declared ineligible by Northeastern because he had allegedly violated the N.C.A.A.'s Principle of Amateurism which is embodied in Article Three of the association's constitution. Article Three, Section 1 reads:

> *Principle of Amateurism and Student Participation.* An amateur student-athlete is one who engages in a particular sport for the educational, physical, mental and social benefits he derives therefrom, and to whom participation in that sport is an avocation.

The Article then goes on to list a number of specific eligibility standards, certain of which the plaintiff has allegedly failed to meet. Prior to his matriculation at Northeastern, the plaintiff had played five seasons of hockey for various non-scholastic Canadian and American teams. During the first three of those seasons, he also attended high school either in this country or in Canada. For the remaining two seasons he played hockey but did not attend school. He received financial aid from his team during each of these five seasons …

The situation in the instant case is an entirely different one. The plaintiff here is an American, not a Canadian. His home town had an active hockey program and was called "Hockey Town U.S.A." The plaintiff therefore, did not have to play Canadian Major Junior A hockey in order to participate in an organized hockey program. It is unnecessary to determine if his decision to do so, standing alone, is fatal to his cause, because the record reflects he has even more serious problems which cast doubt on the likelihood of his prevailing. During the two-year hiatus between his high school graduation and matriculation at Northeastern, plaintiff continued to play for Canadian and American "Amateur" teams and continued to receive the same financial aid from his team. Unlike the situation in *Buckton*, plaintiff's play during those two years cannot be considered as coincidental to or in conjunction with his obtaining an education. The challenged regulations would make ineligible any athlete, American or Canadian, who while not attending school, was given financial assistance to play hockey. Accordingly, a decision to restore plaintiff's eligibility under these circumstances would put him on a superior, and not merely equal, footing with other student-athletes. This the court cannot do …

In the instant case, there is no claim that the N.C.A.A. has defined eligibility in terms that operate as an economic penalty or has imposed costs upon the plaintiff which deprive him of an opportunity to play hockey. Rather, plaintiff claims only that it is relatively more difficult for poor athletes to avoid receiving compensation from private teams. This disparity in economic effect is not the type of absolute deprivation which constitutes unconstitutional discrimination on the basis of wealth …

In the instant case, it is unlikely that the plaintiff will be able to show that such scienter is present. The N.C.A.A. was originally established to promote amateurism in college sports and to integrate intercollegiate athletics into the educational programs of its member institutions. The N.C.A.A. eligibility rules were not designed to coerce students into staying away from intercollegiate athletics, but to implement the N.C.A.A. basic principles of amateurism, principles which have been at the heart of the Association since its founding. Any limitation on access to intercollegiate sports is merely the incidental result of the organization's pursuit of its legitimate goals. Its conduct does not, therefore, rise to the level of a violation of section 1.

Finally, the plaintiff alleges that the actions of the Association amount to an attempt or conspiracy to monopolize in violation of section 2. So far, however, there is no evidence in this case which would allow this court to conclude that there is a substantial likelihood of the plaintiff's showing that the N.C.A.A.'s eligibility decisions were made for the purpose of forming a monopoly. Indeed, there is no evidence presently on the record that the Association's current pre-eminence in the field is the result of anything other than its own skill, foresight and industry.

1. Ineligibility and sanctions again. Should the NCAA have this much power if their mantra is to be player-friendly?

Jones v. National Collegiate Athletic Ass'n, 392 F. Supp. 295 (D. Mass. 1975), U.S. Supreme Court.

⚖ *CASE 12-10 Colo. Seminary v. NCAA*

570 F.2d 320 (10th Cir. 1978)

This action was brought by the University of Denver and by several of its student athletes to enjoin the National Collegiate Athletic Association from imposing sanctions against the hockey team and other DU athletic teams. The trial court denied the plaintiffs' motion for summary judgment and granted a like motion of the defendants with some exceptions. The plaintiffs have taken this appeal. The trial court held that the interest of the student athletes in participating in intercollegiate sports was not constitutionally protected, and that no constitutionally protected right of the University had been violated. We agree with these conclusions, and we agree with the Memorandum Opinion of the trial court appearing at 417 F.Supp. 885. The facts are described in the trial court's Memorandum and need not be repeated here. It is sufficient to say that the dispute began between the University and the NCAA as to the eligibility of several hockey players and culminated with the NCAA placing the hockey team on a two-year probation with no post season participation in NCAA events, and also the probation of all other University athletic teams for a one-year period with similar consequences. We conclude that this appeal is controlled by our decisions in *Albach v. Odle*, 531 F.2d 983 (10th Cir.), and *Oklahoma High School Athletic Ass'n v. Bray*, 321 F.2d 269 (10th Cir.). These two cases, of course, concerned high school athletics, but the same considerations are applicable here. The arguments as to the difference between high school athletic programs and those in the universities have been examined. We have also considered the point that college athletic scholarship arrangements may create a distinction. But all considered, we find no more than a difference in degree. The fundamental positions are the same, the goals are the same, the stakes are pretty much the same. The same relationship also exists between the primary academic functions of the schools in each category and the athletic programs. The differences in degree or magnitude do not lead to a different result. In each, the athletic program is very important, as are the many other diverse functions, programs, and activities not within the academic core. It is obvious that the relative importance of the many school "activities" to each other, and to the academic core, depends on where you sit. The "educational process" is indeed a bundle of diverse situations to which the students are subjected by varying degrees of compulsion, both officially and by their peers. This is basically the *Goss v. Lopez*, 419 U.S. 565, 95 S.Ct. 729, 42 L.Ed.2d 725, assumption. It is then to be applied with the significant conclusion therefrom reached in Albach v. Odle, quoted above, to the effect that if one stick in the bundle is removed, it does not necessarily mean that a constitutionally protected right of a student has thereby been violated ...

The same conclusion was there reached as to the complaint of the school itself against the association. Thus, here also we must hold that there is present no substantial federal question. The equal protection argument, as the trial court observes, is answered by *San Antonio Independent School Dist. v. Rodriguez*, 411 U.S. 1, 93 S.Ct. 1278, 36 L.Ed.2d 16. There is here no valid argument based on classification. In the final analysis, the NCAA reacted to the position taken by the University as a member and in response to the NCAA pronouncements. The matter resulting in the probation sanction became removed from the issue of eligibility of the several hockey players. AFFIRMED in all respects.

1. *Colorado Seminary* establishes the principle that challenges to NCAA-imposed sanctions do not unconstitutionally discriminate against the allegedly offending institution.
2. The NCAA's rules behind the probation in *Colorado Seminary* were not unconstitutional since the offending hockey player's interest in participation did not rise to the level of a constitutionally protected property on liberty interest based on arbitrary classifications that affect race, religion, or national origin. Would it make a difference if the player was Canadian?

Colorado Seminary (University of Denver), Kenneth Bradcarefoot, Mark Louis Falcone, Ernest Johnglanville, David A. Robinson, Appellants, v. National Collegiate Athletic Association and Harry E.troxell, Appellees, 570 F.2d 320 (10th Cir. 1978), U.S. Supreme Court.

⚖ CASE 12-11 *Marshall v. ESPN, Inc.*

111 F.Supp.3d 815 (M.D. Tenn. 2015)

Plaintiffs are eight former college football players (three each from Vanderbilt University and the University of Tennessee, and one each from the University of Washington and the University of Tennessee, Chattanooga) and two former college basketball players (one each from Tennessee State University and the University of Maryland Eastern Shore). Defendants are more than two dozen separate entities that fall into three camps. The assorted athletic conferences, specifically the Atlantic Coast Conference, Big East Conference, Inc., Big 12 Conference, The Big Ten Conference, Inc., Conference USA, Ohio Valley

Conference, Pac-12 Conference, and Southeastern Conference, manage athletic competition among teams and sell the rights to broadcast conference games. The networks, specifically, ESPN Inc., CBS Broadcasting Inc., NBCUniversal Media, LLC, ABC, Inc., Fox Broadcasting Company, Big Ten Network, LLC, SEC Network, and Longhorn Network (the "Network Defendants") purchase media content, including college sports from content owners, or produce it internally, and then telecast that content to television viewers. The licensing agencies, specifically, Outfront Media Sports, Inc. (f/k/a CBS Collegiate Sports Properties, Inc.), IMG Worldwide, LLC, IMG College, LLC, William Morris Endeavor Entertainment, LLC, JMI Sports LLC, Learfield Sports LLC, T3 Media, Inc., and TeleSouth Communications, Inc. (collectively, the "Licensing Defendants"), offer brand development and management and act as a conduit in licensing college teams' intellectual property …

Though the NCAA is alleged to be a part of the conspiracy, it not named as a Defendant in this action. Nevertheless, Plaintiffs' tacitly concede that any discussion of the alleged unlawfulness must acknowledge its existence and the role it plays in college sports. In accordance with NCAA rules, intercollegiate sports are limited to participation of "amateur" athletes …

In order to participate in NCAA sports, Student Athletes are required to sign a "Form 08-3a," that "allows the NCAA to use the Student Athlete's name or picture to 'generally promote' NCAA championships or other NCAA events, activities or programs." Plaintiffs allege that "Student Athletes desiring to extend their athletic careers beyond high school are left with no comparable alternative to accepting a scholarship from an FBS football or Division I basketball school," because "[b]oth the National Football League ('NFL') and the National Basketball Association ('NBA') prohibit high school players from entering their leagues directly after high school." As a consequence, in order to play at a competitive level, Student Athletes have little or no choice but to accept a scholarship and sign Form 08-3a, making the Form "a contract of adhesion and unenforceable." Plaintiffs claim that the NCAA and Defendants have "multi-billion dollar agreements," yet "the Student Athlete, receives nothing or, at most, the cost of attendance." The restrictive NCAA and Conference rule which "even go as far as to place quotas on the number of meals a Student Athlete may eat," allegedly "have deprived Student Athletes from realizing the commercial value of their images." That is, while the NCAA "purports to protect Student Athletes from commercial exploitation, [it] has conspired with Defendants to create an anticompetitive market where Student Athletes are powerless to realize the commercial value of their names, images and likenesses." Plaintiffs contend that the NCAA and Defendants have benefitted enormously from the status quo, all to the detriment of Student Athletes. Just by way of examples, Plaintiffs claim:

- A basketball scholarship at the University of Kentucky is worth approximately $12,000 per year, yet the basketball team consisting of no more than 13 scholarship players, generated approximately $23 million dollars in revenue in 2012.
- Approximately 50% of NCAA football and men's basketball players are left without a college degree.
- According to a study, the average FBS football student athlete has a fair market value of $456,612 "above and beyond" the value of their scholarship, and the average men's basketball player has a fair market value of $1.06 million over four years, not including his scholarship …

III. Conclusion

College basketball and football, particularly at the Division I and FBS levels, is big business. Of that there can be little doubt. Many believe that "amateur" when applied to college athletes today is a misnomer — an artificial label and anathema, placed on players, like Plaintiffs, whose efforts on the court and field lead to untold riches for others, such as Defendants. Cogent arguments have been raised that it is time Student Athletes share in the bounty, above and beyond any scholarships they may receive. In this case, however, the Court is not called upon to address the larger picture of whether, as a matter of recognition, equity or fundamental fairness, Student Athletes should receive "pay for play." Nor is it the Court's task to pass on the wisdom of the NCAA's eligibility rules that bar compensation, or whether those rules capture reality, given the present nature and environment of college sports. The Court expresses no opinion on those issues. Rather, the Court's sole task is to determine whether present Plaintiffs have alleged sufficient facts or stated a viable claim that they are entitled to monetary compensation because they play in televised games. The Court finds that Plaintiffs have not done so under any of the theories that they set forth. Accordingly, the Motions to Dismiss filed by the Network Defendants, the Conference Defendants, and the Licensing Defendants will be granted. Said dismissal will be with prejudice.

1. Should athletes receive profits that are made by the NCAA or by the school, given the substantial revenue that sports events bring to the NCAA and the school itself?

Marshall v. ESPN, Inc. 111 F.Supp.3d 815 (M.D. Tenn. 2015), U.S. Supreme Court.

⚖ CASE 12-12 McCormack v. NCAA

845 F.2d 1338 (5th Cir 1988)

ALVIN B. RUBIN, Circuit Judge:

Finding that the football program of Southern Methodist University had exceeded restrictions on compensation for student athletes, the National Collegiate Athletic Association suspended the program for the 1987 season and imposed other penalties. A group of SMU alumni, football players, and cheerleaders challenges that action, contending that the NCAA violated the antitrust and civil rights laws by promulgating and enforcing rules restricting the benefits that may be awarded student athletes. While we give the loyal students and alumni credit for making a college try, we affirm the judgment dismissing their complaint, for we hold that some of the plaintiffs lack standing and the others have failed to state a claim for which relief can be granted to them.

The NCAA found that Southern Methodist University had violated its rules limiting compensation for football players to scholarships with limited financial benefits. It accordingly suspended the SMU football program for the entire 1987 season and imposed restrictions on it for the 1988 season. David R. McCormack, an attorney and SMU alumnus, then filed this class action suit on behalf of SMU "as an institution," its graduates and current students, several members of its football team, and several cheerleaders.

The complaint, as amended, charges antitrust violations in that (1) the restrictions on compensation to football players constitute illegal price-fixing in violation of the Sherman Act and (2) the suspension of SMU constitutes a group boycott by other NCAA members. The suspension, the complaint alleges, has destroyed the football players' careers and caused the cheerleaders "considerable emotional anguish and distress" by depriving them of the opportunity to conduct their cheerleading activities at games.

In addition, all of the plaintiffs assert that the NCAA has repeatedly imposed penalties on the college football program of SMU in unequal fashion and without due process of law, thereby damaging "the image of the University as an academic institution," endangering "[its] existence . . . as an academic institution," and causing it to lose revenues from donors. The NCAA's actions, it is alleged, have deprived McCormack and others of "their right to associate together in support of the University by attendance at the football games of the University," while the football players have been "forced to discontinue their athlete-academic duties" at SMU and the cheerleaders have lost the opportunity to lead cheers at football games.

The plaintiffs seek (1) injunctive relief; (2) for the injuries suffered by the football players, treble money damages; (3) for the price-fixing violations, $20 million "in the name of the University

▶ Ethical Criticism of "Collegiate Model of Athletics"

The NCAA's "collegiate model of athletics" appears to be a collection of bromides, bon mots, aphorisms, and axioms. *E.g.*, there's no "I" in "team," but it was promoted as the panacea to rampant commercialization of college athletics, of their own making. Southall and Karcher assert that "[f]or a number of years the collegiate model of athletics had been described as an unethical system, within which profit athletes are a vulnerable population subject to a high degree of *undue influence* and economic exploitation."[26] The word exploitation is used in this context as a form of domination to which a group that has an unfair advantage over vulnerable persons for self-enrichment.[27]

There is no clearer example of "exploitation" and "commercialization" than the sexual abuse of minor gymnasts at the hands of Dr. Larry Nassar and his employer, Michigan State University. The NCAA chose not to dramatically penalize Michigan State, perhaps as a result of the backlash against their original draconian response to the Sandusky/Penn State scandal. In *Doe v. Michigan State University*, plaintiffs alleged that "[t]he present action arise from the serial sexual misconduct of pedophile Lawrence Nassar and the institutional failures that caused direct and substantial injury to seemingly countless young girls and women including Jane MPW Doe (hereinafter "Plaintiff" – who was

approximately 7 years old when she was first abused and was victimized dozens of times over the course of years thereafter.)"[28]

The connection to Michigan State and the NCAA was that at all relevant times, Dr. Nassar was acting in the scope of employment with defendant Michigan State and defendant U.S.A. Gymnastics. As an employee of USAG from 1986 to 2015, Dr. Nassar served as: certified athletic trainers, osteopathic physician, National Medical Director, National Team Physician for USAG, and National Team Physician for USAG Women's Artistic Gymnastic Team.

Defendant Nassar received a benefit from his relationship with Defendant USAG in the form of national and global exposures, fame, and increased patients at his office at MSU, which resulted in Defendant Nassar receiving higher compensation … MSU Defendants received a benefit from Nassar's employment with USAG, Twistars, and MSU in the form of medical services rendered to its member athletes, national and global exposure, fame, and increased enrollment. Defendant Nassar was employed by Defendant MSU from approximately 1996 to 2016 in various positions including but not limited to: a. Associate Professor, Defendant MSU's Division of Sports Medicine, Department of Radiology, College of Osteopathic Medicine; b. Team Physician, Defendant MSU's Men's and Women's Gymnastics Team; c. Team Physician, Defendant MSU's Men's and Women's Track and Field Team; d. Team Physician, Defendant MSU's Men's and Women's Crew Team; e. Team Physician, Defendant MSU's Intercollegiate Athletics; f. Medical Consultant, Defendant

MSU's Wharton Center for Performing Arts; g. Advisor, Student Osteopathic Association of Sports Medicine.

As part of Defendant Nassar's employment and contractual duties with MSU, Defendant Nassar was responsible for spending between 50% to 70% of his time engaged in "Outreach" and/or "Public Services". . . . Based on MSU's decision to compensate Nassar for his work with USAG and Twistars, Nassar was acting in the scope of his employment with MSU while he was working at USAG and Twistars and also while he was working with athletes from institutions.[29]

1. The collegiate model has been criticized as unethical since profit-athletes are vulnerable and subject to undue influence and economic exploitation. Are these athletes vulnerable?

2. Profit-athletes are economically exploited since they have no meaningful market choice and must adhere to the NCAA's amateurism guidelines. Do rules such as the one-year rule in basketball and the three-year rule in football defeat the goal of a meaningful market choice and an emphasis on education?

3. The billions in annual revenues of universities, conferences, and the NCAA are in large part derived from rights fees paid by media conglomerates for broadcasting live coverage of sports events. Should the athletes/entertainers receive some monetary benefit from these billions of dollars?

4. "Amateurism" does not have an objective meaning—essentially, "amateurism" is nothing more than a term designating a business model. If that is so, why does the NCAA brandish it as a sacred core value?

5. In *Oliver v. NCAA*, 920 N.E.2d 203 (Ohio App. 2009), a collegiate baseball player successfully enjoined the NCAA from enforcing its player-eligibility bylaws against him. Oliver also disavowed the NCAA's restitution rule, which allows it to impose penalties when an injunction is overturned on appeal.

6. Are these rules athlete-friendly? Remember that the NCAA claims that it is an athlete-friendly organization.

7. The lawsuit of super-Olympian gymnast Aly Raisman tells the tale of the extreme deleterious consequences of an athlete in a predatory system. "This case arises from the serial molestation, sexual abuse of Aly Raisman, three-time Olympic gold medalist by her trusted team physician and former Olympic Team [and Michigan State Doctor] Larry Nassar, while Aly was a young girl and woman competing for the honor of her country." *Raisman v. USOC*, 2018 WL 1129131 (Cal. Super.) (Trial Pleading). Who should be responsible for this predator? Who should protect Aly?

⚖ *CASE 12-13   NCAA v. Board of Regents*

468 U.S. 85 (1984)

The University of Oklahoma and the University of Georgia contend that the National Collegiate Athletic Association has unreasonably restrained trade in the televising of college football games. After an extended trial, the District Court found that the NCAA had violated § 1 of the Sherman Act and granted injunctive relief. 546 F.Supp. 1276 (WD Okla. 1982). The Court of Appeals agreed that the statute had been violated but modified the remedy in some respects. 707 F.2d 1147 (CA10 1983). We granted certiorari, 464 U.S. 913 (1983), and now affirm.

1. The question is, should the NCAA's TV package monies be distributed evenly among all Div. 1A schools. The Court said "No." Is this a correct decision, or a case of the tail wagging the dog?

⚖ CASE 12-14 *White v. NCAA*

2000 WL 8066802 (C.D. Cal.)

INTRODUCTION

Plaintiff Jason White, on behalf of himself and other colleges athletes (collectively "Plaintiffs"), sued the National Collegiate Athletic Association ("NCAA" or "Defendant") for alleged violations of the Sherman Act. Plaintiffs' Second Amended Complaint ("SAC") alleges that Defendant and its member institutions entered into a horizontal agreement to adhere to a grant-in-aid ("GIA") cap in their financial aid awards to student athletes. Under this GIA cap, member schools may give student athletes financial aid for their tuition, room and board, and books. Other expenses, such as travel, insurance, laundry or other incidental expenses may not be covered. Plaintiffs allege that the NCAA uses this GIA cap solely as a cost-saving measure rather than as a means to promote amateur competition. Plaintiffs further allege that this agreement harms competition because, absent any agreement, major collegiate men's basketball and football programs would compete with each other to offer student athletes financial aid packages equal to their full cost of attendance. Presently before the Court is the NCAA's Motion to Dismiss the Second Amended Complaint. For the reasons stated below, the Court denies the NCAA's Motion …

In each alleged market, Plaintiffs assert that colleges and universities compete to attract prospective student-athletes. Plaintiffs claim that student-athletes are potential buyers of the unique combination of coaching-services and academics offered by these colleges and universities. Moreover, Plaintiffs claim that "from the standpoint of student-athletes, there are "no reasonably interchangeable substitutes" for Major College Football or Major College Basketball "because no other alternative combines the opportunity to compete at the highest level of college sports while earning a college degree, together with a greater prospect for advancement to a professional football or basketball career than is available anywhere else." Plaintiffs' relevant product market allegations are legally sufficient. On its face, Plaintiffs' SAC alleges a relevant product market. More importantly, the SAC offers a plausible explanation as to why there are no reasonably interchangeable substitutes for the "unique combination of athletic and academic benefits" which comprise the relevant product market. (SAC ¶¶ 31–33). Assuming all factual allegations to be true and construing the complaint in the light most favorable to Plaintiffs, the Court finds Plaintiffs' allegations legally sufficient to survive the NCAA's motion to dismiss.

1. In White, the question is whether grant-in-aid caps restrict trade. The Court says it does not, but the GIA does not cover other necessary expenses such as travel, insurance, laundry, *etc.*

⚖ CASE 12-15 *Keller v. Elec. Arts*

724 F.2d 1268 (9th Cir. 2012)

BYBEE, Circuit Judge:

Video games are entitled to the full protections of the First Amendment, because "[l]ike the protected books, plays, and movies that preceded them, video games communicate ideas—and even social messages—through many familiar literary devices (such as characters, dialogue, plot, and music) and through features distinctive to the medium (such as the player's interaction with the virtual world)."

Such rights are not absolute, and states may recognize the right of publicity to a degree consistent with the First Amendment. *Zacchini v. Scripps-Howard Broad. Co.,* 433 U.S. 562, 574-75, 97 S. Ct. 2849, 53 L. Ed. 2d 965 (1977). In this case, we must balance the right of publicity of a former college football player against the asserted First Amendment right of a video game developer to use his likeness in its expressive works. The district court concluded that the game developer, Electronic Arts ("EA"), had no First Amendment defense against the right-of-publicity claims of the football player, Samuel Keller. We affirm. Under the "transformative use" test developed by the California Supreme Court, EA's use does not qualify for First Amendment protection as a matter of law because it literally recreates Keller in the very setting in which he has achieved renown. The other First Amendment defenses asserted by EA do not defeat Keller's claims either.

Samuel Keller was the starting quarterback for Arizona State University in 2005 before he transferred to the University of Nebraska, where he played during the 2007 season. EA is the producer of the *NCAA Football* series of video games, which allow users to control avatars representing college football players as those avatars participate in simulated games. In *NCAA Football*, EA seeks to replicate each school's entire team as accurately as possible. Every real football player on each team included in the game has a corresponding avatar in the game with the player's actual jersey number and virtually identical height, weight, build, skin tone, hair color, and home state. EA attempts to match any unique, highly identifiable playing behaviors by sending detailed questionnaires to team equipment managers. Additionally, EA creates realistic virtual versions of actual stadiums; populates them with the virtual athletes, coaches, cheerleaders, and fans realistically rendered by EA's graphic artists; and incorporates realistic sounds such as the crunch of the players' pads and the roar of the crowd.

EA's game differs from reality in that EA omits the players' names on their jerseys and assigns each player a home town that is different from the actual player's home town. However, users of the video game may upload rosters of names obtained from third parties so that the names do appear on the jerseys. In such cases, EA allows images from the game containing athletes' real names to be posted on its website by users.

1. Video games make a lot of money. Keller's right to publicity trumps EA's First Amendment rights. On what should an ethical distribution of the profits be based?

⚖ CASE 12-16   Hart v. Elec. Arts

717 F.3d 141 (3d Cir. 2013)

OPINION
GREENAWAY, JR., Circuit Judge.

In 2009, Appellant Ryan Hart brought suit against Appellee Electronic Arts, Inc. for allegedly violating his right of publicity as recognized under New Jersey law. Specifically, Appellant's claims stemmed from Appellee's alleged use of his likeness and biographical information in its *NCAA Football* series of videogames. The District Court granted summary judgment in favor of Appellee on the ground that its use of Appellant's likeness was protected by the First Amendment. For the reasons set forth below, we will reverse the grant of summary judgment and remand the case back to the District Court for further proceedings.

I. Facts

Hart was a quarterback, player number 13, with the Rutgers University NCAA Men's Division I Football team for the 2002 through 2005 seasons. As a condition of participating in college-level sports, Hart was required to adhere to the National Collegiate Athletic Association's amateurism rules as set out in Article 12 of the NCAA bylaws. *See, e.g.,* NCAA, *2011–12 NCAA Division I Manual* § 12.01.1 (2011) ("Only an amateur student-athlete is eligible for inter-collegiate athletics participation in a particular sport."). In relevant part, these rules state that a collegiate athlete loses his or her "amateur" status if (1) the athlete "[u]ses his or her athletics skill (directly or indirectly) for pay in any form in that sport," *id.* § 12.1.2, or (2) the athlete "[a]ccepts any remuneration or permits the use of his or her name or picture to advertise, recommend or promote directly the sale or use of a commercial product or service of any kind," *id.* § 12.5.2.1. In comporting with these bylaws, Hart purportedly refrained from seizing on various commercial opportunities. On the field, Hart excelled. At 6'2", weighing 197 pounds, and typically wearing a visor and armband on his left wrist, Hart amassed an impressive list of achievements as the Scarlet Knights' starting quarterback. As of this writing, Hart still holds the Scarlet Knights' records for career attempts, completions, and interceptions. Hart's skill brought success to the team and during his senior year the Knights were invited to the Insight Bowl, their first Bowl game since 1978.

Hart's participation in college football also ensured his inclusion in EA's successful *NCAA Football* videogame franchise. EA, founded in 1982, is "one of the world's leading interactive entertainment software companies," and "develops, publishes, and distributes interactive software worldwide" for consoles, cell phones, and PCs. EA's catalogue includes *NCAA Football*, the videogame series at issue in the instant case. The first edition of the game was released in 1993 as *Bill Walsh College Football*. EA subsequently changed the name first to *College Football USA* (in 1995), and then to the current *NCAA Football* (in 1997). New editions in the series are released annually, and "allow[ ] users to experience the excitement and challenge of college football" by interacting with "over 100 virtual teams and thousands of virtual players." (*Id.* at 530.) …

III. Discussion

We begin our analysis by noting the self-evident: video games are protected as expressive speech under the First Amendment …

Appellant's career as a college football player suggests that the target audience for his merchandise and performances (e.g., his actual matches) would be sports fans. It is only logical, then, that products appropriating and exploiting his identity would fare best—and thereby would provide ne'er-do-wells with the greatest incentive—when targeted at the sports-fan market segment. Given that Appellant played intercollegiate football, however, products targeting the sports-fan market would, as a matter of course, relate to him. Yet under Appellee's approach, all such uses would be protected. It cannot be that the very activity by which Appellant achieved his renown now prevents him from protecting his hard-won celebrity …

IV. Conclusion

We therefore hold that the *NCAA Football 2004, 2005* and *2006* games at issue in this case do not sufficiently transform Appellant's identity to escape the right of publicity claim and hold that the District Court erred in granted summary judgment in favor of Appellee. While we do hold that the only apparent use of Appellant's likeness in *NCAA Football 2009* (the photograph) is protected by the First Amendment, Appellant's overall claim for violation of his right of publicity should have survived Appellee's motion for summary judgment. Consequently, we need not address Appellant's desire for additional discovery. We shall reverse the District Court's grant of summary judgment and remand this case back to the court below for further proceedings consistent with this opinion.

1. Hart's commercial rights to his image trumps EA's First Amendment rights based primarily on EA's slavish copying of the actual athlete. Is it ethical for EA to minutely copy Hart's image for monetary gain? Would it make a difference if the video rendering of Ryan Hart was less than an exact copy of the real Ryan Hart? Should it make a difference?

⚖ CASE 12-17 O'Bannon v. NCAA

802 F.3d 1049 (9th Cir. 2015)

OPINION
BYBEE, Circuit Judge:

Section 1 of the Sherman Antitrust Act of 1890, 15 U.S.C. § 1, prohibits "[e]very contract, combination . . ., or conspiracy, in restraint of trade or commerce." For more than a century, the National Collegiate Athletic Association (NCAA) has prescribed rules governing the eligibility of athletes at its more than 1,000-member colleges and universities. Those rules prohibit student-athletes from being paid for the use of their names, images, and likenesses (NILs). The question presented in this momentous case is whether the NCAA's rules are subject to the antitrust laws and, if so, whether they are an unlawful restraint of trade.

After a bench trial and in a thorough opinion, the district court concluded that the NCAA's compensation rules were an unlawful restraint of trade. It then enjoined the NCAA from prohibiting its member schools from giving student-athletes scholarships up to the full cost of attendance at their respective schools and up to $5,000 per year in deferred compensation, to be held in trust for student-athletes until after they leave college. As far as we are aware, the district court's decision is the first by any federal court to hold that any aspect of the NCAA's amateurism rules violate the antitrust laws, let alone to mandate by injunction that the NCAA change its practices.

We conclude that the district court's decision was largely correct. Although we agree with the Supreme Court and our sister circuits that many of the NCAA's amateurism rules are likely to be procompetitive, we hold that those rules are not exempt from antitrust scrutiny; rather, they must be analyzed under the Rule of Reason. Applying the Rule of Reason, we conclude that the district court correctly identified one proper alternative to the current NCAA compensation rules—*i.e.*, allowing NCAA members to give scholarships up to the full cost of attendance—but that the district court's other remedy, allowing students to be paid cash compensation of up to $5,000 per year, was erroneous. We therefore affirm in part and reverse in part.

A. The NCAA

American colleges and universities have been competing in sports for nearly 150 years: the era of intercollegiate athletics began, by most accounts, on November 6, 1869, when Rutgers and Princeton met in the first college football game in American history—a game more akin to soccer than to modern American football, played with "25 men to a side." ... *Fin de siècle* college football was a rough game. Serious injuries were common, and it was not unheard of for players to be killed during games. Schools were also free to hire nonstudent ringers to compete on their teams or to purchase players away from other schools. By 1905, these and other problems had brought college football to a moment of crisis, and President Theodore Roosevelt convened a conference at the White House to address the issue of injuries in college football. Later that year, the presidents of 62 colleges and universities founded the Intercollegiate Athletic Association to create uniform rules for college football. In 1910, the IAA changed its name to the National Collegiate Athletic Association (NCAA), and it has kept that name to this day. The NCAA has grown to include some 1,100 member schools, organized into three divisions: Division I, Division II, and Division III. Division I schools are those with the largest athletic programs—schools must sponsor at least fourteen varsity sports teams to qualify for Division I—and they provide the most financial aid to student-athletes. Division I has about 350 embers. For football competition only, Division I's membership is divided into two subdivisions: the Football Bowl Subdivision (FBS) and the Football Championship Subdivision (FCS). FBS schools are permitted to offer more full scholarships to their football players and, as a result, the level of competition is generally higher in FBS than in FCS. FBS consists of about 120 of the nation's premier college football schools.

B. The Amateurism Rules

One of the NCAA's earliest reforms of intercollegiate sports was a requirement that the participants be amateurs … The NCAA began to strengthen its enforcement capabilities in 1948, when it adopted what became known as the "Sanity Code"—a set of rules that prohibited schools from giving athletes financial aid that was based on athletic ability and not available to ordinary students … In 1956, the NCAA departed from the Sanity Code's approach to financial aid by changing its rules to permit its members, for the first time, to give student-athletes scholarships based on athletic ability … In August 2014, the NCAA announced it would allow athletic conferences to authorize their member schools to increase scholarships up to the full cost of attendance … In addition to its financial aid rules, the NCAA has adopted numerous other amateurism rules that limit student-athletes' compensation and their interactions with professional sports leagues. An athlete can lose his amateur status, for example, if he signs a contract with a professional team, enters a professional league's player draft, or hires an agent. And, most importantly, an athlete is prohibited—with few exceptions—from receiving *any* "pay" based on his athletic ability, whether from boosters, companies seeking endorsements, or would-be licensors of the athlete's name, image, and likeness (NIL).

C. The O'Bannon *and* Keller *Litigation*

In 2008, Ed O'Bannon, a former All–American basketball player at UCLA, visited a friend's house, where his friend's son told O'Bannon that he was depicted in a college basketball video game produced by Electronic Arts (EA), a software company that produced video games based on college football and men's basketball from the late 1990s until around 2013. The friend's son turned on the video game, and O'Bannon saw an avatar of himself—a virtual player who visually resembled O'Bannon, played for UCLA, and wore O'Bannon's jersey number, 31. O'Bannon had never consented to the use of his likeness in the video game, and he had not been compensated for it. In 2009, O'Bannon sued the NCAA and the Collegiate Licensing Company (CLC), the entity which licenses the trademarks of the NCAA and a number of its member schools for commercial use, in federal court. The gravamen of O'Bannon's complaint was that the NCAA's amateurism rules, insofar as they prevented student-athletes from being compensated for the use of their NILs, were an illegal restraint of trade under Section 1 of the Sherman Act, 15 U.S.C. § 1. Around the same time, Sam Keller, the former starting quarterback for the Arizona State University and University of Nebraska football teams, separately brought suit against the NCAA, CLC, and EA. Keller alleged that EA had impermissibly used student-athletes' NILs in its video games and that the NCAA and CLC had wrongfully turned a blind eye to EA's misappropriation of these NILs. The complaint stated a claim under Indiana's and California's right of publicity statutes, as well as a number of common-law claims. The two cases were consolidated during pretrial proceedings …

c. Less restrictive alternatives

Having found that the NCAA had presented two procompetitive justifications for "circumscribed" limits on student-athlete compensation—*i.e.,* increasing consumer demand for college sports and preventing the formation of a "wedge" between student-athletes and other students—the court proceeded to the third and final step of the Rule of Reason, where it considered whether there were means of achieving the NCAA's procompetitive purposes that were "substantially less restrictive" than a total ban on compensating student-athletes for use of their NILs. *Id.* at 1004–05.

1. *O'Bannon* sued the NCAA and CLC for violating antitrust laws by conspiring to prevent former collegiate student athletes' from receiving compensation for their EA videos. Should Ed O'Bannon be compensated for the use of his commercial image?
2. Is this a viable method in the student-athlete's attempt to receive equitable compensation?
3. The O'Bannon case said that the NCAA can be sued on antitrust grounds, and that athletes can be compensated.
4. But, on Appeal, the $5,000 cap was disavowed. Was that a good or bad thing?

Modified from O'Bannon v. NCAA, 802 F.3d 1049 (9th Cir. 2015).

⚖ CASE 12-18   *In re NCAA Student-Athlete Name & Likeness Licensing Litig.*

37 F.Supp.3d 1126 (N.D. Cal. 2014)

Plaintiffs, a group of current and former college athletes, bring this antitrust class action against Defendant National Collegiate Athletic Association. They initially brought claims against Collegiate Licensing Company (CLC) and Electronic Arts Inc. (EA), as well, but agreed in September 2013 to settle those claims. Plaintiffs now move for summary judgment on all antitrust class claims against the NCAA.

BACKGROUND

Plaintiffs are twenty-four current and former student-athletes who played for NCAA men's football or basketball teams between 1953 and the present. All played at the Division I level, the highest level of collegiate athletic competition, and many went on to play professionally, as well. In the present case, four of the Plaintiffs (Right-of-Publicity Plaintiffs) allege that the NCAA misappropriated their names, images, and likenesses in violation of their statutory and common law rights of publicity. The other twenty Plaintiffs (Antitrust Plaintiffs) allege that the NCAA violated federal antitrust law by conspiring with EA and CLC to restrain competition in the market for the commercial use of their names, images, and likenesses. The instant motions address only the latter set of claims, which arise under the Sherman Antitrust Act, 15 U.S.C. §§ 1 et seq.

Antitrust Plaintiffs initiated the first of these consolidated actions in 2009 and filed the operative Third Amended Consolidated Class Action Complaint in July 2013. Docket No. 832. They allege that the NCAA engaged in anti-competitive conduct by conspiring to sell or license the names, images, and likenesses of Division I men's football and basketball players, without their consent, for use in live television broadcasts, archival game footage, and NCAA-branded videogames featuring player-avatars modeled after real student-athletes. They accuse the NCAA, EA, and CLC of engaging "in an overarching conspiracy to: (a) fix the amount current and former student-athletes are paid for the licensing, use, and sale of their names, images, and likenesses at zero; and (b) foreclose current and former student-athletes from the market for the licensing, use, and sale of their names, images, and likenesses." In 2012, Plaintiffs moved to certify a class of current and former Division I football and basketball players to pursue declaratory and injunctive relief. In particular, they sought an injunction barring the NCAA from enforcing any rules, bylaws, or organizational policies that prohibit current and former student-athletes from seeking compensation for the commercial use of their names, images, or likenesses. According to Plaintiffs, these rules, bylaws, and policies form an integral part of the NCAA's price-fixing conspiracy and operate to restrain competition in two distinct but related markets: (1) the "college education" market, in which Division I colleges and universities compete to recruit the best student-athletes to play football or basketball; and (2) the "group licensing" market, in which broadcasters and videogame developers compete for group licenses to use the names, images and likenesses of all student-athletes on particular Division I football and basketball teams in live game broadcasts, archival footage, and videogames. Plaintiffs also moved to certify a subclass of current and former student-athletes to pursue monetary damages. Specifically, they sought compensation for the unauthorized use of student-athletes' names, images, and likenesses in broadcast footage and videogames after July 2005, which is the earliest date on which Plaintiffs could recover damages under the Sherman Act's four-year statute of limitations. In September 2013, while their class certification motion was pending, Plaintiffs reached a settlement in principle with EA and CLC. The parties represented that this settlement would resolve all of Plaintiffs' pending antitrust and right-of-publicity claims against EA and CLC. Based on this representation, the Court vacated EA and CLC's remaining discovery and dispositive motion deadlines in October 2013 so that they could finalize the terms of their agreement and Plaintiffs could move for preliminary settlement approval. As of this date, the parties have yet to finalize their agreement and move for preliminary approval …

Here, the NCAA has not presented evidence to show that there can be no market for clips and highlight footage of Division I football and basketball players because such clips are used exclusively to produce protected, non-commercial speech. Plaintiffs, likewise, have not presented evidence to define a clear market for clips and highlight footage of these student-athletes to produce unprotected, commercial speech. Thus, the Court can neither summarily adjudicate that the First Amendment precludes a market for clips and highlight footage nor can it conclude that, absent the challenged restraint, such a market would actually exist. Accordingly, neither party is entitled to summary judgment on the question of whether the group licensing market includes a market for clips and highlight footage …

3. Integration of Education and Athletics

The NCAA's third stated justification for the challenged restraint is that it promotes the integration of education and athletics. The NCAA contends that the integration of education and athletics not only improves the educational experiences of student-athletes but also advances the educational mission of colleges. While these may be worthwhile goals, they are not procompetitive.

1. Interestingly, the Court held the NCAA's contention that the integration of education and athletics not only improves their educational experience but also advances the schools' educational mission, was undoubtedly worthwhile; however, it was not procompetitive. Your thoughts.

In re NCAA Student-Athlete Name & Likeness Licensing Litig., 37 F.Supp.3d 1126 (N.D. Cal. 2014), U.S. Supreme Court.

▶ References

1. 10cc, "Art for Art's Sake," by Eric Stewart and Graham Gouldman, Mercury Records, 1975.
2. "The Business of Amateurs," directed by Bobby Demars (Sonderful Entertainment, 2015).
3. Ibid.
4. *Arrington v. NCAA*, 2011 WL 4374451 (N.D. Ill.).
5. Case No. 4:14-cv-02758-CW, National Collegiate Athletic Association, U.S. Supreme Court.
6. "Knight Commission on Intercollegiate Athletics, Restoring the Balance, Dollar Values, and the Future of College Sports" (2010), as reprinted in App. 31, Walter Champion, *Fundamentals of Sports Law* 673–96 (2d ed., ann. cum. supp. 2017–18).
7. *O'Bannon v. NCAA*, 7 F.Supp. 3d 955,56 (N.D. Cal. 2014).
8. Richard M. Southall and Richard T. Karcher, "Distributive injustice: an ethical analysis of the NCAA's 'collegiate model of athletics and its jurisprudence," *15 Int'l Sports L. J.*
9. Ibid., at 211.

10. NCAA, "Brand addresses: Fortify bond between academics, *NCAA News* (Jan. 19, 2004).

11. Ibid.

12. Ibid.

13. NCAA, "The 2009 NCAA State of the Association speech," *NCAA News* (Jan. 15, 2009).

14. Ibid.

15. NCAA, "Brand charts course for collegiate model's next century," *NCAA News* (Jan. 16, 2006).

16. Southall & Karcher, "Distributive injustice," *15 Int'l Sports L. J.* 210, 212.

17. Ibid., quoting from NCAA working group on collegiate model – Enforcement at 4 (2012).

18. Southall & Karcher, "Distributive injustice" *15 Int'l Sports L. J.* 210, 212.

19. Ibid. at 213.

20. "Brand charts course for collegiate model's next century," (2016).

21. Ibid.

22. Ibid.

23. Ibid.

24. Ibid.

25. Ibid.

26. Southall & Karcher, "Distributive injustice," *15 Int'l Sports L. J.* 210, 219. Richard T. Karcher, "Broadcast Rights, Unjust Enrichment, and the Student-Athlete," 34 *Cardozo L. Rev.* 107 (2012); and Karcher, "The Battle Outside of the Courtroom: Principles of Amateurism vs Principles of Supply and Demand," 3 *Miss. Sports L. Rev.* 47 (2013).

27. Southall & Karcher 15 Int'l Sports L. J. 210, 219.

28. *Doe v. Michigan State University*, 2018 WL 2753641 at 1 (W.D. Mich.) (Trial Pleading).

29. Ibid., at 3–4. *Raisman v. USOC*, 2018 WL 1129131 (Cal. Super.) (Trial Pleading).

Case Index

Index